CONTEMPORARY CHINESE POLITICS:

an introduction

JAMES C.F. WANG

University of Hawaii at Hilo

Prentice-Hall, Inc., *Englewood Cliffs, New Jersey 07632*

Library of Congress Cataloging in Publication Data

Wang, James C F
   Contemporary Chinese politics.

   Includes bibliographical references and index.
      1.   China—Politics and government—1976-
I.   Title.
DS779.W365   320.9'5105   79-24738
ISBN   0-13-169987-3

© 1980 by PRENTICE-HALL, INC., Englewood Cliffs, N.J. 07632

Printed in the United States of America

10   9   8   7   6   5   4   3   2   1

editorial production/supervision and interior design: CATHIE MICK MAHAR
manufacturing buyer: HARRY P. BAISLEY

PRENTICE-HALL INTERNATIONAL, INC., *London*
PRENTICE-HALL OF AUSTRALIA PTY. LIMITED, *Sydney*
PRENTICE-HALL OF CANADA, LTD., *Toronto*
PRENTICE-HALL OF INDIA PRIVATE LIMITED, *New Delhi*
PRENTICE-HALL OF JAPAN, INC., *Tokyo*
PRENTICE-HALL OF SOUTHEAST ASIA PTE. LTD., *Singapore*
WHITEHALL BOOKS LIMITED, *Wellington, New Zealand*

To

Sally, my wife,
and children Sarah and Eric,
for their tolerance,
patience, and assistance

Contents

Preface

When Hua Guofeng was designated the First Vice Chairman of the Central Committee of the Chinese Communist Party and the Premier of the Central Government of China in April 1976, the world was puzzled not only by the emergence of an obscure personality as China's national leader but also by the ever changing political situation unfolding in China. Although this book is not intended to present predictions about what is going to happen in China, it nevertheless is designed to provide the necessary basic information about politics in contemporary China. The book emphasizes the development of Chinese political institutions and processes. Since most undergraduate students lack background knowledge of China, Chapter I begins with a brief history. It presents a chronological description and analysis of such topics as the traditional Chinese political system, its reform and revolution in modern times, and the rise of the Chinese communist movement. Chapter I also brings the students up to date on the political developments since 1949, with special focus on the Cultural Revolution, the struggle for power among China's top leaders, and the issues surrounding these elite conflicts.

How is the Chinese Communist Party organized? What are the requirements and recruitment patterns for membership in the party? What exactly is the thought of Mao Zedong, and how has this thought been imposed on contemporary Chinese thinking and belief? What is

Mao's legacy to China? Chapters II and III discuss answers to these questions.

What is the State Council; how is it organized and how does the Chinese Communist Party interlock with the government in order to insure its control and direction? What are the characteristics of the Polit-buro members, the top policy-makers in the party and government? What has been the nature of Chinese bureaucracy and the cadre system? How can the Chinese legal system, with its formal structure and informal practices, be explained? What is the status of the autonomous regions where over fifty million ethnic minorities live? What has been the Chinese solution to her national minority problem? Chapter IV and V offer description and analysis of the central and local governments and how they function, as well as the significance of provincial politics in China. Related closely to the subject of provincial politics is the role of the military in Chinese politics. Chapter VI discusses in detail the organization and the modernization effort of the Chinese armed forces, the militia, the military's intervention in the Cultural Revolution, and its continued participation in decision making at the highest level.

How actively do the Chinese masses participate in politics? How are political messages and party/government directions communicated to the masses? What is the nature of a mass campaign? What is a small study group, and how important is it in molding political behavior and thinking? These are specific topics examined in Chapter VII.

What has been China's economic performance? Will China be able to increase her grain production by mechanizing agriculture? What have been China's policies in science and technology? What are the implications of educational reforms introduced during the Cultural Revolution and the subsequent reversal of some of these policies after the death of Mao and the downfall of the radical ideologues in 1976? What is the thrust of China's modernization programs and its implications for China's development? These are the main subjects discussed in Chapters VIII and IX on the politics of modernization, economic development, science and technology, and education.

Finally, Chapter X examines China's role in world politics as perceived by the Chinese leaders, based largely on material from Chinese sources. The discussion on China's foreign policy focuses on the explosive Sino-Soviet relations, the problem of Taiwan in the normalization of relations between China and the United States, and Sino-Japanese relations.

There are several features in this book which need to be mentioned. First, it is hopefully the most up-to-date and informative undergraduate textbook on contemporary Chinese political development; it contains the latest available facts and data about China. Second, while the major objective of this book is to provide basic information about China's political institutions and processes, it also attempts to explain complex organizations and issues by incorporating, whenever appropriate, various interpretative analyses from the works of China scholars. The source material cited in the notes to each chapter contains rich references to enable students to explore specific topics further. Third, the text has been written in simple, readable style to avoid burdening students with an excess of terminology. Lastly, Romanization of Chinese names of persons and places in this book is based on the newly approved standardized Chinese phonetic alphabet or the Pinyin System.

My indebtedness to other China scholars whose works are cited in the text and in the chapter notes is indeed immense. Also my personal gratitude and appreciation are great for the invaluable suggestions made by those who reviewed the sample chapters. Last, and certainly not least, is my sincere appreciation for the guidance and encourangement so generously given to me by Stan Wakefield and Joseph Murray of Prentice-Hall.

JAMES C.F. WANG
University of Hawaii at Hilo

Romanization of Chinese Names of Persons and Places*

CHINESE PHONETIC ALPHABET
OR THE PINYIN SYSTEM

HOW TO PRONOUNCE

Following is a Chinese phonetic alphabet table showing the alphabet pronunciation with approximate English equivalents. Spelling in the Wade system is in parentheses for reference.

"a"   (a), a vowel, as in *far*;
"b"   (p), a consonant, as in *be*;
"c"   (ts), a consonant, as "ts" in *its*; and
"ch" (ch), a consonant, as "ch" in *church*, strongly aspirated;
"d"   (t), a consonant, as in *do*;
"e"   (e), a vowel, as "er" in *her*, the "r" being silent; but "ie," a diphthong, as in *yes* and "ei," a diphthong, as in *way*;
"f"   (f), a consonant, as in *foot*;
"g"   (k), a consonant, as in *go*;

*Based on official version published in *Beijing Review*, no. 1 (January 5, 1979), pp. 18–20. A specific rule requires that the traditional spelling of historical places and persons such as Confucius and Sun Yat-sen need not be changed.

"h"   (h), a consonant, as in *her*, strongly aspirated;
"i"   (i), a vowel, two pronunciations:
    1) as in *eat*
    2) as in *sir* in syllables beginning with the consonants *c, ch, r, s, sh, z,* and *zh*;
"j"   (ch), a consonant, as in *jeep*;
"k"   (k), a consonant, as in *kind*, strongly aspirated;
"l"   (l), a consonant, as in *land*;
"m"   (m), a consonant, as in *me*;
"n"   (n), a consonant, as in *no*;
"o"   (o), a vowel, as "aw" in *law*;
"p"   (p), a consonant, as in *par*, strongly aspirated;
"q"   (ch), a consonant, as "ch" in *cheek*;
"r"   (j), a consonant, pronounced as "r" but not rolled, or like "z" in *azure;*
"s"   (s, ss, sz), a consonant, as in *sister*; and
"sh"   (sh), a consonant, as "sh" in *shore*;
"t"   (t), a consonant, as in *top*, strongly aspirated;
"u"   (u), a vowel, as in *too*, also as in the French "u" in *tu* or the German umlauted "ü" in *Müenchen*;
"v"   (v), is used only to produce foreign and national minority words, and local dialects;
"w"   (w), used as a semi-vowel in syllables beginning with "u" when not preceded by consonants, pronounced as in *want*;
"x"   (hs), a consonant, as "sh" in *she*;
"y"   used as a semi-vowel in syllables beginning with "i" or "u" when not preceded by consonants, pronounced as in *yet*;
"z"   (ts, tz), a consonant, as in *zero*; and
"zh"   (ch), a consonant, as "j" in *"jump."*

SPELLING OF CHINESE NAMES OF PERSONS

In accordance with the Chinese phonetic alphabet, the late Chairman Mao Tsetung's name will be spelled "Mao Zedong"; the late Premier Chou En-lai's name will be "Zhou Enlai"; and the late Chairman of the Standing Committee of the National People's Congress, Chu Teh, and will be "Zhu De."

Following are names of Party leaders of China, romanized according to the chinese phonetic alphabet. The old spelling is in parentheses for reference.

Chairman of the Central Committee of the Chinese Communist Party:
    Hua Guofeng (Hua Kuo-feng)

Vice-Chairmen of the Party Central Committee:
    Ye Jianying (Yeh Chien-ying)
    Deng Xiaoping (Teng Hsiao-ping)
    Li Xiannian (Li Hsien-nien)
    Chen Yun (Chen Yun)
    Wang Dongxing (Wang Tung-hsing)

Members of the Political Bureau of the Party Central Committee:
Hua Guofeng (Hua Kuo-feng)

(The following are listed in the order of the number of strokes in their surnames.)

Wang Zhen (Wang Chen)
Wei Guoqing (Wei Kuo-ching)
Ulanhu (Ulanfu)
Fang Yi (Fang Yi)
Deng Xiaoping (Teng Hsiao-ping)
Deng Yingchao (Teng Ying-chao)
Ye Jianying (Yeh Chien-ying)
Liu Bocheng (Liu Po-cheng)
Xu Shiyou (Hsu Shih-yu)
Ji Dengkui (Chi Teng-kuei)
Su Zhenhua (Su Chen-hua)
Li Xiannian (Li Hsien-nien)
Li Desheng (Li Teh-sheng)
Wu De (Wu Teh)
Yu Qiuli (Yu Chiu-li)
Wang Dongxing (Wang Tung-hsing)
Zhang Tingfa (Chang Ting-fa)
Chen Yun (Chen Yun)
Chen Yonggui (Chen Yung-Kuei)
Chen Xilian (Chen Hsi-lien)
Hu Yaobang (Hu Yao-pang)
Geng Biao (Keng Piao)
Nie Rongzhen (Nieh Jung-chen)
Ni Zhifu (Ni Chih-fu)
Xu Xiangqian (Hsu Hsiang-chien)
Peng Chong (Pen Chung)

Alternate Members of the Political Bureau of the Party Central Committee:

(The following are listed in the order of the number of strokes in their surnames.)

Chen Muhua (Chen Mu-hua)
Zhao Ziyang (Chao Tsu-yang)
Seypidin (Saifudin)

SPELLING OF CHINESE PLACE NAMES

Names of well known places in China are listed as follows. The old spelling is in parentheses for reference.

Municipalities directly under the central authorities:
Beijing (Peking)
Shanghai (Shanghai)
Tianjin (Tientsin)

Provinces, autonomous regions for minority nationalities, and some well-known cities and other places:

Anhui (Anhwei) Province
  Hefei (Hofei)
  Bengbu (Pengpu)
Fujian (Fukien) Province
  Fuzhou (Foochow)
  Xiamen (Amoy)
Gansu (Kansu) Province
  Lanzhou (Lanchow)
Guangdong (Kwangtung) Province
  Guangzhou (Kwangchow)
  Shantou (Swatow)
Guangxi Zhuang (Kwangsi Chuang) Autonomous Region
  Nanning (Nanning)
  Guilin (Kweilin)
Guizhou (Kweichow) Province
  Guiyang (Kweiyang)
  Zunyi (Tsunyi)
Hebei (Hopei) Province
  Shijiazhuang (Shihchiachuang)
  Tangshan (Tangshan)
Heilongjiang (Heilungkiang) Province
  Harbin (Harbin)
  Daquing Oilfield (Taching Oilfield)
  Qiqihar (Chichihar)
Henan (Honan) Province
  Zhengzhou (Chengchow)
  Luoyang (Loyang)
  Kaifeng (Kaifeng)
Hubei (Hupeh) Province
  Wuhan (Wuhan)
Hunan (Hunan) Province
  Changsha (Changsha)
Jiangsu (Kiangsu) Province
  Nanjing (Nanking)
  Suzhou (Soochow)
  Wuxi (Wuhsi)
Jiangxi (Kiangsi) Province
  Nanchang (Nanchang)
  Jiujiang (Chiuchiang)
Jilin (Kirin) Province
  Changchun (Changchun)
Liaoning (Liaoning) Province
  Shenyang (Shenyang)
  Anshan (Anshan)
  Luda (Luta)
Nei Monggol (Inner Mongolia) Autonomous Region
  Hohhot (Huhehot)
  Baotou (Paotou)
Ningxia Hui (Ningsia Hui) Autonomous Region
  Yinchuan (Yinchuan)

Qinghai (Chinghai) Province
Xining (Sining)
Shaanxi (Shensi) Province
Xian (Sian)
Yanan (Yenan)
Shandong (Shantung) Province
Jinan (Tsinan)
Qingdao (Tsingtao)
Yantai (Yentai)
Shanxi (Shansi) Province
Taiyuan (Taiyuan)
Dazhai (Tachai)
Sichuan (Szechuan) Province
Chengdu (Chengtu)
Chongqing (Chungking)
Taiwan (Taiwan) Province
Taibei (Taipei)
Xinjiang Uygur (Sinkiang Uighur) Autonomous Region
Urumqi (Urumchi)
Xizang (Tibet) Autonomous Region
Lhasa (Lhasa)
Yunnan (Yunnan) Province
Kunming (Kunming)
Dali (Tali)
Zhejiang (Chekiang) Province
Hangzhou (Hangchow)

ABBREVIATIONS

APC   Agricultural Producers' Cooperatives
CCP   Chinese Communist Party
Comintern   Communist Third International
CPPCC   Chinese People's Political Consultative Conference
CYL   Communist Youth League
MAC   Military Affairs Committee
NCNA   New China News Agency
NPC   National People's Congress
PLA   People's Liberation Army

Introduction:
The Chinese Revolution
in Historical Perspectives

1

TRADITIONAL CHINESE POLITICAL SYSTEM

We begin a review of China's modern history with a discussion of the Chinese traditional political system prior to the 1911 revolution to provide the necessary historical background for an understanding of contemporary China. The traditional Chinese political system was based upon a predominantly agrarian society. It was administered by an officialdom of scholars and was controlled, theoretically, by an authoritarian emperor. Although the Chinese empire was centralized, there was a great deal of regional and local autonomy. In the following pages we will examine some of the major characteristics of the traditional Chinese political system: the emperor, Confucian ideology, the gentry-officialdom, and the nature of local autonomy.

The Emperor: Mandate of Heaven and Dynastic Cycle

The Chinese emperor ruled with unlimited power over his subjects. His power and legitimacy to rule the vast empire derived from the belief that he was the "Son of Heaven" with a mandate to rule on earth. The mandate of heaven was legitimate as long as the emperor ruled in a righteous way and maintained harmony within the Chinese society and between the society and nature. A corollary to the mandate of heaven theory was the right to rebel if the emperor failed to maintain harmony. It was, therefore, an unwritten constitution providing for rebellion as a means of deposing an intolerable imperial ruler. But rebellion was legitimate only if it succeeded.

Rebellions in Chinese history fall into two general patterns: peasant uprisings with religious overtones and military insurrections. The peasant uprisings, such as the Taiping Rebellion of 1850, while at times widespread, only once led directly to the founding of a new imperial dynasty. The Ming Dynasty, which succeeded that of the Mongols in the fourteenth century, was founded by a laborer.[1] Peasant unrest and rebellions did, however, contribute indirectly to new dynasties by further weakening declining reigns and providing evidence of the loss of the mandate of heaven. These new dynasties, with the exception of the Ming, were founded either through a takeover by a powerful Chinese military figure, who had exploited peasant discontent and obtained the support of the scholars, or by foreign invasion.

While dynastic changes were effected through rebellion or invasion, the form and substance of government remained essentially unchanged. Each new emperor accepted the Confucian ideology, claiming the mandate of heaven for himself by virtue of success. He governed the empire through the established bureaucratic machinery administered by career officials. Each ruler was dependent upon these officials to administer the vast, populous empire. Dynasties rose and fell, but the officialdom remained intact. Each of the twenty-four historic dynasties followed a common pattern of development, the dynastic cycle. At the beginning of a new dynasty, a period of national unity under virtuous and benevolent rule flourished and usually was accompanied by intellectual excitement and ferment; then mid-way in the cycle, a period of mediocre rule, accompanied by signs of corruption and unrest, emerged; finally at the end of the cycle, natural disasters occurred for which the ruler was unable to provide workable remedies, and a successful rebellion or invasion was mounted. A new dynasty was born and the cycle repeated itself.[2]

Confucian Ideology

Confucianism, which permeated traditional Chinese society, is basically conservative and establishment-oriented in nature. The central concepts stress the need to achieve harmony in society through moral conduct in all relationships. The mandate of heaven implied explicit adherence to the Confucian theory of "government by goodness."[3] This code of proper behavior for the emperor and all government officials was prescribed in detail in the writings of Confucius and his disciples. The officials were recruited on the basis of competitive examinations designed to test mastery of the Confucian classics. It was assumed that once the Confucian ethic was mastered and internalized by the scholar-officials, a just and benevolent government would result. Since the government was administered by those who possessed the required ethics and code of conduct, there was really little need for either the promulgation of laws or for the formal structuring of government institutions.

As the officially sanctioned political ideology, Confucianism conditioned and controlled the minds of the rulers and the ruled alike; it became the undisputed "orthodox doctrine of the imperial state."[4] It was perpetuated by the scholars as the basic foundation for the education of young men of means. Traditional Confucian ideology made its greatest impact on the wealthy elite. It left an "ideological vacuum" among the peasantry, the bulk of the population then as now, who were more concerned with the burden of taxes and the hardship of life than with theories of government.[5] In later chapters we will discuss in detail how the Chinese Communist Party has successfully molded in the minds of the Chinese people a different but equally orthodox political ideology. It is sufficient to note here the central role of political ideology in both imperial and communist Chinese systems.

The Gentry-Officialdom

Under the imperial system, the government officials—the mandarins—dominated the political and economic life of China. The mandarins were those individuals who held office by virtue of imperial degrees obtained by passing the civil service examinations. They came almost solely from the wealthy landholding class with the resources to provide extended education for their sons. Because of the status and the power of the office, the mandarin officials were able to acquire fortunes in landholdings for themselves and their families. They constituted the small, privileged upper class of the Chinese agrarian society. Under the imperial civil service for the Manchu Dynasty—the last dynasty before the revolution of 1911—these officials were estimated to total not more than forty thousand, or only about two percent of the population.[6] These officials of the imperial civil service wielded complete and arbitrary power over their subjects, the vast majority of whom were peasants living in the countryside. A typical magistrate for a Chinese county, according to one study, was responsible for the lives and well-being of about a quarter of a million subjects.[7] The magistrate, therefore, had to seek the cooperation and support of the large landholders to administer the county on behalf of the emperor and the central administration in Beijing. This administrative setup illustrates the gulf that existed between the educated elite and the illiterate peasants and indicates the hierarchical structure of the Chinese imperial rule.

The Chinese bureaucracy was classified into ranks and grades, each with a special set of privileges and a compensation scale. A voluminous flow of official documents and memoranda moved up and down the hierarchical ladder. At each level of the hierarchy a certain prescribed form and literary style had to be observed—a multiplication of bureaucratic jargon. To control the huge bureaucracy, the emperor designated special censors in the various levels of the government to report on the conduct of public officials. The provincial governor or the top man in a branch of the central bureaucracy in Beijing could become a bottleneck in the policy initiation and implementation process. At the lowest level of administration—the Chinese county—all important decisions affecting the community were made by the elites with the blessing of the magistrate. These decisions often disregarded, or were contrary to, the wishes of the earth-bound peasants, who constituted the majority. Arbitrary decision making, unresponsive to the uneducated masses in the villages, remains to this day a basic problem in the relationship between the leaders and the led in China. In traditional Chinese politics, as in modern China, the elites or officials exercised control over the mass of peasants.

Local Autonomy

While the Chinese imperial government was centralized at the court in Beijing and was hierarchical in structure, the system did permit some degree of autonomy at the local level, provided that this did not interfere with the absolute authority of the emperor. A magistrate for a county, the lowest administrative unit in traditional China, could not possibly carry out his duties without working with and through the "local power structure."[8] This power structure was headed by the large landowners but included merchants, artisans, and other persons of wealth and power in the community. As a convenient administrative arrangement, these groups were sanctioned by the magistrate to manage their own affairs within their own established confines. The magistrate naturally reserved the right to intervene if he deemed it necessary. Under this pragmatic arrangement, spokesmen for special interest groups in the community, such as the clan, the merchants' guilds, and the secret societies, often articulated their views and positions before the magistrate by informal and unofficial means but never overtly by heavy pressure. It was considered an unforgivable sin for officials to organize themselves into factions which advocated competing interests of groups in the community. But articulation of interest for groups often was made by officials within the bureaucratic framework.[9] Thus, there was keen competition and maneuvering by officials, within the bureaucratic setup, to gain favorable decisions on a particular matter. In all instances, politics of this sort was conducted in secrecy and was influenced by the personal ties which competing officials might have with the local power structure, by their own rank within the bureaucratic hierarchy, and by their finesse in the maneuverings.

THE CHINESE REVOLUTION, 1911–1937

Long before the Manchu Dynasty reached its lowest ebb in the cyclical decline, reform efforts were made to arrest further spread of its decay. The reform movements were largely remedial measures aimed at the inefficient and corrupt bureaucracy. They attempted to strengthen the imperial government's capability to meet unrest and rebellion in the countryside, the source of China's manpower, food supply, and government revenues. Unrest and rebellion were triggered by the demands of an increased population on the limited supplies that the land could produce and by the perennial occurrences of drought, flood, and famine. Confidence in the Manchu Dynasty's ability to govern received a severe blow in 1842 when European governments forced open the closed doors of China with unequal treaties that provided for special territorial concessions to foreigners for trade and missionary activities. Reformers then sought to strengthen the old Chinese empire by making changes in the traditional institutions, such as the examination system and the military establishment. The optimism of the reformers was dashed when China received her greatest humiliation—defeat by Japan in 1895. This defeat convinced some that reform alone could not possibly save the empire, and marked the beginning of the idea of revolutionary change to overthrow the traditional imperial system.

Revolution of 1911

One leader who advocated revolutionary change was Dr. Sun Yat-sen. In 1894 he founded a small secret society among overseas Chinese for the purpose of overthrowing the decaying Manchu dynasty. As a revolutionary with a price on his head, Sun was forced to operate and organize abroad much of the time. After many years of hard work in southeast Asia, Japan, and Hawaii, Sun's movement took hold among educated young Chinese abroad. In 1905, four hundred of Sun's followers gathered in Japan to form the first viable revolutionary movement, the Tung Meng Hui.[10] The members took a solemn oath to bring down the alien Manchu empire and to replace it with a Chinese republic. Ten different attempts were organized and financed by the group, headquartered variously in Tokyo and Hanoi, to strike down the vulnerable Manchu rule by assassinating imperial officials. As these revolutionary attempts failed, one by one, and more revolutionaries lost their lives, the movement became demoralized and ran low on funds. On October 10, 1911, an eleventh attempt was made. It resulted in a successful uprising by discontented and dissatisfied provincial officials, merchants, and im-

6

perial army commanders. The Manchu emperor abdicated, and shortly thereafter the Chinese imperial dynastic system was ended.

While Dr. Sun's revolutionary movement, comprised largely of students, youths, and overseas Chinese, gave impetus and momentum to the revolution, it was not the force which brought down the empire. It was the new imperial army, headed by Yuan Shihkai, that forced the abdication. Yuan Shihkai assumed the power of the government immediately after the abdication, and stayed on to become the first president of the Chinese republic, under an agreement with Dr. Sun who had little bargaining power. The new republic floundered from the start. Very few Chinese had any real understanding of Western democracy. All of the Chinese political traditions and institutions were designed for imperial rule and, therefore, were ill suited for constitutional democracy. Yuan Shihkai increasingly disregarded the constitution, and finally attempted to establish himself as emperor. The Chinese nation disintegrated as the new government proved incapable of commanding allegiance from the people in the midst of mounting domestic problems and the constant meddling in Chinese internal affairs by European powers and Japan. Yuan's death in 1916 marked the final collapse of the central government's effective authority.[11]

Warlordism and the Nationalist Revolution

The disintegration of the Chinese nation actually meant the emergence of a warlord period, which prevailed for two decades from 1916 to 1936. At Yuan's death, some of his officers and others with sufficient power seized control of various regions. These territories were controlled by the warlords, who maintained private armies manned with conscripted peasants, to protect and extend their provincial domains. Even Sun Yatsen and his followers had to seek refuge under the protection of the warlord in Canton. Sun's revolutionary program now called for the eventual establishment of constitutional government in three stages: 1. unification of the nation through elimination of warlordism by military force and termination of foreign intervention in China, 2. a period of political tutelage to prepare the people for democratic government, and 3. the enactment of a constitution by the people. Neither the European powers nor the warlords paid any attention to Dr. Sun, who had become disillusioned and desperate for a way to save China from further disintegration.

The political turmoil in China provided the impetus for an intellectual awakening. In 1919 this intellectual ferment culminated in the May Fourth Movement, instigated by high school and university students and their teachers to search for a model for building a new China. The May Fourth Movement led the reform in the written Chinese language, from the archaic classical style to use of the vernacular, or everyday spoken form. It also introduced the study of Western science, technology, and political ideologies, including Marxism. The movement was closely tied in with demonstrations by university students against foreign intervention in Chinese affairs and against warlordism. These activities gave impetus to the new nationalistic and patriotic feeling emerging among the general population.

It was in this atmosphere of ferment and feelings of anger, humiliation, and disillusionment that a nationalist revolution took form. Dr. Sun fled from the southern warlord in Canton to Shanghai in 1922. There he was contacted by an agent of the Communist Third International (the Comintern), who offered assistance to the Chinese revolutionary movement. Sun accepted the offer and signed an agreement to receive, from the Soviet Union through the Comintern, personnel to reorganize Sun's ineffective political party along the lines of the Communist Party of the Soviet Union, and limited arms and training in Soviet military schools for members of the revolutionary armies to be organized by Dr. Sun's followers. In addition, the agreement called for an alliance with the infant Chinese Communist Party under the new National People's Party (the Nationalists), the *Kuomintang*. A military academy was established in Whampoa, not far from the city of Canton, to train an officer corps to lead the newly recruited armies. Although Dr. Sun died in 1925, a military expedition was launched in 1926 to unify China by defeating the warlords. News of the expedition did unify the people with nationalistic feelings and aroused the populace against foreign imperialism.

The expedition was launched under an uneasy alliance between Sun's followers, who were receiving financial backing from merchants in coastal cities and from large landowners in the countryside, and the members of the Chinese Communist Party, controlled by the Comintern. By March of 1927, the new nationalist government had been dominated by the left-wing elements of the Kuomintang and the communists with headquarters in Wuhan in central China. When the expedition had gained control of eastern China on its push north, Chiang Kaishek, commander of the revolutionary armies and successor to Sun Yatsen, decided to end the internal schism between the left and right by first eliminating members of the Chinese Communist Party within the revolutionary movement. In April 1927, a lightning strike massacred communists in the cities under Chiang's control. This surprise blow, known as the "Shanghai Massacre," was so effective that it practically decimated the communist ranks. Chiang also expelled the Soviet advisers from China. Then in Nanjing he established the nationalist government, which was recognized by most nations as the legitimate government of China in the 1940s. The remaining Chinese communists sought refuge in the mountainous regions in central China after 1930.

China Under the Nationalists: 1927–1937

During the decade of Kuomintang rule from 1927 to 1937, there was modest progress made in many areas of modernization, initiated by the Nationalists under the leadership of Chiang Kaishek and his Western-trained advisers and administrators. For the first time, China had a modern governmental structure. As soon as major provincial warlords were eliminated or coopted into the system, the transportation and industrial facilities were improved and expanded in the area. Earnest attempts were made to expand elementary school education and to provide political indoctrination for the young. Most important, from Chiang's point of view, was the building of a more efficient and dedicated modern army for a host of purposes, including the eventual elimination of warlords and the communist guerrillas in mountainous operating areas of central China, as well as protecting China's borders from foreign attack.

There were glaring negative features in the Nationalist balance sheet. First, no real efforts were made to provide progressive economic and social programs to improve the lot of the people. Land reform measures to alleviate the plight of the peasants were mostly on paper. Second, the regime alienated the intellectuals by its repressive measures against them in the guise of purging any elements of communist influence from their ranks. Third, enormous expenditures from the national treasury were devoted to the "extermination" of the Chinese communists operating in remote mountain regions. The Nationalists steadfastly refused to seek a nonmilitary solution to the problem of insurrection by the communists. Nor were they willing to seek consultation with other political groups, let alone share political power with other elements of the Chinese society to pave the way for termination of their "tutelage rule." The Kuomintang's modest accomplishments in nation building were soon obliterated by its obsession to eliminate all opposition.

Time was not on the side of the Nationalists. In 1931, when they had achieved some measure of national unification and modernization in the midst of waging encirclement campaigns against the communist guerrilla forces, the Japanese militarists annexed resource-rich Manchuria and made advances into northern China, inside the Great Wall. The Nationalist regime faced a hard choice in allocating its limited resources between the Japanese aggressors and the communist insurgents. In the early 1930s Chiang's strategy was to rapidly annihilate the communist guerrilla forces and then turn to face the Japanese. However, rising public sentiment, expressed in frequent demonstrations, demanded that the regime prevent further territorial losses to the Japanese, and in December 1936, Chiang was forced to join in a united front with the Chinese communists to fight the Japanese.

THE ORIGIN AND RISE
OF THE CHINESE COMMUNIST MOVEMENT

Although Marxism was introduced in China about the time of World War I, this ideology, which called for revolution by an urban proletariat under mature capitalism, elicited little attention. Fabian socialism—progressive and social change through gradual constitutional means, developed in England in 1884—became the most popular liberal ideology from the West. For example, Dr. Sun's program incorporated socialist planks, including nationalization of land, a welfare state, and a planned economy. Interest in Marxism suddenly flowered among Chinese intellectuals after the 1917 Bolshevik Revolution in Russia. They saw in Lenin's revolution a relevant solution to China's political and economic problems. The keen interest in Bolshevism also reflected disillusionment with Western democracy as a model for Chinese development. In addition, it expressed Chinese bitterness over the imperialist activities of the Western democracies in China.

The early Chinese Marxists and the founders of the Chinese Communist Party were leading intellectuals in the Beijing National University (Beita). In 1918, Li Dazhao, the university's head librarian, formed a Marxist study group to which many young students, including a library assistant named Mao Zedong, were attracted. These young students were more interested in learning how to make a revolution than in theorizing about Marxism. With some urging from Comintern agents, the Chinese Communist Party was formed on July 1, 1921. The group of thirteen intellectuals and revolutionaries, representing a total of fifty-seven members, were called together by Chen Duxiu, who became the first secretary general. Meetings for the first two party congresses were held secretly in the French concession in Shanghai to prevent harassment from the police. This was the very modest beginning of the party and the movement that took root in later years.

The CCP and the Comintern

For the first six years of the CCP's existence, 1921–1927, the movement was under the control and direction of the Third International, or the Comintern. The Comintern was formed in 1919 at the insistence of Lenin, who wanted a new international organization, controlled by Moscow, to provide direction for all proletariat parties and to promote anti-imperialist revolutions throughout the world. Moscow directed and controlled the CCP and its leadership through Soviet Comintern agents who came to China with financial aid and military materiel. The leadership of the CCP before 1934, with few exceptions, was in the hands of the "returned Chinese bolsheviks," trained for party work in Moscow under the sponsorship of the Comintern.

The Comintern's doctrine insisted that revolutions in colonial areas must be based on industrial workers. Its strategy called for the participation of nonproletariat elements, such as the bourgeoisie, in a united front alliance to lead national revolutions. The manifestos adopted by four consecutive CCP congresses, from 1922 to 1925, echoed the Comintern line, calling for a revolutionary alliance with the landlord-merchant based Kuomintang, Dr. Sun's Nationalist Party. This Comintern strategy, which limited the communist base to urban industrial workers and called for individual communists to join the Kuomintang under a united front, enhanced the CCP's growth as a viable political party during its early years.

By 1927, the united front alliance had become unworkable. Chiang Kaishek's power as Commander in Chief and head of the Kuomintang was threatened by leftist elements in control of the revolutionary government, which was supported by the communists. As pointed out earlier, Chiang decided to purge the communists from his organization in the famous "Shanghai Massacre" and to set up a rival government in Nanjing. Not long after, the leftist-dominated Wuhan government also turned on the communists when it became known that the Comintern, under direct orders from Stalin, had instructed the CCP to eliminate the landlord elements and militarists in order to transform the alliance into a new revolutionary force. This also turned out to be a bloody mass execution of the communists who were caught.

Instead of admitting the mistake of his China policy, Stalin blamed the CCP leaders for their failure to prepare the workers in Wuhan for action.[12] Partly as a rebuttal to criticism raised by Leon Trotsky, Stalin ordered the Comintern agents in China to plan a series of armed insurrections in the hope that quick victories would silence any criticism of the failure of his united front policy.[13] On August 1, 1927, now celebrated as founding day of the People's Liberation Army, Zhou Enlai and Zhu De led a mutiny of communist troops within the Kuomintang forces in Nanchang in central China. After occupying the city briefly, the communists were forced to seek refuge as guerrillas in the hills of eastern Guangdong province. The CCP also authorized a number of "Autumn Harvest Uprisings" in the fall of 1927 in central and southern China.

One of these was led by Mao Zedong in his home province of Hunan. These uprisings were ill-fated misadventures which ended in defeat and brought heavy losses to the already decimated CCP ranks. When Mao and his group sought refuge in the mountain stronghold of Chingkanshan on the Hunan-Jiangxi border in central China, he repudiated the Comintern-inspired strategy. As a reprimand, Mao was dismissed briefly from his membership on the Politburo, the executive and policy making body of the party.

After the united front between the CCP and the Kuomintang ruptured, the Chinese communist movement fragmented into two areas of operation: one in the cities as an underground movement, with close links to the Comintern; the other in rural areas as experimental soviets, operating almost autonomously and feuding constantly with the Comintern advisers. By the end of 1930, the party had been driven out of the cities, and only pockets of guerrilla bands operated in remote mountain regions of central and southern China, plus a pocket of operation in northern Shaanxi. The plight of the CCP was evidenced by the fact that its central committee had to operate underground in Shanghai's foreign concessions and the Sixth Party Congress had to meet in Moscow in 1928. The leadership of the party was still in the hands of the returned Bolsheviks who adhered to the Comintern policies. In a last attempt to recapture an urban base for a proletarian revolution, the CCP leadership, under Li Lisan, launched an attack from the rural bases in the summer of 1930, with the objective of capturing a number of cities on the Changjiang (Yangtse) River. Like previous Comintern-instigated misadventures, this one also ended in failure, with the small bases in rural mountain regions under blockade by Chaing Kaishek's forces. The Chinese communists' future at this juncture seemed bleak.

The Rise of Mao Zedong and Military Communism

The future of the Chinese communist movement hinged on the survival of the small pockets of experimental soviets in the remote rural areas, mostly in central and southern China. The CCP's decision, in the fall of 1931, to establish a Chinese Soviet Republic, which would unite the scattered bases, was both a political necessity and an admission that a revolution based on an urban proletariat was no longer possible in China. Thus, by 1931 when the CCP's central committee moved from urban Shanghai to the rural Jiangxi soviet, a decade-long quarrel within the Chinese communist movement, regarding the theoretical correctness of a revolutionary strategy based on the peasants, officially ended. The foremost proponent of a peasant base was the leader of the Jiangxi soviet, Mao Zedong. Mao had developed a strategy for victory during the six years he operated the Jiangxi guerrilla base. Besides the need for a highly disciplined united party, Mao's strategy contained three indispensable ingredients: 1. the development of a strong and mobile peasant-based Red Army for a protracted armed struggle, 2. the selection of a strategic terrain for military operations, and 3. the establishment of a self-sufficient economic base in the Red Army-controlled soviet areas to provide manpower and supplies for the armed struggle.[14] Mao believed that a highly disciplined party could only be built by a recruitment policy that would draw into the party the tough and dedicated guerrilla soldiers of the Red Army, who were predominantly poor peasants. The party became "militarized" as Mao began to build a new base for revolution.[15]

The Kuomintang intensified its attack against the guerrilla base in its fifth and most extensive military campaign, which included an effective blockade that deprived the guerrilla base of outside supplies, particularly salt. By 1934 the guerrilla base had to be abandoned. The communists broke out of the Kuomintang encirclement and moved the surviving forces, numbering not more than 150,000, westward and then north to the Great Wall. This was the legendary Long March of more than six thousand miles over treacherous terrain of high mountains and rivers, amidst ambushes from warlords, the Kuomintang troops, and hostile minorities enroute.[16] In October 1935, after almost a year's march, the greatly reduced forces of about 20,000 survivors arrived in Yanan in the north-western province of Shaanxi and established a new base for guerrilla operations. By this time the stormy Politburo meeting, held at Zunyi in southwest Guizhou Province in January 1935, had selected Mao as the undisputed leader of the CCP, including the cells operating in some urban areas, mainly industrial centers such as Shanghai and Wuhan. This marked the end of Comintern dominance and the beginning of Mao's supremacy as the CCP's political and military leader, which lasted for over forty years, until his death in 1976.

Expansion of Communism Under Mao and Final Victory

When Chiang Kaishek learned that the communists had established a base in Yanan, he sent a force of crack troops to Shaanxi. The Kuomintang force included soldiers that had been driven from Manchuria by the Japanese army in 1931. The Manchurian troops began to show signs of low morale and a reluctance to fight the communists. This was largely due to effective political propaganda by the communists, which stressed the urgent need for a united front against Japan. In an effort to step up the offensive, Chiang Kaishek went to Xian in Shaanxi to direct the campaign personally. The mutinous Manchurian troops seized Chiang as a hostage in order to force him to agree to a united front policy. The Chinese communists by then had established contact with the Manchurian troops. Both Mao Zedong and Zhou Enlai served as mediators for the release of Chiang Kaishek under an agreement for a united front to fight the Japanese. This was the Xian Agreement, which temporarily terminated the civil war and marked the beginning of a second alliance between the CCP and the Kuomintang.

When Japan attacked North China in the summer of 1937, the Red Army was swiftly brought into action under the united front agreement. The cessation of the civil war gave the CCP the needed respite to expand its base of operations and to strengthen its military forces for the eventual showdown with the Kuomintang.[17] As China suffered repeated military defeats by the Japanese, the CCP-controlled Red Army expanded its guerrilla operations behind enemy lines. Party membership grew rapidly from a little over twenty thousand at the end of the Long March in 1935, to over eight hundred thousand in 1939, and to about 1.2 million at the end of the war in 1945. Of this enlarged party membership, perhaps a million were party members of the "military supply system," peasants and patriotic students who served the Red Army without salary but under strict military discipline.[18] They were the backbone of the leadership, not only for the communist guerrilla forces, but also for the militarized border-region governments established in the areas under Red Army control. In each of these border regions, experiments in mild land reform and self-government by popular election were introduced. It was during this period that many of the practices and experiences became revolutionary traditions which persist today under the overall label of the "Yanan spirit."

When the Japanese surrendered in 1945, open clashes occurred between the Kuomintang and the communist forces in many parts of China. China was once again engulfed in civil war, but this time the communists were in a much stronger position in terms of discipline, numerical strength, and the will to combat—not to mention the support of the intellectuals and a large segment of the rural population. The policy of President Truman of the United States was to bring the parties together for a political settlement. A series of cease-fire agreements were reached under the U.S. supervision. The mediation efforts by General Marshall for the United States soon deteriorated. Neither side had any intention of observing the truce and settling the future of China by political means. As the strength and morale of the Kuomintang forces ebbed, the People's Liberation Army won victories over the Nationalist troops, equipped and supplied by the United States. By the summer and fall of 1948, the People's Liberation Army had overrun Manchuria and most of north China. Kuomintang forces were surrendering in divisional strength. With captured American military hardware, a large-scale military offensive was launched by the communists in the spring of 1949 against the remaining Kuomintang forces in central and southern China. Although the Nationalists did not flee to the island of Taiwan until December 1949, the communists convened the People's Political Consultative Conference on October 1, to establish a new People's Republic of China in Beijing. At last the Chinese communist movement, which began as a Marxist study group, had seized power in China. A new search now began to find a suitable development model to build an industrially powerful China.

CHINA'S SEARCH FOR A DEVELOPMENT MODEL

After almost eight years of war with Japan and four years of civil war, the initial years of the new republic were preoccupied with the immediate problems of consolidation and reconstruction. In the beginning, the CCP permitted a partial sharing of the political power it had seized with twenty-three other political elements and groups, under a coalition government, along the lines first formulated by Mao Zedong in his "New Democracy" in 1940 and "On Coalition Government" in 1945.[19] The central government in Beijing proliferated with ministries on economic affairs. More than fifty-five percent of the top national administrative posts were reserved for leaders of the CCP; the remainder were distributed among experienced and talented liberal noncommunist intellectuals. During these early years, the new regime also relied heavily on the regional pattern of government to superintend the provinces. The regional government was in turn bolstered by the military field armies which had conquered and remained stationed in these regions after the civil war.

The enormous task of reconstruction called, first of all, for a solution to the mounting inflation. During the last few months of the Nationalist regime, prices had risen eighty-five thousand times.[20] The inflation abated somewhat when the new regime came into power, but with huge budget deficits from increased governmental expenditures, inflation remained a serious problem. By a variety of fiscal and monetary devices, including the central control of local taxes and the measuring of prices and wages in terms of commodity units, prices were finally stabilized by the summer of 1950.

Private industry and commerce, while restricted, was rehabilitated and developed along with the socialistic national economy. National ministries of economic production saw to it that the privately owned industries obtained needed raw materials to make their products and that they received orders from private or state-owned enterprises for these goods and services. Rapid economic recovery was made, and by 1952 production had reached China's peak pre-1949 levels. This rapid recovery was attributable to the policy of gradualism in nationalization, with no outright confiscation of private industry. Privately owned industries were eventually transformed into joint state and private enterprises and finally into completely state-owned operations through the "buying-off" policy, under which former owners of private enterprises were paid interests on their shares at a rate fixed by the state.[21]

Land Reform: Transformation of the Countryside

By far the most important program enacted by the new regime, from 1950 to 1953, was agrarian reform. Land redistribution, a basic plank in the CCP programs, had been carried out in the early Soviet phase in the Jiangxi border areas, and later in the northwest, with varying degrees of intensity. In 1949, when the CCP took over the country, some five hundred million people were living in the rural villages. The land tenure system was such that "half the cultivated land was owned by less than one-tenth of the farm population, while two-thirds of the population owned less than one-fifth."[22] This serious problem of uneven land distribution was further aggravated by the large number of landless tenants who had to pay exorbitant annual rents, as high as sixty percent of their production. The 1950 Agrarian Reform Law was basically a mild reform measure which permitted rich peasants to retain their land and property (Article 6), and landlords to retain the land for their own use (Article 10). The later harsh treatment to the landlords, which accompanied the implementation of the land redistribution through the "struggle meetings" and the "people's tribunals" to settle accounts by the peasants, was attributable to the speedy implementation needed to prevent "foot dragging" by cadres and activists assigned to do the job and by the peasants themselves.[23] The Korean War also generated some fear on the part of the peasants of the possible return of the Nationalists.[24] The land redistribution was completed in 1952 when 113 million acres, plus draft animals and farm implements, were distributed to over three hundred million landless peasants.[25]

It soon became obvious that land redistribution was only a step toward collectivizing the countryside. The millions of new land-owning peasants realized very quickly that their small plots of land were too small to produce even enough to feed their families. The individual peasants simply did not have the means to acquire modern tools, much less to build irrigation projects. Having committed themselves to the party's cause by participating in the land redistribution, the peasants had to accept the party's new appeal for mutual aid teams, the pooling together of draft animals, implements, and shared labor. In 1953–1954, the mutual aid teams gave way to larger and more complicated cooperative ventures, the voluntary agricultural producers' cooperative (APCs). An agricultural producers' cooperative was, in essence, a unified management of farm production. The individual peasants pooled their land, draft animals, implements, and houses in return for shares in the enterprise. Detailed accounting was kept, and after deductions were made for expenses incurred and taxes to be paid, income was distributed to the members on the basis of their contributions, stated in terms of shares. While the movement was voluntary, the party conducted massive campaigns to persuade and sometimes to coerce peasants to join the APCs. Although an overwhelming majority of the peasants had joined the cooperatives by 1957, official accounts show resistance to the program. In some parts of the country peasants deliberately consumed what they produced to avoid forceful delivery to the government purchasing agencies.[26]

The APCs enabled the peasants to better utilize resources and labor. During the slack seasons, surplus labor could be mobilized easily to carry on small-scale irrigation works, such as making ditches, ponds, and dams. Combined surplus labor could reclaim land through irrigation and reforestation. The APCs certainly allowed the peasants to realize greater savings and investment. Even more important was the sharing of the risks of crop failure. Individual peasants no longer had to face the possibility of bankruptcy if crops failed. But there were also many problems inherent in the APCs: Many peasants were too poor to contribute funds to the cooperatives; there was a lack of such qualified technical personnel as accountants among the illiterate peasantry to provide efficient management; peasants were frequently unhappy when centralized purchasing and marketing operations were imposed on the cooperatives by the state, leading to intensified animosity toward the party, and a reluctance to cooperate.[27]

The First Five-Year Plan, 1953–1957, and the Soviet Model

By 1953 the regime had completed the immediate tasks of rehabilitating the war-torn economy and consolidating their control over the nation. With the end of the Korean War, the regime was confident enough to embark on a rapid industrialization program. The approach selected was the Stalinist strategy of long-term centralized planning, a proven socialistic model which had enabled the Soviet Union to emerge from World War II as the second most powerful nation in the world. For ideological reasons it was the only logical strategy comprehensible to the

Chinese communists at the time, particularly in view of the emerging bipolarization of the world into Soviet and Western orbits. The pragmatic Chinese were aware of the benefits in Soviet aid, in terms of both financial credit and technical assistance, which would be forthcoming to promote this model.[28]

Fundamental to the Stalinist model was the rapid build-up in the heavy industry sector through the concentrated allocation of investment into capital goods industries. The model also called for highly centralized decision making at the top to determine targets and quotas to be fulfilled by the various economic sectors.[29] In many ways, this strategy required basic structural change in the agricultural sector, from which the bulk of savings for investment must come. The introduction of agricultural producers' cooperatives was a necessary step in this structural change to accumulate these savings through increased agricultural production and controlled consumption. The First Five-Year Plan allocated fifty-eight percent of the twenty-billion-dollar investment fund to capital goods for heavy industries.[30] The bulk of these investment funds was financed by the Chinese themselves. The Soviet Union made considerable contributions in the form of technical assistance, construction and equipment of 154 modern industrial plants which were paid for by the Chinese, and the training of Chinese technicians. Soviet-trained Chinese technicians numbered about ten thousand by June 1960, when Soviet aid was suddenly withdrawn. By 1957, when the First Five-Year Plan was completed, it had brought an annual growth rate of eight percent to China's economic growth,[31] an impressive achievement by any standards. In addition, the First Five-Year Plan made a lasting investment in education (130,000 engineers graduated) and public health (the control of the communicable diseases, such as cholera and typhoid, which formerly had plagued the Chinese people).[32]

The First Five-Year Plan also had a number of drawbacks. First, the plan was rather costly when one considers that the bulk of the twenty billion dollars in investments came from the Chinese. Second, the plan required large forced savings from the agricultural sector. Third, the Stalinist model placed undue concentration of investment in such heavy industries as steel, at the expense not only of agriculture but also of light and consumer-goods industries. Fourth, the model required a high degree of centralization and the development of an elaborate bureaucratic structure to implement, control, and check the plan according to fixed targets and quotas. Fifth, since planning and implementation of the model emphasized the roles of technocrats, engineers, and plant managers, it thus neglected the need to politicize the millions of uneducated and tradition-oriented peasants for the rapid construction of an industrial socialistic state. After an agonizing reappraisal of the First Five-Year

Plan, Mao and his followers launched the Great Leap Forward in an attempt to obtain a faster rate of growth and to develop a socialistic economic model more suited to China's conditions and needs.

The Great Leap Forward and Communization Program, 1958-1959

Under the Great Leap Forward, the regime was to mobilize the creative enthusiasm of the Chinese masses for economic growth and industrialization in the same way it had mobilized the masses for the communist revolution.[33] The Great Leap would substitute its most plentiful resource, manpower, for capital goods in the same way that it had successfully substituted committed men for modern weapons during the guerrilla and civil war days. The unemployed were to be put to work, and the employed were to work much harder, under military discipline to make the gigantic leap to become an industrial power through the widespread use of labor-intensive, small-scale production. The emphasis was placed on the techniques of mass mobilization.

The program called for use of "dual technology." The Chinese economy at the end of the First Five-Year Plan consisted of a mixture of modern sectors (capital-intensive and large-scale) and traditional sectors (labor-intensive and small-scale). These two types of economic sectors in a typical developing country like China are more or less independent of each other. In the modern sectors, goods produced are mostly exported to earn foreign exchange to pay for the imported machines. In the traditional sectors, small-scale industries in villages are self-sufficient, providing virtually all of their own consumptive and productive needs. Under the Great Leap strategy, the modern sector would not need to supply capital goods for the traditional sector, but the traditional sector would increase its flow of food and raw materials to build up the industrial sector. This is the meaning of the Chinese slogans so familiar during the Great Leap period: "walking on two legs" and "self-reliance in the simultaneous development of industry and agriculture." Land was to be reclaimed, and irrigation systems were to be built by the peasants, using simple tools at their disposal. Rural communities were to build "backyard furnaces" to produce enough pig iron to allow China to surpass Great Britain in steel production. Other popular small-scale projects were electric power generators and chemical fertilizer plants.

Conceptually, the Great Leap model was not only rational, but had some economic validity.[34] However, there were unrealistic expectations and overzealous implementation of the program. In an effort to fulfill the required quotas, workers often sacrificed quality for quantity. Quality also suffered from a lack of technical knowledge among the peasants.

Some statistics on increased production were based on exaggeration and fabrication. Millions of tons of pig iron, much substandard and all a long way from being steel, were produced by backyard furnaces. Pig iron accumulated along railways, which could not possibly handle its movement, causing a serious bottleneck in the entire transport system.[35]

Merging of cooperatives into people's communes was an integral part of the Great Leap Forward program. The communes were, in essence, a device to collectivize the agricultural production on a scale much larger than the cooperatives. Unlike the APC, the commune became a local government, performing a multiplicity of functions in agriculture, industry, education, social welfare, public health, public works, and military defense. The peasants turned over to the collective entity their ownership in land, tools, draft animals, houses, and shares in the cooperatives. They then became members of a commune, of which they claimed collective ownership. In return, they were to receive five guarantees: food, clothing, housing, medical care, and education. During the early stage of the commune development in 1958, communal kitchens were installed to free more women for production. In some extreme cases, men and women lived in segregated communal dormitories, with their children in communal nurseries. The people's communes were hailed with great fanfare as the ideal collective life described by classical Marxism: "from each according to his ability and to each according to his needs."

By the spring of 1959 there were twenty-six thousand communes. Although there was no uniform size, an average commune consisted of about two thousand households, or about ten thousand peasants. Within each commune, peasants were organized into production brigades and production teams, the basic unit of the commune. This radical experiment encountered a host of problems. For instance, the peasants could not adjust to communal kitchens and dormitories. The discipline imposed by the cadres, those selected for leadership positions, for long hours of work at a feverish pace sapped the peasants' energy and enthusiasm. Without their tiny private plots for vegetables to supplement their meager diet, the peasants' general health declined. Initially, the peasants were neither willing nor able to make decisions under the commune setup, which required their participation. Their inexperience in the management of complex productive activities also made them reluctant to assume responsibilities. In 1959, some corrective measures were implemented: private garden plots were permitted, forced communal living was halted, and commune members were given adequate time for rest and recreation.

The numerous problems implicit in the Great Leap and communization, accompanied by natural disasters of flood and drought, should have doomed the program. In 1958, when the Great Leap and commune programs were launched, there was a good harvest. In 1959, heavy floods and drought laid waste almost half of the cultivatable land. Then, in 1960, floods, drought, and pests ravaged millions of acres. To make matters worse, the Soviets withdrew all their technicians and advisers from China in June 1960 because of their disagreement over the development strategy. The drastic reduction in agricultural production stalled the drive for rapid development of industry. Famine was averted by the imposition of rationing in the communes and by large purchases of grain from abroad. China's experience was typical of an agricultural setback in developing nations: Scarce foreign exchange had to be diverted from capital goods to food imports. A new policy had to be adopted to give first priority to a minimally sufficient food supply rather than to industrialization.

Post-Great Leap: Leadership Dissension and Economic Recovery

The failure of the Great Leap brought to a head growing division within the Chinese leadership, not only over development strategy, but also over the ideological implications of the strategy. This division is frequently referred to as the "red" (politics) versus "expert" (technology) controversy. Mao contended that sheer human will and determination, coupled with the correct puritanical mentality of a new "socialist man," could develop China. He felt that material incentives were not only unnecessary but undesirable. Mao's most outspoken critic was Marshal Peng Dehuai, the Defense Minister and a Politburo member.[36] Peng's criticism focused on three effects of the Great Leap: 1. the damage to the long-term economic development of China, which must rely on technical proficiency rather than sheer mobilization of the masses, 2. rejection of the Soviet development model would cause a deterioration in Sino-Soviet relations, and 3. the obvious decline in morale and efficiency he had observed in his inspection of the armed forces. Marshal Peng's central concern seemed to be that China needed a modern army, which must rest on the development of heavy industries and technical skills to produce and operate advanced weapons, including nuclear weapons. Peng delivered his criticisms at an enlarged meeting of the Politburo in Lushan in July and August of 1959. Red Guard pamphlets, circulated later during the Cultural Revolution, revealed that Mao admitted some mistakes in the implementation of the Great Leap, but, in the main, vigorously defended his role and policies associated with the program. He demanded a showdown at a subsequent enlarged meeting of the Central Committee, and won. After these Lushan meetings, Marshal

Peng was purged. Mao later was criticized for the purge of Peng. As planned before the Lushan meetings, Mao stepped down as the President of the People's Republic and handed the powerful position over to Liu Shaoqi, a leading party theoretician and able administrator.[37]

The policies initiated by Liu Shaoqi reversed and corrected the Great Leap programs. It should be noted that before Liu assumed office, the Central Committee and its Politburo, in close consultation with the party's provincial secretaries, had already made a number of recommendations to correct the mistakes of the Great Leap. Some of these measures are given here as a background to the policy dissension that came into full bloom during the Cultural Revolution. First, Liu called for a reintroduction of personal incentives, such as the private plots and free markets to spur agricultural production. Second, he issued directives to those who managed state enterprises, to pay strict attention to profits and losses: All enterprises must be managed and evaluated in terms of efficiency. Third, Liu insisted that technical "expertise" must command ideological "redness": Managers must have more authority in their plants than the ideologues. Fourth, he declared a relaxation of centralized planning by giving local units more freedom in setting their production quotas and targets. Fifth, he demanded that basic-level cadres observe strict discipline and report accurate statistics. Sixth, Liu introduced measures to reorganize the party by placing more emphasis on party discipline and institutional control mechanism; these measures helped him to consolidate his power and to place his supporters in key positions.

Soon the economic recovery took shape under Liu Shaoqi's direction.[38] Agricultural development was now the top economic priority. With the introduction of material incentives and a good harvest in 1962, economic conditions improved in the countryside. With hard work and an end to the constant ideological and political interference, many of the industrial projects were completed and new ones were initiated, despite the withdrawal of the Soviet technical assistance. The new economic policy continued to encourage the development of medium- and small-size industries in the countryside, such as farm equipment factories and rural electrification plants. In order to reduce China's dependence on Soviet imports, self-reliance was stressed by encouraging technological innovation and exploration for such new resources as petroleum, found in Daqing. By 1964, Premier Zhou Enlai announced that the recovery was complete, and a new Third Five-Year Plan was ready for implementation in 1966. The Chinese had learned that, with some realistic adjustment to suit the Chinese conditions, the centralized, planned economy, based on the Stalinist model, worked for China.

The Socialist Education Campaign, 1962–1965

The Socialist Education Campaign was the prelude to the Cultural Revolution.[39] It was a campaign of ideological education and of rectification of cadre behavior (which displays honest, hard-working leadership qualities). The main theme of the campaign was class struggle, a theme for which Mao fought hard when he resumed an active political role in the party at the tenth session of the Eighth Central Committee in 1962. Mao and other top leaders had become alarmed at reports of widespread corruption among the rural cadres. They feared that the free markets and private vegetable plots were fostering the growth of economic individualism, which posed a serious threat to the collective economy. The Socialist Education Movement consisted of three interrelated mass campaigns: 1. an educational campaign to assist the formation of poor and lower-middle peasant associations in order to prevent the rise of a class of well-to-do middle peasants, 2. a rectification campaign aimed at eliminating the corrupt practices of rural cadres, such as embezzlement, large wedding parties, and misuse of public property, and 3. a purification movement for the nation, with the People's Liberation Army (PLA) heroes as models, which stressed the virtues of self-sacrifice, the collective good, and endurance of hardship.

There was a great deal of controversy with respect to the directives and guidelines issued by the Central Committee. Mao's original instructions, the "earlier ten points," were altered by the central secretariat on instructions from Liu Shaoqi and Deng Xiaoping, who were then responsible for the day-to-day operation of the party. There were debates and quarrels among the top leaders, primarily between Mao and Liu, on methods of investigating corrupt cadres in rural communes.[40] Mao advocated open investigation in the communes by work teams of top cadres from the center; Liu wanted in-depth investigation by covert infiltration among the peasants, both to gather true information and to ferret out the corrupt cadres.[41] There was also divergence between Mao and Liu in terms of the party's role and its leaders in the Socialist Education Movement. Mao intended it to be a mass education movement. Liu wanted a party-controlled rectification operation with emphasis on corrective and remedial measures, in accordance with established norms within the party organization.

The entire Socialist Education Movement was carried out under a cloud of uncertainty and contradicting instructions. The local cadres, most of them recruited after land reform in the early 1950s, had developed strategies for survival; they knew how to play the game and how to protect themselves against outside investigations by work teams dispatched from far away Beijing or provincial capitols. If necessary, these bureaucratized cadres would withhold information or intimidate poor peasants. By 1965 most of the Socialist Education Movement had ended in failure, mainly because of disagreements over the proper implementation for the campaign.

Only the campaign to emulate PLA heroes was a success. It began in the military where the soldiers were required to form small groups to systematically study Mao's writings, particularly three essays on self-sacrifice and self-negation, written for the cadres during the Yanan days. Exemplary PLA companies were formed to demonstrate their living application of the thought of Mao. This ideological education campaign within the PLA was personally supervised by the new Defense Minister, Lin Biao. With its campaign's success in the military, a nation-wide movement to emulate the PLA was launched.

The battle lines for the Cultural Revolution were now clearly drawn. Although the party apparatus under Liu Shaoqi and Deng Xiaoping had shown its disdain for Mao's mass mobilization approach (seeing it as disruptive to the routine operation of the party and government), the PLA, under Lin Biao, had not only embraced Mao's style but applied Mao's teachings to their activities. Mao now saw that the cadres who monopolized the party apparatus, and the career-oriented status seekers, had become resistant to change and were reluctant to accept the new socialist values. The party could no longer be considered an effective instrument for the revolutionary change Mao so much desired.

THE CULTURAL REVOLUTION AND THE LIN BIAO AFFAIR

Before describing the events of the Cultural Revolution, let us look briefly at some of the issues underlying this great upheaval. If we survey the voluminous literature about the Cultural Revolution, we may find several basic themes which serve to explain the causes of the upheaval.[42] One popular theme depicted the Cultural Revolution as an "ideological crusade" aimed at preventing gradual erosion of the revolutionary spirit fostered by the early guerrilla experience of reliance on the masses and egalitarianism. Closely related to this was the theme that a thorough rectification campaign had to be waged in order to halt further growth of bureaucratic tendencies within the party and government. Another theme contended that, as the regime moved toward further development, its leaders inevitably would reach a point where resolution of policy differences regarding strategy and priority would become more difficult. Prolonged dissension among the top leadership generally resulted in a power struggle between contending groups, with each jockeying for position and eventual vindication of its views. Thus policy differences and power struggle among a divided leadership became intertwined. In addition, the contest for power among the top leadership in China probably had been intensified by the question of succession to Mao as the leader of the party.

There is some evidence that the launching of the Cultural Revolution coincided with deterioration of Sino-Soviet relations and the escalation of the Vietnam War by the United States. Some scholars contend that the Soviet Union's offer to China, in 1965, of a joint action to counteract the United States' escalation in the Vietnam War served as the catalyst that triggered the policy debate among China's top leaders.[43]

Events of the Cultural Revolution

The Cultural Revolution was officially launched on August 8, 1966, when the eleventh session of the Eighth Central Committee approved a sixteen-point guideline for conducting a thorough revolution. The revolution was to be concerned not only with the economic base (the socialist collectivized economy) but also with the superstructures (education, the arts, literature, and institutional arrangements).

Some nine or ten months before the Central Committee approved the guidelines, the battle had actually begun with a controversy over the political implications of a play by a historian and playwright, Wu Han. Wu Han, who was also deputy mayor of Beijing, and his superior, Peng Zhen, mayor of Beijing and a member of the Politburo, were politically allied with Liu Shaoqi. The play, *Hai Rui's Dismissal from Office,* was a historical allegory about a Ming official's final vindication after his dismissal from office. Mao and his supporters charged that the purpose of the play was to vindicate Marshal Peng Dehaui, who had been purged for his 1959 criticism of Mao and the Great Leap program. When a lengthy critique of the play by Yao Wenyuan, a radical writer from Shanghai and a supporter of Mao, was refused publication in the party press, Lin Biao had it published in the PLA paper, the *Liberation Army Daily.* This action forced publication in the leading party paper, the *People's Daily,* for nationwide circulation. At first, the party leaders refused to admit the political implication in the play, saying it was a purely academic matter. After Mao's supporters intensified their attack, Liu Shaoqi and Peng Zhen appointed a team to investigate the matter. The team's final report, known as the "February Outline Report," written under the direct supervision of Peng Zhen and subsequently approved by the Politburo under the acting leadership of Liu Shaoqi, called for toleration of ideas within the party, less stress on the class struggle in academic and literary fields, and a rectification campaign against the radical left. Mao rebuked the "February Report" and asked for mass criticism of art and literature.

The literary debate was followed by mass criticism, which led to purges of top party and military leaders. The purged party leaders included Beijing municipal party committee members Peng Zhen and Wu Han. General Lo Juijin, the chief-of-staff for the PLA, was also purged because of his advocacy of military professionalism and his reluctance to conduct Socialist Education Movement in the army. The attack then spread to the party committees in China's two leading universities, Beita and Qinghua. The university students organized themselves as Red Guards, Mao's "revolutionary successors."[44]

Soon high school and university students throughout China formed their own Red Guard groups to investigate cadres' behavior and attitudes.[45] This gave the students an opportunity not only to air their grievances against school officials and teachers but also to vent their frustrations with the system's inability to absorb the large number of graduating youths into appropriate jobs and to provide advancement opportunities.[46] By late August and early fall of 1966, the Red Guard movement had grown to such proportions that normal schooling had to be abandoned. Mass criticism, led by Red Guards against the party leaders and their apparatus, became an everyday occurrence. Party leaders were dragged out on the street for failing to provide the answers that the students wanted to hear. To counter the roaming Red Guards organized by university students, party leaders in many localities formed their own Red Guards. This was a period of chaos and violence as factional Red Guard groups feuded endlessly with each other. All functions of the party and some of government were at a standstill. The only organization that was intact was the military. The Red Guard movement was supported by the radical leaders loyal to Mao and was fueled by access to confidential information about the leaders and their policy differences. From this movement, the tabloid Red Guard wall posters became a major source of insight about the policy debates to the outside world. The Central Committee and its secretariat had by now ceased to function. In its place, a Central Cultural Revolution Group had been formed, dominated by the radicals with shifting membership, to act as the party's most authoritative spokesmen with direct lines of communication to Mao.[47]

To outside observers, China in January and February of 1967 was a gigantic spectacle of big-character posters, slogans, and endless processions and meetings in the sea of banners and portraits of Mao. Factionalized Red Guard groups openly employed physical force in their frequent skirmishes against each other all over China after the party machinery had been effectively paralyzed. The established party authorities, in some cases with the active support of the local PLA commands, mounted their counterattack against the radical Red Guards, which resulted in more bloodshed. This stage of chaos and violence reached such alarming proportions that the only alternative left was to call in the military to restore order and to prevent any more violence. The PLA was ordered by Mao to intervene in domestic turmoil in January 1967. The main tasks in the military's intervention were to fill the power vacuum created by the dismantled party and government organizations in the provinces, to supervise economic production, and to prevent violence by the rampaging Red Guards. The PLA was also to provide ideological training in universities and schools and to thereby exercise control over the students after their return to campuses. Military control commissions, a device that had been employed for control and consolidation of the country in the early 1950s, reappeared in order to provide supervision and control in industries and many other institutions of the party and government. By the end of 1967, the military was effectively in control of China and began, rather uneasily, to govern.[48]

Once the military was in control, it intervened in provincial politics to establish provincial revolutionary committees—a new power structure to temporarily replace the provincial party committees. The provincial revolutionary committees were made up of representatives of the PLA commands, the Red Guards as a mass organization, and the repentant veteran cadres—the "three-way alliance." With the inception of the revolutionary committees, the military became the real power. The success of the revolutionary committees was dependent upon the PLA's active intervention on behalf of Mao's supporters in Beijing. Order was gradually restored in the provinces as new revolutionary committees were formed to operate as party committees, purged and cleansed, at least for the moment, of "revisionist" tendencies.

When the Ninth Party Congress met in Beijing in April 1969, it signaled the end of the Cultural Revolution and the reestablishment of the party structure. The party congress, dominated by Lin Biao and his military supporters, sanctioned "a revolutionary seizure of power," as described by Edgar Snow.[49] Unity, proclaimed by Lin Biao, was the major, but short-lived, theme of the Ninth Party Congress.

Effects of the Cultural Revolution

Although the effects of the Cultural Revolution on the Chinese political system will be discussed in later chapters, it may be helpful to outline here some of the long-term effects the upheaval had on the Chinese political scene.

First, one direct and far reaching effect of the Cultural Revolution was the change it brought about in the relationship between the power center in Beijing and the provinces. Beginning in 1969, there was a steady increase in the representation of provinces at the central decision-making level, as evidenced by the number of provincial party secretaries elected to the party's central committees (see Table 5 in Chapter 5). Second, the political prominence of the military at both the central and provincial levels was more apparent during and immediately after the Cultural Revolution. The increase of provincial and military authorities in decision making, both at the center and in the provinces, benefitted the more pragmatic veteran administrators (who had been allies of the regional and provincial military power) in their conflict with the more radicalized party ideologues. This rise in political influence by the provincial leaders, many of whom had their power base in the military establishment, certainly must be attributed to the military intervention in the Cultural Revolution.[50] Third, the greatest impact of the Cultural Revolution was on education.[51] As we shall see in later chapters, not only curriculum content and teaching methods were reorganized, but educational opportunities were opened up for those of rural nonelite background. However, abolition of the examination system for university entrance and for measuring competence at the higher education level contributed to low academic quality in students and, in the long run, impeded the country's advanced scientific and technological development and research. Fourth, the Cultural Revolution's stress on decentralization in decision making and on mass participation in economic development programs called attention to the evils of bureaucratization, so common in all planned economic systems. To some analysts, participation in economic decision making contributed to both more institutional responsiveness and institutional accountability to the masses.[52]

The Lin Biao Affair, 1969–1973

In a rare occurrence in the regime's history, a complete and nationwide halt of all civilian and military flights was ordered by the central government of the People's Republic of China for three days, from September 11–13, 1971—an unprecedented event in terms of the intensity and duration. The halt was accompanied by the sudden orders cancelling all furloughs for the People's Liberation Army, which were monitored by the Japanese. A week later, the British Foreign Office was advised by its charge d'affaires in Beijing that the annual October 1 National Day parade and reception were to be cancelled. There were reports of unusual troop movements and of an army alert throughout China.[53] The ubiquitous Premier Zhou and the familiar top military leaders were conspicuously absent from public view and became inaccessible to foreign visitors. As the unresolved Chinese mystery deepened, the outside world could only speculate on what was happening inside China.

Then, on September 30, as the Chinese kept their silence, the Soviet news agency Tass reported from Moscow that a Chinese air force jet plane had crashed on September 13 at Unden Khan, west of Ulan Bator, the capital of the Mongolian People's Republic. The Mongolian government accused the Chinese of violating its air space and demanded an explanation from the Chinese. The crashed air force plane contained, Tass reported, nine charred bodies with firearms, documents, and equipment identified as belonging to the Chinese air force.

For ten months, from September 1971 to June 1972, the world outside continued to be confused, and focused its speculation on what was going on inside China by linking the plane crash in Mongolia with the probable downfall of Lin Biao and his lieutenants in the military hierarchy. Then, in 1972, [54] in separate meetings with Prime Minister Bandaranaike of Ceylon in June and Foreign Minister Schumann of France in July, Chairman Mao revealed that Lin Biao was killed in a plane crash while fleeing from China after his unsuccessful attempt to assassinate the chairman and to carry out a coup d'etat. Simultaneously, statements were issued by the Chinese embassy in Algiers and by Wang Hairung, an Assistant Foreign Minister and Mao's niece, confirming Lin Biao's death in a plane crash and the reason for the flight abroad. Subsequently, Premier Zhou, in an interview with visiting members of the American Society of Newspaper Editors and Publishers, elaborated further on the manner by which Lin Biao had met his death.[55]

Although semi-official revelation to foreign visitors by Mao and Zhou about Lin Biao's death had solved the ten-month mystery for the outside world, the reasons for Lin's demise remained a puzzle. It must be noted here that these semi-official revelations were made primarily for external consumption. Internally, an intensive rectification campaign had begun in September 1971, which involved study, discussion, and criticism based upon official documents and directives about the Lin Biao affair. The debate and intensive criticism, which engaged all the cadres of the party and government, culminated in the secret convocation of the Tenth National Congress of the Chinese Communist Party in August 1973. It was then that the death of Lin Biao was officially announced, along with a list of his crimes of conspiracy against the party.

It is rather instructive to read Premier Zhou Enlai's political report to the secretly convened Tenth National Congress of the CCP in August 1973. An important portion of Zhou Enlai's political report dealt with Lin Biao's "anti-party" activities. Zhou dates Lin's disagreement with the leadership to the Second Plenum of the party's Ninth Central Committee in August 1970. Premier Zhou's report revealed only in general terms the abortive military coup engineered by Lin Biao, and confirmed officially Lin's flight that resulted in his death on September 13, 1971. Zhou's report gave neither clues as to how Lin Biao attempted to assassinate Chairman Mao nor any details about the military's attempted coup. What the political report to the party congress presented was an official version of Lin Biao's death and his anti-party conspiracy. The report also indicated that the rectification campaign, launched soon after Lin's demise, emphasized not only the correct revolutionary line but also work style, particularly for the PLA. In language which was couched in general theoretical and ideological terms, Zhou indicted Lin Biao for being an "ultra-rightist" and a "conspirator" who had attempted to "split" the unity of the party.

While Premier Zhou gave no details in his report to the party congress on Lin Biao's abortive coup, he nevertheless admitted in the report that "the course of the struggle to smash the Lin Biao anti-party clique and the crimes of the clique are already known to the whole party, army, and people." What this implied was the intense discussion, criticism, and rectification campaign that had been waged inside China, leading up to the convocation of the Tenth Party Congress.

In addition to the purge which followed the demise of Lin Biao, the Politburo of the CCP appointed a top level investigation committee on the Lin Biao affiar. A series of documents were said to have been issued by the Central Committee on the findings of the investigation—these were considered internal reading material for the cadres in conducting the rectification campaign against Lin Biao and his followers.[56] One document, dated January 13, 1972, contained an outline of the "571 Engineering Project," the military coup plan of Lin Biao's group, mentioned in Zhou's political report as evidence of the conspiracy against the party. The document also contained an excerpt of a confession by a Lin Biao co-conspirator on the execution of the plan.

Much more revealing information about the inner struggle among the top leaders, particularly between the chairman and his designated successor Lin Biao, was contained in another document. It was a summary of, or notes on, Mao's talk with provincial military and party cadres during his inspection trip to the interior, conducted from mid-August to mid-September 1971, on the eve of Lin Biao's alleged attempted assassination of Mao. Mao presumably made the trip in order to use his personal charisma to rally support of military and party leaders in his struggle with Lin.

This particular document revealed in Mao's own words his view of the power struggle and disagreement on the issues of leadership direction and the loyalty and command of the army at the Second Plenum of the Ninth Central Committee held in Lushan in August 1970.

In reading these internal documents and the many interpretations by China scholars, it seems obvious that Mao and Lin Biao had disagreed and confronted each other on a number of issues: the need for collective leadership after Mao, the dominance of the military in the party and the government with the resultant erosion of party authority, the failure by the military to expedite Mao's orders, and preferential appointments of Lin Biao's proteges to important positions at the expense of experienced veteran cadres. These confrontations evidently took place at party gatherings in March 1970.

A detailed discussion of the rise of military power in Chinese politics since the Cultural Revolution, and its implication in the Lin Biao affair, will be found in Chapter 6. What needs to be pointed out here is that expansion of the military political role was the basis of top leadership's disagreement and conflict. The purge of a large number of senior military officers, and the attempts to restore party control over the military, became the focal concerns of the post-Lin Biao collective leadership of Premier Zhou and the radicals who survived the onslaught of the army during the Cultural Revolution. This new coalition of forces (factions), although accepted by the Tenth Party Congress, proved to be temporary and illusory. The contest for power between the forces behind Premier Zhou and the radicals, led by Mao's wife Jiang Qing, eventually culminated in the Tian An Men Square incident after Zhou Enlai's death in January 1976 and in the arrest of the radical leaders in October of that year, a month after Mao's death. The elimination of the radicals ushered in not only a new leader to succeed Mao, but a new era of moderation and pragmaticism. It is this story of China after Mao that we must now examine.

THE "GANG OF FOUR" AND THE ASCENDENCY OF HUA GUOFENG[57]

The top radical leaders, later known as the "Gang of Four" included Jiang Qing, Zhang Chunqiao, Yao Wenyuan and Wang Hungwen. Aside from having been Mao's wife, Jiang Qing had been a member of the Central Committee's Cultural Revolution Group, which directed the Red Guards and the upheaval, and a vice chairman of the Cultural Revolution Committee in the PLA under Lin Biao. Zhang Chunqiao and Yao Wenyuan were active in the Shanghai Municipal Party Committee and had used Shanghai as a bastion for Mao's counterattacks against Liu Shaoqi's forces during the Cultural Revolution. It was Yao who wrote the first critique of the play, *Hai Rui's Dismissal from Office,* that served as the first salvo against Liu Shaoqi at the beginning of the Cultural Revolution. Both Yao and Zhang, along with Jiang Qing, subsequently became key members of the Central Committee's Cultural Revolution Group. Wang Hungwen was a young leader of the Shanghai Congress of Revolutionary Workers Rebels, a workers' group which supported the radical activities in Shanghai during the Cultural Revolution.

The radicals were a minority group within the party who advocated continuous class struggle under the dictatorship of the proletariat. Their greatest strength came from activists and young university students. As a group, the radicals had little institutional support within the society. Their survival after the Cultural Revolution was dependent upon two factors: personal support from Chairman Mao and their fragile alliances, first with Lin Biao and then with Zhou Enlai's forces. The fact that they served as Mao's spokesmen on ideological matters during and after the Cultural Revolution gave the radicals an aura of strength. While Mao remained mentally alert, few dared to oppose their views openly for fear of incurring Mao's wrath. The radicals' control over the mass media and over the fields of art, literature, and drama added to their strength. Hua Guofeng later charged that they had "spread a host of revisionist fallacies" and that "metaphysics" ran wild and "idealism went rampant." The radicals' base of operation was limited to a few urban centers, primarily the municipalities under the direct administration of the central government: Beijing, Shanghai, Tianjin. Their activities were mainly concentrated in the trade union federations in these cities.

Realizing their weakness in case of a showdown, the radicals helped to build an urban militia in an attempt to secure a countervailing force to the PLA. The urban militia, which were organized and controlled by the various trade union federations and municipal party committees allied with the radicals, appeared to be a potentially powerful political instrument for the radical elements within the party.[58]

During and after the Cultural Revolution, the top radical leaders acquired influence and position in the party. The Ninth Party Congress in 1969 elected all four radical leaders/members of the Central Committee. Zhang Chunqiao, as first secretary of the party's Shanghai Municipal Committee, was also elected to the Politburo. With the demise of Lin Biao, the four leaders were elected to the Politburo of the Tenth Central Committee in August 1973. In addition, Wang was said to have been Mao's personal choice for vice chairman of the party, the post previously held by Lin Biao.

When the much delayed Fourth National People's Congress, China's equivalent to parliament, convened in January 1975, it presented an appearance of surface unity. However, behind the scenes, the radicals, led by Jiang Qing, were jockeying for power against the moderate forces supporting Premier Zhou Enlai. At first, Zhou made some compromises with the radicals. Zhang Chunqiao was made a vice premier and a director of the PLA's General Political Department, responsible for the political and ideological education of the troops. But at Zhou's insistence, Deng Xiaoping was brought back and rehabilitated as a vice premier and the chief-of-staff for the PLA. Deng, considered a chief villain by the radicals, had been purged along with Liu Shaoqi during the Cultural Revolution. Zhou, in failing health, wanted Deng, who was a capable and trusted colleague, to provide the needed leadership and experience in the central government.

The Fourth National People's Congress was dominated by Zhou and his party and government veterans. Zhou made it very clear at the session that in order to speed up development and modernization of the economy, it was necessary to make changes, including implementing wage differentials to spur production, placing decision making in factories into the hands of plant managers and experts, and emphasizing scientific research through the upgrading of university education. Zhou even invoked one of Mao's statements on the need for a technical revolution and for borrowing scientific and technical know-how from abroad.[59] These changes were viewed by the radicals as reversals of the Cultural Revolution gains.

The radicals' offensives soon converged on the individual that they considered most vulnerable in the Zhou Enlai group, the rehabilitated Deng Xiaoping, who had been designated by Zhou to implement the economic acceleration and modernization. As Zhou became increasingly incapacitated by cancer and was hospitalized most of the time as 1975 progressed, the attacks against him and Deng intensified in the radical-controlled media. The radicals were very much concerned about who would take over the premiership in the event of Zhou's death. Wang Hungwen was said to have been dispatched on several occasions to see Chairman Mao to persuade him to designate either Zhang Chunqiao or Jiang Qing to succeed Zhou.[60] Their aim was to at least prevent Deng Xiaoping from assuming the premiership in case Zhou should die in office. In the radicals' eyes, Deng was the "capitalist roader" who had long advocated that hard work, not politics in command, was what really mattered: "Never mind about the color of the cat as long as it catches mice." In January 1976 Zhou Enlai died. There was an outpouring of genuine affection and respect by the masses for Zhou. But as soon as the nation had paid final tribute to the leader, the battle for succession began in earnest. Wall posters in the streets of Beijing demanded that

Deng Xiaoping be purged again for his efforts to restore the "bourgeois rights." The campaign of villification against Deng culminated in April in the Tian An Men incident.

The entire incident at Tian An Men Square was a large, spontaneous demonstration during the traditional festival in honor of the dead. The crowd, reportedly more than one hundred thousand at its height, was angered by the removal of flower wreaths placed in the square to honor the late Premier Zhou. The demonstrators created disturbances and damaged property belonging to the public security units stationed at public buildings on the square. The incident was a spontaneous show of support for the late Premier's policies on material development and incentives. It could also be considered a show of support for Deng Xiaoping, who was a major target for attack by the radical leaders. Toward the end of the demonstration, the radicals entered this round-of-power contest by dispatching some units of the urban militia, presumably to quell the riots. By all accounts, this show of strength by the urban militia was rather feeble and unimpressive.[61]

The radicals used the incident for their own purposes. They labeled the disorderly conduct of the demonstrators in support of Zhou and Deng as "counterrevolutionary," and blamed Deng for instigating the incident. The radicals at this time had the support of Mao and enough Politburo members to have Deng dismissed from all positions of power and, thereby, to remove him as a candidate to succeed Zhou Enlai for the premiership. The spontaneous outburst of the huge crowd in the Tian An Men Square incident demonstrated the radicals' alienation from the masses. The radicals, nevertheless, won this first round of the succession struggle by removing Deng Xiaoping from the seat of power for the second time. The compromise choice of Hua Guofeng as first vice chairman of the CCP, a newly designated position, and as acting premier may have been made personally by Mao, who surely by then had realized the danger of a split within the top echelon of the party. While Mao lived, he somehow kept the factions in balance, even, at times, tipping the balance slightly in favor of his radical disciples.

The campaign to criticize Deng Xiaoping sputtered forward without arousing any genuine mass support or enthusiasm from April through July, ending in August when a series of a major earthquakes began in the Beijing area. The ancient Chinese saying that unusual natural phenomena generally precede some earthshaking event seemed prophetic: Chairman Mao died on September 9, 1976, at the age of 82. While the nation again mourned the loss of a great leader, political maneuvering for the succession contest reached its peak. At first the open dispute revolved around Mao's will. The radicals claimed that the will called for the gains and values of the Cultural Revolution to be upheld by Mao's successors. The moderates, now a close alliance of party, government, and military veteran cadres, claimed that Mao had designated in writing that Hua Guofeng be named his successor: "With you in charge, I am at ease."[62] These were merely skirmishes of the pen. The real combat took place from the end of September to the first week of October at Politburo meetings, which included some heated debates. Reportedly, the radical leaders proposed that Jiang Qing be named the new party chairman, and Zhang Chunqiao, the new premier. It has also since been reported that the radical leaders mapped out a military coup to be staged in Shanghai as a last recourse in the contest for power.[63]

The final decision of the Central Committee on October 7 was firm and direct: Hua Guofeng was to succeed Mao as chairman of the party, and all opposition to this decision must be silenced. Almost simultaneously, the four radical leaders were placed under arrest by the special security force No. 8341, directly under the supervision of the Central Committee and the Politburo and under the personal command of Politburo member Wang Dongxing. Swiftly, regular PLA units, all under the command of Politburo members, moved into Beijing, Shanghai, and other cities to disarm the urban militia. The PLA placed these cities under temporary military control to prevent any disturbances. By October 24, Hua's successful move against the radicals was complete, and an estimated one million Chinese gathered in Tian An Men Square to cheer a new leader and to celebrate the dawn of a new era for China.

Hua Guofeng[64]

When Hua Guofeng arrived in Bucharest, Romania, in August 1978, he was the first Chinese party leader ever to travel further west than Moscow. As millions watched a worldwide television broadcast of this relaxed and plain, middle-aged Chinese folk dancing in a public square in Bucharest, the image of Hua Guofeng was one of supreme confidence in himself and in his ability to mix well with people. This trip abroad said something about China's political stability and about Hua's confidence in his firm control over the country. Prior to Zhou's death, the world knew very little about this man who would emerge as chairman of the party, premier, and chief of the military complex in China. His rise to one of the most powerful positions in the world is not really very spectacular. Let us look briefly at his background from the information now available to us.

Hua was born in 1920 of a peasant family in the northwestern province of Shanxi. He joined the communist guerrillas in his home province at a young age, and by 1947, at the age of twenty-seven, was a young party secretary for a county and a leader of a local guerrilla band with considerable experience in making explosives. In 1949 he moved with the PLA forces to Hunan where he remained as a local and provincial party leader until 1971. During this period, Hua, who is now a widower, raised four children.

In 1952, Hua was appointed party secretary for Xiang-tan Special District, which included Mao's birthplace, Shaoshan. In this post, Hua supervised the planning and construction of a memorial hall, which was formally dedicated to Mao in 1955. By 1959 Hua had carved out an impressive administrative record in Hunan in a number of posts in diverse functional areas, giving him a wealth of knowledge about party and government affairs. These areas included agriculture, education, cultural affairs, water conservation, finance, and trade. Each new position was a promotion in responsibility, if not always in grade.

When Mao visited his birthplace in June 1959, for the first time in thirty-seven years, he was impressed with the memorial and beautification of the village, and undoubtedly mentioned this to Hua when they met. Then, during the summer, Hua participated in the Lushan Conference, where Mao was being criticized for the Great Leap and the commune programs. Hua, as a leading figure in the Hunan provincial government, wrote at least two investigative reports supporting the communes and defending the Great Leap. Reportedly, because of his staunch defense of Mao at Lushan, Hua was appointed to the position of provincial party secretary for Hunan on Mao's recommendation.[65]

In rising to the position of provincial party secretary, Hua had to be adept at coping with intraparty conflicts. On the major questions of cooperatives, communes, and the purge of Peng Dehuai, Hua supported Mao's policies. He also supported the Great Leap Forward program in Hunan but cautioned against excesses. He was one of the few provincial bosses who survived the Cultural Revolution and emerged intact to lead the formation of one of the first provincial revolutionary committees in China. Hua was also involved at the provincial level in preventing military supporters of Lin Biao from exerting influence in provincial affairs in 1969 and 1970. Hua by then had been elected by the Ninth Party Congress to full membership on the Central Committee.

By 1971 Hua's political activities had extended beyond Hunan. Either because of his personal contacts with Mao or the impression he had made on such key central leaders as Ye Jianying and Li Xiannian, Hua was called to Beijing to direct the staff office of the State Council. In that capacity, Hua was one of the top aides to Premier Zhou. Hua's stay in Beijing was short; he returned to Hunan in the summer of 1971 to resume his duties as the provincial party chief. His experience in serving directly under Zhou Enlai in the State Council was most likely an important factor in his promotion to the chairmanship of the State Council in April 1976 and, hence, his subsequent selection as head of the party.[66]

Nineteen seventy-one was a turbulent year in which the Lin Biao affair surfaced. The Politburo established a special committee to investigate Lin Biao's alleged attempted coup. Hua was appointed to the investigation committee, along with six senior Politburo members. Apparently, Hua, who was noted for his investigative skills, did a good job on the committee, which indicted Lin Biao for anti-party crimes. Perhaps as a reward for Hua's work in the Lin Biao investigation and also perhaps as a recognition of the need to promote talented provincial leaders to the center, Hua was elected to the all-powerful Politburo in August 1973. He was soon brought into the State Council in 1974 in a position of considerable importance and power as the Minister for Public Security, the nation's chief law enforcer.

By now, Hua Guofeng was recognized by the leaders at the center as a capable administrator with expertise in a variety of areas. In October 1975, he was called upon by the central leadership to deliver a policy speech on agriculture.[67] Hua's speech indicated his stand on the question of modernization of agriculture. His pitch was that China needed to strengthen her material base against war and natural disasters, and this could be accomplished only by modernizing agriculture, which would effectively push forward the modernization of industry, national defense, and science and technology. In that speech, Hua called for renewed efforts in scientific research for improved seeds, new techniques in multiple cropping, and rational use of fertilizer. Hua also urged that all-around planning be undertaken by party organizations at the county levels. Hua's 1975 speech on agriculture clearly indicated that he endorsed the views advocated by Zhou Enlai on China's future economic development.

For Mao Zedong and the radicals, Hua was, nevertheless, a compromise choice in January 1976 when Premier Zhou died. The other choice, Deng Xiaoping, was a bitter pill to swallow. The selection of Hua as acting premier immediately after Zhou's death might be considered Mao's way of keeping the contending groups in balance. The compromise became the only possible choice when the Tian An Men Square demonstration occurred in April. After the Tian An Men incident, Hua Guofeng must have sensed that his political future rested with the coalition of party and government administrators and the military. As a shrewd leader who had engaged in and survived many power contests as a provincial party secretary, Hua must have realized by the spring of 1976 that the radicals had neither the popular support for their revolutionary causes nor the institutional base for the power contest, particularly in view of the poor showing by the urban militia at Tian An Men. He marked his time until the appropriate moment arrived to deal a mortal blow to the radicals at the urging and with the support of the military.

Hua Guofeng certainly cannot fill Mao's shoes as the charismatic leader and theoretician. Hua, however, could be another Zhou Enlai, the organizer, mediator, and pragmatic administrator in the ever changing but always complex Chinese political scene. For the future of China, there may be more need for pragmatic planners and skilled administrators than for visionary revolutionaries.

NOTES

[1]Charles P. Fitzgerald, *Revolution in China* (New York: Holt, Rinehart & Winston, 1952), pp. 12–16.

[2]John King Fairbank, *The United States and China*, 3rd ed. (Cambridge, Mass.: Harvard University Press, 1971), pp. 90–95.

[3]Fairbank, *The United States and China*, p. 55.

[4]Fitzgerald, *Revolution in China*, p. 23.

[5]Kung-chuan Hsiao, *Rural China: Imperial Control in the Nineteenth Century* (Seattle, Wash.: University of Washington Press, 1960), pp. 253–54.

[6]Fairbank, *The United States and China*, pp. 20–34.

[7]Fairbank, *The United States and China*, p. 103.

[8]Fairbank, *The United States and China*, p. 103; and James Townsend, *Politics in China* (Boston: Little, Brown and Company, 1974), pp. 35–36.

[9]Townsend, Politics in China, p. 37.

[10]Fairbank, *The United States and China*, p. 191.

[11]Fitzgerald, *Revolution in China*, p. 38; and Fairbank, *The United States and China*, pp. 197–98.

[12]For a detailed account of the events in 1927 see Franklin Houn, *A Short History of Chinese Communism* (Englewood Cliffs, N.J.: Prentice-Hall, Inc., 1967), pp. 21–33.

[13] Houn, *A Short History of Chinese Communism*, pp. 35–38.

[14]Hsiung, *Ideology and Practice: The Evolution of Chinese Communism* (New York: Praeger Publishers, 1970), pp. 61–62. See also Edgar Snow, *Red Star Over China* (New York: Grove Press, Inc., 1961).

[15]John M.H. Lindbeck, "Transformation in the Chinese Communist Party," in *Soviet and Chinese Communist: Similarities and Differences,* ed. Donald Treadgold (Seattle: University of Washington Press, 1967), p. 76; and Stuart Schram, "Mao Tse-tung and the Chinese Political Equalibrium," *Government and Opposition,* vol. 4, no. 1 (Winter 1969), 141–42.

[16]Hsiung, *Ideology and Practice*, pp. 45–46; and Dick Wilson, *The Long March 1935: The Epic of Chinese Communism's Survival* (New York: Avon Books, First Discus Printing, 1973). Also see Edward E. Rice, *Mao's Way* (Berkeley, Calif.: University of California Press, 1972), pp. 83–88.

[17]Hsiung, *Ideology and Practice*, pp. 52–53, and Fairbank, *The United States and China*, pp. 269–70.

[18]John Lindbeck, "Transformation in the Chinese Communist Party," p. 76.

[19] See *The Selected Works of Mao Tse-tung* (Peking: Foreign Language Press, 1967), II, 339–84; III, 205–70.

[20] Fairbank, *The United States and China,* p. 313.

[21] Houn, *A Short History of Chinese Communism,* pp. 173–77.

[22] E. Stuart Kirby, "Agrarian Problems and Peasantry," in *Communist China, 1949–1969: A Twenty Year Appraisal,* eds. Frank N. Trager and William Henderson (New York: New York University Press, 1970), p. 160.

[23] Ezra Vogel, "Land Reform in Kwangtung 1951–1953: Central Control and Localism," *The China Quarterly,* 38 (April–June 1969), 27–62.

[24] Vogel, "Land Reform in Kwangtung 1951–1953," pp. 27–62.

[25] Houn, *A Short History of Chinese Communism,* p. 159.

[26] Houn, *A Short History of Chinese Communism,* p. 164; and Kirby, "Agrarian Problems and Peasantry," p. 162.

[27] See the official documents issued dealing with the debate over the cooperatives. The texts of these documents are in Robert R. Bowie and John K. Fairbank's, *Communist China, 1955–1959: Policy Documents With Analysis* (Cambridge, Mass.: Harvard University Press, 1965), pp. 92–126.

[28] Discussion on the First Five-Year Plan was based on the following sources: Alexander Eckstein, *China's Economic Revolution* (London and New York: Cambridge University Press, 1977), pp. 31–66; E.L. Wheelwright and Bruce McFarlane, *The Chinese Road to Socialism: Economics of the Cultural Revolution* (New York: Monthly Review Press, 1970), pp. 31–65; and Franklin Houn, *A Short History of Communist China,* pp. 177–85.

[29] Houn, *A Short History of Chinese Communism,* pp. 178–79; Wheelwright and McFarlane, *The Chinese Road to Socialism,* p. 35.

[30] Houn, *A Short History of Chinese Communism,* pp. 178–79.

[31] Houn, *A Short History of Chinese Communism,* pp. 178–79.

[32] Wheelwright and McFarlane, *The Chinese Road to Socialism,* p. 36.

[33] Discussion in this section on the Great Leap program is based on these sources: Houn, *A Short History of Chinese Communism,* pp. 181–82; Fairbank, *The United States and China,* pp. 369–75; Eckstein, *China's Economic Revolution,* pp. 54–65; Roderick MacFarquhar, *The Origin of the Cultural Revolution: The Contradictions among the People, 1956–1957* (New York: Columbia University Press, 1974), pp. 57–74; Hsiung, *Ideology and Practice,* pp. 185–99.

[34] Eckstein, *China's Economic Revolution,* p. 59.

[35] Byung-joon Ahn, *Chinese Politics and the Cultural Revolution: Dynamics of Policy Processes* (Seattle, Wash. and London: University of Washington Press, 1976), pp. 31–47.

[36] *The Case of Peng Teh-huai* (Hongkong: Union Research Institute, 1968); and J.D. Simmons, "Peng Teh-huai: A Chronological Re-examination," *The China Quarterly,* 37 (January–March 1968), 120–38.

[37] There are many accounts of the Lushan decision, the latest is in Ahn, *Chinese Politics and the Cultural Revolution,* pp. 38–44.

[38] The brief survey here is based on Eckstein, *China's Economic Revolution,* pp. 202–205, and Houn, *A Short History of Chinese Communism,* pp. 182–85. Also see Ahn, *Chinese Politics and the Cultural Revolution,* pp. 48–86 for a more detailed account of the recovery for the period, 1962–1965.

[39]Discussion on the socialist education campaign is drawn from these sources: Hsiung, *Ideology and Practice*, pp. 200–16; Richard Baum and Frederick C. Teiwes, *Ssu-Ch'ing: The Socialist Educational Movement of 1962–1966* (Berkeley, Calif.: Center for Chinese Studies, University of California, 1968); Ahn, *Chinese Politics and the Cultural Revolution*, pp. 89–122; Philip Bridgham, "Mao's 'Cultural Revolution': Origin and Development," *The China Quarterly*, 29 (January–March 1967), 1–35; and Richard Baum and Frederick Teiwes, "Liu Shao-chi and the Cadres Question," *Asian Survey*, vol. VIII, no. 4 (April 1968), 323–45; and Richard Baum, *Prelude to Revolution: Mao, the Party and the Peasant Question, 1962–1966* (New York: Columbia University Press, 1975).

[40]C.S. Chen, ed., *Rural People's Communes in Lien-chiang*, Trans. Charles P. Ridley (Stanford, Calif.: Hoover Institution, 1969); Baum and Teiwes, "Liu Shao-chi and the Cadres Question," and Ahn, *Chinese Politics and the Cultural Revolution*, pp. 99–108. Also see Hsiung, *Ideology and Practice*, pp. 206–208.

[41]Ahn, *Chinese Politics and the Cultural Revolution*, p. 103; and for an insight into the interpersonal behavior of the cadres, see Michel Oksenberg, "The Institutionalization of the Chinese Communist Revolution: The Ladder of Success on the Eve of the Cultural Revolution," *The China Quarterly*, 36 (October–December 1968), 61–92.

[42]For a listing of the bibliography on the subject, see James C.F. Wang, *The Cultural Revolution in China: An Annotated Bibliography* (New York and London: Garland Publishing, Inc., 1976).

[43]See Donald Zagoria, *Vietnam Triangle: Moscow, Peking, Hanoi* (New York: Pagasus, 1967); Uri Ra'amam, "Peking's Foreign Policy 'Debate,' 1965–1966," in *China's Policies in Asia and America's Alternatives*, ed. Tang Tsou (Chicago: University of Chicago Press, 1968), pp. 23–71; Robert Scalapino, "The Cultural Revolution and Chinese Foreign Policy," in *The Cultural Revolution: 1967 in Review* (Ann Arbor, Mich.: Michigan Papers in Michigan Studies No. 2, Center for Chinese Studies, University of Michigan, 1968), pp. 1–15.

[44]For an account of the struggle at these two universities during the Cultural Revolution, see Victor Nee, *The Cultural Revolution at Peking University* (New York: Monthly Review Press, 1969); and William Hinton, *Hundred Day War: The Cultural Revolution at Tsinghua* (New York and London: Monthly Review Press, 1972).

[45]See Gordon Bennett and Ronald N. Montaperto, *Red Guard: The Political Biography of Dai Hsiao-ai* (New York: Anchor Books, Doubleday, 1972).

[46]See Michel Oksenberg, "China: Forcing the Revolution to a New Stage," *Asian Survey*, vol. vii, no. 1 (January 1967), 1–15; and John Israel, "The Red Guards in Historical Perspective: Continuity and Change in Chinese Youth Movement," *The China Quarterly*, 30 (April–June 1967), 1–32.

[47]See Lowell Dittmer, "The Cultural Revolution and the Fall of Liu Shao-chi," *Current Scene*, vol. xi, no. 1 (January 1973), 1–13; Israel, "The Red Guards in Historical Perspective: Continuity and Change in the Chinese Youth Movement," 1–32.

[48]Philip Bridgham, "Mao's Cultural Revolution in 1967: The Struggle to Seize Power," *The China Quarterly*, 34 (April–June 1968), 6–36; Ellis Joffe, "The Chinese Army in the Cultural Revolution: The Politics of Intervention," *The Current Scene*, vol. II, no. 18 (December 7, 1970), 1–25; William Whitson, *The Chinese Communist High Command: A History of Military Politics, 1927–69* (New York: Holt, Rinehart & Winston, 1971); Jean Esmein, *The Chinese Cultural Revolution* (Garden City, N.Y.: Anchor Books, Doubleday, 1973); Stanley Karnow, *Mao and China: From Revolution to Revolution* (New York: Viking, 1972), 276–316.

[49]Edgar Snow, "Mao and the New Mandate," *The World Today*, vol. 25, no. 7 (July 1969), 290.

[50]Parris H. Chang, "Regional Military Power: The Aftermath of the Cultural Revolution," *Asian Survey*, vol. XII, no. 12 (December 1972), 999–1013, and "The Revolutionary Com-

mittee and the Party in the Aftermath of the Cultural Revolution," *Current Scene*, vol. viii, no. 8 (April 15, 1970), 1–10.

[51]"Recent Development in Chinese Education," *Current Scene*, vol. X, no. 1 (July 1972), 1–6.

[52]See Richard M. Pfeffer, "Serving the People and Continuing the Revolution," *The China Quarterly*, 52 (October–December 1972), 620–53.

[53]*The New York Times*, September 23, 1971, sec. 1, pp. 1, 6.

[54]*The New York Times*, July 28, 1972, sec. 1, p. 1.

[55]*The New York Times*, July 29, 1972, sec. 1, p. 1; and *The New York Times*, October 12, 1972, sec. 1, p. 1.

[56]For the texts of these internal documents, see Y.M. Kau, *The Lin Piao Affair, Power Politics and Military Coup* (White Plains, New York: International Arts and Sciences Press, 1975), and also *The New York Times*, July 23, 1972, sec. 1, pp. 1, 6.

[57]Suggested reading about the downfall of the Gang of Four: Jurgen Domes, "China in 1976: Tremors of Transition," *Asian Survey*, vol. xiii, no. 1 (January 1977), 1–17; Peter R. Moody, Jr., "The Fall of the Gang of Four: Background Notes on the Chinese Counter-revolution," *Asian Survey*, vol. xvii, no. 8 (August 1977), 711–23; Jurgen Domes, "The 'Gang of Four' and Hua Kuo-feng: Analysis of Political Events in 1975–76," *The China Quarterly*, 71 (September 1977), 473–97, and James C.F. Wang, "The Urban Militia as a Political Instrument in the Power Contest in China in 1976," *Asian Survey*, vol. xviii, no. 6 (June 1978), 541–59; Andres D. Onate, "Hua Kuo-feng and the Arrest of 'Gang of Four'," *The China Quarterly*, 75 (September 1978), 540–65.

[58]Wang, "The Urban Militia in China," p. 550.

[59]Chou En-lai, "Report on the Work of the Government," *Peking Review*, 4 (January 24, 1975), 24.

[60]"The Crux of 'Gang of Four's' Crimes to Usurp Party and State Power," *Peking Review*, 2 (January 7, 1977), 30.

[61]Wang, "Urban Militia in China," pp. 552–53.

[62]See "Chairman Mao Will Live For Ever in Our Hearts," *Peking Review*, 39 (September 24, 1976), 35; and "Comrade Wu Teh's Speech at the Celebration Rally in the Capitol," *Peking Review*, 44 (October 29, 1976), 12.

[63]Wang, "Urban Militia in China," pp. 555–58.

[64]Michel Oksenberg and Sai-cheung Yeung, "Hua Kuo-feng's Pre-Cultural Revolution Hunan Years, 1949–66: The Making of a Political Generalist," *The China Quarterly*, 69 (March 1977), 3–53; "Hua Kuo-feng," *Issues and Studies*, vol. xii, no. 3 (March 1976), 80–88; Jen Hua, "Comrade Hua Kuo-feng in Hunan," *Peking Review*, 9 (February 25, 1977), 5–11; and "Comrade Hua Kuo-feng in The Years of War," *Peking Review*, 15 (August 8, 1977), 9–12.

[65]Jen Hua, "Comrade Hua Kuo-feng in Hunan," p. 6.

[66]Hua's experience at local and national levels were the points mentioned in Yeh Chien-ying's endorsement of Hua for party chairmanship. See "Report on the Revision of the Party Constitution," p. 24.

[67]Hua Kuo-feng, "Build Tachai-Type Counties Through the Country," *Peking Review*, 44 (October 31, 1975), 7–10.

The Chinese Communist Ideology: Marxism-Leninism, Mao's Thought, and De-Maoization

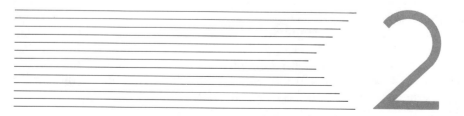

2

Let us begin by defining the term ideology. It may be defined as the manner by which an individual or a group thinks. Ideology is a set of political values, feelings, and knowledge which provides direction for individuals to act or behave in a certain manner for the purpose of achieving a particular goal. It has been said that the success of the Chinese communist movement rests on two basic elements: an effective set of organizations, guided by a set of clearly stated principles.[1] Schurmann differentiates ideologies in terms of the consequences the ideas may generate. If an idea leads to the formulation of a policy or an action, it is a "practical" ideology; but if an idea is employed for the sole purpose of molding the thinking of the individual, it is a "pure" ideology.[2] Pure ideology is a set of theories; practical ideology is based on experiences and practices. The Chinese make a clear distinction between these two sets of ideologies in their political communication. To the Chinese, the ideas of Karl Marx and of Lenin are pure ideology which has universal application. In the Chinese language, pure ideology is called *lilun* or *chuyi*, and practical ideology is *suxiang*.

The Chinese communist ideology consists of three basic elements: 1. the influence of the Chinese revolution, particularly the intellectual ferment of the May Fourth Movement; 2. the ideas of Marxism-Leninism; and 3. the thought of Mao Zedong. Let us keep in mind that, while the thought of Mao constitutes a major portion of the Chinese communist ideology, it is by no means the only element. In the sections to follow we shall briefly discuss the origin and the nature of these main elements which constitute the Chinese communist ideology today.

THE MAY FOURTH MOVEMENT

As was pointed out in Chapter 1, there was very little interest in Marxism among the Chinese intellectuals before 1917. The rapid rise in the study of Marxism was brought about by the 1917 Bolshevik revolution and by the appeal of Lenin's thesis on anti-imperialism. The anti-imperialist plank struck a responsive chord among the Chinese intellectuals, who were already committed to saving China from imperialism through a nationalist revolution. The early founders of the Chinese Communist Party—men like Li Dazhao and Chen Duxiu—were exponents of anti-imperialism and a "new culture" for a modern China. Many of the ideas which were translated into concrete programs after the establishment of the People's Republic in 1949 had their roots in the May Fourth Movement. The May Fourth Movement was a reaction by intellectuals to the imperialist West and its economic system of exploitation. It represented the search for ways to develop a modern Chinese nation. Programs of the May Fourth Movement included reform of both the written language and the educational system; introduction of scientific methods; and exploration of political ideologies, including Marxism. It was a populist appeal to the innate goodness of the common people, particularly the earth bound peasants whose well-being had been always neglected by the intellectual urban elite. Many of the movement's young students went into the countryside to work with the peasants. The ideas from the May Fourth Movement have been continuous threads that run through modern Chinese revolution, including the communist revolution.[3]

MARXISM-LENINISM[4]

The theoretical foundation of the Chinese communist ideology is Marxism-Leninism. It is the guiding principle for both the party and the state. It is the pure theory with universal application. Let us examine briefly the essential features of Marxism.

The first key Marxist concept is historical materialism. Karl Marx began with the assertion that the character of any society is determined by the manner or the mode of production by which man makes his living. The mode of production determines social structure and political order; it also determines social ideas and customs. Therefore, to change the minds of men, it is necessary to change the mode of production or the economic system. This, Marx said, is the universal truth and the "evolutionary laws of human history." Even human society has at its foundation an economic base, the mode of production which produces goods and services to support human life. This economic basis, in turn, is supported by superstructures of culture, law, courts, and governmental institutions.

Having asserted that materialism determines the nature of society, Marx described how human history evolves in a predictable pattern. This is dialectical materialism. For this Marx borrowed the dialectical development of history from the German philosopher Hegel. Hegel proposed that every idea or thesis, once started, goes too far and becomes exaggerated or false. When this inevitably happens, the thesis is met with an opposing idea, the antithesis. These two opposing ideas clash, and out of the conflict comes the synthesis, an entirely new idea which contains the essential truths of both opposing ideas. Soon this synthesis becomes a thesis, and the process of change continues, ad infinitum. Marx used the Hegelian dialectics to predict that a communist society would inevitably result from this historical development after the society had passed through certain stages: first, the primitive communal society, in which there is no class differentiation; then the slave society, in which there is ownership and class status separating the slaves and the masters; the slave society would give way to the feudal society, with pronounced class distinction between the lord and his serfs; and the fourth stage of development, the capitalistic society, in which the owners of the means of production are pitted against the impoverished workers who lead a meager existence under the exploitation of the capitalists. Marx predicted that this struggle between the capitalists and the working class would result in a communist society where there would be no class distinction. The economy would be operated under Marx's dictum: "from each according to his ability, to each according to his need." Finally, the state, with its coercive instruments, would no longer be needed and would wither away.

Marx believed that the course of human history must pass through these stages; but before the arrival of the communist stage, there must be intense class struggle. In fact, Marx maintained that human history is a history of class warfare. As long as property or the means of production is owned by private individuals for the purpose of exploiting the work of others, there will always be a struggle between the two classes. It is an unfair struggle since all of the superstructures of society—laws, police, courts, and other political institutions—support the property-owning class. The property-owning class has all of the privileges, sanctioned by social customs and mores. Marx argued that this situation cannot endure long; the working class has no alternative except to forcefully overthrow the existing social order. He concludes the Communist Manifesto with a call for revolution: "Workers of the world unite, you have nothing to lose but your chains."

It is not the purpose of this section to engage in a critique of Marxism. However, we need to keep in mind that two basic historic responses have developed under different sets of circumstances, in answer to the appalling conditions of the early industrialization that he criticized. One is the evolution of social democracy in the West, which brought changes through constitutional reform and progressive social legislation. The other is the Russian Bolshevik Revolution, which brought change through violent revolution.

Lenin made two basic modifications to Marxism. One was his treatise on imperialism, published in 1916. Marx had predicted that a forceful but spontaneous workers' revolution would descend upon the capitalistic European societies, such as England, France, and Germany. But for over seventy years, no revolution by the working class occurred in continental Europe. When the revolution came, it came to Russia, an industrially backward country. Even more significant was the fact that the lot of workers in the advanced capitalist countries had improved through progressive social legislation. How could the disciples of Marx explain this phenomenon? Lenin answered this question in his treatise, *Imperialism.* Lenin argued that capitalism had broken away from the cycle of contradiction as prescribed by Marx in his dialectical materialism theory. Capitalism had expanded and grown by seeking new sources of raw material abroad, in undeveloped parts of the world, and by setting up factories with cheap labor in colonies, which in turn became the ready markets for the manufactured goods. Lenin rationalized the situation by claiming that the capitalist nations had developed a monopoly which accumulated enormous profits from the backward areas of the world and then rewarded labor at home with better wages and working conditions from these profits. By making concessions to labor at home, the capitalists were able to maintain the status quo and to prevent a workers' revolution. Therefore, the imperialists' exploitation of the backward areas of the world had sustained capitalism. Capitalism would not collapse as long as colonial power and monopolistic capitalism could successfully exploit the backward areas of Russia, China, India, and Africa. From this analysis, Lenin thought that the first blow of the revolution must be dealt to the weakest part in the system, the colonial complex in Asia and Africa. The Bolshevik Revolution and Lenin's treatise on imperialism made sense to the Chinese intellectuals who were frustrated by their previous effort in revolution making. Now there was a meaningful and emotional link between nationalism on one hand and anti-imperialism on the other.

Lenin's second major modification of Marxism was in regard to organization for the revolution, which Marx had not discussed beyond saying that it would be spontaneous. In *What's To Be Done?* Lenin outlined his strategy for the working class to achieve and to maintain political power. His first key principle was that a revolutionary party was needed, led by a highly disciplined and dedicated corps of professional revolutionaries to serve as the vanguard of the proletariat. Lenin insisted on professionalism and self-discipline in the vanguard to be organized for the proletariat. Another key organizational principle was the doctrine of "democratic centralism." This calls for centralized decision making, with free discussion at the policy formulation level. Once a decision is made at the top, however, all must abide by it without dissent. Lenin insisted on strict discipline within a "single unified party." The Leninist organizational model is hierarchical and pyramidal, with the supreme power vested in the hands of a few at the apex. At the base of the pyramid is the level of primary organizations—units or cells. Between the base and the apex are a myriad of intermediary organizations (see Chapter 3).

We must now turn to a discussion about the thought of Mao Zedong.

Mao Zedong, The Man

Wind and thunder are stirring,
Flags and banners are flying
Wherever men live.
Thirty-eight years are fled
With a mere snap of the fingers
We can clasp the moon in the Ninth Heaven
And seize turtles deep down in the Five Seas;
We'll return amid triumphant song and laughter.
Nothing is hard in this world
If you dare to scale the heights.[5]

This is the second stanza of a poem written by Mao in May 1965 when he revisited Jinggangshan, the mountain retreat where he had gathered the remnants of the defeated and disillusioned urban revolutionaries in 1927 before reorganizing them into a fighting guerrilla force. This poem shows a familiar image of Mao: a man with infinite faith in the ability of human beings to accomplish any task, no matter how difficult. Mao Zedong was a much more complex person than has been commonly portrayed. In this section we will look at Mao, the man, by focusing on his background.

Mao was born in 1893 of a middle, not poor, peasant family in the village of Shaoshan, Hunan Province, in central China. He was brought up in the traditional Chinese family environment where his father exercised almost dictatorial power over the family. Mao usually submitted to his father's wishes, but on occasion rebelled. As a boy, he learned the value of hard labor by helping his father on the farm. His primary school curriculum centered on recitation of the Confucian classics, but he enjoyed reading popular romantic literature depicting heroic adventures, peasant rebellions, and the contests of empires. At the time of the 1911 revolution, Mao was eighteen, a fledgling youth not too sure of what was happening to China. His social awakening did not begin until he went to the provincial capital of Changsha for his secondary education in 1912. In Changsha he learned about the various revolutionary activities of Sun Yatsen and others from the newspapers. Excited by these events, Mao wrote his first wall poster, already a popular medium for expressing political opinions. Following local uprisings in Changsha and Wuhan, he joined the revolutionary army. Military life with its regimentation and authoritarianism did not suit young Mao, who was alert and impatient with the world around him. For some months after his short sojourn in the army, Mao read and toyed with the idea of becoming a lawyer. Finally, in 1918, at the age of twenty-five, he settled for a teaching career and obtained a degree from a teacher training school. Stuart Schram, an authoritative biographer of Mao, views the five years in teacher training school as an important landmark in the shaping of Mao's future.[6] The greatest and perhaps most successful role that Mao played was as a teacher to his people: He showed them how to learn by themselves and how to learn together.[7] In later years, schoolmates described Mao of this period as a loner, but a well behaved person.[8]

The most important change that occurred in Mao's life was his move from his native province of Hunan to Beijing, the center of political and intellectual ferment. Toward the end of the first World War, Mao went to Beijing with some thirty fellow Hunanese as members of a society to study new ideas. Through his former teacher in Changsha, Mao obtained a menial job as a librarian's assistant at Beijing National University to support himself. Although he shared a room with seven other students from Hunan, Mao was lonely. As a means of meeting people, he joined the Marxist Study Group, organized by Li Dazhao, founder of the Chinese communist movement. As Mao later admitted to Edgar Snow, at that time he was rather confused by the new ideas proliferating like mushrooms at Beijing National University, and leaned toward anarchism while "looking for a road."[9] Before becoming a Marxist in the summer of 1920, Mao had read only three Chinese translations of major works on Marxism: *The Communist Manifesto* by Marx, *Class Struggle* by Kautsky, and *History of Socialism* by Kirkupp. A year later, Mao was a delegate to the founding of the Chinese Communist Party in Shanghai. From 1921 until 1927 he was an obedient Chinese communist, following the orders of the Comintern. During the years of 1927 to

1935, he began to shape a different movement, with reliance on the peasantry as a base. Mao's rise to leadership of the Chinese Communist Party and his tenure of that position until his death in 1976 are discussed in Chapter 1 and in other parts of this book.

As Lucian Pye has pointed out, Mao must be seen at various times and under various conditions.[10] In his youth he was a loner and exhibited signs of "aloofness and solitariness."[11] When he went into the field as organizer among the workers and peasants, Mao not only dressed but acted like them. As Mao gained power and grew as a leader, he was distinguished as a "man of decisive action, great energy, and increasing aloofness."[12] He developed his maturity as a student of Marxism-Leninism and as a theoretician of guerrilla warfare during the Yanan years of 1935 to 1940 when he wrote and lectured to the soldiers and cadres. He was then looked upon by his followers as a scholar, a teacher, and a man of wisdom, an image that remained with him long after the establishment of the People's Republic in 1949. This image of a scholar and a man with answers to problems became veiled with an aura of mysticism and magic, the image of a charismatic leader. But the private Mao remained a Chinese scholar, reading books and reports or writing poetry in the traditional style. As many foreigners who interviewed him testified, he was a good conversationalist and was remarkably well informed. Interestingly, he engaged in philosophic conversations about the existence of a god or gods with the late Edgar Snow.[13] Mao personally seemed to have detested the campaigns to build an image of him as comparable to a god or to an emperor, to be worshipped by the people. The epithet that Mao preferred was that of a "great teacher."[14] There is really no appropriate epithet to describe such a complex man as Mao. The recent attempt to measure Mao in the scale of history has produced a number of themes on major areas of Mao's public life: philosopher, Marxist, theorist, political leader, soldier, teacher, economist, partriot, statesman, and innovator.[15] Mao's contribution to the development of the Chinese communist ideology is truly enormous. The following discussion represents only some of the salient aspects of his thought.

THE THOUGHT OF MAO ZEDONG

Before examining Mao's thought, the importance of the Yanan years from 1935 to 1945 in the development of Mao's thinking must be stressed. About half of the articles in the first four volumes of the *Selected Works of Mao Tse-tung* were written during this period. Mao, as leader of the communist movement, was under great pressure from 1939 to 1940 to develop ideas and to provide leadership not only for the communists but also for all the Chinese who would listen.[16]

Peasantry as the Base for Revolution

In 1927, Mao reported on his investigation of the peasant movement in Hunan province. In the report, Mao made a strong appeal to the party, then dominated by the Comintern, to exploit discontent in the countryside and to organize peasant associations as a vanguard for the revolution.[17] Mao noted that poor peasants had been fighting the landlords and feudal rule and that the countryside was on the verge of an agrarian revolution. Mao urged that "a revolutionary tidal wave" must be generated in the countryside to mobilize the masses and to "weld them into this great force" for revolution.

The thrust of Mao's guerrilla efforts in the 1930s and 1940s was the mobilization and welding of the peasants into a formidable revolutionary force for the CCP in its quest for the eventual control of a nation. This concept and practice of mobilizing the peasantry as a revolutionary base has created some controversy among scholars as to whether Mao was a heretic or an original thinker and contributor to communist theory.[18] We may attribute the origin of the idea not to Mao but to Lenin, who recognized the potential of the Russian peasants as a revolutionary force in 1905. We may also say that Mao probably was influenced by Li Dazhao, who saw the peasantry as a possible base for the revolution. The importance of Mao's contribution, as some scholars have noted, was the timing. Mao was the first orthodox Marxist-Leninist to advocate using the peasantry as a major rather than a secondary force, and he made his appeal at the time when the CCP leadership had committed the party to relying on the urban proletariat.[19] With the benefit of hindsight, we might argue that reliance on the peasants was not a conceptual contribution but obviously the only practical revolutionary strategy that could be effective. Practical ideas based on experience were the keynote of Mao's practical ideology.

Mass Line and Populism

At the heart of Mao's political philosophy is the concept of "from the masses, to the masses," commonly known as the mass line. Briefly stated, the concept of mass line specifies that a party policy is good only if the ideas of that policy come originally from the masses—the peasants and the workers—and only if the interests and wishes of the people are taken into account and incorporated into the policy. The implementation of a policy, no matter how good it is, must have the wholehearted support of the masses. The mass line concept is applied in several stages to achieve the enthusiastic support of the masses for its implementation. These stages have been described by John W. Lewis as "perception, summarization, authorization, and implementation."[20] First, the party cadres list the "scattered and unsystematic" views of the masses. Second, the cadres study these ideas and put them into systematic and summary form in their reports to higher authorities. Third, the higher authorities make comments or give instructions based on these systematic ideas and return them to the masses. During this stage, political education or propaganda is carried on by the cadres among the masses, not only to explain the ideas, but also to test their correctness. Finally, when the masses have embraced the ideas as their own, the ideas are translated into concrete action.[21] According to Mao, this is not the end; the proper application of mass line must repeat the process several times "so that each time these ideas emerge with greater correctness and become more vital and meaningful."[22]

The mass line concept, formulated during the Jiangxi soviet days of the 1930s, was an effective method for securing the support of the masses. The application of the mass line requires that both the leaders and the masses go through an educational process, learning from and supporting each other. It provides a continuous dialogue between the leaders and the led. In going through the various stages of the mass line process, the masses are given ample opportunity to participate in the decision-making process, and the leaders are able to obtain popular commitment for policies and programs.

While Mao had immense respect for the virtues of the masses, this did not mean that there were no limits to what the masses could do. The Red Guards' demonstrations and big character posters during the Cultural Revolution were applications of the mass line.[23] As we saw in Chapter 1, however, when the fighting between the various factions of Red Guards reached a state of anarchy, Mao did not hesitate to call in the army to restore order in the tradition of Lenin's democratic centralism. Stuart Schram writes that Mao, who clearly opposed unrestricted mass rule, prevented the Shanghai radicals from organizing leaderless people's committees.[24] Within limits, the concept of mass line does provide a monitoring device on the bureaucratic elite and their tendency to rule the inarticulate masses by party and governmental sanction.[25]

Mass line is considered Mao's theoretical contribution to populism.[26] At the root of this concept is the assertion that simple people—peasants and workers—possess virtue and wisdom. Mao again seems to agree with Li Dazhao, who once said that one becomes more humanistic as one gets closer to the soil. The methods of mass campaigns and small study groups, developed for applying the mass line, have been what Townsend terms "the primary institutions of Mao's populism."[27]

Closely associated with the mass line is Mao's belief in the intellectual tradition of voluntarism: Human will and determination will, in the end, remove all obstacles in making a better world. To Mao, it was this human will—diligence, hard work, and self-reliance—which must be inculcated into the minds of China's impoverished masses, whose potential had been inhibited by centuries of ignorance and superstition. Before and particularly during the Cultural Revolution, repeated references were made to Mao's favorite folk tale about a foolish old man who did succeed in moving mountains through faith and perseverance. The tale, or parable, conveys the idea that it is necessary to rely on one's own strength and to have faith in one's own ability to accomplish revolutionary tasks in building a new society.[28]

Theory and Practice

"We should not study the words of Marxism-Leninism, but study their standpoint and approach in viewing problems and solving them," Mao wrote in a theoretical essay in 1943.[29] He warned that too much reliance on purely abstract ideas or theory yields nothing but dogmatism, for theory is of no value if it does not involve practice. For Mao, the process of cognition involves more than merely what one observes and conceptualizes from observations. There is a third element, which is action or practice for the purpose of making changes in the material world. Knowledge cannot be separated from practice, since it begins with men's experience. For example, Mao wrote that Marxism as a theory did not experience imperialism, and therefore, was good only up to a point. When Lenin, who had perceived and experienced imperialism, added imperialism to the body of Marxist theory, it became meaningful to the Chinese situation. Theory must be subject to modification as changes occur and as new experiences enter into the situation. Marxism, according to Mao, must take into account the historic experience of China and the characteristics of China in order to discover solutions to that country's problems. If one compares Mao's essay on practice with the writings of American pragmatists, such as John Dewey and William James, one will find many interesting parallels. As John Bryan Starr has noted, the philosophy of American pragmatists is not only to discover the world around us but "to know how to remake it."[30]

An example of application of the theory and practice can be seen in Chinese education during the 1950s and the Cultural Revolution, when students split their time into half study and half work. Another example is revealed in Mao's attitude toward students' participation in the Cultural Revolution. He would fondly tell the millions of students that they were the "revolutionary successors," and that the only way they could learn about revolution was to dare to make revolution in the streets. Perhaps the most important point to remember about Mao's treatise on practice is that Mao thought that we can discover knowledge and truth only through practice, which must become an integral part of theory, or conceptual knowledge. This conceptual knowledge will be changed by additional experiences and practices. If knowledge comes from practice, as Mao argued, then practice means action, or at the very least, action orientation.

Contradiction

Mao's theory of contradiction begins with the assertion that society has always been full of contradictions: life-death, sun-moon, darkness-lightness, black-white, individual-collective, and red-expert. It is from the juxtaposition of these contradictions that changes can take place in society. Change takes place because the opposites, or contradictions, have a tendency for one aspect of the contradiction "to transfer itself to the position of its opposite" through some type of a struggle between the two opposites. Adhering to Marxist theory, Mao said that all conflicts are class conflicts between social groups: prior to socialism, peasants versus landlords; now, proletariat versus bourgeoisie. The origin of this theory, sometimes known as the "law of unity of opposites," can be traced to Hegelian dialectics and Marxian dialectical materialism. As others have noted, Mao probably was also influenced by the traditional Chinese concept of opposites, yin and yang.[31] The idea that conflict and change are normal was certainly revolutionary. As was said in Chapter 1, the traditional Chinese society, under Confucianism, had been told to strive for harmony and to maintain the status quo. The theory of contradictions is considered by many to be the core of the thought of Mao Zedong.

Mao felt that the interplay of contradictions would continue even though society had advanced into the higher level of socialism. In 1957, Mao said that none of the socialist countries, including China and the Soviet Union, could transcend the contradictions of social classes by forgetting the class struggle. In an essay entitled "On the Correct Handling of Contradictions Among the People,"[32] Mao advanced the idea that class struggle would continue for an indefinite period of time. It would no longer be in regard to the contradictions between "friends" and "enemies," but on the contradictions between proletarian and bourgeois thinking and behavior. In 1957, Mao explained that there are two types of contradictions: "antagonistic contradiction" between ourselves and the enemy; and "nonantagonistic contradiction" among working people, between peasants and workers, or between cadres and the masses. The nonantagonistic contradictions are essentially matters of ideological and political right and wrong. Since there are two different types of contradictions, Mao proposed two different methods of resolving these conflicts. For antagonistic contradictions, the proletariat dictatorship must suppress the reactionary elements in society; but for the nonantagonistic contradictions among the people, a continuous process of struggle and criticism must be employed to "raise the level of consciousness" and to correct erroneous thinking and behavior of the people. It is through this continuous process of struggle and criticism that unity can be achieved. The key objective of struggle and criticism is to proletarianize the behavior and thinking of the individual, no matter from what economic class background he or she may come. It is the "proletarian consciousness" which is important in the final determination of one's class status.[33] Several major nonantagonistic contradictions or problems which the Chinese must resolve, as defined by Mao, are: 1. between heavy industry and agriculture, 2. between central and local authorities, 3. between urban and rural, 4. between national minorities and the Han peoples over pluralism or radical assimilation.[34]

Mao made it clear that there were bound to be conflicts and struggles to resolve issues within the party:

> Opposition and struggle between different ideas constantly occur within the Party, reflecting contradictions between the classes and between the old and new in society. If in the Party there were no contradictions and no ideological struggles to solve them, the life of the Party would come to an end.[35]

The intra-party disputes, which have beset the party since the 1930s, usually are to be resolved by rectification campaigns; but when the contradictions within the party are so severe that they cause a serious "cleavage of opinion" among the members of the Politburo, the contradictions must be resolved by some type of mass campaign.

The Cultural Revolution has been viewed as both a rectification campaign and a mass campaign for class struggle to resolve the contradictions between the proletariat and the bourgeoisie. It is called the Cultural Revolution because, according to both Marx and Mao, the construction of a total socialist society demands transformation in the superstructure of culture, customs, and habits to eliminate the contradictions between proletarian collectivism and bourgeois individualism.[36]

Most Americans tend to be very skeptical about the utility of Mao's theory on contradictions, treating it as a piece of incomprehensible diatribe. It is very difficult for our highly technological and analytical minds to understand why, for instance, the workers and staff in a blast furnace attribute their breakthrough to higher output to simply studying the dialectics on contradiction. But the Chinese say, first, the theory of contradiction helps the peasants and workers develop "a habit of analysis." In the case of the blast furnace, the workers and staff sat down and analyzed why the conventional way of increasing temperatures of the furnace brought about an increase in output only up to an optimal level.

By altering the structure of the layers of the furnace through analysis, they were able to control the flow of coal gas and to realize a greater yield after the standard level of pressure had been applied.[37] Another example is of a peasant who has just been thrust into a position of leadership in his village and is daily confronted by a host of conflict-of-interest situations for which he must provide resolution. By studying the theory of contradiction, he is able to carry on some analyses of his own and to feel more confident in providing resolution to the conflicts.[38] Second, the theory of contradiction is useful, as pointed out by Schurmann, in a struggle and criticism session where the deviant individual's erroneous thinking is brought into sharp focus to facilitate correction through thought reform.[39] Finally, the theory on contradiction, by focusing on the law of unity of opposites, compels those involved in a conflict situation to agree on the proper means for resolving the conflict. Schurmann describes how discussion of a controversial issue at the Politburo level first produces two opposite sets of opinions and then results in the adoption of one set of opinions as a majority view and the other set as a minority view. Before a decision is reached, however, there must be what Schurmann calls the "juxtaposition" or polarization of opinion as a logical consequence of the application of the theory of contradiction.[40] By recognizing and accepting that there are contradictions in Chinese society, in the party, and in the political system, and by requiring that these contradictions be resolved through the continuous process of struggle and criticism, Mao's theory of contradiction has contributed enormously to the dynamism that is present in the Chinese political process.

Permanent Revolution.[41]

The ideas about change and struggle, contained in Mao's essays on practice and contradictions, logically lead to his concept of a permanent, or continuous, revolution: If society is rampant with contradictions, then "ceaseless change and upheaval" must be the normal condition to enable the society to reach a higher level of proletarian consciousness. The continuous class struggle is therefore necessary to create the "new socialist man."

Mao emphasized that his concept of the permanent revolution was different from Leon Trotsky's, a point which Krushchev seemed to have missed. In 1959, Krushchev compared the two concepts, labeling Mao's concept of a permanent revolution as a mixture of anarchism, Trotskyism, and adventurism. One essential difference was that Trotsky was merely concerned about "the transition from the democratic to the socialistic stage of the revolution," while Mao was concerned about "a separate stage of social transformation" during which the revolutionary environment must be maintained to eliminate all bourgeois influences and tendencies and to rebuild the superstructures.[42] Another difference was that Trotsky and Stalin would permit a new class of technocrats to emerge in order to establish the new economic base. Mao, on the other hand, argued that a new economic base does not necessarily bring about new superstructure; class struggle must continue from the beginning to the end when the society is undergoing transformation. Mao believed that "Politics must take command so that the elites understand the correct ideological line." The contradictions must be solved by continuous struggle or revolution. Mao would insist: "We must destroy the old basis for unity, pass through a struggle, and unite on a new basis." Viewed from this perspective, both the Socialist Education Movement and the Cultural Revolution were important examples of the theory of permanent revolution. At the heart of Mao's theory of permanent revolution is the thesis that even after the establishment of a new economic base, both individuals and institutions still can acquire bourgeois tendencies and thus change the color of the revolution.

MAO'S LEGACY AND DE-MAOIZATION

Something unusual has happened recently in China: the move by the present leadership to deemphasize the "personality cult" of Mao. On July 1, 1978, the fifty-eighth anniversary of the founding of the Chinese Communist Party, the major mass media published the text of Chairman Mao's 1962 talk to some seven thousand cadres at an enlarged central work conference.[43] What is so significant about the publication of the talk is that it was at that 1962 gathering that Mao admitted he had made serious mistakes and should be criticized for the ill-fated Great Leap programs. Mao admitted frankly that he knew very little about "economic construction" or about industry and commerce. Some of the policies of the Great Leap, Mao confessed, had been mistakes on his part, and he took full responsibility for them. There have been many other small signs or signals of the downgrading of some of Mao's teachings: For instance, the *People's Daily* no longer carries Mao's quotations on the front page.

But there is also continued veneration for Mao as a great leader. One need only look at the thousands of people who filed silently into the memorial hall in the Tian An Men Square in Beijing everyday since it opened in 1977 to realize the profound affection Mao had with his people. None of the new leaders of China today has ever made a speech without quoting a line or two from Mao, either to illustrate or to justify their own position. In the post-Mao era, as well as in those periods when he was alive and active, Mao Zedong still is a unifying symbol for the

Chinese. More than any other leader in modern China, Mao has left an enormous legacy for his people.

The thinking of Mao Zedong is very complex as we have pointed out. His ideas have their roots in the Chinese intellectual tradition, particularly in the May Fourth Movement, in the Marxist-Leninist tradition, and in the revolutionary experiences of the Chinese Communist Party. Yet Mao's populist approach, contained in the concept of mass line, is distinct and goes beyond Marx, Lenin, and the Chinese tradition. The vision that the semi-literate peasants and workers—collectively, the masses—can be the source of ideas and inspiration for the leaders was truly revolutionary. The application of this core concept of Mao enabled the CCP to secure the popular support from guerrilla operations in the 1930s and 1940s through the land reform and the communization in the 1950s and 1960s. The failure of the Great Leap and the questions raised about the results of the Cultural Revolution make it appear doubtful that Mao's concept has been realized. Yet, in spite of the dampening effect of the Great Leap and the Cultural Revolution, Mao's prescription for a proper relationship between the leaders and the led in the mass-line formula remain a fundamental work style for the Chinese leaders. Both the state constitution of 1978 and the party charter of 1977 enshrine this Maoist vision of relying on the masses for inspiration, support, and implementation of policies and programs. It is the mass line as an ideological concept which has given the Chinese their national identity.[44]

Mao's practical ideology also has functioned as a guide, if not the basis, for individuals in Chinese society to shape their attitudes and to regulate their behavior. These ideas serve as a set of preferred societal values on which actions and thoughts are gauged. Mao's philosophical ideas and teachings, such as human will and determination, self-sacrifice, and service to the people, have become an integral part of today's value system, governing behavior. These preferred values have been instilled in the minds of the people by means of the ceaseless class struggle called for in the theory of contradictions. The result of these ideas is an evolving and dynamic society for which Mao must be given a large amount of the credit. To many Americans and to some of Mao's own colleagues, his ideas of a permanent revolution and ceaseless change may be too unsettling, bordering on anarchy; but in Mao's vision, the revolution is like a pair of straw sandals which have no definite pattern, but "shape themselves in the making." Stuart Schram's tribute to Mao is worth quoting: "Mao has left the sandal of the Chinese revolution unfinished, but it has already begun to take shape, and for a long time to come it can scarcely fail to bear his stamp."[45]

Ideology alone could not have had such a great impact on China. In the final analysis, it takes a man like Mao, with exceptional skill and acumen as a political leader, to translate ideas into concrete actions and to make people do what the leader wants over a long period of time. No other Chinese leader in modern times has been involved directly in so many important issues over such a long period of time as has Mao Zedong.[46] When he died in 1976, he left behind a unified, strong, and vital society.

It has been fashionable, since Mao's death and the arrest of the radical leaders in October 1976, to detect signs of deemphasizing Mao's ideology and programs he supported during the Cultural Revolution. The newly coined word "de-Maoization" has come into vogue.[47] There is even some debunking about "Maoism." "Maoism" has been termed as a "myth" and is considered too abstract to be understood.[48] However, we must use caution in assessing Mao's ideas and programs. There are several reasons for issuing this caution. First, the function of a political ideology is to serve a unifying purpose, and the thought of Mao, perhaps more than anything else, has done just that. Mao's ideas have given the Chinese people the hope that they can do something about their lives on their own initiative and hard work. The enormous accomplishments of the Chinese, during the past forty years, in finding solutions to some of the most pressing and difficult problems of mankind cannot be dissociated from Mao's ideology and the organizations he established for translating these ideas into concrete programs. Second, because of the enormity of these human problems for so large a populace, who for centuries had been living in stagnation, inertia, and pessimism, Mao's ideas offered not only a ray of hope but the message that they must constantly experiment, think afresh, and be willing to take risks.

The efforts to deemphasize the more radical aspects of Mao's teachings raises questions about the durability of Mao's legacy and the future of China. It does appear that some of Mao's ideas that emerged from the Cultural Revolution have been altered or modified. For example, the new leadership under Hua Guofeng has called for higher academic standards in schools and for industrial enterprises to be operated on the basis of profit and material incentives to spur production. Some Western analysts have argued that there is really no clear-cut "left" and "right" in describing political change in China, but rather that there is only disagreement with speed or direction. Only time will reveal the impact of the modifications which are bound to evolve; but whatever modifications are made, Mao's example of self-reliance and innovative experimentation to develop a better society will remain.

Mao once told Edgar Snow that he would like his epithet to be that of "teacher" for the Chinese people. An essential quality of a good teacher is to encourage his pupils to learn and not to be discouraged, to correct mistakes and to move on. Mao's thought and ideas have been an inspiration to his people and have provided methods by which solutions can be found to their staggering problems. Stripping off its Marxian cover, some of his thought might conceivably become a model of thinking for a new China of which Mao Zedong was the most influential architect and visionary designer.

Mao, however, is not invulnerable to criticism. Under the leadership of Hua Guofeng and Deng Xiaoping, there will be opportunities for some free expression in the name of "a more democratic way of life," now that the radical ideologues and their "oppression" have been swept away by arrests and purges. The appearance of a sudden flurry of wall posters in Beijing in late November 1978, denouncing Mao's role in the 1976 Tian An Men incident, is a case in point. As time goes on, the Chinese probably will have a more balanced view about Mao, both as a person and as a leader. It is interesting to note the recent publication of a speech made by Zhou Enlai to the First All-China Youth Congress in 1949, in which Zhou had warned the youth not to look upon Mao as a demigod.[49] Zhou related a story about how unhappy Mao was when he learned that a school textbook had said that he had been opposed to superstition when he was a boy of ten. On the contrary, Zhou explained, Mao believed in gods when he was a little boy and "prayed to Buddha for help" at one time when his mother became ill.[50] Zhou's message to the youth in 1949 was twofold: They should not regard Mao as an infallible leader, and they should seek truth from facts. It is this blind worship of Mao which, in time, will be deemphasized or eliminated altogether. Truth, including Mao's thought, as the leaders now insist, must eventually be tested by practice—this is the major theme in China's policy of moderation.

After a lengthy debate at the Third Plenary Session of the Eleventh Central Committee meeting in December 18–22, 1978, China's new leadership agreed that the time had come for the people to "emancipate their thinking, dedicate themselves to the study of new circumstances, things, and questions, and uphold the principle of seeking truth from facts."[51] While paying tribute to Mao's "outstanding leadership," the party's Central Committee nevertheless found that Mao had made mistakes: "It would not be Marxist to demand that a revolutionary leader be free of all shortcomings and errors."[52] This was the beginning of the process to deemphasize Mao and to dispel the myth of his infallibility, which had been built up over the years by the radicals. Anti-Mao posters appeared in Beijing in late 1978 and early 1979, along with the party's admission of "erroneous" action in the Tian An Men Square incident in April 1976 and its reexamination of the events of the Cultural Revolution. In December 1978, the Central Committee exonerated and rehabilitated a host of top leaders purged in 1959 and during the Cultural

Revolution for opposing Mao or his policies, including Peng Dehuai, Peng Zhen, Bo Yibo, and Tao Zhu. Deng Xiaoping, who repeatedly endured Mao's wrath, has been quoted as saying that Mao was perhaps "seventy percent correct and thirty percent wrong."[53] The process of reevaluating Mao in China has yielded, and will continue to yield, important facts as well as varied perspectives on the ramifications of Mao's leadership, which should produce a more complete and balanced picture of the man and his impact on history.

NOTES

[1]Franz Schurmann, *Ideology and Organization in Communist China* (Berkeley, Calif.: University of California Press, 1966).

[2]Schurmann, *Ideology and Organization in Communist China,* pp. 21–22.

[3]See Lawrence Sullivan and Richard H. Solomon, "The Formation of Chinese Ideology in the May Fourth Era: A Content Analysis of Hsin ch'ing Nien," in *Ideology and Politics in Contemporary China,* ed. Chalmers Johnson (Seattle and London: University of Washington Press, 1973), pp. 117–60. Also see "Chairman Hua Guofeng on May 4th Movement," *Beijing Review,* 19 (May 11, 1979), pp. 9–11.

[4]Alfred G. Meyers, *Communism,* 3rd ed. (New York: Random House, 1967).

[5]Mao-Tse-tung, "Ching Kanshan Revisited," *Peking Review,* 1 (January 2, 1976), p. 5.

[6]*Mao Tse-tung* (London: Penguin, 1970), p. 36.

[7]See Enrica Collotti Pischel, "The Teacher," in *Mao Tse-tung in the Scale of History,* ed. Dick Wilson (London: Cambridge University Press, 1977), pp. 144–73.

[8]Lucian Pye, *Mao-Tse-tung, the Man in the Leader* (New York: Basic Books, Inc., 1976), pp. 20–21.

[9]Edgar Snow, *Red Star Over China* (New York: Grove Press, 1961), p. 151.

[10]*Pye, Mao Tse-tung, the Man in the Leader,* pp 17–38.

[11]Pye, *Mao Tse-tung, the Man in the Leader,* pp. 17–38.

[12]Pye, *Mao Tse-tung, the Man in the Leader,* p. 23.

[13]Edgar Snow, *The Long Revolution* (New York: Vintage Books, 1973), pp. 170–71.

[14]Snow, *The Long Revolution,* p. 169.

[15]Dick Wilson, ed., *Mao Tse-tung in the Scale of History* (London and New York: Cambridge University Press, 1977).

[16]James Chieh Hsiung, *Ideology and Practice: The Evolution of Chinese Communism* (New York: Holt, Rinehart & Winston, 1970), p. 67.

[17]Mao Tse-tung, "Report on an Investigation of the Peasant Movement in Hunan," in *Selected Works of Mao Tse-tung* (Peking: Foreign Language Press, 1967), vol. I, pp. 23–59.

[18]Benjamin I. Schwartz, *Communism and China: Ideology in Flux* (Cambridge, Mass.: Harvard University Press, 1968), p. 41; James Hsiung, *Ideology and Practice,* pp. 61–62; and Chester

C. Tan, *Chinese Political Thought in the Twentieth Century* (Garden City, N.Y.: Doubleday, 1971), pp. 345–46.

[19]James Hsiung, *Ideology and Practice*, pp. 61–62; and Conrad Brandt, Benjamin Schwartz, and John Fairbank, *A Documentary History of Chinese Communism* (New York: Antheneum, 1966), pp. 80–93.

[20]John W. Lewis, *Leadership in Communist China* (Ithaca, N.Y.: Cornell University Press, 1963), p. 72.

[21]Mao Tse-tung, "Some Questions Concerning Methods of Leadership," in *Selected Works of Mao Tse-tung* (Peking: Foreign Language Press, 1967), vol. III, pp. 117–22.

[22]Mao Tse-tung, "Some Questions Concerning Methods of Leadership," p. 113.

[23]See Lowell Dittmer, "Mass Line and Mass Criticism in China: An Analysis of the Fall of Liu Shao-chi," *Asian Survey* (August 1973), vol. xiii, no. 8, 772–92.

[24]Schram, "The Marxist," in *Mao Tse-tung in the Scale of History*, p. 48. Also in John W. Lewis, *Leadership in Communist China*, p. 79.

[25]Lewis, *Leadership in Communist China*, pp. 84–86.

[26]James R. Townsend, "Chinese Populism and the Legacy of Mao Tse-tung," *Asian Survey* (November 1977), vol. xviii, no. 11, 1006–11.

[27]Townsend, "Chinese Populism and the Legacy of Mao Tse-tung," p. 1009.

[28]See James C.F. Wang, "Values of the Cultural Revolution," in the *Journal of Communication* (Summer 1977), vol. 27, no. 3, 41–46. Also see Maurice Meisner, "Utopian Goals and Ascetic Values in Chinese Communist Ideology," *Journal of Asian Studies* (November 1968), vol. 28, no. 1, 101–10.

[29]Mao Tse-tung, "On Practice," *Selected Works of Mao Tse-tung* (Peking: Foreign Language Press, 1967), vol. I, pp. 295–309.

[30]Starr, *Ideology and Culture*, p. 30.

[31]Hsiung, *Ideology and Practice*, pp. 102–103; Pye, *Mao-Tse-tung: the Man in the Leader*, p. 45; Schram, "The Marxist," in *Mao Tse-tung in the Scale of History*, p. 60.

[32]*Selected Works of Mao Tse-tung* (Peking: Foreign Language Press, 1977) vol. V, pp. 384–421.

[33]Starr, *Ideology and Culture*, p. 128.

[34]Mao Tse-tung, "On the Ten Major Relationships, April 25, 1956," *Peking Review*, 1 (January 1, 1977), 10–25.

[35]Mao Tse-tung, "On Contradiction," in *Selected Works of Mao Tse-tung* (Peking: Foreign Language Press, 1967), vol. I, p. 317.

[36]William Hinton, *Turning Point in China: An Essay on the Cultural Revolution* (New York: Monthly Review Press, 1972).

[37]Shih Kang, "Dialectics in Blast Furnaces," *Peking Review*, 41 (October 12, 1973), 19–20.

[38]The illustration is given by Gray and Cavendish *Chinese Communism in Crisis* (New York and London: Holt, Rinehart & Winston, 1968), pp. 59–60.

[39]Schurmann, *Ideology and Organization*, p. 54.

[40]Shurmann, *Ideology and Organization*, p. 55.

[41]"Talks at the Chengtu Conference, March 1958" in Stuart Schram, ed., *Chairman Mao Talks to the People*, p. 108. For further insights into the concept, see Stuart Schram's two

articles, "Mao Tse-tung and the Theory of Permanent Revolution," *The China Quarterly,* 46 (April–June 1971), 221–44, and "The Marxist," *Mao Tse-tung in the Scale of History,* pp. 56–62. Also, see John Bryan Starr, "Conceptual Foundations of Mao Tse-tung's Theory of Continuous Revolution," *Asian Survey,* vol. XI, no. 6 (June 1971), 610–28.

[42]Starr, "Conceptual Foundations of Mao Tse-tung's Theory of Continuous Revolution," p. 612.

[43]Mao Tse-tung, "Talk at an Enlarged Working Conference Convened by the Central Committee of the CCP," *Peking Review,* 27 (July 7, 1978), 6–22. The version has been, however, included in translation form in Stuart Schram, *Chairman Mao Talks to the People, Talks and Letters, 1956–1971* (New York: The Pantheon Asia Library, 1974), pp. 158–87.

[44]Townsend, "Chinese Populism and the Legacy of Mao Tse-tung," p. 1011.

[45]Schram, "The Marxist," in *Mao Tse-tung in the Scale of History,* p. 69.

[46]Mike Oksenberg, "Mao's Policy Commitments, 1921–1976," *Problems of Communism,* vol. xxv, no. 6 (November–December 1976), 19–26. Also see his article "The Political Leader" in *Mao Tse-tung in the Scale of History,* pp. 88–98.

[47]Fox Butterfield, "China Disputes Legacy of Mao More Directly," *The New York Times* (May 17, 1978), pp. 1–2; Linda Mathews, " 'Demaoization' Extends to People's Daily," Los Angeles Times Service, reprinted in *Honolulu Advertiser* (January 13, 1978), p. E-15; and David Bonavia, "Dismantling Parts of Maoism—But Not Mao," *Far Eastern Economic Review,* vol. 98, no. 40 (October 7, 1977), 39–41.

[48]Simon Leys, *Chinese Shadows* (Middlesex, England: Penguin, 1978).

[49]Chou En-lai, "Learn from Mao Tse-tung," *Peking Review,* 43 (October 27, 1978), 7.

[50]Chou En-lai, "Learn from Mao Tse-tung," p. 8.

[51]"Communiqué of the Third Plenary Session of the Eleventh Central Committee of the Communist Party of China Adopted on December 22, 1978," *Peking Review,* 52 (December 29, 1978), 14–15.

[52]"Communiqué of the Third Plenary Session of the Eleventh Central Committee of the Communist Party of China," p. 15.

[53]*Ming Pao Daily* (Hongkong) November 30, 1978, p. 1.

The Basic Political Organization: The Chinese Communist Party

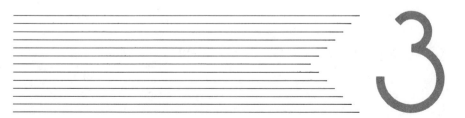

3

The Chinese Communist Party (CCP) is the source of all political power and has the exclusive right to legitimize and control of all other political organizations. The Chinese Communist Party alone determines the social, economic, and political goals for the society. The attainment of these goals is pursued through careful recruitment of its members and their placement in party organs which supervise and control all other institutions and groups in the society. All other institutions in China are controlled by the elites, who are themselves leaders of the party hierarchy.

HIERARCHICAL STRUCTURE OF THE PARTY

One of the most salient characteristics of the party as an organization is that it is hierarchical, pyramidal, and centralist in nature. A simplified representation of the structure of the CCP is shown in Figure 3.1. The pyramidal structure of the CCP has four main levels of organizations: 1. the central organizations, 2. the provincial and autonomous regional organizations, 3. the xien (county) or district organizations, and 4. the basic and primary organizations—party branches in schools, factories, and communes.

CENTRAL-LEVEL PARTY ORGANIZATION

In this section the central level of the party organization will be discussed in some detail.

66

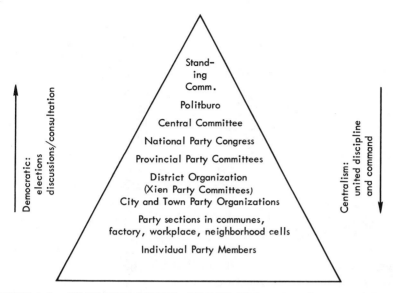

FIGURE 3.1: SIMPLIFIED MODEL OF CCP ORGANIZATIONAL PYRAMID

Source: Modified version of Joseph L. LaPalombara, Politics Within Nations *(Englewood Cliffs, N.J.: Prentice-Hall, Inc., 1974), p. 527. By permission of publisher.*

National Party Congress

In conformity with the tradition of a Leninist party, the CCP vests its supreme authority, at least nominally, in the National Party Congress. During its fifty-eight-year history, only eleven such National Party Congresses have been convened. The 1969, 1973, and 1977 party constitutions have all stipulated that it must meet every five years. The two longest intervals between congresses were eleven years and thirteen years, between the Seventh Congress in 1945 and the Eighth Congress in 1956, and between the Eighth Congress and the Ninth Congress in 1969. The party constitutions of 1956, 1969, 1973, and 1977 contain a proviso, an escape clause, which states that "under special circumstances, it (the National Party Congress) may be convened before its due date or postponed" by the Central Committee. Since the Party Congress generally meets in a perfunctory manner to approve policy changes being recommended by the Central Committee, its sessions have generally been short, a week or two in duration.

We do not know how the delegates are chosen. The procedures for selection are generally determined by the Central Committee. Presumably, delegates are selected at the provincial and district levels to reflect the "constellation of power" at the central level. It is also possible for the power at the center to engage in slate-making. The process of packing the congress at the various levels of the party organization to represent factionalized leaders may also be in operation. Wang Hungwen, one of the arrested radical leaders from Shanghai, has been accused of pressuring his close supporters to run for the position of delegate for the Tenth Party Congress.[1] However, it was revealed in 1968 by Xieh Fuchi, the Minister for Public Security, that delegates to the Second through the Seventh Party Congress had been appointed.[2]

The sheer size of the party congress—1,249 delegates for the Tenth Congress (1973) and 1,510 for the Eleventh Congress (1977)— makes an unwieldly body to be truly deliberative. However, the party congress does have certain basic functions to perform; these can be seen from the agenda for each session. Generally speaking, each session of the Party Congress has three standard items which constitute the entire agenda: a political report by the party chairman or his designee, a report on the revision of the party constitution, and the election of the Central Committee and its Standing Committee.

A major task of the National Party Congress is to select the new Central Committee. Selection perhaps is not the proper term to describe the actual process involved: a preliminary list of those to become members of the Central Committee is usually drawn up by the key leaders in the hierarchy, and then the list is presented to the Party Congress for formal ratification. For instance, the draft list for members of the Eighth Central Committee (1956) was prepared by Liu Shaoqi supporters— Peng Zheng and An Ziwen.[3] The membership of the Central Committee elected in 1977 clearly reflects the power line-up within the party. Omissions from the powerful Central Committee membership are indicative of power shifts or simply of a reduction of influence within the party's hierarchy.

In the preparation of the party constitution to be ratified by the Party Congress, inputs have been made by all party organizations. We now know that, beginning in 1967, party organizations at levels below the Central Committee participated in the revision of the constitution, at Mao's insistence.[4] Both the 1969 and 1973 party constitutions involved participation and discussion by party cadres at all levels before the final version was enacted by the delegates to these congresses. Wang Hungwen gave a detailed account of the revision process of the party constitution adopted in 1973 by the Tenth Party Congress.[5]

Some students of Chinese politics have pointed out that, in addition to the important tasks of ratification of the party constitution and election of the Central Committee, the Party Congress accepts and reviews political reports from party leaders.[6] Reports presented at the National Party Congress have been published, and one can infer policy shifts and program emphasis from them. Since the Central Committee debates are never published, except for occasional communiques summarizing policy formulations and personnel changes, reports of the National Party Congress provide a unique source of information with some inkling about the issues and programs of concern to the party. For example, the political report delivered by Hua Guofeng to the Eleventh Party Congress in August 1977 presented the official version on the wrongdoings committed against the party by the purged radical leaders led by Jiang Qing, Mao's widow. The four-hour report contained an eight-point program of "musts" for establishing party stability and unity to enable the Party to lead the nation to modernization in agriculture, industry, and national defense by 1980. The report also called for a concerted effort in stepping up scientific research in an atmosphere of "freedom and discipline" and of "less empty talk and more hard work."

Finally, there has always been a great deal of fanfare and publicity focused on the Party Congress. This is more than mere public relations work by the party; the convocation of the congress serves as a rallying point for the party members and for the populace in general. It creates a feeling of participation in the important decisions of the party among the delegates themselves, many of whom come from very humble backgrounds and remote regions of China. It instills in them the "sense of commitment" to and unity with their leaders and the party.[7]

In view of the limited duration and agenda of the Party Congress, the question arises as to how preparations for it are made. Technically, the outgoing Central Committee is responsible for preparing the forthcoming congress. In practice, however, the Politburo or the Standing Committee of the Politburo, prepares the agenda and designates members to draft the political reports and to work on the new party constitution under its supervision. We know, for instance, that Lin Biao's original draft of his political report to the Ninth Party Congress was rejected by the Central Committee or Chairman Mao.[8] Evidently, the final report, as read by Lin Biao to the delegates at the 1969 Party Congress, was drafted "under Chairman Mao's guidance." We probably can assume that political reports from the Seventh Party Congress, in 1945, to the Tenth Party Congress, in 1973, received personal approval from Mao. There have been admissions of hasty preparation for the proceedings of the Party Congress. Mrs. Liu Shaoqi (Wang Guangmei) admitted, under Red Guard interrogation during the Cultural Revolution, that "everything was done in a hurry" in preparation for the Eighth Party Congress, in 1956.[9]

Central Committee

The party constitution vests in the Central Committee the supreme power to govern party affairs and to enact party policies when the Party Congress is not in session. The large size of the Central Committee makes it an unwieldly body for policy making. Although the Central Committee as a collective body rarely initiates party policy, it must approve or endorse policies, programs, and major changes in membership in leading central organs. Thus, with a few exceptions, the Central Committee usually holds annual plenary sessions, either with its own full and alternate members in attendance, or with non-Central Committee members, as well, in enlarged sessions. The few deviations from the norm were during the Korean War (1950–1953), the turbulent period prior to the Cultural Revolution (1962–1966), and the Lin Biao affair (1971–1973). These regularized plenums of the Central Committee are the forums through which party and state policies and programs are discussed and ratified. On at least two occasions—the October 1955 plenum (enlarged), and the August 1959 plenum (enlarged)—the Central Committee became the "ultimate" body which decided agricultural policies to be implemented when there was dissension among top leaders of the party.[10]

There has been a steady increase in the size of the Central Committee. The Eighth Party Congress, first session (1956), expanded the full membership of the Central Committee from 44 to 97; the Ninth Party Congress (1969) almost doubled the size to a cumbersome 170; the Eleventh Party Congress (August 1977) elected 201 full, and 132 alternate, members to the Central Committee, for a total of 333. There are several reasons that the membership of the Central Committee has increased to the present enormous proportions. First, increased membership in the Central Committee reflects the phenomenal growth of the party membership as a whole since the Cultural Revolution, from approximately seventeen million in 1961 to over twenty-eight million at the time of the Tenth Party Congress in August 1973. Second, like its counterpart in the Soviet Union, membership in the Central Committee has been used as a reward for loyal service to the party and to the government. Preeminent scholars and scientists have been recognized and elevated into the Central Committee membership. Third, the Ninth and Tenth Party Congresses expanded the Central Committee membership in order to make it reflect the post-Cultural Revolution party leadership recruitment policy—increased representation by workers and peasants who have rendered significant political service for the party. As shown in Table 3.1, of the full members elected to the Ninth Central Committee in April 1969, 32 (19 percent) were from mass organizations representing workers and peasants. This representation of full members increased to 58, or 30 percent, in the Tenth Central Committee in August 1973. But the representation for mass organizations—the source of support for the radical wing of the party—was reduced to 32, or 16 percent, in the Eleventh Central Committee full membership in August 1977. Veteran cadre representation increased slightly by about one percent in the

TABLE 3.1: Groups Represented By Members of 9th–11th Central Committees

Group Represented	9th Full	Central Committee Alternate	Total	10th Full	Central Committee Alternate	Total	11th Full	Central Committee Alternate	Total
				Number					
PLA	74	49	123	63	37	100	62	41	103
Veteran Cadres	59	20	79	71	20	91	107	28	135
Mass Organizations	32	23	55	58	49	107	32	63	95
Unknown	5	17	22	3	18	21	—	—	—
Total	170	109	279	195	124	319	201	132	333
				Percent					
PLA	43%	45%	44%	32%	30%	31%	31.8%	31%	31%
Veteran Cadres	35	18	28	36	16	29	53	21	41
Mass Organizations	19	20	20	30	40	34	16	48	29
Unknown	3	16	8	2	15	7	—	—	—
Total a	100%	100%	100%	100%	100%	100%	100%	100%	100%

aTotals may not equal 100%, due to rounding

Sources:

Ninth Central Committee: Figures are based on the published list in Hung-qi (Red Flag), 5 (May 1, 1969), 49–50.

Tenth Central Committee: Figures are based on the published list in Hung-qi (Red Flag), 9 (September 3, 1973), 32–35.

Eleventh Central Committee: Figures are based on the published list in Remin Ribao (People's Daily) (August 21, 1977), p. 3.

Tenth Central Committee, but their representation in the full membership of the Eleventh Central Committee leaped to 107, or 53 percent of the total—a clear evidence of the veteran cadres' dominance in the party after the purge of the radicals in 1976. While PLA representation in the full membership on the Tenth Central Committee declined eleven percent from the Ninth Central Committee (from 43 to 32 percent), its representation in the Eleventh Central Committee full membership remained almost the same at 31.8 percent. The combined representation of the PLA and the veteran cadres in the Eleventh Central Committee full membership is now over 84 percent. A fourth reason for membership expansion in the Central Committee is related to increased female representation at the Ninth and Tenth Central Committees. There were 23, or 8.2 percent, female members on the Ninth Central Committee. This representation was increased to 41, or 12.8 percent, on the Tenth Central Committee. However, female representation was reduced to 38, or 11.4 percent in the membership of the Eleventh Central Committee.

There has been a marked continuity in the membership of the Central Committees in recent years. For instance, the Tenth Party Congress in 1973 failed to reelect only 39 of the 170 full members of the Ninth Central Committee to the new Tenth Central Committee—all of them were supporters of Lin Biao. The Eleventh Party Congress in 1977 reelected 111 of the 195 full members of the Tenth Central Committee to the new Eleventh Central Committee, which had a full membership of 201. In other words, close to half of the Eleventh Central Committee full membership was carried over from the old Tenth Central Committee elected in 1973. The ones who were not reelected to the Eleventh Central Committee were apparently the supporters of the Gang of Four. The Eleventh Central Committee has a preponderant representation of the old veterans of the party, government, and the military. The average age of both full and alternate members of the Eleventh Central Committee is over sixty-five.[11]

The Politburo and Its Standing Committee

The principle of Lenin's democratic centralism calls for decision-making power for the party to be vested in a small number of key leaders who occupy positions at the apex of the power structure, the Political Bureau (Politburo). The formal language in the party constitution does not reveal the actual power of this top command for the CCP. The party constitutions of 1969, 1973, and 1977 simply stipulated that the Politburo shall be elected by the Central Committee in full session and shall act in its behalf when the Central Committee is not in session. Day-to-day work of the Politburo is carried out by its Standing Committee, the apex of the pyramidal structure of the party.[12] In essence, it is the Politburo and its Standing Committee which possess "boundless" power over the general policies of the party and all important matters of the regime that affect the government organs.[13] It is the Politburo which selects top personnel to direct the vast apparatus of the party, the government, and the military.

The Politburo holds frequent meetings; discussion is free and unrestrained. It has been compared to a corporate board of directors.[14] Decisions of the Politburo are generally reached by the group's consensus after thorough discussion of the available alternatives.

When the party took power in 1949, the CCP Politburo consisted of eleven members, and its operation very closely resembled Lenin's inner circle of key leaders who made all of the important decisions for the Soviet party, government, and state.[15] By 1956, the CCP Politburo membership had increased to seventeen full and six alternate members, paralleling the enlargement of the Party Congress and the Central Committee. With fluctuations, as a result of deaths and purges, its membership rose to over twenty full members in later years. The Eleventh Party Congress in 1977 elected a twenty-six member Politburo which was expanded to thirty in 1978. As we have seen with the Party Congress and Central Committee, enlargement reflected a shift in function. The 1956 party constitution introduced the concept of the "apex of the apex:" the formation of the Standing Committee of the Politburo, which became the top ruling clique. The membership for the Standing Committee has varied from five to nine. In many instances the Standing Committee makes decisions without even consulting the Politburo.[16]

The dynamics of decision making, involving key leaders and cadres of the party and government, will be discussed in Chapter 4. It should be noted here, however, that prior to the Cultural Revolution, the decision-making process was institutionalized, to a large extent, by the frequent use of work conferences under the sponsorship of the Politburo or the Central Committee.[17] Since the purge of the radical leaders in October 1976, this institutionalized device for policy formulation has been revived so that at least several dozen national conferences have been convened to develop national policies on various matters, including modernizing agriculture and industry, national defense, and science and technology.

Although, according to the party constitution, the Central Committee elects members to the Politburo and its Standing Committee, the actual selection rested in the hands of Chairman Mao from 1935 to 1975. In fact, the determination of which Central Committee members were to sit on the powerful Politburo had been termed Mao's "personal prerogative."[18] Franklin Houn points out that Mao followed a general set of guidelines in his selection of candidates to Politburo membership: seniority in the party, contributions made to Mao's own rise to power, and loyalty and usefulness to Mao and the party.[19] To what extent Hua Guofeng had a decisive role in the selection of the twenty-six-member Politburo for the Eleventh Central Committee (1977) is difficult to determine. But sixteen of the members were reelected from the previous Politburo membership, and the ten newly elected members all have backgrounds of long service in the party, government, and military bureaucracy. Thus, administrative experience may have been an important factor in Politburo membership selection.

Other Principal Organs of the Central Committee

The Central Committee and its Politburo are serviced by a host of centralized organs, responsible for executing party policies and managing party affairs. Some of this machinery deals with the routine matters of party organization, propaganda, and united front work. However, three principal central party organs need to be briefly mentioned here: the Central Secretariat, the Military Affairs Commission, and the Control Commission.

The Central Secretariat, as it existed from 1956–1966, was the administrative and staff agency that supervised the party's numerous functional departments, paralleling the functional ministries of the central government. The total number of these central party functional departments may once have reached more than eighteen. Membership of the Central Secretariat was not fixed; it ranged from six or seven to ten or eleven top ranking Central Committee members. For over a decade, the Central Secretariat was under the control of Deng Xiaoping, who served as its general secretary. Deng and the members of the Central Secretariat used the machinery for making or influencing many important party decisions without even consulting Mao, the chairman of the party.[20] In the aftermath of the Cultural Revolution, the Central Secretariat, as a formal unit, was abandoned, probably at the insistence of Mao who felt that it had overstepped its authority. From then until 1977 or 1978, the administrative functions of the party secretariat were absorbed by the General Office for the Politburo, headed by Politburo member Wang Dongxing. In the winter of 1978, Wang was replaced by Tao Yilin. At the same time, a newly elected Politburo member, Hu Yaobang, a trusted protégé of Deng Xiaoping, was appointed as secretary-general of the Central Secretariat, which has been reestablished in its pre-Cultural Revolution form.

Although the Military Affairs Commission (MAC) is a subunit of the Central Committee of the CCP, it reports directly to the Politburo and its Standing Committee. The MAC supervises the administration of the armed forces and makes policies in national defense. The MAC directly controls the General Political Department (GPD), the party's political agent within the PLA, which in theory is a branch of the Ministry of Defense but in practice operates independent of it. The General Political Department is responsible for the political education of the troops and publishes the *Liberation Army Daily,* the military's own daily newspaper.

The basic function of the MAC has been its exclusive responsibility in directing the party's military activities, including the power to appoint and remove military personnel. As a subunit of the Central Committee, with responsibility for strategy and tactics of the Chinese army, it can be traced back to the guerrilla days of the early 1930s.[21] After the 1935 Zunyi Conference, Mao assumed the chairmanship of the Revolutionary Military Committee, the predecessor of the present MAC. By that time the committee had assumed the responsibilities of educating the troops in political matters and of approving the party's political commissars assigned to the various armies. The MAC operates through a standing committee; the members of that committee regularly conduct inspection trips to the thirteen regional military commands and submit reports directly to the Politburo. Throughout the years, the MAC has held periodic special work conferences for military leaders from all regions and provinces on military and political-ideological topics. New policies and directives are explained at these conferences to insure proper implementation. From possibly 1954 on, the MAC has also been responsible for conducting numerous political training schools for army officers. Ralph Powell points out that the MAC supervision of the PLA is extensive and diverse, covering even the most routine matters.[22]

Although no official list of the MAC members has been published, two general guidelines seem to determine its composition: 1. members include most of the senior military figures, particularly the PLA marshals, and 2. members usually reflect the composition of the Politburo. The size of the MAC ranges from at least ten to perhaps nineteen or twenty. Traditionally, the first vice chairman of MAC concurrently serves as the minister of defense. The chief of staff for the PLA is usually a member of the Standing Committee of the MAC. There is also an interlocking membership situation which exists among the MAC, the Politburo, and the Central Committee. The high degree of interlocking membership between the MAC and the Politburo is such that at least nine members of the Politburo elected by the Eleventh Central Committee (August 1977) have been members of the MAC.

The true functions of the Control Commission have not been spelled out anywhere, not even in the informative party constitution of 1956, which gave the hierarchical structure of the Control Commission. However, based on recent revelation, the reestablished party control mechanism seems to have the following main functions: 1. maintenance of party morality and discipline, 2. control over the performance of party organizations, and 3. investigation of breaches of party discipline.[23]

As the party's internal rectification campaigns became more numerous and intensified, as they did in the late 1950s and 1960s, the Control Commission at all levels became more active in conducting investigations. This was particularly true on the eve of the Cultural Revolution, when a disunited party at the center caused confusion about the direction of·party policies for the lower-level organizations. By the time the Cultural Revolution was in full swing in 1966, the entire party control mechanism simply fell apart. The end result was the abolition of the old Control Commission by the Ninth Party Congress. Both the ninth and tenth party constitutions directed that the masses, not the party's control machinery, must provide overall supervision and control on matters of party discipline and the correctness of party policy or line. The Cultural Revolution practices provided at least three forms of mass supervision over party discipline and unity: 1. direct contact between the party cadres and the masses when investigation was required, 2. mass criticisms when policy was being implemented, and 3. mass participation in the management of the party's affairs through their representation in the revolutionary committee.

The party constitution of 1977 created a new control device—the Central Commission for Inspecting Discipline—to strengthen party discipline and internal party democracy, in the aftermath of the abusive practices instituted during the Cultural Revolution by the recently purged radical leaders. The new commission for party discipline is charged with the task of enforcing party rules and regulations, as well as the development of sound party style, including the inculcation of all the requisite party virtues. In 1978 the third Plenary Session of the Eleventh Central Committee elected the first hundred-member Central Commission for Inspecting Discipline, headed by veteran party administrator Chen Yun.[24] Prior to the Cultural Revolution, the sixty-member Control Commission operated through a standing committee of nine or ten members.[25] The standing committee for the newly formed Central Commission for Inspecting Discipline consists of twenty-four party veterans, all purged or mistreated during the Cultural Revolution. In their first report published in March 1979 the party's inspection commission urged that any false charges, wrong punishments, and frame ups leveled against any party members be corrected and the victims rehabilitated. Thus a first step has been taken to tighten the slackened party discipline and to restore internal party democracy.

REGIONAL PARTY ORGANS AND FUNCTIONS

Administratively speaking, China is governed, as it always has been, by provinces, the most immediate and important subunit below the central level. The party organization below the Central Committee level is the provincial party apparatus in each of the twenty-one provinces and the five autonomous regions and three municipalities (Beijing, Shanghai, and Tianjin), administered directly by the central government. From 1949 to 1954, and again from 1960 to 1966, the party established an intermediate layer of organs to supervise the provincial party affairs on behalf of the Central Committee. These were the six regional bureaus for the northeast, north, east, central south, northwest, and southwest, as shown in Figure 3.2.

FIGURE 3.2: REGIONAL BUREAUS OF THE CCP CENTRAL COMMITTEE

Source: Li Shih-fei, "The Party's Middleman: The Role of Regional Bureaus in the Chinese Communist Party," Current Scene: Developments in Mainland China, *vol. iii, no. 25 (August 15, 1965), 15.*

The party regional bureaus were formed in 1949 to parallel the regional administrative bureaus for the central government. The party constitution of 1956, in formally establishing the regional bureaus, said little about their functions except that they were to serve as a linkage between the party, centered in Beijing, and the vast regional areas administered traditionally as provinces. The operation of the party's regional bureaus from 1949 to 1954 showed that the regional party secretaries and the functional departments of these bureaus had enormous power over the provincial party affairs. In fact, it was mainly the growth of the regional bureaus' power that became a threat to the center and led to the abolition of the regional bureaus in 1954, following the purge of Gao Gang and Rao Shushih. Gao Gang, the party secretary for the Northeast Bureau, had exercised a considerable amount of independence in supervising party activities of the three provinces bordering the Soviet Union. Gao, who was also a member of the Politburo and a vice chairman of the central government, was charged by the Central Committee with creating an "independent kingdom" for the northeast. Both Gao Gang and Rao Shushih, as spokesmen for the vital regions of China's northeastern and eastern provinces, had attacked Mao's collectivization and agricultural and economic policies and had challenged the leadership of both Liu Shaoqi and Zhou Enlai; this brought on the combined wrath of the top leaders in the party's hierarchy.[26] The purge of these two "regionally based" party leaders in 1954 strengthened the position of the "centrally based" leaders, Liu and Zhou, and resulted in a "high degree of centralization" of control in Beijing.[27]

The six regional bureaus were reestablished in 1960, presumably to provide better coordination and supervision by the party over the economic recovery activities in the provinces in the aftermath of the Great Leap. The new regional bureaus of the Central Committee, which existed until the Cultural Revolution, maintained a close relationship with the thirteen regional military commands: in most cases regional bureau secretaries concurrently served as political commissars for the military commands, and military commanders frequently concurrently served as the party's regional bureau secretaries.[28] This relationship became a major obstacle in implementing the directives from the center during the Cultural Revolution. Regional bureau leaders and provincial party leaders defied orders issued from Beijing and maintained their own local predilection. For instance, before he was finally purged, Li Jingchuan, the first secretary of the Southwest Bureau and the political commissar for the Chengdu Military Region, defiantly spoke against the Cultural Revolution by saying, "Give prominence to politics? No, we should give prominence to fertilizer. Fertilizer can solve problems."[29] Li had refused to receive emissaries from Beijing and tried very hard to protect his party leaders from attacks by the students.[30] The purge meted out by the students and the radicals to the regional bureaus' secretaries was so complete that by 1968 the structure itself once again was abandoned. The party constitutions of 1969 and 1973 make no reference to the regional bureaus, which began as the intermediate link between the center and the far-flung provinces, but ended up as "mountain-strongholds" or "independent kingdoms" which occasionally obstructed the will of the center.

With the all-out effort of the modernization program launched in 1978, party regional bureaus seem to have been revived in order to coordinate and effectively implement the various economic programs.

PROVINCIAL PARTY ORGANS AND FUNCTIONS

Theoretically speaking, provincial party committees derive their power from the party congresses at the provincial level. The party constitution of 1956, adopted by the Eighth Party Congress, stipulated the convening of provincial party congresses once a year (Article 38). The 1969, 1973, and 1977 party constitutions mandated the party congresses at the provincial level and below to meet every three years. Each provincial party committee is generally run by a standing committee consisting of the first secretary and a number of subordinate secretaries within the hierarchy of the provincial party structure.

The provincial party committee is responsible for supervision and provides direction over four basic areas: organization and control of the party; economic activities in agriculture, industry, finance and trade; capital construction; mobilization of women and youth; and research for policy development. Initially, the provincial party committees played a subordinate role in supervising provincial economic development. This was more pronounced during the period of high centralization of the First Five-Year Plan (1953–1956) when the national functional ministries had a great deal of authority and control over the provincial party activities. During and after the Great Leap Forward (1957–1959), there was a period of decentralization when the provincial party committees were given greater responsibility and more power in managing economic activities in the provinces. In many respects, the provincial party committees behaved as though they were "underdeveloped nations" in bidding for resources to develop economic and productive activities.[31]

Since the provincial party committees and their subordinate primary party organs within the provinces are responsible for implementing party policies, they hold a unique position within the party structure. The first secretary of the provincial party committee wields an enormous amount of power. Provincial party secretaries, as pointed out by one study, on occasion have deliberately refused to carry out directives from the center.[32] This power is reflected and enhanced by the provincial party secretaries' participation in central party affairs (see Chapter 5).

PRIMARY PARTY ORGANS AND FUNCTIONS

Below the provincial party committees are the primary units at the county level and below. They are the "fighting bastions" (to use the phraseology in the 1977 party constitution) for carrying out the party policies and line. It is here that the party makes its immediate contact with the rest of the society. Like the provincial party structure, all basic units of the party are headed by a party secretary who in turn is guided by a party committee. Party units at the primary level rarely rubber-stamp policies and programs imposed from above. On the contrary, the need for "creativity and autonomy" at the lower level of party organization has always been emphasized. Honest and vigorous discussion often prevails at these lower-level party meetings.

The lowest level of party organization, the so-called primary party units or cells, are party branches formed in "factories, mines and other enterprises, people's communes, offices, schools, shop, neighborhoods, and companies of the People's Liberation Army," in accordance with Article 18 of the 1977 party constitution. While there are no official figures on the total number of party branches at the lowest level, one source estimated the total number in 1959 at 1,069,000.[33] It is at this level that the organization functions of the party are carried out: membership recruitment, political and ideological education about the party line, exercise of party discipline, and maintenance of "close ties with the masses." It is generally the party branch in a given enterprise, commune, or office which provides leadership, supervision, and guidance in the party affairs. Like the first secretaries in the higher party organizations, the party branch secretary exercises the overall leadership. In addition, a party branch secretary also serves as a "friend, counselor, and guardian of all the people under his jurisdiction."[34] Popular literature and drama often depict the party branch secretary as one who is always fearless, fair, firm, and devoted to the welfare of his or her people in the unit.

The party branches operate somewhat differently in rural and urban areas. The party committee in a commune is the leading organizational unit which provides leadership, supervision, and management of all political and economic activities in the countryside; this function and power was shared with the revolutionary committees representing the masses. The party committee at the basic level directs party organization work and is responsible for general policy. It also controls the assignment of personnel at the local level. It is a standard practice for some members of the commune revolutionary committee to hold simultaneous membership in the commune party committee.

A few words must be said about the Cultural Revolution's impact on the party. The upheaval was more than a power struggle and a purge of such top leaders as Liu Shaoqi, Deng Xiaoping and Peng Zhen, a key Politburo member and former mayor of Beijing. Certainly, a primary objective of the upheaval was to shake up the party machine for its increasing bureaucracy and routinization. There were also extensive purges of the party personnel at the middle and lower levels for their lack of understanding of mass line in their work with the people. One remedy which came out of the Cultural Revolution was the structural reform, the formation of revolutionary committees at the party's central, provincial, and primary levels as a temporary substitute for the party machine. What was novel about the experiment was the introduction of the masses from outside the party into these revolutionary committees, which, for the duration of the Cultural Revolution and thereafter, were performing the functions of both the party and government.[35] Party and government administrative structures were also reduced under the slogan of "simplified administration."

How fundamental and lasting has been the structural change in the party? Events in China since Mao's death, and the subsequent purge of the radical Gang of Four in 1976, have indicated a restoration of the basic structures which existed prior to the Cultural Revolution. The Eleventh Party Congress (August 1977) reemphasized many of the familiar practices and structures of the party that had operated quite effectively prior to the Cultural Revolution. An example of this is the reinstitution of the Control Commission at all levels of the party in order to maintain and strengthen inner-party discipline.[36]

After a considerable period of confused jurisdiction, the revolutionary committees were legalized in 1978 to become executive organs of local government. We can summarize by saying that the party was highly institutionalized from the 1950s to the early 1960s. This was interrupted for the turbulent years of 1966 to 1976 by the Cultural Revolution. The process of reinstitutionalization now appears to be accelerating under the leadership of Hua Guofeng and Deng Xiaoping. This process can be expected to lead to a period of stability and moderation, for China is now again under the leadership and control of professionally oriented, veteran party administrators.

RECRUITMENT OF PARTY MEMBERS

When the Eleventh Party Congress convened in August 1977, almost a year after the downfall of the Gang of Four, it was announced that the party had a membership of more than thirty-five million. In his speech, Ye Jianying pointed out that seven million of the thirty-five million party members had been recruited since the last party congress in 1973.[37] He admitted that there was a serious problem in party organization and discipline, which resulted from the rapid recruitment of so many party members by the Gang of Four. The old soldier, now a vice chairman of the party, bluntly indicated that the radicals had recruited a large number of new party members in accordance with their own standards. What Ye was demanding was tighter requirements for party membership. What he failed to mention was that the Chinese Communist Party membership had been steadily increasing since it came to power in 1949, and this phenomenal rise in party membership (see Table 3.2) had not always insisted on ideological purity and correctness as the most important criterion in membership admittance. Let us now discuss the factors which contributed to the party membership expansion.

TABLE 3.2: CCP Membership Growth Pattern

Party Congress	Year	Number of Members
1st Congress	1921	57
2nd Congress	1922	123
3rd Congress	1923	432
4th Congress	1925	950
5th Congress	1927	57,967
6th Congress	1928	40,000
7th Congress	1945	1,211,128
8th Congress	1956	10,734,384
	1961	17,000,000
9th Congress	1969	20,000,000
10th Congress	1973	28,000,000
11th Congress	1977	35,000,000

Sources: Figures from 1921 to 1961 are based on John W. Lewis, Leadership in Communist China *(Ithaca, N.Y.: Cornell University Press, 1963), pp. 108–20.*

The 1969 party membership figure is an estimate calculated on the basis of about forty percent increase in 1973 over 1969 given by Jurgen Domes, "A Rift in the New Course," Far Eastern Economic Review, *October 1, 1973, p. 3.*

The 1973 total party membership figure is taken from Zhou Enlai's "Report to the Tenth National Congress of the CCP," Peking Review, *nos. 35–36 (September 7, 1973), p. 18.*

The 1977 party membership figure is based on Ye Jianying, "Report on the Revision of the Party Constitution to the Eleventh Party Congress, August 13–18, 1977," Peking Review, *36 (September 2, 1977), 36.*

Factors for Party Membership Expansion

Several general remarks may be made with respect to the growth of the CCP membership. First, for the period from 1920 to 1927, from the party's First Congress to the Fifth Congress, members of the party were

primarily urban intellectuals, intermixed with some members of the proletariat from coastal cities and from mines in the inland provinces. When
the Sixth Party Congress convened in 1928, most of its members had
been driven underground by the Nationalists. There was a significant
reduction in membership, by as much as 17,900, between the Fifth Party
Congress in 1927 and the Sixth Party Congress in 1928. This reduction
can be attributed to the slaughter by the Nationalists in the 1927 coup
and to the subsequent defections.

Second, from the Sixth Congress in 1928 to the Seventh Congress
in 1945, the primary membership recruitment shifted from intellectuals
to peasants, who became the mainstay of the guerrilla armies. In fact,
beginning in 1939, the CCP, under the firm leadership of Mao, under-
took to militarize the party membership. The 1.2 million members
reached by the Seventh Congress in 1945, at the termination of the war
with Japan, was largely operating under the appropriate description of
"military communism." Party members were essentially recruited from
the famed Eighth Route and the New Fourth Armies. The late John
Lindbeck noted the profound impact of the recruiting pattern on the
character building of the party membership as follows:

> The result of the militarization policy was that dedication, fighting spirit,
> and responsiveness to discipline and orders became the hallmark of Com-
> munity Party members, as well as the harsher virtues of a soldier—
> ruthlessness, toughness, and a will to override and subdue other people.
> They held the guns out of which Mao's political power and everything else
> grew. By the time the party had conquered China, the bulk of its member-
> ship was made up of triumphant warriors.[38]

Lindbeck also pointed out that the militarization of the party membership created many problems which have beset Chinese party politics.
These problems of the army, as a special political power and as an
independent interest group, will be discussed in later chapters. What we
need to point out here is that the army has always been the model for the
CCP to emulate in organizational disciplinary matters.

Third, party recruitment from 1945 to 1956, or from the Seventh
to the Eighth Party Congress, represented the most rapid growth period
in the party's history: from a little over 1.2 million to just under 11
million, or approximately an 886 percent increase. The years of 1955–
1956 saw another sudden rise in membership recruitment, followed by a
temporary lull and a gigantic rise in 1956–1957, when party organizational work was intensified in all rural areas of China preceeding the
Great Leap Forward, launched in 1958. Although party recruitment
took some great strides quantitively—by 1961, some 90 percent of the
seventeen million party members had been recruited since 1949, and 70
percent had been since 1953—the ideological purity of the new party
recruits was questionable.

Fourth, during the period from the Eighth Party Congress in 1956 to 1961, recruitment of party members became institutionalized to insure that party members possessed both ideological redness and technical expertise. Membership expansion during 1954 and 1956–1957 was designed to recruit personnel needed to direct and manage the extensive political and economic activities. The rapid recruitment of those who possessed the needed technical skill resulted in a shift in the recruitment pattern of new party members in terms of social background. This trend is clearly discernible in the limited data available, presented in Table 3.3. From 1956 to 1957, only the "intellectuals" gained in relative representation in party membership, rising from 11.7 percent to 14.8 percent and accounting for over 31 percent of all new recruits. All other groups declined in relative representation. While peasants retained a clear majority of new party members, their representation is well below their proportion of the total population. Conversely, the intellectuals are vastly overrepresented.

TABLE 3.3: Background of Party Members, 1956 and 1957

	Numbers			Percent of Total		
			Increase			Increase
	1956	1957	1956–1957	1956	1957	1956–1957
	(Thousands)			(Percent)		
Workers	1,503	1,740	237	14.0	13.7	11.9
Peasants	7,417	8,500	1,083	69.1	66.8	54.5
Intellectuals	1,256	1,880	624	11.7	14.8	31.4
Others	558	600	42	5.2	4.7	2.1
Total	10,734	12,720	1,986	100.0	100.0	100.0

Source: Modified version of Franz Schurmann, Ideology and Organization in Communist China, *(Berkeley, Calif.: University of California Press, 1966), p. 132. By permission of publisher.*

Following this changed pattern of recruitment, the party cadre system was institutionalized to make it more attractive to intellectuals who were being coopted into the party. By 1955 a rank system for cadres' work assignments had been instituted, based on the acquisition of technical skills. In addition, a salary scale system was promulgated, along with the rank system for cadres. Recruitment and promotion rules were also instituted in the late 1950s. Recent studies have pointed out the bureaucratization of the party. One study concludes that by 1965 China was no longer a revolutionary society because, by initial contact with the political systems and a careful selection of education and occupation, a careerist could very well predict the outcome of his life.[39] Another study points out that one inevitable result of the institutionalization of the party in the late 1950s and the 1960s was bureaucratization, which stressed order, discipline, and routine as organizational virtues.[40] While no detailed official statistics on party membership have been released since 1961, when membership stood at seventeen million, the general level of party membership has been indicated, as shown in Table 3.2. During the Cultural Revolution, aggregate membership remained around seventeen million, virtually unchanged from 1961. Membership for 1969 was approximately twenty million, a net increase of only three million from 1961. However, after 1969 the party membership resumed its rapid rise, with the addition of eight million from 1969 to 1973 when the total stood at twenty-eight million, and the addition of seven million from 1973 to 1977 when the total stood at thirty-five million. This means, as Marshal Ye has indicated, that over half of the thirty-five million party members in 1977 were recruited after the Cultural Revolution.[41]

Without detailed data, we cannot be sure of the background of the new members recruited since the Cultural Revolution. However, fragmentary official figures, showing the characteristics and social composition of new party members, have been reported.[42] The party membership for the Beijing municipality may be used here as an illustration. From the Cultural Revolution to 1973 some sixty thousand new members were added to the party membership roster for Beijing. Of the total new recruits, about seventy-five percent were "workers, former poor and lower-middle peasants or children of such families," and just under five percent were "revolutionary intellectuals working in the fields of culture, health, science and education." The overwhelming majority of these new Beijing municipality party members was under thirty-five years of age, and women constituted twenty-five percent of the total.

Another important element in the recruitment pattern following the Cultural Revolution was the effort made to recruit members of the minority groups in the autonomous regions. We were told that 143,000 new members from minority nationalities were admitted to party membership from 1969 to 1973. Although we do not have comprehensive official statistics for the entire CCP membership from 1961 to 1976, we may surmise, based on fragmentary data, that the new membership recruitment pattern placed greater emphasis on 1. industrial workers of peasant origin, 2. women, 3. minority nationalities, and 4. youths. If the above conclusion is correct, and I believe it is not too far off target, then the CCP has greatly broadened its base regardless of the shifting recruitment requirements.

Membership Requirements: Changing Emphasis

There is a marked difference in the party constitutions of the Eighth Congress (1956) and the subsequent congresses (1969, 1973, and 1977) with regard to eligibility for party membership. The Eighth Party Constitution stipulated no class base or origin for party membership: It was open to "all Chinese citizens" who qualified. The party constitutions approved in 1969 by the Ninth Party Congress, at the end of the Cultural Revolution, and the ones adopted by the Tenth and Eleventh Party Congresses in 1973 and 1977 required that only those who are "workers, poor peasants, lower-middle peasants" are eligible to become members of the CCP. In addition, PLA soldiers and "other revolutionary elements" may also be eligible for membership. Both the 1973 and the 1977 party constitutions prescribe four steps by which an applicant for party membership must be scrutinized: 1. recommendation by two party members, after filing the application individually, 2. examination of the application by a party branch which solicits opinions about the applicant from both inside and outside of the party, 3. acceptance of the application by the party branch at its general membership meeting, and 4. approval of the party branch's acceptance of membership by the next higher party committee. It has been a frequent practice, dating back to the late 1940s, for an applicant to be admitted to party membership solely upon the recommendation of top party leaders.[43]

All party members were obligated by both the 1969 and 1973 party constitutions to live up to the five requirements that Chairman Mao advanced for worthy revolutionary successors: to conscientiously study the works of Marx, Lenin, and Mao's thought; to always serve the collective interests of the people and never work for private gains; to strive for united front work; to consult the masses; and to be willing to engage in criticism and self-criticism. The 1977 party constitution added three more requirements: to never engage in factional activities to split the party unity, to observe party discipline, and to always perform well tasks assigned by the party and to set examples as a vanguard. The added demands in the 1977 party constitution were designed to strengthen the standards for recruitment of party members and to tighten admission policy in order to avoid the "crash admittance" program allegedly practiced by the purged radical leaders. In his report on the need to tighten requirements for party members, Marshal Ye said

> ... In recent years the "gang of four" set their own standards for party membership and practical "crash admittance" and as a result some political speculators and bad types have sneaked into the party.[44]

That the provisions for "purification of the ranks" and strict party discipline, as well as for tightening admission standards, have been written into the 1977 party constitution illustrates the importance of the recruitment process to the party leaders and their awareness that the pattern of recruitment has great influence on the character of the party.

NOTES

[1]*Renmin Ribao,* March 1, 1977, and *Ming Pdo* (Hongkong), March 3, 1977, p. 3.

[2]*Survey of Chinese Mainland Press,* 4097 (January 11, 1968), 1–4.

[3]Roderick MacFarquhar, *The Origins of the Cultural Revolution, Vol. 1: Contradictions Among the People, 1957–1967* (New York: Columbia University Press, 1974), p. 144.

[4]Lin Piao, "Report to the Ninth National Congress of the CCP," *Peking Review,* 18 (April 30, 1969), 16–35.

[5]Wang Hung-wen, "Report on the Revision of the Party Constitution," *Peking Review,* 35–36 (September 7, 1973), 29–33.

[6]William Brugger, "The Ninth National Congress of the CCP," *The World Today,* vol. 25, no. 7 (July 1969), 297–305; Roderick MacFarquhar, "China After the 10th Congress," *The World Today,* vol. 29, no. 12 (December 1973), 514–26; Richard Wich, "The Tenth Party Congress: The Power Structure and the Succession Question," *The China Quarterly,* 58 (April–May 1974), 231–48.

[7]Houn, *A Short History of Chinese Communism,* p. 87.

[8]For text of Chou En-lai's political report to the Tenth Party Congress, see *Peking Review,* 35–36 (September 3, 1973), 17–21.

[9]Roderick MacFarquhar, *The Origins of the Cultural Revolution,* p. 101.

[10]Parris Chang, *Power and Policy in China* (University Park, Penna. and London: The Pennsylvania State University Press, 1974), p. 184.

[11]See Jill Lai, "The Power Structure After China's 10th Party Congress," *Far Eastern Economic Review* (October 1, 1973), p. 5. Her calculation for the Tenth Central Committee members' average age was 65 and since close to half of the Eleventh Central Committee members are carried over from the Tenth, the average for the Eleventh is probably from 65 to 68. Also see Jurgen Domes, "China in 1977: Reversal of Verdict," *Asian Survey,* vol. xviii, no. 1 (January 1978), 7.

[12]"Constitution of the Communist Party of China, adopted by the 11th National Congress on August 18, 1977," in *Peking Review,* 36 (September 2, 1977), 21–22.

[13]Houn, *A Short History of Chinese Communism.* p. 89.

[14]"Board of Directors, China, Inc.," *Far Eastern Economic Review* (September 2, 1977), p. 9.

[15]Robert J. Osborn, *The Evolution of Soviet Politics* (New York: The Dorsey Press, 1974), pp. 213–14.

[16]Houn, *A Short History of Chinese Communism,* p. 93.

[17]Chang, *Power and Politics in China,* p. 184.

[18]Houn, *A Short History of Chinese Communism,* pp. 91–92.

[19]Houn, *A Short History of Chinese Communism, p. 89.*

[20]"Talk at the Report Meeting, 24 October 1966," in *Chairman Mao Talks to the People—Talks and Letters: 1956–1971,* ed. Stuart Schram (New York: Pantheon, 1974), pp. 266–67.

[21]Gittings notes on the formation of this organ in 1931 by the First All-China Soviet Congress, see John Gittings, *The Role of the Chinese Red Army* (London: Oxford University Press, 1967), pp. 263–265.

[22]Ralph Powell, "Politico-Military Relationships in Communist China," External Research Staff, Bureau of Intelligence and Research, Department of State, October 1963.

[23]Yeh Chien-ying, "Report on the Revision of the Party Constitution," *Peking Review,* 36 (September 2, 1977), 32.

[24]Yeh Chien- ying, "Report on the Revision of the Party Constitution;" and "Communiqué of the Third Plenary Session of the 11th Central Committee," *Peking Review,* 52 (December 29, 1978), 6, 16.

[25]John W. Lewis, *Leadership in Communist China* (Ithaca, N.Y.: Cornell University Press, 1963), p. 134.

[26]Jurgen Domes, "Party Politics and the Cultural Revolution," in *Communist China 1949– 1969: A Twenty Year Appraisal,* eds. Frank Trager and William Henderson (New York: New York University Press, 1970), p. 65.

[27]Chang, *Power and Politics in China,* pp. 48–49.

[28]Li Shih-fei, "The Party's Middlemen: The Role of Regional Bureaus in the Chinese Communist Party," *Current Scene: Development in Mainland China,* vol. iii, no. 25 (August 15, 1965), 6.

[29]See Thomas Jay Mathews, *"The Cultural Revolution in Szechwan"* in *The Cultural Revolution in the Provinces,* East Asian Monographs No. 42, (Cambridge: Harvard University Press, 1971), pp. 106–10.

[30]Ibid.

[31]Schurmann, *Ideology and Organizations,* p. 210.

[32]Chang, "Provincial Party Leaders Strategies for Survival During the Cultural Revolution" in *Elites in the People's Republic of China,* ed. Robert A. Scalapino (Seattle, Wash. and London: University of Washington Press, 1972), pp. 501–39.

[33]Houn, *A Short History of Chinese Communism,* p. 106.

[34]Houn, *A Short History of Chinese Communism,* p. 106.

[35]See Gordon Bennett, "China's Continuing Revolution: Will It Be Permanent?" *Asian Survey,* vol. x, No. 1 (January 1970), 2–17; Parris H. Chang, "The Revolutionary Committee in China—Two Case Studies: Heilungkiang and Honan," *Current Scene,* vol. vi, no. 9 (June 1, 1968), 1–37; Jurgen Domes, "The Role of the Military in the Formation of Revolutionary Committees, 1967–68," *The China Quarterly,* 44 (October–December 1970), 112–45; Garbel Feurtado, "The Formation of Provincial Revolutionary Committees, 1966–68: Heilungkiang and Hopei," *Asian Survey,* vol. xii, no. 12 (December 1972), 1014– 31.

[36]Yeh Chien-ying, "Report on the Revision of the Party Constitution," p. 32.

[37]Yeh Chien-ying, "Report on the Revision of the Party Constitution," p. 36.

[38]John Lindbeck, "Transformation in the Chinese Communist Party," in *Soviet and Chinese Communism: Similarities and Differences,* ed. Donald Treadgold (Seattle, Wash.: University of Washington Press, 1967), p. 76.

[39]Ezra Vogel, "From Revolutionary to Semi-Bureaucrat: The 'Regularization' of Cadres," *The China Quarterly,* 29 (January–March 1967), 36–40; Michel Oksenberg, "Institutionalization of the Chinese Communist Revolution: The Ladder of Success on the Eve of the Cultural Revolution," *The China Quarterly,* 36 (October–December 1968), 61–92.

[40]Charles Neuhauser, "The Chinese Communist Party in the 1960s: Prelude to the Cultural Revolution," *The China Quarterly,* 32 (October–December 1967), 3–36.

[41]See Yeh Chien-ying, "Report on the Revision of the Party Constitution," p. 36.

[42]"New Party Members—A Dynamic Force," *Peking Review,* 27 (July 6, 1973), 6–7; "Millions of New Cadres Maturing," *Peking Review,* 52 (December 1973), 3; "Commemorating the 10th Anniversary of the CPC Central Committee's May 16 'Circular,' " *Peking Review,* 21 (May 21, 1976), 3.

[43]Red Guard interrogation of Wang Guangmei, wife of Liu Shaoqi, revealed the practice of admission to party membership by recommendation by top party leaders. See Chao Tsung, *An Account of the Great Proletarian Cultural Revolution,* ii (Hongkong: Union Research Institute, 1974), 836–39.

[44]Yeh Chien-ying, "Report on the Revision of the Party Constitution," p. 36.

The Government and the Party: Interlocking Structure and Decision-Making

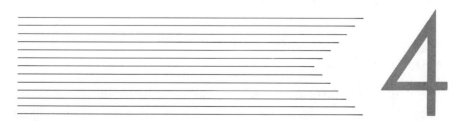

4

In this chapter we shall examine the structure of the Chinese central government by focusing on the central government complex. Subjects to be discussed include constitutions, the National People's Congress, the State Council and its multifarious agencies, the legal system, and the cadre system. Before we take up these topics, two general comments must be made about the Chinese national government. First, as discussed in the previous chapter, the Chinese Communist Party controls and directs the complex system of government machinery. It is through the agencies of the government that the policies and programs approved by the party are implemented. The CCP closely monitors the government's execution of its directives. Second, the People's Republic of China is a unitary state. In a federated system, such as that in the United States or the Soviet Union, certain governmental powers and responsibilities are reserved for local governments. Under a unitary system, all powers theoretically are vested in the central government and must be specifically delegated to local governments by the central authority. This centralization of power in the national government has led to perennial debate in China over the degree and nature of power to be allocated to local governments. The governments in the provinces and local units generate constant pressure for decentralization by seeking to increase their discretional power over such local affairs as finances and allocation of resources. The subject of provincial and local politics and government will be discussed in detail in Chapter 5.

POLITICAL CONSULTATION AND CONSTITUTION MAKING

The CCP first participated in constitution making with the Kuomintang in January 1946 under the cease-fire agreements mediated by General Marshall. The various political parties participated in the Political Consultative Conference, which resolved to draft a revised version of the 1935 Kuomintang constitution and to establish a constitutional government through an elected national assembly. These plans were shattered by the eruption of full-scale civil war.

In 1948, with victory in sight, the CCP Politburo passed a resolution calling for a united front of all parties and groups, for a new political consultative conference to form a coalition government, and to establish a people's congress.[1] The new Chinese People's Political Consultative Conference (CPPCC) convened in Beijing in September 1949 with Mao presiding over the 662 delegates from more than 20 political parties and mass groups. This national conference established the People's Republic of China and promulgated the Common Program and the Organic Law. On October 1, 1949, Mao proclaimed the new government by raising the now familiar red flag with one large gold star beside four small ones, symbolic of the dominant CCP and the four classes of people—peasants, petty bourgeoisie, owners of enterprises, and workers. The Common Program and the Organic Law became a provisional constitution for the People's Republic until the new regime could consolidate its power. The Common Program was a set of guiding principles for the affairs of state, couched in moderate language acceptable to all of the cooperating parties. The Organic Law prescribed the power and structure of the national government.

From 1949 until 1954, the People's Republic operated under two specific organs established to exercise the power of the central government. One was the fifty-six member Central Government Council, the executive organ of the CPPCC, chaired by Mao. The Central Government Council assumed a supervisory function with power to enact laws and to make appointments. The second was the Government Administrative Council, headed by Premier Zhou Enlai. The Government Administrative Council was charged with the daily administration of the central government and operated through a multitude of functionally specific ministries. A majority of these ministries were concerned with economic and financial affairs.

With the formation of these two governmental organs as the interim de facto central government, the People's Political Consultative Conference faded rapidly into the background as an instrument for political consultation. Nevertheless, the CPPCC still exists, primarily to carry on united front work in support of CCP policies, often serving as a liaison between the CCP and minor political parties. The CPPCC was given the responsibility of rehabilitating the 293 war criminals, mostly civil war Kuomintang army officers, who were released from prison under the 1975 special amnesty.[2] In early 1978, the mass media gave prominent coverage to CPPCC participation in preliminary discussions with delegates to the Fifth National People's Congress, in regard to the revised constitution.[3] This renewed political consultative role for the CPPCC is interesting, in view of charges that the Gang of Four deliberately sabotaged the normal functions of political consultation.[4]

The Common Program provided for nationwide general elections to elect representatives to a national congress, which was to draft and enact a constitution. This process did not begin until 1953, for a variety of reasons. First, time was needed for the regime to consolidate its control over the vast territory and population. We must remember that the land reform program was not completed until 1953, about the time the Korean War reached its stalemate. Second, time was needed to reorganize local governmental units. During the initial years of the republic, from 1949 to 1951, provincial and local government functions were generally carried out by the army through the Military Control Commission, a type of military rule. Gradually, military rule was replaced in rural areas by people's congresses, with limited authority for conducting local governmental affairs, under close supervision of the local CCP. Third, the regime had to prepare and lay the ground for an elaborate election law that would demonstrate to the world that China's first national election was a legitimate exercise of the people's will.

The Election Law, enacted in March 1953 by the Central People's Government Council on behalf of the CPPCC, called for universal suffrage for persons eighteen years old or older except for those classified as counterrevolutionaries or those otherwise deprived by law of their right to vote. Voters participated directly only at the lowest basic level, in the selection of representatives to people's congresses for the village or local unit. The representatives on the local people's congress then elected representatives to provincial people's congress, who then elected representatives to the 1,226-member First National People's Congress. This indirect election system, which has continued to be used for electing National People's Congresses, will be discussed further in Chapter 7.

The 1954 Constitution[5]

A great deal of effort went into the 1954 constitution presented to the First National People's Congress for enactment. The initial draft was prepared by a committee of the party's Central Committee, with considerable input from Mao. Reportedly, the constitution's draft was submitted to some 8,000 individuals for comment, and was circulated to over 150 million people for discussion before it was completed.[6] This process took over twenty-one months. The constitution was a lengthy one, with 106 articles detailing the general principles of government, the structure of the national and local governments, and the fundamental rights and duties of citizens.

The constitution created a "People's Democratic Dictatorship," which was to practice democratic centralism. The National People's Congress (NPC) was designated the highest organ of state power and the only legislative power for the state. The NPC was to elect a chairman and vice chairman for the People's Republic of China. Since the NPC was to meet only once a year, its standing committee was designated the "permanent body" of the NPC. The executive functions of the government were to be carried out by the State Council, the Central People's Government, headed by a premier and vice premiers appointed by the NPC. Provisions were also made for local people's congresses and councils, as well as for organs of self-government for the autonomous areas. The local governments will be discussed in Chapter 5. The judicial functions were to be exercised by a Supreme People's Court, local people's courts, and special people's courts.

The 1954 constitution was modeled on the Soviet constitution of 1936 and, therefore, was representative of the "socialist legality," a phrase denoting the legal responsibility of the dictatorial state to its citizens. The constitution stated

> . . . the fundamental tasks of the state are, step by step, to bring about the socialist industrialization of the country and, step by step, to accomplish the socialist transformation of agriculture, handicrafts, industry, and commerce.

The planned economy with its gradual transition to socialism, would allow for the "gradual abolition of systems of exploitation." While the constitution sought to protect the ownership of ordinary peasants' land and handicraftmen's means of production as well as other property, such as savings and houses, it called for the restriction and gradual elimination of rich peasants and industrialists. Work was exhorted as a "matter of honor" and was to be carried out with enthusiasm and creativity.

The constitution provided a list of fundamental rights and freedoms for citizens: the rights to vote and for due process of law; and the freedoms of speech and press, assembly, association, procession, demonstration, religion, privacy, residence and change of residence, scientific research, and artistic creativity. Economic rights listed were the rights to work; to rest from work; to education; of assistance in old age, illness, and disability; and finally, to bring complaints against any person working in organs of the state. The first duties listed were to uphold the constitution and the law, to maintain discipline at work, to keep public order, and to respect social ethics. Others included respecting public property, paying taxes, and defending the homeland.

The basic principles of the 1954 constitution were incorporated in the revised constitutions of 1975 and 1978. Changes made in these revisions reflected both the maturing and consolidation of the system and the political climates of the periods.

The 1975 Constitution[7]

The 1975 constitution was submitted to the NPC for the party's Central Committee by Zhang Chunqiao, the radical leader from Shanghai who was later arrested as one of the Gang of Four. Apparently constitutional revision had been prepared as early as 1970, with Lin Biao as a key drafter, but the revisions were not acceptable to Chairman Mao. The NPC, which had not met since 1965, was postponed until after the Lin Biao affair. It finally convened in secret in January 1975 under the supervision of Zhou Enlai. Zhang explained that a new constitution was needed to reflect the transition to socialism, the gains of the Cultural Revolution, and the defeat of Liu Shaoqi and Lin Biao.[8]

With the consolidation of power completed after the demise of Lin Biao, the constitution, which was streamlined and shortened to only thirty articles, no longer needed to be so specific nor to play down the role of the CCP, Zhang reported. Article 2 of the 1975 constitution stated

> The Communist Party of China is the core of leadership of the whole Chinese People. The working class exercises leadership over the state through its vanguard, the Communist Party of China.

> Marxism-Leninism-Mao Zedong Thought is the theoretical basis guiding the thinking of our nation.

The role of the CCP was made more specific in Article 16: "The National People's Congress is the highest organ of state power under the leadership of the Communist Party of China." The list of functions and powers of the NPC were condensed and abridged. In addition, the position of chairman for the republic was abolished, thus eliminating the most powerful position of the government, which might be used as a base for power contention with the party chairman. Mao had held the chairmanship of the republic, as well as that of the party, and had used it to his advantage. For instance, he convened at least fifteen supreme state conferences as chairman of the republic, bypassing the established party channels of consultation to obtain support for his views on crucial policy matters. Soon after the Great Leap, Mao relinquished, as planned, the chairmanship of the republic at the 1959 NPC session in favor of Liu Shaoqi. Liu, who was the vice chairman of the party, used the position to acquire considerable power in the central government and the party until his purge during the Cultural Revolution. Liu's successful use of the chairmanship contributed to Mao's antagonism toward him and his corps of senior cadres. As discussed in Chapter 1, the chairmanship of the republic may have been one of the contentious issues between Mao and Lin Biao. Certainly Mao, who remained party chairman until his death, had no desire to return to the pre-Cultural Revolution conditions of "two chairmen" competing for power. The crucial role of the army was also recognized by designating the chairman of the CCP as commander of the armed forces, rather than the chairman of the republic, as required in the 1954 version. In his report, Zhang Chunqiao explained that these changes were to help strengthen the party's centralized leadership over the structure of the state.[9] At the local level, the constitution recognized the revolutionary committees as the "permanent organs of the local people's congresses and at the same time the local people's governments at various levels."

With the socialist transition complete, as explained by Zhang, the constitution of 1975 called for carrying on the three great revolutionary movements of class struggle, the struggle for production, and scientific experiment, using self-reliance as the main mode of operation. The document affirmed right of ownership by the whole people and socialist collective ownership by working people. While restricted nonagriculture individual labor was allowed, the individual laborers were to be "guided on the road of socialist collectivization, step by step." The people's communes were recognized as the legitimate form of land ownership, but members were given permission to farm small plots, engage in limited household sideline production, and keep a small number of livestock. Article 9 described the work-play relationship: " 'He who does not work, neither shall he eat' and 'from each according to his ability, to each according to his work.' "

Accomplishments of the Cultural Revolution were incorporated into the 1975 constitution: " . . .put proletarian politics in command, combat bureaucracy, maintain close ties with the people." Culture, education, literature, art, physical education, health work, and scientific work must all serve the proletarian politics. Encouragement and specific rights, such as the right for debate and for putting up large character posters, to carry on the revolution were given.

The rights of citizens were condensed from the 1954 constitution in 1975 with a few deletions. The rights to residence and change of residence were eliminated, in view of the programs to send people to the countryside for manual labor. Also the rights of scientific research and artistic creativity were eliminated, since these were to serve the proletarian politics. The duties to maintain discipline at work, to maintain public order, and to respect social ethics were eliminated in the 1957 constitution. The right to strike was added.

The 1978 Constitution[10]

The draft of the 1978 constitution was prepared by a committee composed of all twenty-six members of the party's Politburo, with repeated consultation with "the broad masses both inside and outside of the party." After adoption by the party's Central Committee, Marshal Ye Jianying, a vice chairman of the party and a powerful supporter of Hua, introduced the sixty articles of the revised constitution to the Fifth NPC in February 1978. Among the reasons given by Ye for a new constitution were eliminating any vestige of influence of the Gang of Four, facilitating implementation of the decision of the Eleventh Party Congress to accelerate development of China's economy by moderating and liberalizing cultural and educational policies, and returning to an orderly state of affairs after more than a decade of turmoil.[11]

The constitution states the general task for the new period of development:

> To persevere in continuing the revolution under the dictatorship of the proletariat; to carry forward the three great revolutionary movements of class struggle—the struggle for production and scientific experiment, and to make China a great powerful socialist country with modern agriculture, industry, national defense, and science and technology, by the end of the century.

While the CCP is still included as the "core leadership of the whole Chinese people," there is no mention of the NPC being under the leadership of the CCP. In addition, the functions and powers of the NPC are again listed separately. For the first time, NPC delegates are to be elected "by secret ballot after democratic consultation." The moderation in politics is summed up:

> We should endeavor to create . . . a political situation in which there are both centralism and democracy, both discipline and freedom, both unity of will and personal ease of mind and liveliness.

Much attention is given in the 1978 constitution to developing education, science, and technology. While cultural undertakings must serve socialism, the arts and sciences are to be promoted by "letting a hundred flowers blossom and a hundred schools of thought contend."

In the 1978 constitution, there are admonitions not only against undermining the economy, as in 1975, but also against disrupting the economy. Wage incentives and professional competency are specifically sanctioned. While the right to strike remains, provisions in the 1954 constitution were reintroduced: to preserve labor discipline, to keep public order, and to respect social ethics. The constitution of 1978 recognizes the state's duty to protect the environment.

NATIONAL PEOPLE'S CONGRESS

The NPC is the highest government organ and has constitutional duties similar to those of many parliamentary bodies in other nations. It is empowered to amend the constitution, to make laws, and to supervise their enforcement. Upon recommendation of the party's Central Committee, the NPC designates, and can remove, the premier and other members of the State Council, elect the president of the Supreme People's Court and Chief Procurator of the Supreme People's Procuratorate. These structural relationships are reflected in Figure 4.1.

Since 1954, five national people's congresses have been convened, as shown in Table 4.1. The first three congresses, which then were elected for four-year terms rather than the present five-year terms, met

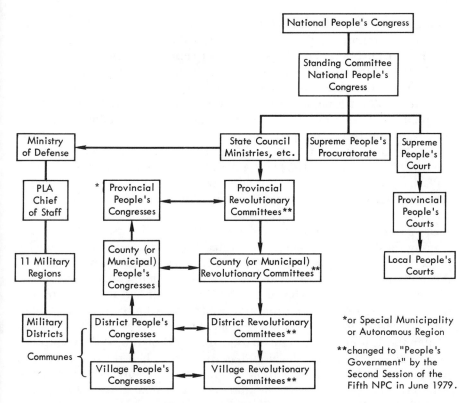

FIGURE 4.1   GOVERNMENTAL STRUCTURE OF PEOPLE'S REPUBLIC OF CHINA (1978 CONSTITUTION)

A modified version based on Kim and Ziring, An Introduction to Asian Politics *(Englewood Cliffs, N.J.: Prentice-Hall, Inc., 1977), p. 74. By permission of publisher.*

TABLE 4.1: The National People's Congress, 1954–1978

NPC	Year Convened	Number of Delegates	Chief of State	Constitution Promulgated
1st	1954	1,226	Mao Zedong	Constitution of 1954
2nd	1959	1,226	Liu Shaoqi	
3rd	1964 (Dec.)			
	1965 (Jan.)	3,040	Liu Shaoqi	
4th	1975	2,885	—	Revised, 1975
5th	1978	3,459	—	Revised, 1978

Source: Delegate number is based on "Brief Notes About the People's Congresses" in Renmin Ribao *(February 27, 1978) p. 2.*

annually from 1954 through 1964. After 1964 the regular annual meetings were interrupted first by the Cultural Revolution and then by the Lin Biao affair. The Third NPC was not replaced by the Fourth NPC until 1975. After the Fourth NPC promulgated the 1975 constitution, the work of the congress was again interrupted by the radicals' attack against the Zhou Enlai dominated government. The Fifth NPC, which adopted the 1978 consitution, seems to have achieved stability under a moderate and pragmatic program.

The large size of the NPC has increased markedly over the years, from 1,226 members in 1954 to 3,459 in 1978. Apparently the size of the NPC has been expanded to broaden the representation and to allow greater participation in the government. The Fifth NPC has the following class or occupational representation: workers, 26.7 percent; intellectuals, 24 percent; peasants, 20.6 percent; and soldiers, 14.4 percent. Among these groups, women constituted 21 percent and minorities, 10 percent.[12] The enormous size of the NPC raises the question of whether the NPC was ever intended to be a genuinely deliberative body. The argument can be made that if the NPC was intended to be a "rubber stamp" for the CCP, then it might as well be very large and representative. However, the NPC cannot be totally dismissed as a rubber stamp. Under the leadership of Liu Shaoqi, the NPC at times did scrutinize proposals on economic development programs before giving its approval. On at least one occasion, at the 1957 session, NPC delegates attacked Mao in relation to the anti-rightist campaign and the party's meddling in the affairs of a Shanghai university.[13] However, the fact remains that no programs of any importance have ever been initiated by the NPC.

When the NPC is not in session, its Standing Committee serves as the executive body to act on behalf of the congress (The Second Session of the Fifth NPC in June 1979 approved a constitutional change which required the establishment of standing committees for people's congresses at and above the county level). While the Standing Committee is elected by the NPC, it is the Standing Committee which has the power to conduct elections of the deputies to the NPC and to convene the NPC sessions. Since the NPC meets once a year at most, the Standing Committee controls a great deal of that body's powers. The 1954 constitution provided for as many as sixty-five members on the Standing Committee. In recent times, it has had about twnty members drawn from the chairman, numerous vice chairmen and the secretary-general for the NPC. The Standing Committee of the Fifth NPC has a membership of 175. Since neither the 1975 nor the 1978 constitutions provided for a chief of state, the functions of the chief of state are placed in the hands of the Standing Committee in a collective leadership role. The chairman of that committee, in practice, assumes many of the ceremonial functions of the chief of state. In 1978 the venerable Ye Jianying, a powerful member of the party's Politburo, was elected chairman of the Standing Committee. The powers of the Standing Committee under the 1978 constitution have been curtailed somewhat in comparison with the 1954 constitution. Article 13 of the 1954 constitution gave the NPC's Standing Committee the power to declare decrees and policies of the State Council unconstitutional. Article 25(5) of the 1978 constitution (see Appendix A) grants the Standing Committee the power "to change and annul inappropriate decisions" adopted by the provincial and local government only. Thus, theoretically, under the 1978 constitution, the Standing Committee cannot restrain the State Council, the executive and administrative arm of the central government. However, Article 25(3) of the 1978 constitution does authorize the Standing Committee of the NPC to interpret the constitution.

THE STATE COUNCIL

The State Council, the nation's highest executive organ, administers the government through functional ministries and commissions, as indicated in Table 4.2. The constitution stipulates that the State Council be comprised of a premier, vice premiers, and heads of national ministries and commissions. The State Council may also include others, such as vice ministers. The membership of the State Council has ranged from a low of thirty to over one hundred. As the government expanded over the years, the number of ministries and commissions expanded to a peak of forty-nine just prior to the Cultural Revolution. Administrative reduction and simplification, major aims of the Cultural Revolution, were instituted by the Fourth NPC in 1975 when the number of ministries and commissions was reduced to twenty-nine. With the downfall of the Gang of Four and the launching of an extensive modernization program, some of the old ministries reappeared under the Fifth NPC, such as the state planning and science and technological commissions. The constitutionally mandated membership of the State Council, appointed by the Fourth and Fifth NPCs, are presented in Table 4.2.

TABLE 4.2: Composition of the State Council

| | State Council Appointed by | |
	4th NPC (1975)	5th NPC (1978)
Premier	1	1
Vice Premiers	12	13
Ministers and Commissioners	29	36
Secretary-general	—	1
Total	42	51

*Exclude the three new vice premiers (Chen Yun, Bo Yibo, and Yao Yilin) approved by the Second Session of the Fifth NPC in June 1979.

Since the full State Council is too large for effective decision making, in practice this role has been assumed by an inner cabinet of the premier and his vice premiers.[14]

The personnel of the State Council has remained relatively stable over the years. During the Cultural Revolution it suffered much less than the party apparatus, largely due to the leadership of Zhou Enlai, who was premier from 1949 until his death in 1976. Zhou stayed away from the debates during the initial stage of the revolution but joined Mao and Lin Biao when he realized their faction would emerge dominant. For Zhou's support, concessions were made for the State Council, including exemption from participation in the upheaval by scientists and technicians. As Thomas Robinson points out, Zhou was Mao's and Lin's "Chief problem solver, troubleshooter, negotiator, organizer, administrator, guide-advisor to revolutionary groups, and local enforcer of Central Committee policy."[15] It has been estimated that between one-half and two-thirds of the 366 ministers, vice ministers, commissioners, and vice commissioners kept their posts during the turbulent period from 1966–1968.[16] Another reason for the stability of the State Council, whose members represented a concentration of administrative and technical expertise, was for production to continue unimpeded. The ability of the State Council to issue directives, often jointly with the party's leading committees, is evidence that central civil bureaucracy was quite institutionalized and functionally effective in spite of the turmoil during the Cultural Revolution. The current leaders of the State Council have been working closely together for at least a decade. Since many of the vacant positions are filled through promotions of those with on-the-job training, this situation is likely to continue in the foreseeable future.

Doak Barnett has described the State Council aptly as the "command headquarters" for a network of bureaus and agencies staffed by cadres who administer and coordinate the government's programs at the provincial and local levels.[17] The degree of centralization of authority has fluctuated over the regime's history. During the First Five-Year Plan from 1953 to 1957, the ministries had enormous power over the provincial authorities in terms of quota fulfillment, allocation of resources, and management of such enterprises as factories and mines. The increasing complexity of coordinating the economy and the gravitation of power to the individual ministries, the "ministerial autarky," led to numerous problems and a continuing debate over centralization versus decentralization.[18] In 1957, during the Great Leap, decentralization was instituted by giving the provinces authority to administer and coordinate consumer-goods oriented industries. The decentralization of the Great Leap hampered central planning and resulted in inefficiency. Following the failure of the Great Leap, a modified version of centralization was adopted until the Cultural Revolution ushered in another period of decentralization.[19] With the reestablishment of planning operations and the emphasis on research and development under the Ten-Year Development Plan, endorsed by the Fifth NPC in March 1978, the pendulum most likely will swing back to greater centralization. In his speech to the Fifth NPC, one of the six points made by Hua Guofeng about the economy, was to strengthen centralized planning with due regard for initiative by local authorities: "Power is to be centralized where necessary, while active support is to be given to the local authorities in undertaking what should be put in their charge."[20]

A large majority of the ministries under the State Council is concerned with economic affairs; a minority deals with matters such as defense, foreign relations, public security, civil and minority affairs, education, and public health. The ministries on economic matters can be grouped into the categories shown in Figure 4.2.

FIGURE 4.2   Ministries on the Economic Functions of the State Council

Planning	Economic/Finance	Ministries of Machine-building	Special Industries
State Planning Commissions	State Economic Commissions Capital Construction	First Second Third	Metallurgical Coal Petroleum
Scientific/Technological Commissions	Foreign Trade	Fourth	Chemical

FIGURE 4.2   Continued

Planning	Economic/Finance	Ministries of Machine-building	Special Industries
	Economic Relations with Foreign Countries	Fifth	Power and Water
Statistical	Agriculture and	Sixth	Textile
Commissions	Forestry	Seventh	Light
Geology	Railways		Farm
	Communications		machinery
	Posts and Telecommunication	Eighth (1979)	
	Finance		
	People's Bank		
	Commerce		
	Co-op Marketing		

*Source: "Proclamations of National People's Congress," * Peking Review, *10 (March 10, 1978), 42.*

INTERLOCKING STRUCTURE OF THE GOVERNMENT AND PARTY

To students who are familiar with Western constitutions, it is often a surprise to read in the Chinese constitution the stipulation that the party is "the core of leadership of the whole Chinese people," and that "the working class exercises leadership over the state through its vanguard, the Communist Party of China." This, of course, means that the governmental institutions in China exist to serve the party.

The Chinese Communist Party controls and directs the machinery of state through an interlocking system of party personnel and a structure parallel to that of the state government. The best example of interlocking personnel is Hua Guofeng, who is both chairman of the CCP and premier of the government. In addition, as party chairman Hua automatically becomes the chairman of the party's Military Affairs Commission, which supervises the armed forces and sets military or defense policies. The first vice chairman of the party's Military Affairs Commission becomes, by tradition, the Minister of Defense. One of the party's vice chairmen, Deng Xiaoping, is also the chief of staff of the armed forces. Of the thirteen vice premiers of the State Council elected by the Fifth NPC in 1978, nine were members of the powerful CCP Politburo, and all were members of the CCP Central Committee elected in 1977. Of the thirty-six ministers in charge of the various governmental agencies,

104

twenty-nine, or eighty-one percent, were members of the Central Committee. All major economic ministries, including economic planning, capital construction, research and development, foreign trade, and heavy and light industries, were in the hands of ministers who were members of either the Politburo or the Central Committee. In fact, the party's highest policy-making body, the Politburo, is functionally organized to parallel the government ministries, with members specializing in the various governmental activities. In each state bureaucracy there is always the presence of the party cell of leading CCP members who provide direction for the state organ. The party has always been able to exercise its control in a state bureaucracy by supervising its personnel. Thus, the state structure and the party are not truly parallel entities since they interlock from top to bottom.

The party control over the state bureaucracy has been the subject of much discussion among scholars. Too often, students of Chinese politics look at the bureaucracy under the State Council as if it were an independent power base competing with the party. The fact that all of the thirty-six ministers approved by the Fifth NPC are members of the CCP's Central Committee demonstrates that the State Council is not only interlocked with the party, but is controlled by it. Conflicts that do occur are not primarily between the gvernment and the party, but are intraparty conflicts between high ranking party members.

Interlocking Relationships of the Politburo Members

The interlocking relationships of the members of the Politburo, the highest decision-making body of the party, not only demonstrates how the party exercises its control over the central government but also gives an indication of possible areas of specialty and power base for the top elites who are members of the Politburo. Figure 4.3 lists the members of the Politburo elected by the Eleventh Party Congress in 1977 and 1978 by their affiliation with either the military, the central government administration, or the provincial party administration.

One way of measuring the role of these individual Politburo members as key policy makers is to identify the number of institutions and levels of administration with which they have been known to have a close relationship. The six-member Standing Committee of the Politburo is at the policy making apex. The institutions and offices with which these Standing Committee members are or have been associated yeilds the

FIGURE 4.3 Politburo Members Elected in 1977 and 1978 by Their Affiliation with the Military, Central Government Administration, or Provincial Party Committees and Mass Organizations

	Hua Guofeng		
Standing Committee of Politburo:	Ye Jianying Wang Dongxing	Deng Xiaoping Li Xiannian	dChen Yun
	Professional Military	Central Administrators	Provincial Party Administrators
1.	Liu Bocheng	b1. Fang Yi	b1. Peng Chung
2.	Xu Shiyou	b2. Yu Qiuli	(Shanghai)
c3.	Su Zhenhua (died)	b3. Chen Yonggui	a2. Zhao Ziyang
4.	Li Desheng	b4. Geng Biao	(Sichuan)
b5.	Zhang Tingfa	ab5. Chen Muhua	
6.	Chen Xilian	6. Ji Dengkui	
b7.	Nie Rongzhen	7. Wei Guoqing	
b8.	Xu Xiangqian	8. Ulanhu	
d9.	Wang Zhen	a9. Seypidin	
		10. Wu De	
		c11. Ni Zhifu (labor)	
		d12. Hu Yaobang (youth)	
		d13. Deng Yingchao (women)	

a. Elected as alternate members of the Politburo

b. Newly elected for the first time to the Politburo

c. Promoted from alternate status in the Tenth Central Committee in 1973 to full membership on the Politburo in 1977

d. Elected by the Third Plenary Session of the Eleventh Party Congress on December 22, 1978. The addition of Chen Yun as a vice chairman of the CCP to head the Central Commission for Inspecting Discipline of the party also means that his administrative experiences in the past as an economic expert in the areas of commerce and capital construction could be utilized in the thrust for modernization.

following interlocking pattern of relationships:

1. Hua Guofeng   Chairman of the CCP
                    Chairman of the Military Affairs
                        Committee (MAC)
                    Premier of the State Council
                    (Formerly) First Party Secretary for
                        the Hunan Province

2. Ye Jianying   Vice Chairman of the CCP
                    Vice Chairman of the MAC
                    Vice Premier of the State Council

106

	Chairman, Standing Committee, Fifth NPC
	President of Military Science Academy
3. Deng Xiaoping	Vice Chairman of the CCP
	Vice Chairman of the MAC
	Chief of Staff for the PLA
	Vice Premier of the State Council
4. Li Xiannian	Vice Chairman of the CCP
	Vice Premier of the State Council
	Finance Minister
	(Formerly) Member of the Party's Central Secretariat
	(Formerly) Director of Office of Finance and Commerce of the Party
5. Wang Dongxing	Vice Chairman of the CCP
	(Formerly) Director of the Central Office for the Party
	Member of Standing Committee of MAC
	(Formerly) Commander of Central Security Force #8341
	(Formerly) Director of Central Security of the Party
	(Formerly) Minister for Public Security
6. Chen Yun	Vice Premier of the State Council (June 1979)
	First Secretary, Central Commission for Inspecting Discipline
	(Formerly) Vice Premier, State Council
	(Formerly) Chairman of State Capital Construction Commission

The leadership, under the direction of Hua Guofeng and Deng Xiaoping, has launched a program to modernize China, by the end of this century, in four areas: agriculture, industry, national defense, and science and technology.[21] This means emphasis must be placed on the development of science and technology, foreign trade and economic relations, and the whole gamut of activities associated with economic planning and development. The areas of expertise of the new members elected to the Politburo in 1977 and 1978 reflect these priorities:

7. Fang Yi	Vice Premier of the State Council
	President, Chinese Academy of Sciences (June 1979)

	Director, Part's Nucleus Group on Science and Technology Minister for the Science and Technological Commission, State Council
8. Yu Qiuli	Vice Premier of the State Council Minister for State Planning Commission (Formerly) Minister for Petroleum Industry
9. Chen Yonggui	Vice Premier of the State Council (Formerly) Leader of Dazhai commune and considered a self-made agricultural expert
10. Geng Biao	Vice Premier of the State Council Director, Party's International Liaison Office
11. Chen Muhua	Vice Premier of the State Council Minister for Foreign Economic Relations (Formerly) Deputy Director, Office for Liaison with Foreign Economic Relations
12. Ji Dengkui	Vice Premier of the State Council
13. Ni Zhifu	Vice Chairman of Beijing Revolutionary Committee First Vice Chairman of Shanghai Revolutionary Committee Director of Beijing Trade Union Federation Director of newly reorganized All-China Trade Union Federation Party Secretary for both Beijing and Shanghai
14. Wei Guoqing	Director of the General Political Department of the PLA (Formerly) First Party Secretary for Sichuan and Guangzhou Provinces
15. Ulanhu	Director of General Logistics Department of PLA (Formerly) First Party Secretary for Inner Mongolia
16. Seypidin	(Formerly) First Party Secretary for Xinjiang (Formerly) Chairman of Xinjiang Revolutionary Committee (Formerly) Political Commissar for Xinjiang Military Region
17. Wu De	(Formerly) Party Secretary for Beijing

	(Formerly) Chairman of Beijing Revolutionary Committee
	(Formerly) Political Commissar for Beijing Garrison Command
18. Hu Yaobang	Secretary-General for the Central Secretariat (as of December 1978)
	Third Secretary, Central Commission for Inspecting Discipline
	Director, Propaganda Department, CCP
19. Deng Yingchao	Vice Chairman, Fifth NPC
	(Formerly) Second Secretary, All-China Women's Federation
	(Wife of Zhou Enlai)

Again, we can measure their role as key policy makers by identifying the number of institutions and the level of administration with which they have been affiliated, as well as by their areas of expertise. Of the four new Politburo members added by the Third Plenary Session of the Eleventh Central Committee in December 1978, Hu Yaobang is the most important in terms of the pivotal position he occupies: secretary-general of the party's Central Secretariat, a position occupied by Deng Xiaoping before he was purged in 1966. Hu has been a trusted and devoted protégé of Deng for many years. His star seems to rise and fall with that of Deng. Hu, now only 63, may be considered a likely successor to Deng who is in his late 70s.

In addition to Politburo Standing Committee members Deng Xiaoping, Ye Jianying, and Wang Dongxing, who have close ties with the powerful military establishment, the following nine members of the Politburo elected in 1977 are active senior military leaders who represent the professional military viewpoints:

20. Liu Bocheng	Vice Chairman of the MAC
21. Xu Shiyou	Deputy Minister of National Defense
	Commander of Guangzhou Military Region
22. Su Zhenhua	Political Commissar for the Navy
	First Party Secretary for Shanghai Municipal Party Committee (died in February 1979)
23. Li Desheng	Commander of Shenyang Military Region (Manchuria)
24. Zhang Tingfa	Commander of the Air Force
25. Chen Xilian	Vice Premier of the State Council

	Commander for Beijing Garrison Command
26. Nie Rongzhen	Vice Chairman of the MAC
27. Xu Xiangqian	Vice Chairman of the MAC
	Vice Premier of the State Council
	Minister of National Defense (since 1978)
28. Wang Zhen	Vice Premier of the State Council
	(Formerly) First Army Corps, PLA First Field Army and Commander for the Xinjiang Military Region
	(Formerly) Minister for State Farms and Land Reclamation

As of 1979 only two provincial figures were represented on the Politburo:

29. Peng Chong	Party Secretary for Shanghai
	Second Vice Chairman of Shanghai Revolutionary Committee
	Political Commissar for the Nanjing Military Region
30. Zhao Ziyang	First Party Secretary for Sichuan Province
	Chairman of Sichuan Revolutionary Committee
	Political Commissar for Chengdu Military Region

Seypidin (Xinjiang) and Wu De (Beijing) were removed from some of their party and government positions in the fall of 1978 for their past cooperation with the Gang of Four. However, both seemed to have maintained their Politburo membership at least for the moment. Wang Dongxing, Chen Xilian, Ji Dengkui, Ni Zhifu, and Chen Yonggui were criticized during the winter of 1978 in wall posters for their past relationship with or support of the radicals. They, too, have not been dropped from their Politburo membership mainly because of the need to maintain party unity. It is reasonable to expect periodic reshuffling in the Politburo membership to reflect possible divergent views which may emerge in regard to modernization and other crucial policy issues or priorities. All signs seem to indicate that the seasoned veteran administrators of the pre-Cultural Revolution days, at the urging of Deng Xiaoping, are returning to their positions of influence in the party and government. For the foreseeable future they will play a large part in China's surge for modernization.

CHINESE LEGAL SYSTEM
AND LAW ENFORCEMENT

We begin this section on the Chinese legal system with two case illustrations: one, a criminal case of deviance; the other, a civil case of divorce. The purpose of these case illustrations is to enable those who are not familiar with the Chinese concept of law to have some understanding of how it works and why. Outsiders looking in at the Chinese legal institutions and the proceedings may get the impression that either the Chinese legal system today is nonexistent or there is no need for law at all since there are few, if any, criminals in their society. Both of these impressions are, of course, misconceptions. The Chinese legal system is quite different from that in the West, and the manner by which deviance and disputes are handled has been shaped to a large extent by their own revolutionary experiences of past decades, as well as by the communist political ideology.

In the criminal case,[22] a worker had stolen about $250 worth of material and equipment from his factory. A colleague and neighbor reported his deviant behavior to the factory revolutionary committee, which referred the matter to the public security unit. An investigation was made by a procurator, who in accordance with Chinese legal practice, served as both prosecuting attorney and public defender. The procurator then presented a dossier of the case to an intermediate court. The court ordered an open trial to be held in the factory so that other factory workers could participate in the proceedings. At the trial, the judge, with the help of two community elected lay assessors, examined the charges and the evidence as presented by the procurator. A trade union leader who personally knew the defendant testified about the defendant's good character and appealed for leniency. After the defendant made a confession about his crime, the judge solicited the opinion of the masses, the workers in the factory. The consensus of the masses in attendance at the trial was that the defendant was a good worker but that his crime must be punished. Upon the suggestion of the masses, the judge sentenced the defendant to two years of labor in the factory under the supervision of his fellow workers.

The civil case[23] is a divorce case. While divorce cases are not frequent, they represent sixty percent of all civil cases in China. The case came to trial at a lower court after reconciliatory attempts had been made, first by the committee that handles misdemeanors, then by the procurator, and finally by the judge's department. The hearings were held in a store front, and included a judge, two lay assessors, and a procurator. The judge heard arguments from both the husband and the wife, and then retired for an hour with the two assessors to reach a decision. The verdict was that a final reconciliation attempt was to be made over forty-eight hours, and that a divorce would be granted if this last effort failed.

The Chinese legal system is operated on two basic approaches: one, the formal set of structure and procedures seen in the two cases summarized above; the other, a set of what Professor Jerome Cohen calls the "extrajudicial" structure and practices, which generally emphasize continuous education on acceptable social norms, peer pressure dynamics, and persuasion to correct deviant behavior. These two approaches, or "models," interact and coexist within the Chinese legal system.[24] From 1954 to 1956 the formalized legal structure and procedures were dominant. From the Great Leap in 1958 through the Cultural Revolution, the extrajudicial structure and practices increased in importance. Following the convocation of the Fifth NPC and promulgation of the 1978 constitution, there has been a reversion to more formalized structure and procedures, including the revising of civil and criminal codes by a group of experts headed by Peng Zhen, a former Politburo member purged during the Cultural Revolution but now rehabilitated.[25]

The Courts: Formal Structure and Functions

The 1978 constitution provides that judicial authority be exercised by a Supreme People's Court, local people's courts at the various levels, and special people's courts. The Supreme People's Court is responsible and accountable to the NPC and its Standing Committee. It supervises the administration of justice of the local people's courts and the special people's courts. The local people's courts are the provincial, county, and district levels. The local people's courts at the higher levels supervise the administration of justice of the people's courts at lower levels. The local people's courts are responsible and accountable to the local people's congresses at the various levels of local government. Representatives of the masses must participate in the administration of justice as assessors. All cases are to be heard in public, "except those involving special circumstances, as prescribed by law." The accused always has the right to defense.

Alongside of the court system is a parallel system of people's procuratorates, headed by the Supreme People's Procuratorate, which is responsible to the NPC and supervises the local procuratorates at the various levels. The system of procuracy is rooted both in the Chinese imperial practices and in the Napoleonic civil code, which was used in part by the Soviets and many other continental European nations in their legal systems.[26] As was mentioned earlier, the procurator serves the dual functions of prosecuting attorney and public defender during a trial. The procurator also is responsible for monitoring and reviewing the government organs, including the courts, to provide a legal check on the civil bureaucracy.[27] The procuratorate also is responsible for authorizing the arrests of criminals and counterrevolutionaries.

The 1954 constitution provided for independence, under the law, of the courts and procuratorates. These provisions were eliminated by both the 1975 and 1978 constitutions. The 1954 to 1957 period witnessed the strong development of judicial independence. Judges frequently made their own decisions, disregarding the views and wishes of the party in important cases. This independence illicited much criticism from the party and resulted in increased tension between the courts and the party.[28] Coupled with the development of judicial independence was a movement to develop legal professionalism and expertise. Law schools were established, and offices of "people's lawyers" were formed in cities to provide legal aid to citizens. In 1957, the party countered judicial independence with a two-pronged attack: first, it purged or transferred to other branches of government those court cadres who advocated strengthening judicial independence and professionalism; and second, it introduced many of the extrajudicial institutions and practices for handling cases, in order to bypass the formal court system. In addition, in 1959 the functions of the local procuratorates were merged into the party's political and legal departments at the local levels. Thus, for all practical purposes, local procuratorates disappeared during the Cultural Revolution, and the Supreme People's Procuratorate existed in name only.[29]

Extrajudicial Institutions: Informal Practices

The party cadres who came from the guerrilla background had acquired a different set of legal experiences, which relied heavily on the use of reeducation, persuasion, and social group pressure. As Victor Li has pointed out, the informal handling of deviance by guerrillas had its roots in traditional China.[30] Except for very serious cases, the traditional settlement of a dispute was one of informality, compromise, and face-saving for everyone involved. Disputes were settled largely by mediation of elders in a family, clan, or village, with consultation all around. In China today, we see similar mediation roles assigned to organizations, such as street or neighborhood committees, in settlement of disputes or in cases concerning deviant behavior. For instance, if a man steals a bicycle, his family is notified, and the family elders impose minor disciplinary action. If the man refuses to admit his wrongdoing or refuses to accept the sanction from the family, his neighborhood committee becomes involved. The leaders of the neighborhood committee then guide a group of his neighbors in attempts to reeducate the offender. If the man is a first-time offender and confesses his wrongdoing, his action is usually forgiven, and he is given a chance to amend his behavior under the supervision of the group. If he repeats his deviant act, the public security unit would be called in. The public security, or police, would not jail the man, but would instead attempt to reeducate him. Only the incorrigibles are incarcerated in labor reform camps.[31] In a more serious criminal case, such as the one illustrated at the beginning of this section, the judicial proceedings are informal and emphasize mass participation in reaching a verdict. In fact, the illustration points out that the judge's sentence was handed out after the view of the masses—the fellow workers in the factory of the defendant—had been solicited.

In summary, a large percentage of both civil and criminal cases are settled in China by this type of informal method without going through a court trial. The reliance on informal settlements through local level organs has eliminated the use of trained lawyer's services, but persons accused of wrongdoing are permitted to speak for themselves.

Public Security Bureau: Law Enforcement

The Public Security Bureau performs all of the police tasks in China (national, provincial, and local), and is responsible for maintaining law and order. The operation of public security is headed by a national Ministry of Public Security Affairs, and has local branches in cities, towns, and villages. Its responsibilities include surveillance of the movements of citizens and foreigners and the investigation of all criminal cases. Since 1957, it has been empowered to pronounce sentence in criminal cases, including internment in labor reform camps under its control. The power of the public security to sentence is another major type of extrajudicial practice, instituted in 1957 to bypass the courts. Local public security personnel are usually all members of the party or the Communist Youth League.[32] At times, public security offices have even been operated as organizations of the local party apparatus. Because of close ties with the party, the public security bureaus usually reflect the view of the party leaders in control.

Just prior to the Cultural Revolution, the procuratorate functions were carried out from the public security units. During the upheaval, the attacks by Red Guards on the party frequently focused on the public security bureaus, disrupting, if not paralyzing, their functions. When the People's Liberation Army intervened in January 1967, the functions of the public security bureaus were placed under military control. During this period it became a common practice for the PLA to perform police work: arresting criminals, stopping riots, supervising prisons and labor reform camps, and even directing traffic.[33] The 1975 constitution again placed the procuratorate functions and powers in the local public security units. That constitution also prescribed that citizens could be arrested either by a decision of the courts or "by sanction of the public security organ." The constitution of 1978 restored the sanction of arrest of criminal offenders to the people's procuratorate, but assigned the duty of arrest to the public security unit. This fine distinction may not mean very much since both the public security units and the procuratorate operate from the same administrative office of the party, at the local levels. In June 1979 the Second Session of the Fifth NPC enacted the new organic laws for the courts and criminal procedure which delineated further the relationship between public security organs and the courts as follows: the public security organ is responsible for investigation of crimes and detention of criminals; the procuratorate has the power of approving arrests and prosecuting criminal cases; the people's court is to try cases.

The restoration of the procuratorate and the enunciation of citizens' fundamental rights and duties in the 1978 constitution (see Articles 44–59 in Appendix A) seem to have provided a new framework of law and justice in post-Mao China. A campaign for human rights and equal justice for all was launched soon after the promulgation of the 1978 constitution, and reached its height in the winter of 1978, just prior to the convening of the Third Plenary Session of the Eleventh Central Committee. Meanwhile, the Central Committee reevaluated the events of the Cultural Revolution and corrected erroneous decisions with respect to the purge of a number of top leaders. Special articles in mass media and wall posters in Beijing focused on human rights and injustices to those who had been arbitrarily arrested and mistreated from the days of the Cultural Revolution to the time of the arrest of the Gang of Four. A special group of legal specialists was formed to undertake the major task of codifying and revising some thirty codes and regulations, including criminal and civil justice procedures, as mentioned earlier. The release and rehabilitation of over 100,000 "right deviationists" (a convenient label used by the radicals for those who refused to conform to the appropriate political or ideological line) demonstrates the new leadership's intention to observe and enforce "socialist legality and democracy." The many exposés revealed by the mass media in 1978 and 1979 pointed out clearly how widespread were the abuses sanctioned and practiced by the radicals in arbitrarily arresting and detaining cadres and masses alike. From this campaign for law and justice came the approval of regulations governing the arrest and detention of persons, by the Second Session of the Fifth NPC in June 1979. The specific prohibitions contained in the new law on arrest and detention give us some idea of the state of lawlessness that had existed in China for some time. The new law provides that no person shall be arrested without a specific decision of a people's court or the approval of the procurate. Within three days of detention or arrest, the police (public security bureau) must submit the evidence to the procurate or make formal charges for the detention. The new law requires that interrogation of the detainee must commence within twenty-four hours of the arrest and that the person detained must be released immediately if there is no evidence against him. In Beijing a lawyers' association has been formed to provide legal services, including arrangement for defence counsel in criminal cases, to people who need them. We will probably see more efforts being made to formalize the legal procedures.

There are two compelling reasons for what the Chinese term "new beginnings" in restoring and strengthening the legal system, particularly in providing some protection for the cadres and the masses against arbitrary arrest and detention. One is the new regime's desire to bring some order from the anarchical conditions created and fostered by the radicals. Hua Guofeng told the delegates of the Fifth NPC that "It is essential to strengthen the socialist legal system if we are to bring about great order across the land." In addition to order and stability, which are necessary conditions for China's modernization, there also must be created an atmosphere free from fear of arbitrary arrest and detention, if China's intellectuals, can dare to think, explore, and make innovations.

THE CHINESE TOP ELITE AND THE CADRE SYSTEM

In this section we shall first discuss the characteristics of China's top elite, the members of the Politburo in terms of their socio-economic background. A discussion of the development of the Chinese bureaucracy, the cadre system, will follow.

Profile of the Chinese Top Political Elite

Considerable data has been compiled by scholars in the West on the elites of China, particularly on members of the Eighth and Ninth Central Committees and their Politburos.[34] One of the most comprehensive studies of the Eighth and Ninth Central Committees found that the members were largely from China's interior and rural areas, generally had received less formal education than most modern elites, were predominantly administrative cadres of a generalist type, and were mostly past their middle years.[35]

Table 4.4 presents a frequency tabulation of characteristics of the twenty-six members of the Politburo elected by the Eleventh Party Con-

TABLE 4.4: Characteristics of the Chinese Top Elite—Politburo Members Elected By the Eleventh Party Congress, 1977

Age	Number		Percentage of Total
80 and over	2		7.6
70s	8		30.7
60s	11		42.3
50s	4		15.3
40s	1		3.8
	26	average: 65.2	
Sex			
Male	25		96.2
Female	1		3.8
	26		
Nationality			
Chinese	24		93.4
National Minorities	2		7.6
	26		
Geographic Origin			
Central	9		34.6
East	2		7.6
North	3		11.5
Northeast	—		—
Northwest	3		11.5
South	3		11.5
Southwest	3		11.5
	26		
Occupational Background			
Provincial	8		30.7
Central Party apparatus/ State apparatus	4		15.4
Military/Public Security	10		38.5
Economic specialists/Scientific academic/intellectual	2		7.6
Workers	1		3.8
Peasants	1		3.8
	26		

Source: Compilation is based on the biographic sketch in Ming Pao Daily News (Hongkong) August 24, 1977, p. 3.

gress in 1977. Almost eighty percent of the members were over 60, and the average age was sixty-five years. Only one woman, Chen Muhua, was elected to this top policy-making body in 1977. Over half of the members are from the interior provinces of central, northwest, and southwest China.

117

The summary of primary occupational background reveals the largest representation, thirty-eight percent, are from a predominantly military background. The second largest representation, thirty percent, are or have been provincial party secretaries. They can be expected to serve as spokesmen for their regions and provinces, where they have built up strong ties over the years. Of the last major representation, twenty-three percent are from the central apparatus, either top administrators or economic specialists. Only one member, Chen Yonggui, a self-made agricultural expert and former leader of Dazhai commune, has close vocational ties with the peasants. Similarly, only Ni Zhifu, who emerged from the trade union organization and urban revolutionary committees, has a labor background. What strikes one as the most important characteristics of this policy-making group is the large number of senior administrator-bureaucrats: Over fifty-four percent hold senior directorships in central and provincial apparatus. When these administrator-bureaucrats are combined with the military elements, they comprise ninety-two percent of the total Politburo membership. One might describe this as China's bureaucratic-military complex. It is the same combination which dominates the Eleventh Central Committee, as shown in Table 3.1.

No one can really predict the future cohesiveness of the top elite elected to membership on the Politburo in 1977 and 1978. As we have seen, some Politburo members have had to make self-criticisms for their support of the radicals, particularly with respect to their role in the April 1976 Tian An Men Square incident that resulted in the second purge of Deng Xiaoping. The reversal of the verdict on theTian An Men incident has tarnished the prestige and perhaps reduced the power of Hua Guofeng, who has made self-criticism for his support of the radicals, even though he did finally help to mobilize the forces for the arrest of the radical leaders after Mao's death. By contrast, Deng Xiaoping's star has been rising steadily in the collective leadership that is now governing China.

The Development of the Chinese Bureaucracy: The Cadre System

The tasks of a government's policies and programs are generally carried out by the functionaries who staff the administrative agencies. In the noncommunist world, we call these people bureaucrats, the "vast impenetrable and well-paid" corps of paper shufflers.[36] The Chinese call these bureaucrats "cadres" or "kanpu" which denotes leadership skill and capability in an organizational set-up. Thus, we may refer to Zhou Enlai, Hua Guofeng or Deng Xiaoping as the party and central government's leading cadres. The intermediary layer of bureaucrats is the middle-level cadres; and those on the bottom layer, who must deal directly with the masses, are the basic-level cadres.

It should be kept in mind that not every cadre is a party member, nor is every party member a cadre. In short, cadres are the functionaries who staff the various party and government bureaucracies and have authority to conduct party or government business. When we use the term "elite" in discussing Chinese politics, it generally refers to the cadres at various levels.

On the basis of their employment, the cadres are divided into three general broad categories: state, local, and military. Each group has its own salary classification system with ranks and grades, similar to civil service systems in noncommunist countries. Urban state cadres have a system with twenty-four grades, while local cadres have twenty-six grades. Local cadres at the commune level or below are paid directly by the organizations they work for. This ranking system also is associated with status, privileges, and the degree of upward mobility in the career ladder. A cadre's rank, particularly at the state level, is determined not necessarily by length of service or seniority but frequently by educational background, expertise, or technical competence. Those cadres who have served the party since the days of the Long March and the war against Japan naturally command more prestige than those who joined after the liberation in 1949. During the Cultural Revolution the term "veteran cadres" was widely used to denote cadres who had acquired administrative experience in managing party and government affairs prior to the Cultural Revolution.

It is difficult to obtain precise figures for the total number of state, local, and military cadres in China today. We know that in 1958 there were about eight million state cadres, or one state leader for every eighty persons in China. If we use the ratio of 1:80 as a basis for a rough estimate, the total number of state cadres may now be over eleven million. This figure does not include the millions of cadres at the local level and in the military, and it includes only some of the thirty-five million party members, many of whom are cadres. The leadership nucleus in China may well total between fifty and sixty million cadres. These are the Chinese elites who must provide leadership for the masses.

Development of the Cadre System

In the early days when the Chinese communist movement was engaged in guerrilla activities, the vast majority of the cadres were basic level. They were the link between the party and the masses, the middlemen in the execution of party directives. They were expected then, as now, to conscientiously apply the principle "from the masses, to the masses" and to always be attentive and responsive to the wishes of the masses. Most of these basic-level cadres then were peasants with experience mainly in managing governmental affairs of a rural nature. Because of the guerrilla operation, it was necessary to require all cadres to be dedicated party members and to adhere strictly to the party principle of democratic centralism. In implementing policies, these cadres supervised the tasks called for by the policies. They were required, from time to time, to conduct investigations into the results of programs and to make reports to the party. The ideal cadre, during the guerrilla days, was also a combat leader who lived among the masses and exemplified the traits of modesty and prudence.

After the communist takeover in 1949, a new type of cadre was needed to manage the complex social and economic affairs of the vast nation. This required persons with administrative skills and experience not possessed by the cadres who came from the rural environment and guerrilla background. A massive infusion of both party members and government cadres took place from 1949 into the early 1950s. As a stopgap measure, party membership and loyalty were no longer required for the government cadres. Instead, education, technical skill, and experience became the prerequisites for cadre rank. The cadres from the guerrilla experience were placed in special training programs to prepare them for work in complex governmental agencies. By 1953, about fifty-nine percent of the 2.7 million cadre force were graduates of either regular or people's universities; the remaining forty-one percent had attended special training courses to prepare for their work in various government agencies.[37]

The transformation of cadres from revolutionary leaders, engaged in guerrilla warfare, to government bureaucrats, concerned largely with paper work, became formally institutionalized in 1955 when the State Council promulgated a rank classification system for the cadres.[38] Rank within the system was based on the acquisition of technical skills and on the time when the cadre had joined the revolution. As the need for manpower in government service grew, a salary system with a promotional ladder was also established to attract career-oriented young people.[39] It has been said that by this time a cadre could predict with some accuracy his future promotions and status.[40] These developments in the bureaucracy presented a host of problems for a society dedicated both to egalitarian principles and to modernization, with its concomitant requirement for specialization and expertise, which could only be administered in a complex hierarchical structure. In an effort to maintain the egalitarian society and to correct various abuses, the regime developed three major strategies aside from the use of persuasion through education and the dispatch of special work teams to correct specific local abuses. These strategies were rectification campaigns, the xia-fang movement, and May Seventh Cadre Schools.

Rectification Campaigns

Rectification campaigns have been used to correct deviant behavior of both party and government cadres. The campaigns generally have involved education, reform, and purge. These campaigns have been undertaken periodically to strengthen the cadres' discipline, to raise their political and ideological awareness, and to combat corruption and inefficient work performance.[41]

The first rectification campaign, conducted by Mao from 1942 to 1944 following his selection as party chairman, was designed to remove lingering opposition to Mao's strategy for revolution. This was followed by the 1950 rectification campaign aimed at correcting deviant attitudes among party cadres at all levels. The party cadres were criticized for "commandism," or issuing orders without proper consultation with the masses; tendencies of bureaucraticism, including excessive paper shuffling; distrusting the masses; and lack of direction and coordination in their work. The campaign was also an attempt to resolve differences between cadres from the guerrilla days and those recruited after 1949, which had created friction and tensions within the party. The 1950 campaign required the cadres to systematically study selected key party documents, to analyze China's situation, and to participate in self-criticism during small group discussions. These two campaigns were followed by at least six more rectification campaigns, including the Socialist Education Campaign in 1963, prior to the Cultural Revolution. As Teiwes has pointed out, the measures used in these successive rectification campaigns ranged from educational persuasion, to reduction of rank and pay, to punishment by purge or even death.[42]

Despite these rectification campaigns, the cadres as bureaucrats and administrators were committed more to efficiency and orderly completion of tasks than to revolutionary enthusiasm and vision, on the eve of the Cultural Revolution.[43] As careerists, the cadres as a whole had established political power, comfortable income, and security as life goals.[44] There were particular problems which included difficulties in actual implementation of the mass-line principle, deviant behavior, acquisition of special privileges, declining morale, and increased tensions.[45] The Cultural Revolution can be considered both as a gigantic rectification and as a mass campaign aimed, to a large extent, at these bureaucratic problems. These numerous rectification campaigns have created fear and uncertainty among the cadres and have led to administrative chaos and waste in the management of government activities.

The Xiafang, or "Downward Transfer" Movement and the May Seventh Cadre Schools

The temporary transfer of party cadres down to a lower-level assignment or to a rural village or factory was introduced in the 1940s. Originally, the primary purpose of the movement was to reduce bureaucratic machinery and to strengthen the basic-level leadership. The system of temporary downward transfer of party and government cadres became institutionalized in 1957, when the movement's primary purpose shifted to the "education and reform of cadres through labor." From 1961 to 1963, as many as twenty million education cadres, a large number with technical skills, were sent to work in villages with the peasants.[46] The movement was intensified during the Cultural Revolution, when it became fashionable for cadres to opt for downward transfer to rural villages and communes. The major objective then was two fold: 1. to combat the cadres' bureaucratic tendencies, through physical labor in the fields, alongside the peasants, and 2. to develop the mass line by enabling the cadres to understand the masses' problems and aspirations by living and working among them. The program resulted in a marked change in the cadres' attitudes toward the masses. Interestingly, the manual labor also improved the participating cadres' health.[47] While the downward transfer of skilled cadres must be considered an underemployment of resources, the xia-fang movement represents an innovative technique to check the perennial problem of elitism in China.

One of the most innovative devices that came out of the Cultural Revolution was the May Seventh cadres schools for the reeducation and rehabilitation of incorrect attitudes and ideological thoughts. Thousands of these cadre schools were formed under a directive, issued by Mao on May 7, 1966, that emphasized the need to reeducate and to rusticate cadres for ideological remolding. The schools' curriculum consisted of manual labor, including working in the fields with commune production teams, performing duties required to run the school, and theoretical studies of works by Mao, Marx, and Lenin. Life at the May Seventh cadres schools was initially spartan, and provisions for daily living had to be obtained by the participants through their own labor. A cadre was usually sent to a school for three, six, or twelve months. Occasionally their stay was for more than a year. These schools were innovative in combining physical labor and ideological study, aimed at curbing tendencies toward bureaucratic elitism.[48] They were a unique addition to the broad xia-fang movement.

Trends in the Cadre System

Over the past decade and a half, life for a cadre as a middle man was not easy. The cadre was not able to please either those at the top of the party nor the masses at the bottom. Since all decisions were subject to criticism from many directions, frequently the wisest choice was to make no decision at all. The cadres who came from the intellectual class, but who possessed technical expertise, were subject to special abuse as China's privileged "new class."[49] To redeem themselves, cadres opted for physical labor in the countryside, putting aside their professional development, at least temporarily.

The pendulum has now swung back to the moderation of the mid-1950s, when China's economic development demanded the rapid recruitment of capable, skilled persons as cadres to manage the complex economic activities. The attacks against the new "bourgeoisie right" of elites and intellectuals have been silenced now with the downfall of the radical Gang of Four. Hua Guofeng has called for the rapid formation of an army of "technical cadres and of professors, teachers, scientists, journalists, writers, artists, and Marxist theorists." The new leadership in post Mao China seems to say that there need not be a contradiction between "red" (ardent ideologues) and "expert" (skilled technocrats); Hua Guofeng has proposed to educate a vast corps of cadres who can be both ideologically correct and professionally competent.[50] Attempts have been made since 1977 not only to reduce the number of cadres and educated urban youth sent to the communes for physical labor but to improve the living conditions of the xiafang personnel. There are two main reasons why these remedial measures have been taken with regard to the xiafang movement: one is the need for the nation, which has embarked on a very ambitious modernization program, to utilize fully the technical skills of the educated, and the other is to minimize the constant complaint and resentment by the xiafang personnel, particularly the educated urban youth, on the poor living conditions that existed in the countryside. The new leadership in the post Mao China also recognized the need that the intellectuals, who constitutes a major proportion of the cadre system, may have to undergo periodically some thought remolding, perhaps not as so prolonged and intense as in the past. But, what is more important, as the new leadership seems to be saying, is that the work of the educated elite and their professional achievements must be acknowledged, if not praised. Hua Guofeng and Deng Xiaoping have made a pledge that the educated elite must be treated fairly and that their working conditions and facilities must be improved, if not guaranteed.[51] All of these changes about the cadre system may lead to a new pattern of political and intellectual life in China, one in which there is perhaps some liberation of the mind.

NOTES

[1]See Houn, *A Short History of Chinese Communism* pp. 72–73; and Chou Erh-fu, "The CPPCC: Consulting on Affairs of State," *China Reconstructs,* vol. xxvii, no. 8 (August 1978), 3–4.

[2]"Granting Special Amnesty to and Releasing All War Criminals in Custody," *Peking Review,* 12 (March 21, 1975), 11–12; and Chou Erh-fu, "The CPPCC," p. 5.

[3]For a summary of activities in English, see *Peking Review,* 9 (March 3, 1978), 4–5.

[4]Chou Erh-fu, "The CPPCC." p. 5.

[5]For text of 1954 constitution, see Jerome Chen, *The Chinese Communist Regime,* pp. 75–92.

[6]Houn, *A Short History of Chinese Communism,* p. 138.

[7]For the text of 1975 constitution, see *Peking Review,* 4 (January 24, 1975), 17

[8]Chang Chun-chiao, "Report on the Revision of the Constitution," *Peking Review,* 4 (February 24, 1975), 15–16.

[9]Chang Chun-chiao, "Report on the Revision of the Constitution."

[10]See Appendix A.

[11]Yeh Chien-ying, "On the Revision of the Constitution," *Peking Review,* 11 (March 17, 1978), 15–16.

[12] Renmin Ribao, (February 26, 1978), p. 1. Also see"China's Structure of State Power," *Beijing Review,* 20 (May 18, 1979), p. 19.

[13]See MacFarquhar, *The Origins of the Cultural Revolution,* pp. 273–78.

[14]Donald Klein, "The State Council and the Cultural Revolution," *The China Quarterly,* 35 (July–September 1968), 78–95.

[15]"Chou En-lai and the Cultural Revolution in China," *The Cultural Revolution in China* (Berkeley: University of California Press, 1971), p. 279.

[16]Klein, "The State Council," p. 81.

[17]See Doak Barnett, *Cadres, Bureaucracy, and Political Power in Communist China* (New York: Columbia University Press, 1967), pp. 3–17.

[18]Chang, *Power and Politics in China,* p. 50.

[19]Chang, *Power and Politics in China,* pp. 63–64, 106–108; also see Barnett, *Uncertain Passage,* pp. 136–43.

[20]"Unite and Strive to Build a Modern Powerful Socialist Country," *Peking Review,* 10 (March 10, 1978), 25.

[21]See Hua Kuo-feng's "Political Report to the 11th National Congress of the CCP," *Peking Review,* 35 (August 26, 1977), 48–52.

[22]Franklin P. Lamb, "An Interview with Chinese Legal Officials," *The China Quarterly,* 66 (June 1976), 323–37.

[23]Frank Pestana, "Law in the People's Republic of China," *Asian Studies Occasional Report,* no. 1 (Arizona State University, June 1975).

[24]J. Cohen, "The Party and the Courts: 1949–1959," *The China Quarterly,* 38 (April–June 1969), 131–40. Discussion of the "models" in the Chinese approaches to legal system is based on Victor Li's article "the Role of Law in Communist China," *The China Quarterly,* 44 (October–December 1970), 72–110.

[25]See "Socialist Legal System Must Not Be Played Around With," *Peking Review*, 24 (June 16, 1978), 28; and "Discussion on Strengthening China's Legal System," *Peking Review*, 45 (November 10, 1978), 5–6. Also see "Speeding the Work of Law-making," *Peking Review*, 9 (March 2, 1979), 3.

[26]Frank Pestana, "Law in the PRC," p. 2. Also see Victor Li, "The Role of Law," p. 78; and George Gingurgs and Arthur Stahnake, "The People's Procuratorate in Communist China: The Institution Ascendant, 1954–1957," *The China Quarterly*, 34 (April–June 1968), 82–132.

[27]Ginsburgs and Stahnake, "The People's Procuratorate in Communist China," pp. 90–91.

[28]For an account of these tensions and criticisms, see Cohen, "The Party and the Courts: 1949–1959," pp. 131–40.

[29]Gerd Ruge, "An Interview with Chinese Legal Officials," *The China Quarterly*, 61 (March 1975), 118–26. Also see Frank P. Lamb, p. 324–25.

[30]Li, "The Role of Law," p. 92.

[31]Martin King Whyte, "Corrective Labor Camps in China," *Asian Survey*, vol. xiii, no. 3 (March 11, 1973), 253–69.

[32]Barnett, *Cadres, Bureaucracy, and Political Power in Communist China*, p. 227; and Ralph Powell and Chong-kun Yoon, "Public Security and the PLA," in *Asian Survey*, vol. xii, no. 12 (December 1972), 1082–1100.

[33]Barnett, *Cadres, Bureaucracy, and Political Power in Communist China*, p. 227; and Powell and Yoon, "Public Security and the PLA," pp. 1082–1100.

[34]See Robert A. Scalapino, ed., *Elites in the People's Republic of China* (Seattle: University of Washington Press, 1972).

[35]Robert A. Scalapino, "The Transition in Chinese Party Leadership: A Comparison of Eighth and Ninth Central Committees," in *Elites in the People's Republic of China*, pp. 67–148.

[36]Robert Sherrill, *Governing America: An Introduction* (New York: Harcourt Brace Jovanovich, Inc., 1978), p. 412.

[37]See Ezra Vogel, "From Revolutionary to Semi-Bureaucrat," p. 45.

[38]Vogel, "From Revolutionary to Semi-Bureaucrat," p. 45.

[39]Oksenberg, "The Institutionalization of the Chinese Communist Revolution," pp. 61–92.

[40]Oksenberg, "The Institutionalization of the Chinese Communist Revolution," pp. 61–92.

[41]For a fuller discussion of the rectification campaigns, see Frederick C. Teiwes, "Rectification Campaigns and Purges in Communist China, 1950–61," unpublished doctoral dissertation, Columbia University, 1971, in University Microfilms, Ann Arbor, Michigan. Also see S.J. Noumoff, "China's Cultural Revolution as a Rectification Movement," *Pacific Affairs*, vol. xi, nos. 3 and 4 (Fall and Winter 1967–68), 221–33.

[42]Teiwes, "Rectification Campaigns and Purges in Communist China," 150–61.

[43]Ezra Vogel, "From Revolutionary to Semi-Bureaucrat."

[44]Oksenberg, "The Institutionalization of the Chinese Communist Revolution."

[45]See Richard Baum, *Prelude to Revolution: Mao, the Party, and the Peasant Question, 1962–66* (New York and London: Columbia University Press, 1975); and Richard Baum and Frederick Teiwes, "Liu Shao-chi and the Cadres Question," *Asian Survey*, vol. viii, no. 4 (April 1968), 323–45.

[46]See Jan S. Prybyla, "Hsia-fang: The Economics and Politics of Rustication in China," *Pacific Affairs*, vol. 48, no. 2 (Summer 1975), 153. Also see Paul E. Ivory and William R.

Lanely, "Rustication, Demography Change, and Development in Shanghai," *Asian Survey*, vol. xvii, no. 5 (May 1977), 440–55.

[47]Notes of conversation with cadres in Peking during my visit in 1973.

[48]See James C.F. Wang, "The May Seventh Cadre School for Eastern Peking," *The China Quarterly*, 63 (September 1975), 522–27.

[49]See Theoretical Group of the Chinese Academy of Sciences, "A Serious Struggle in Scientific and Technical Circles," *Peking Review*, 16 (April 15, 1977), 24–27.

[50]Hua Kuo-feng, "Political Report to the 11th National Congress of the CCP," *Peking Review*, 35 (August 26, 1977), 51–52.

[51]Hua Kuo-feng, "United and Strive to Build a Modern Powerful Socialist Country—Report on the Work of the Government to the First Session of the Fifth NPC," *Peking Review*, 10 (March 10, 1978), 30.

Provincial and Local Government and Provincial Politics

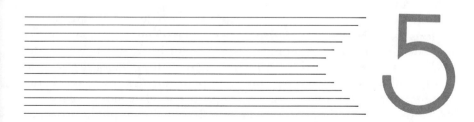

5

OVERVIEW OF PROVINCIAL
AND LOCAL GOVERNMENT

The government of China is administered through twenty-one provinces, five autonomous regions, and the three municipalities—Beijing, Shanghai, and Tianjin. The five autonomous regions of Inner Mongolia, Ningxia, Xinjiang, Guangxi, and Xizang are located on China's borders with neighboring countries and are inhabited by minority groups.

The constitution of 1978 specifies three layers of local political power: the province, the county, and the commune. The source of constitutional power at these levels is the people's congress. We must keep in mind that the deputies of the provincial and county people's congresses are elected indirectly. The constitution states that the deputies to the provincial and county people's congresses are to be elected by "people's congresses at the next lower level by secret ballot after democratic consultation." Eligible voters at the lower level of government (in this case, the communes) directly elect only the deputies to the counties-level people's congress, which then elects the people's congress above it. The county congress elects the provincial people's congress. A simple chart of the provincial and local government is shown in Figure 5.1. Deputies to the provincial congress are elected for a five-year term; deputies to the commune and county congresses are elected for three-year term.

It would be wrong to assume that the people's congresses at the various local levels are legislative bodies. These congresses do not make any laws and, in fact, meet only once a year for between a few days and two weeks. Their main responsibilities fall into three major areas: 1. to ensure the implementation of the state plan, such as the ten-year development plan for 1976–1985; 2. to approve local economic plans and development, including the budget; and 3. to maintain public order. In their deliberations on such matters as fulfillment of state quotas or the

128

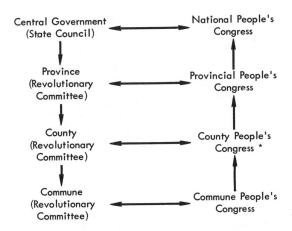

FIGURE 5.1   Provincial and Local Government Structure

*Change to "people's government" by the Second Session of the Fifth NPC, June 1979.

local economic development budget, the deputies are subject to the influence, if not the dictates, of the local party committee. The local party committee is, in turn, subject to the directives of the party authorities above it. The people's congresses also elect the chairman, vice-chairmen, and members of the revolutionary committees.

It will be recalled from Chapter 1, that the revolutionary committee was originally established as a temporary organ to replace the regular party structure dismantled by the Cultural Revolution, and that, thereafter, it remained as a grass-root organization through which the masses could participate directly in making decisions at the basic level. With the reestablishment of the party structure in the early 1970s, many of the functions of the regular party were duplicated by the revolutionary committees. Then, when the Gang of Four were arrested in the fall of 1976, the status of the revolutionary committees at the basic level became rather unclear. Visitors to China during 1977 and the first few months of 1978 observed little evidence of the revolutionary committees in factories and communes. Before the Fifth National People's Congress convened, there was even talk about abolishing the revolutionary committees. This confusion and uncertainty about the status of the revolutionary committees was clarified when the Fifth National People's Congress approved the constitution revision, which provided that the revolutionary committees at the local levels were to become executive organs of the local people's congresses and "local organs of state administration" (Article 37). They were to perform administrative work at their respective levels and areas under the overall direction of the State

129

Council. Thus, the revolutionary committees, an important legacy of the Cultural Revolution, became governmental administrative units at the local levels. Furthermore, the revolutionary committees under the 1978 constitution were empowered to appoint and remove the personnel of the people's courts and procuratorates. The local party committees were responsible only for decisions concerning general line and principle of the party. Despite this constitutional delineation of responsibility for the revolutionary committees at the provincial and local levels, confusion remained over which organ should make what decisions. A large part of this confusion seems to have stemmed from the appointment of individuals to hold concurrent parallel positions on both the party and revolutionary committees. It has become a standard practice, for instance, to have the party secretaries at the various local levels hold the chairmanship or vice-chairmanship of the revolutionary committees as well. We need to bear in mind, however, that the original rationale for the formation of the revolutionary committee was to insure some participation and representation by the masses on matters of strictly local concern. The revolutionary committees at the local level also afforded young cadres an opportunity to acquire leadership skills. Since 1973, a deliberate effort has been made to have both veteran and younger cadres in leadership positions.

But the actual political power in the provinces resides in the party provincial committees, as discussed in Chapter 3. The provincial party committee ensures that the provincial revolutionary committee is controlled by the party by nominating and electing deputies to the provincial people's congress, which in turn elects members to the provincial revolutionary committee. As previously mentioned, it is common to find the first party secretary for a province or an autonomous region concurrently holding the position of chairman for the provincial revolutionary committee, the local organ of administration. Thus, when we speak of provincial politics, we refer almost exclusively to the role played by provincial party committees in the direction and management of provincial affairs.

ISSUES IN PROVINCIAL POLITICS

Chinese provincial politics is a very complex subject. Three interrelated issues that have dominated provincial politics in China have been selected for discussion here.

Regionalism, Provincialism, Localism

We have noted that China is a unitary state with political power concentrated at the central government level, and that throughout China's long history there have been many incidents of the centrifugal forces attempting to pull away from the center because of geography and sectional interests. The warlord period of 1916–1926 represents the epitome of regional separation in recent history. Another general characteristic of Chinese politics has been the trend for local initiative and self-government. In this section we will briefly examine the development of regionalism in provincial politics.

The terms "provincialism," "regionalism," and "localism," have been used to describe the problems of regions versus the center, or the central authority in Beijing, in China. These terms are used here somewhat interchangeably because they all denote the centrifugal force constantly at play in Chinese politics. Regionalism has been defined as "the phenomenon whereby distinct groups, living in discrete territorial enclaves within larger political communities, exert pressures for recognition of their differences."[1]

The presence of regional forces that tend to pull away from the center in Chinese politics may be accounted for, to a large extent, by China's vast size and the variations in the cultures represented in her different geographic areas. It is common to speak of China as divided geographically into the north, south, central, east, west, and the Asian portions of Inner Mongolia, Xinjiang, and Xizang.[2] Each of these regions may be considered an entity dominated by features of climate, drainage systems, soil composition, or dialect variations. A visitor who enters China by train from Hongkong will notice the subtropical climate of southern China, which permits the harvest of two rice crops each year. The rugged hills and mountains of the south tend to foster a variety of dialects among the inhabitants. When the visitor arrives at Beijing in the north, he sees an entirely different China in terms of both climate, which is temperate and thus cold in the winter, and soil formation, which is the dry powdery loess of the Huanghe (Yellow) River basin. Wheat, millet, and cotton are the main crops grown in the north and northeast. Central and east China are watered by the Changjiang (Yangtse) River, whose vast plains permit the cultivation of rice and other crops that support a large population. The mountainous west and southwest is sparsely populated, except for the fertile valley of Sichuan, one of the richest but most difficult provinces to govern because of its geographic isolation and its relative economic self-sufficiency. These geographic and topographic variations are primary factors that have contributed to the feelings of sectional independence.

Centralization vs. Decentralization

In a continuous search for an appropriate administrative formula, China has alternated emphasis between decentralization and centralization since 1949. When the communists took over in 1949, the provincial and local governments were built upon the base of the guerrilla army and governments, which, by their very nature, had operated with a great deal of autonomy in implementing government policies and programs. These new governments were staffed largely by local residents, both for convenience and to avoid accusations of a takeover by outsiders. To aid the central government's administration in Beijing and the coordination of the provinces, the six regional districts (shown in Figure 3.2) were established. Each region was governed by both a military and an administrative committee. A corps of veteran party military leaders headed these committees, which had considerable authority and flexibility in their supervision of the provinces. A good deal of local autonomy was permitted under this regional arrangement while the regime consolidated its rule. The communists had neither the administrative personnel nor the experience to mount a tight central administration over the vast population and area. Under these conditions, the ever-present local tendencies exerted themselves, which frequently resulted in political factions at the local level.[3] Local officials often manipulated party officials at the regional level.

The conflict between the central and regional power structures came to a head with the introduction of the First Five-Year Plan. Centralized planning, with allocated resources, production quotas, forced savings, and formation of the voluntary agricultural producers' cooperatives (APCs), required strong central control. Gao Gang, chairman of the Manchurian Military and Administrative Committee as well as the area's party chief, was purged for opposing the APCs and for disagreeing with the party over allocation of investment funds for Manchuria. Similarly, Rao Sushih, chairman of East China Military and Administrative Committee and party chief, was purged for demanding a slower pace in introducing the APCs into his area. It was alleged that both powerful regional leaders had attempted to solicit support from the military stationed in their respective areas. The six regional government bureaus and the six party bureaus were abolished following these purges.[4] The 1954 constitution specifically stipulated that China was to have a single form of government with headquarters in Beijing. Under the constitution, the provincial authorities were the agents of the central government, with limited power to implement and execute the plans and directives from the center.

The years of 1953 to 1957 turned out to be a period of overcentralization, with excessive control over the provinces by the central authority in Beijing, particularly by those central functional ministries that proliferated under the First Five-Year Plan. All economic enterprises were placed under the direct control and management of the central ministries. Regulatory control devices were promulgated at the center, and all important decisions had to be made in Beijing. Even the acquisition of fixed property, worth about one hundred dollars, needed specific permission from the central ministry concerned.[5] This frequently resulted in delay and frustration in decision making. Even worse, the centralization of decision making resulted in ministerial "autarky." A ministry became an independent economic system that tightly controlled the supply of materials and the allocation of resources under its jurisdiction. Instead of regional independent kingdoms, there were centralized, ministerial independent kingdoms, which interfered with provincial and local administration, drew up ill-conceived plans, and made repeated revisions of the plans, resulting in the neglect of priorities and the waste of raw materials.[6]

At the end of the First Five-Year Plan, the Chinese leaders made an agonizing reappraisal of their experience with the Stalinist model of development. In advocating the return to decentralization, Mao spoke out openly for the extension of power in the regions. In his 1956 speech on the ten major relations or contradictions, Mao criticized the central functional ministries' habit of issuing orders directly to their counterparts at the provincial and municipal levels without even consulting the State Council and the party's Central Committee. He pointed out that local interests must be given due consideration if the central authority was to be respected and strengthened at the provincial and local levels.[7]

While Mao was genuinely concerned about the excess in centralization and the loss of local and provincial initiative, he may have been motivated also by purely political considerations. Centralism had placed tremendous power in the centralized ministries and the members of the State Council, who, from time to time, challenged Mao's policies and were at that time opposed to rapid collectivization. By advocating the return of power to the provinces, Mao would receive support from the provincially based political forces, which could serve as a counterweight in a showdown with the top party-government officials at the center.[8] Mao's view on the return to decentralization was evidently accepted by the party leadership when it met in the fall of 1956 to endorse the Second Five-Year Plan, which provided for local initiative and administration appropriate to local needs and interests.

The Great Leap of 1958 marked the beginning of real efforts at decentralization. Under the decentralization policy, the provincial and local authorities were granted a variety of powers in the administration and management of economic enterprises. Control of enterprises in consumer goods industries was transferred from the Ministry of Light Industry to provincial authorities. While certain basic industries of economic importance, such as oil refining and mining, were still controlled by the central ministries, the provincial authorities were given some say in their operations. In the area of finances, the provincial and local governments gained considerable power. Under the decentralization plan of 1957, provincial and local authorities were granted their own sources of revenues from profits of local enterprises and taxes, freeing them from complete dependence on central government grants for their budgets. The provincial authorities were to retain twenty percent of the profits from the enterprises transferred to the local authorities and a share of local taxes on commodities, commercial transactions, and agriculture. The provinces were even allowed to levy new taxes and to issue bonds, as long as the methods were approved by the center. Even more important for the initiative and growth of the provinces, local authorities were allowed to rearrange or adjust production targets within the framework of the targets of the overall state plan.[9] Thus, in the latter part of the 1950s, the top leaders, including Mao, recognized that the provinces had a definite role to play in the top-level decision-making process. By 1956, Mao had formulated a set of guidelines to be applied in the debates over central versus local issues. A key provision of these guidelines was Mao's insistence that the center must consult the provinces: "It is the practice of the Central Committee of the Party to consult the local authorities; it never hastily issues orders without prior consultation."[10]

A direct consequence of the 1957 decentralization under the Great Leap was the emergence of the provinces as independent entities. The provinces behaved as though they were little "underdeveloped nations"; each wanted to build its own self-sufficient industrial complex.[11]

The inevitable result of the weakened centralized ministerial supervision over economic activities in the provinces was the rapid growth of localism, with provincial leaders acquiring an economic power base to challenge the center on policies and programs. In addition to being the agents of the party at the center, the provincial party secretaries also became spokesmen for the particular interests of their own provinces in dealings with the center at Beijing.

With the failure of the Great Leap in 1959, the Central Committee enacted a recentralization program to strengthen the leadership of the center over the provincial leaders. In 1961 the regional bureaus were reestablished to supervise the provinces and to control their tendencies to become "subnational administrations."[12] These regional bureaus also were mandated to supervise the rectification campaign launched by the Liu Shaoqi group to purge the radicalized provincial party leaders who supported the Great Leap program.[13] The recentralization in the early 1960s did not restore the center-local relationship to the pre-1957 status of overcentralization. Many of the powers granted to the provincial and local authorities during the Great Leap remained intact. However, the crucial functions of economic planning and coordination were largely returned to the central authority.[14] Provincial politics remained a very important force during the early 1960s. For the period from the end of the Great Leap in 1961 to the eve of the Cultural Revolution in 1966, the provincial leaders were active participants at regularized central work conferences, a form of enlarged meetings of the Politburo or the Central Committee, which included selected party leaders who were not members of the highest decision-making body.

Tensions in Provincial-Center Relations

On the eve of the Cultural Revolution, the new center-provincial relationship showed signs of uneasiness as the dissension within the top leadership deepened. The upheaval soon revealed a number of areas of tension between the provinces and the center. Two major areas of tension were the allocation of resources and the types of economic activities to be carried on in the various provinces. For example, the party leader in the southern province of Guangdong was accused of insisting on the development of a complete industrial complex for his province rather than concentrating on the development of light industries as dictated by the center.[15] On occasion, particular local conditions were used by provincial leaders as justification for resisting certain economic programs initiated by the center. Kansu province used its backwardness as justification for not embarking on a rapid program of economic development.[16]

The degree of provincial autonomy or independence from the center varied, according to the province's share of China's total industrial and agricultural resources and the stature of the provincial leaders in the hierarchy of the party and the central government. Thus, provinces of the northeast, the massive industrial base in Manchuria, and the provinces of eastern and central China, with their commanding share of the resources, were in a better bargaining position when it came to allocation and distribution of these resources. For example, the southwestern province of Sichuan has been traditionally known as a difficult province for the center to govern because of its rich resources and its remoteness from Beijing. The party leader in Sichuan before the Cultural Revolution was an old revolutionary veteran with close supporters at the center. He was Li Qingchuan, the party secretary for the southwest region before the Cultural Revolution. He enjoyed considerable autonomy and independence in governing the province of Sichuan and the southwest region.[17] Ulanhu, a powerful member of the Politburo at the beginning of the Cultural Revolution who had long governed the affairs of Inner Mongolia, could be described as an overlord for the autonomous region. Ulanhu not only identified himself with, but banked on, local nationalism to provide local resistance to orders from the center during the Cultural Revolution.[18] Prior to their purges during the Cultural Revolution, both Li Qingchuan and Ulanhu had been brought into the decision-making process at the Central Committee level.

Provincial Representation at the Center

The turmoil of the Cultural Revolution created the need for an extensive "cooperative and consultative style of policy making" between the provinces and the center, to restore order as well as to reduce the tensions.[19] The cooperative role played by the provincial leaders during the Cultural Revolution had enhanced their position in relation to the center. By the time the Ninth Central Committee was formed in 1969, a significant percentage of provincial party secretaries had been elected to that body.

As Table 5.1 shows, the provincial leaders' link with the center was strengthened further by their increased representation as full members

TABLE 5.1: Provincial and Muncipal Party Secretaries Serving On the Central Committees, Ninth–Eleventh

Position in Provincial/Municipal Party Committees	Central Committee					
	Full Members			Alternate Members		
	9th (170)	10th (195)	11th (201)	9th (109)	10th (124)	11th (132)
Provincial First Secretaries	26	22	24	5	7	0
Lesser Provincial Secretaries	28	49	62	17	22	31
Total Provincial Secretaries	54	71	86	22	27	31
Provincial Secretaries Percent of Total	32	36	43	20	22	24

Source: Peking Review, *14 (April 4, 1969), 9;* Peking Review *35 and 36 (September 7, 1973), 9–10; and* Peking Review, *35 (August 26, 1977), 14–16.*

on the Tenth (1973) and Eleventh (1977) Central Committees—from thirty-two percent to thirty-six percent and from thirty-six percent to forty-three percent, respectively. Under these circumstances, Hua Guofeng, as the new party chief and premier of the central government, sought a balance in the relationship between the provinces and the center. He cautioned about the tendency of the central departments and ministries to hamper local initiatives, but at the same time warned against the tendency of the provinces and regions to "attend only to their own individual interests to the neglect of the unified state plan."[20]

THE LOCAL GOVERNMENTS IN CHINA

The County Government[21]

Above the commune is the administrative unit called county, or xien. There are approximately two thousand counties in China; each has a population of about half a million or fewer. The revolutionary committees elected by the People's Congress at the county level supervise a host of local government activities. First, the county government exercises, for the party, control over the personnel assignments for the entire county. In this manner the party manages to keep an eye on all the cadres working for the various units of the county government. It is at the seat of the county that a people's court hears and handles serious deviant cases. It is at the county level that we find the procuratorate operating when serious crimes are to be prosecuted. It is also at the county level that the public security bureau maintains a station for the surveillance of the county populace and to arrest criminals and counter-revolutionaries. Militia activities and relations with the regular PLA are handled at the county level.

The Commune as a Local Government Unit[22]

The lowest level of government is the commune. In China there are about seventy-five thousand communes, varying in size in terms of both the number of households and the total acreage under production. Each commune is organized into production brigades and teams.

A typical production team has from one hundred to two hundred members and is subdivided into work groups. The work groups are led by team cadres, who are seldom members of the party. The team members elect a committee to conduct the team's affairs. Frequently, group leaders are placed on the nomination slate and elected to the committee. We should note that the slate of candidates for the committee election must be approved by the party cell. The team serves as the basic accounting unit on the commune. Team committee members are assigned specific jobs, such as treasurer, accountant, work-points recorder, or security officer. The most important are the accountant and work-points recorder, who must keep detailed books on expenditures and income and on team members' earned work points, respectively. The work points usually range from zero to ten, with an able bodied adult earning between eight and nine points per unit of time worked. The number of work points earned by a team member for a unit of time worked is determined at the beginning of each year by a meeting of all team members. Each member makes a claim to this worth. This claim is evaluated by the assembled team members and a decision is reached on the points to be earned for each member for the coming year.

An average production brigade consists of five or six production teams—over one thousand people. Each production brigade has an elected people's congress, whose main responsibility is to elect a brigade chief and a revolutionary committee to assist the chief in administering the brigade's daily affairs. Frequently, the brigade chief is also chairman of the revolutionary committee and the party secretary. The revolutionary committee and its staff are responsible for managing economic and financial affairs, including planning, budgeting, record keeping, and accounting. The committee is also in charge of providing social welfare, and medical and educational services. Brigades with the use of agricultural machinery also maintain repair service units. In a number of communes that I visited, a small-scale research-and-development unit was attached to the brigade's revolutionary committee.

At either the team or brigade level, interpersonal disputes and deviant behavior are generally reconciled through group discussions. The party and the brigade cadres often serve as mediators in settling disputes. Only rarely do serious cases go beyond the confines of the brigade.

At the commune level, the local government structure becomes more complex. Again, as we find at the production brigade and team levels, the commune people's congress is symbolically and constitutionally the source of power for the people in the commune. Once elected, the congress elects a revolutionary committee, which in practice is the organ that administers the commune's activities. Under the commune revolutionary committee's supervision are distinct functional departments responsible for local government activities, such as maintaining law and order, public security, census taking, and controlling residents' movements. The commune also has a staff to manage financial affairs, including credits and banking. Other functional departments deal with the agricultural, commercial, and industrial activities of the commune. Under decentralization, economic functions of the commune have been transferred to the brigade and team levels. Each commune generally maintains a commune clinic. Its educational department supervises the primary schools located at the brigade level.

Local Government in the Urban Areas

There are two types of municipalities in China. One type includes the important urban centers—Beijing, Shanghai, and Tianjin—administered directly by the central government. The other type is subdivisions of the provincial governments.

A municipal government of a city like Beijing or Guangzhou is administered by the municipal revolutionary committee, elected by the municipal people's congress. For instance, the chairman of the Revolutionary Committee for Beijing was Wu De, who was also the mayor of Beijing. As a municipal government, the revolutionary committee for the city must supervise a large number of functional departments or bureaus dealing with law and order, finance, trade, economic enterprises, and industries located within the city limits. We also find in these cities subdivisions of state organs, such as the people's court, procuratorate, and the public security bureau for social control and law and order. Because of the size of some of the larger municipalities, the administration of the municipal government is subdivided into districts. The municipality of Beijing, with a total population of more than seven million, is divided into four districts as administrative subunits. Each district has a district people's congress, which elects a district revolutionary committee as the executive organ for district affairs.

Within each district of a city there are numerous street committees or offices, the lowest level of urban local government. Each street committee has a staff of trained cadres whose work is to mobilize and provide political education for the residents in the area. Generally, a street committee has twenty-five hundred to three thousand residents.

The street committees perform a variety of functions including organizing workers, teachers, and students in the neighborhood for political study and work; organizing and managing small factories in the neighborhood; providing social welfare services, such as nurseries and dining halls, to supplement those provided by the cities; and administering health, educational, and cultural programs. It also performs surveillance activities in cooperation with the public security units in the area.[23]

Below the street committee are the self-governing units—the resident or neighborhood committee and the resident group—organized and staffed voluntarily by the residents. A typical resident group has about twenty families, or approximately one hundred persons. It is generally headed by an elderly or retired woman, and it can deal with any matter of concern to the residents. It is common in the cities to find that a resident group is linked to a city hospital for family planning or birth control: The resident group disseminates information about the need for family planning. Meetings of all residents decide how many new babies are to be born and who may have them.

ETHNIC POLITICS: AUTONOMOUS
REGIONS AND NATIONAL MINORITIES

One of the interesting things about China is that she too has a minority problem. Similar to many of China's policies on major political, economic, and social matters, policies toward the ethnic minorities also have been subject to the periodic pendulum swings over the past two decades. This section will discuss the development of China's policies on national minorities and the reasons for policy changes, the status of autonomous regions, and minority group representation in party and government.

First, a few essential facts about China's national minorities are in order. There are about 52 million people in China who are considered to be national minorities. The largest of the 55 minority groups are the Zhuangs (7.7 million); Hui, or Chinese Muslims (3.9 million); Uygur (3.9 million); Yi (3.2 million); Tibetan (3.2 million); Miao (2.6 million); Manchus (2.5 million); Mongols (1.6 million); Bouyei (1.3 million); and Koreans (1.2 million).[24] Although these minority groups—the non-Han people—total only 52 million, or six percent of China's population, they inhabit almost sixty percent of China's territory, covering sixteen different provinces. In two autonomous regions, Xizang and Inner Mongolia, the minority people constitute the majority. An extremely important element in understanding China's policies toward the minorities is that over ninety percent of China's border areas with neighboring countries are inhabited by these minority people. When we discuss the border dispute between China and the Soviet Union, we inevitably are reminded that the disputed areas are inhabited by the Manchus, Mongolians, Uygurs, Kazakh, and Koreans. China's relations with Laos, Cambodia, and Vietnam brings to mind the minority people of Zhuang, Yi, Miao, and Bouyei in the autonomous region of Guangxi and provinces of Yunnan and Guizhou. The border dispute between India and China involves the Tibetans living in the Chinese territory in Xizang, Sichuan, and Qinghai. The changes in China's minority policies in recent years have been influenced, to a large extent, by considerations for the security of her border areas.[25]

When the Chinese People's Republic was established in October 1949, the regime followed a policy which can best be described as one of gradualism and pluralism. Primarily for the purpose of a united front to consolidate control of the nation immediately after the civil war, minority customs and habits were tolerated in regions inhabited by minorities. Compromises were made to include prominent minority elites of feudal origin as political leaders in the newly formed autonomous areas for the minority nationalities. At the same time, modern transportation and communication networks were constructed to link the autonomous regions with the adjacent centers of political and economic power populated by the Chinese. The nomadic Mongols in pastoral areas were exempt from the application of land reform measures. The concept and practices of class struggle, so prevalent in other parts of China, were purposefully muted when applied to minority regions. However, no serious attempts were made to assimilate the national minorities into the main throes of the revolutionary movement in other parts of China.

The period of the Great Leap ushered in a rapid change in policies toward the national minorities. For the period of 1956 to 1968, the policy shifted from gradualism and pluralism to one of radical assimilation. For the first time, the Chinese spoken language was introduced in the minority areas. Training of minority cadres was intensified. More importantly, socialist reforms, such as cooperatives and communization were introduced. The campaign against the rightists was also extended in the minority areas, aimed at those who advocated local nationalism. These policies of assimilation resulted in tension and violent clashes in the early 1960s between the Hans (Chinese) and the minority groups, particularly in Xizang and Xinjiang. It was precisely because of these disturbances in the minority areas that the assimilation programs were relaxed in the mid-1960s, prior to the Cultural Revolution. Radicalized communization programs in certain minority areas were disbanded. The slowdown did not last long. The Cultural Revolution brought back the radical line of assimilation for minority groups. Many prominent minority leaders in the border areas were subject to purges and vilification by the Red Guards, who were encouraged by the radicals. Ulanhu, of Inner Mongolia, Li Qingchuan, of Xizang; and Wang Enmao, of Xinjiang, were purged by the time the Cultural Revolution had run its full course from 1966–1968.[26] But the Sino-Soviet border dispute, according to Lucian Pye, made the Chinese realize the necessity of winning over the minority groups for reasons of national security.[27] The policy of assimilation was again modified to provide for diversity. In addition to having minority nationalities learn Chinese, the Chinese cadres were asked to learn the minority language. Minority customs, dress, music, and dance were encouraged as expressions of ethnic diversity. It was within this policy of pluralism and diversity in the post-Cultural Revolution era that we began to see an increase in the representation of China's minority groups in party and government organs.

Both the constitution of 1954 and its revision in 1978 provide identical detailed provisions for self-government in autonomous regions, in marked contrast to the brevity of such provisions in the 1975 constitution. This can be interpreted as a return to the policy of pluralism and gradualism. The people's congresses and revolutionary committees, as local organs of self-government for the autonomous regions, can make specific regulations in light of the special characteristics of the national minorities in these areas. This concept of diversity and pluralism was not mentioned in the 1975 constitution. In addition, both the 1954 and 1978 constitutions mandate the local organs of self-government in these minority areas to employ their own ethnic language in the performance of their duties. This represents a marked departure from past policies of assimilation, which urged the use of the Chinese language, both written and spoken, as the official medium of communication.

There has been increased recognition of minority groups in both the party and the government. Special efforts evidently were made to recruit new party members for the minority regions. We have figures which show that, from 1964 to 1973, over 140,000 new members from the minority areas were admitted into the party.[28] There is no precise breakdown of party membership distribution over the various autonomous regions, but there appears to have been a steady increase of party membership. Three minority leaders (Wei Guoqing, a Zhuang; Seypidin, an Uygur; and Ulanhu, a Mongol) were elected to the presidium of the Eleventh Party Congress, and thirteen minority representatives were elected to the Eleventh Central Committee (seven full and six alternate members). Similarly, the Fifth National People's Congress, which promulgated the 1978 constitution, had eleven percent of its deputies from the fifty-five national minority groups. At least four of the minority leaders (Wei Guoqing, Ulanhu, Seypidin, and Ngapo Ngawang-jigme) were elected as vice-chairmen of the congress. Thus, after more than two decades of policy vacillation in search of an appropriate formula for dealing with the minority groups in the border areas, China seems to have found a solution which stresses the preservation of the cultural diversity of the fifty-two million national minority peoples and at the same time opens up the channels for minority participation in decision making at the highest levels in the Chinese political process.

NOTES

[1]See Dorothy J. Solinger, *Regional Government and Political Integration in Southwest China, 1949–1954: A Case Study* (Berkeley: University of California Press, 1977), p. vii.

[2]George Cressey, *Asia's Lands and Peoples* (New York: McGraw-Hill, 1951), pp. 96–165.

[3]Schurmann, *Ideology and Organization*, p. 214.

[4]For an account of the purge of Gao and Rao, see Jurgen Domes, "Party Politics and the Cultural Revolution," pp. 64–65; Edward E. Rice, *Mao's Way* (Berkeley, Calif.: University of California Press, 1972), pp. 130–32; Albert Ravenholt, "Feud Among the Red Mandarins," American University Field Service, East Asia Series, N:2 (February 1954); Chang, *Power and Policy in China*, pp. 47–48; Jurgen Domes, *The Internal Politics of China* (New York: Holt, Rinehart & Winston, 1973), pp. 24–25.

[5]Chang, *Power and Policy in China*, p. 50.

[6]Chang, *Power and Policy in China*, p. 51; and Audrey Donnithorne, *China's Economic System* (London: Allen and Unwin, 1967), p. 460.

[7]The text, "On the Ten Major Relations," is to be found in *Peking Review*, 1 (January 1, 1977), 16, and *Selected Works of Mao Tse-tung*, vol. V (Peking: Foreign Language Press, 1977), p. 293.

[8]Chang, *Power and Policy in China*, pp. 52–53.

[9]For detailed discussion on the powers granted to the provinces, see Chang, *Power and Policy in China*, pp. 55–61, and Victor C. Falkenheim, "Decentralization Revisited: A Maoist Perspective," *Current Scene*, vol. xvi, no. 1 (January 1978), 1–5.

[10]"On the Ten Major Relations, April 25, 1956," in *Selected Works of Mao Tse-tung*, vol. V (Peking: Foreign Language Press, 1977), p. 293.

[11]Schurmann, *Ideology and Organization*, p. 210.

[12]Schurman, *Ideology and Organization*, p. 210.

[13]See Chang, *Power and Politics in China*, pp. 129–30.

[14]Chang, *Power and Politics in China*, pp. 144–45.

[15]See Frederick C. Teiwes, "Provincial Politics in China: Themes and Variations," in John Lindbeck, ed., *Management of a Revolutionary Society* (Seattle, Wash.: University of Washington Press, 1971), pp. 126–27.

[16]Teiwes, "Provincial Politics in China," pp. 126–27.

[17]See Thomas Jay Mathews, "The Cultural Revolution in Szechwan," in *The Cultural Revolution in the Provinces* (Cambridge, Mass.: Harvard University Press, 1971), pp. 94–146.

[18]See Paul Hyer and William Heston, "The Cultural Revolution in Inner Mongolia," *The China Quarterly*, 36 (October–December 1968), 114–28.

[19]Falkenheim, "Decentralization Revisited: A Maoist Perspective," p. 7.

[20]Hua Kuo-feng, "Unite and Strive to Build a Modern, Powerful Socialist Country!" *Peking Review*, 10 (March 10, 1978), 25.

[21]Information on the local government structure and functions is based on Barnett, *Cadres, Bureaucracy, and Political Power in Communist China;* Chu Li and Tien Chien-yun, *Inside a People's Commune* (Peking: Foreign Language Press, 1975); personal notes of my visits to China in 1972–73 and 1978; and "Our Neighborhood Revolutionary Committee," *China Reconstructs*, vol. xxii, no. 8 (August 1973), 2–3.

[22]Barnett, *Cadres, Bureaucracy, and Political Power in Communist China;* Li and Chien-yun, *Inside a People's Commune;* personal notes of my visits to China; and "Our Neighborhood Revolutionary Committee."

[23]"Our Neighborhood Revolutionary Committee," p.3.

[24]Figures here are based on June Terfel Dreyer, *China's Forty Millions* (Cambridge, Mass.: Harvard University Press, 1976), p. 279. Also see "China's Minority Peoples," *Beijing Re-*

view, 6 (February 9, 1979), 17–21. The State Council in June 1979 recognized the Jinuo people, numbered over 10,000 in Yunnan province in the southwest, as the 55th nationa minority. See *Beijing Review*, no. 25 (June 22, 1979), pp. 5–6.

25Lucien W. Pye, "China: Ethnic Minorities and National Security," *Current Scene: Developments in the People's Republic of China*, vol. xiv, no. 12 (December 1976), 7–10.

26For an account of the change of policies toward the minority groups from 1957–1969, see Dreyer, *China's Forty Millions*, pp. 140–259; "China's Quest for a Socialist Solution," *Problems of Communism*, xxiv (September–October 1975), 49–62; Pye, "China: Ethnic Minorities," pp. 5–11; and Hung-mao Tien, "Sinicization of National Minorities in China," *Current Scene*, vol. xii, no. 11 (November 1974) 1–14.

27Pye, "China: Ethnic Minorities," pp. 9–10.

28"New Party Members—A Dynamic Force," *Peking Review*, 27 (July 6, 1973), 6–7.

The Military's Role in Chinese Politics

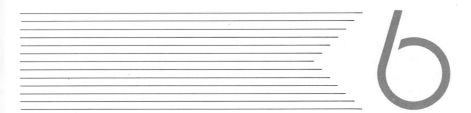

Chinese politics has been complicated by the participation of the military establishment at both the central and the provincial levels. In fact, following the Cultural Revolution, the military assumed the dominant political role in the local levels of government. In this chapter we shall examine first the structure of the PLA, focusing on the regional and provincial military commands as important factors in China's provincial politics; and second, the military's political role, with particular emphasis on the Cultural Revolution and its aftermath.

ORGANIZATION OF
THE PEOPLE'S LIBERATION ARMY

The 1975 and 1978 constitutions stipulate that the chairman of the CCP is commander-in-chief of the armed forces. He exercises control over the military through the CCP's Military Affairs Committee. The minister of defense, who operates under the State Council and the premier, is the administrative head of the PLA. Under the defense minister is the chief of staff for the PLA General Headquarters in Beijing, who is responsible for the execution and coordination of combat operations of all the services and commands. The PLA General Headquarters has a general logistic and procurement service. The party exercises its ideological and political control over the armed forces through the General Political Department. The GPD, as it is called, is responsible for the party cells within the PLA and propaganda, education, and cultural activities of the troops. Under the General Staff Office, the various service arms, such as the air force, naval headquarters, engineer corps, railway corps, armored command, and artillery, maintain their central headquarters for supervision of the armed forces.

At the regional level, the approximately 3.5 million troops are organized under the thirteen military regions, twenty-three provincial military districts, and nine garrison commands for principal population centers (see Table 6.2). Elements of the PLA are assigned to these regions and districts on an almost permanent basis. For instance, troops for the Shenyang Military Region station almost permanently in the northeast and are responsible for the defense of the northeastern provinces of Jilin, Liaoning, and Heilongjiang—each of the three is a military district by itself. In addition, the principal population city in the northeast— Shengyang—is a garrison command, which is in charge of all ground, air, and naval forces in the area. The Shengyang Garrison Command reports directly to the Shengyang Military Region. The autonomous region of Inner Mongolia, like Xizang and Xinjiang, is a military region. Because of the tension and open clashes along the Ussuri and Amur Rivers on the Sino-Soviet border, the Inner Mongolian Military Region is now under the direct jurisdiction of the Beijing Garrison Command.

Each military region has a regional military commander and at least a political commissar (see Table 6.2). Sometimes the military commander for the region simultaneously holds the post of political commissar. Regional military commanders and commissars can be shifted from region to region or can be promoted up to the central headquarters in Beijing. Provincial military district commanders report to their respective regional commands, which in turn delegate responsibilities for local administrative, logistical, recruitment, and mobilization matters to the districts. In addition, the military commands in the provinces and garrison commands in large cities are responsible for maintaining law and order, as was so vividly demonstrated during the Cultural Revolution.

A close relationship between the regional military commands and the civil authorities in the provinces dates back to the days of the civil war against the Kuomintang, when the armies operated in a specific region of the country. During the guerrilla days, the field armies, divided into five major groupings, provided civil and military administration for the regions they occupied: the First Field Army under the command of Marshal Peng Dehuai in the northwest region, the Second Field Army under Marshal Liu Bocheng in the southwest region, the Third Field Army under Marshal Chen Yi in east China, the Fourth Field Army under Marshal Lin Biao in the central and southern regions, and the Fifth Field Army under Marshal Nie Rongzhen in the north and northeast regions.[1]

The close linkage of the military and the civil authorities in the provinces was cemented by the use of the military control commission.[2] The military control commission was a device to take over administrative functions from the defeated Koumintang government during the gradual transition from civil war to normalcy. Each liberated town, county, and city was placed under a military control commission, established by the commanders of the newly arrived field army units. The ranking military officer for a particular locality concurrently held the chairmanship of the military control commission and the top political administrative post for the local government. Local administrative machinery, schools, factories, economic enterprises, and communications were placed under the jurisdiction of the military control commission. On the regional level, congruent with the six major administrative regions, were the six military regions under the control of the field armies. The highest organ of government in these regions was the regional military control commission. The chairman of the regional military control commission was the senior military officer in charge of the military region and the field army headquarters.

While dissolution of military control began in 1953 and was completed in 1954, the close link between the military and the regional, provincial, and local authorities continued. These field army units largely have remained stationed in these areas, although after the Lin Biao affair in 1973 there was a reshuffling of some officers. Following the Korean War, most units sent to the front were reassigned to the regions from which they had been recruited.[3]

Today local military commands still maintain local ties and concerns which have been established through the years and which are shared by the local civil authorities.

The field army system has been seen by some scholars as a partial explanation for factionalism in the military. They see the elite field army systems competing with each other for power and for representation of their regions.[4] Other scholars have found very little evidence, within the field army system, of political powerplays or of competition for assignments to the various military regions.[5] At any event, it must be kept in mind that the Military Affairs Committee controls directly a main or central force, as distinct from regional forces, of about sixteen army corps. These units can be employed under direct orders from the cental authorities in Beijing.

THE PEOPLE'S MILITIA

The militia was founded, during the Jiangxi soviet days, as an elitist organization to augment the Red Army and guerrilla units in combat and logistic support. During the civil war period, the militia's strength was not more than eight percent or ten percent of the total population under communist control. There have been six distinct stages of development of the people's militia since the establishment of the People's Republic in 1949.[6]

After liberation and during the Korean War, the activities of the militia were expanded to include maintenance of law and order, participation in joint defense measures with the PLA forces in border areas, and spearheading land reform activities.[7] This expansion of militia activities in no way altered its basic character as an elite force subordinated to the PLA command and discipline.

The people's militia acquired a new role and increased status when the people's commune and the Great Leap Forward programs were launched during 1958–1959. The militia became a nationwide mass movement, integrated into the structure of the communes in the countryside, growing enormously to a total of approximately 220 million by 1959. Under the concept of "everyone a soldier," members of the communes simultaneously engaged in agriculture, industry, trade, and military work. The militia became the vehicle for mass mobilization for collective action as military organizational techniques and discipline were incorporated into the communes.[8] During this period, the PLA had at first to share, and then gradually to relinquish, its authority and control over the militia to the communes and the party leadership within the communes. Simultaneously, the militia's status was elevated to a position coequal with that of the PLA in defending the countryside against possible enemy attack. These power shifts signalled the party's dissatisfaction with the army's desire to seek modernization in the midst of radicalized crash programs, and generated resentment and hostility within the PLA. At this stage of development, the notion of the militia as a countervailing force to the regular army had not yet surfaced.

In early 1960, following the failure of the Great Leap, substantial changes were made in the militia's role.[9] The militia's priorities were reordered to place productive tasks before military training. To ensure responsible behavior of the militia and its cadres and to curb its wide-ranging activities, overall control of the militia's structure and training was returned to the PLA provincial and district commands. For the period of 1960–1961, the militia was under tight political control and both its size and its activities were curtailed.[10]

On the eve of the Cultural Revolution, efforts were made to strengthen the political education of the militia so that it could become an instrument for political struggle. In 1967, during the midst of the Cultural Revolution, the army journal, then under the control of the radicals, defined the roles of the militia as not only "a partner and assistant to the PLA" but "an important instrument for the dictatorship of the proletariat and a revolutionary weapon of the masses." The militia was asked to work with the regular army and the public security forces to suppress and smash the reactionaries and revisionists who wanted to restore capitalism.[11] The nature of the militia's participation in the Cultural Revolution, however, was largely dependent upon the stand taken by the local party authority and the PLA units in a given locality. In most rural areas, local militia functioned as an integral part of the established party apparatus. When the authority of the party became disrupted as a result of the upheaval, the militia organization also became disrupted or simply vanished. In other instances, the local militia organization and personnel, which had established close ties with the county or municipal party committees, gave support to the established authorities in a showdown. We have well-documented case studies of the role played by the military and the militia in the provinces and cities, illustrating dissident local armed resistance against the central authority during the Cultural Revolution.[12]

The Sino-Soviet border clashes in 1969 served as the primary reason to reactivate and strengthen the militia for war preparation.[13] The campaign for war preparedness also revived charges against Liu Shaoqi and Peng Dehuai for their alleged inattention to building up the militia and for their overemphasis on development of a professional and modernized army. Many work conferences were held during 1969–1970. A constant theme at these conferences, as laid down by Chairman Mao, was that the organizational control of the militia must be under the local party committees because these party committees had a better grasp of the role of the militia in a "people's war."[14] To ensure the party's control over the militia, party committee members at the local level were designated to serve as leading cadres of the militia; only party members could serve as commanders of the militia. Since the role of the militia was to assist the regular armed forces in defending against foreign incursion, the PLA Chief of Staff Office was responsible for developing a system of utilizing and managing militia weapons.[15]

The urban militia, as mentioned briefly in Chapter 1, was formed in 1973 by the radicals for the ostensible purpose of providing auxiliary service for war preparedness in case of foreign aggression. It soon became apparent that the real purpose of the urban militia was to provide the radicals with an "armed force"—a politically reliable instrument among the industrial workers in urban centers—for use in the political struggle for power.[16] Since the radical leaders, such as Zhang Chunqiao and Wang Hungwen, did not trust the political reliability of the regular PLA armed forces, an independent command structure was set up to direct the activities of the urban militia. For the cities of Shanghai, Beijing, Guangzhou, and Tianjin, the command headquarters of the workers' militia were headed by leaders identified with the trade union federations in these cities. Both the urban militia and the trade union federations were under the control of the municipal party committees, which were bastions of the radicals. The Shanghai urban militia was singled out by the radical-controlled mass media as a model for others to emulate. Although the alleged coup plan of the Shanghai radicals to oppose Hua Guofeng's appointment as successor to Mao never materialized in the crucial weeks of late September 1976, there can be no doubt about the radicals' intention to use the urban militia as a political instrument in the contest for power.[17]

The command structure and work of the militia as a whole was reorganized following the arrest of the Gang of Four. Its overall role as an auxiliary to the regular armed forces in the event of a war has once again been revived.[18]

MILITARY IN CHINESE POLITICS

Militarism, as one of the major problems facing the Chinese, at least in the first half of this century, continues to play an important if not decisive role in Chinese politics. The presence of militarism, its relation to social and political organizations, and its effect upon the process of social and political transformation in the Chinese communist society can be a useful framework for analyzing the military's role in politics. Martin Wilbur defined militarism in the Chinese political development as a "system of organizing political power in which force is the normal arbiter in the distribution of power and in the establishment of policy."[19] Modern Chinese political development is, to a large extent, influenced by the power of armies, on one hand, and by the technique in the use of armies and in military organization, on the other.

For decades prior to the unification effort undertaken by the Chinese Nationalists in 1926, a system of regional military separatism dominated the political scene in China. Under the system, independent military-political groupings, each occupying one or more provinces, functioned as separate political entities and engaged in internecine warfare with each other in order to preserve their own separate regions and to prevent their rivals from establishing a unified and centralized political system. That contemporary China has been plagued by the problem of control of armies is really an understatement. It is largely by military means and through military organization and technique that the Chinese Nationalists tried and that the Chinese communists succeeded in reestablishing a "unified hierarchical and centralized political system."[20] The military thus constitutes a dominant group in society, and the military institution has played a dominant role in political develop-ment.[21] The military has always occupied a special position in the Chinese communist society. As mentioned in Chapter 3, the Chinese Communist Party, for a long time, was the army. The party membership grew from the forty thousand Long March survivors in 1936 to over 1.2 million in 1945. Over one million of the total membership in 1945 consti-tuted the military supply system.[22] These people were regular members of either the army or the party, working without salary and under a military type of discipline. Robert Tucker has labeled this unique system of militarizing the party as military communism to distinguish it from all other forms of communism.[23] It has been evident in recent years that party leadership has depended upon party members in the army to carry on political work, to restore order, and to use the army as a coercive instrument in the contest for political power and succession.

The PLA's Political Role from 1949 to 1966

As we have noted, for the years right after the new regime came to power, the PLA continued to govern the provinces under the Military Control Commission.[24] Before the dissolution of military government in the provinces during 1953 and 1954, China became involved in the Korean War. The war made the military leaders painfully aware of the need to modernize the armed forces with the most up-to-date weaponry and combat skills. Figuring prominently in the issue of modernizing the military was the pressing policy question of whether to develop a nuclear strategy to confront the United States in the Pacific.[25] These concerns of the military were the basis of Marshal Peng Dehuai's criticism of Mao and the Great Leap programs. Peng's strategy for modernization was defeated at the Lushan party conference in the summer of 1959, and he was purged for daring to disagree with Mao's policies on mass mobiliza-tion and the communes.

Lin Biao, who succeeded Peng as defense minister, launched a two-fold ideological campaign under the Socialist Education Cam-paign.[26] The first part of the campaign was aimed at tendencies toward professionalism, reliance on technical skills and weaponry, and elitism within the PLA. Party cells, or committees, were formed at the company level to supervise the work of the professionally trained military officers. Simultaneously, an intensive study of Mao's thought on politics and revo-lutionary military strategy was required of all PLA officers and men. A massive printing of millions of copies of the "little red book," *Quotations from Chairman Mao Zedong,* was distributed first to the PLA ranks and later to the general public under the second part of the campaign: emu-lation of the PLA by the whole nation. The PLA was to be a model, a paradigm, of the new communist life. Under the direction of the military, political and ideological verbal symbols, or abbreviated slogans, were disseminated throughout the nation to reshape societal values and attitudes. PLA heroes and their diaries became key material in the campaign. The symbols, such as "self-sacrifice," "determination will prevail," and "primacy of politics," were closely related to Mao's policies for developing China.[27]

In 1965, politization of the military reached its peak with the abolition of ranks and insignia for the PLA. This symbolized the PLA's return to its guerrilla image of a "proletarian army" of the masses waging class struggle under the firm control of the Mao-Lin faction of the party. The political and ideological work in the military was emphasized as the only way for the party to control governmental bureaucracies. Military officers increasingly were assigned positions of importance in the administrative agencies of the party and government.[28] These developments made it fairly clear to the rest of the Chinese society that it was the military, not the regular party under Liu Shaoqi and others opposed to Mao's concepts of reliance on politics, that was in control. It was also clear that Mao's and Lin's strategy of "people's war," with its emphasis on reliance on the human factor and guerrilla tactics, was to be used in any possible confrontation with the United States in Indo-China. The strategy had been elaborated to include a plan for China's survival in the event of nuclear war.[29] The acceptance of the strategy for people's war served as the basis for purging those senior PLA officers who advocated military professionalism and modernization. The stage was set for Mao, then a minority voice within the party, to mount a concerted attack against the bureaucratic party establishment, in the form of the Cultural Revolution.

The PLA in the Cultural Revolution, 1967–1969

At the initial stage of the Cultural Revolution from April to December of 1966, it was not the intention to directly involve the military in the Cultural Revolution. Throughout the early stage of the Cultural Revolution, the major actors at the center invoked the military's power, prestige, and authority only to provide a powerful backing on the side of the radicalized students against the established party apparatus. The initial role of the military was essentially to present guidelines and to identify targets for the attack. At this initial phase, the military's own newspaper, *The Liberation Army Daily,* became the authoritative source of messages concerning the course of the upheaval. The military also provided, at this initial phase, the logistic support for the students who were moving *en masse* all over China to gain revolutionary experience by revolting against the party apparatus. The logistic support included the use of military vehicles for transportation and army barracks for lodging.

The occasion for the PLA to intervene in the Cultural Revolution came in the early part of 1967 with the widespread breakdown of party and state authority, which resulted in bloodshed and disorder, for, in January 1967, the Cultural Revolution had transformed into a gigantic onslaught on the party's machinery. The call for the PLA to intervene in the Cultural Revolution resulted primarily from rising resistance to the seizure of established party and government apparatus by revolutionary rebel groups. In many instances the struggle for power involved rival groups and contending factions within the ranks of the revolutionary masses. The intervention of the PLA thus served two interrelated purposes: to restore law and order and to throw the army's weight behind the Maoist radicals. The latter meant, in essence, the PLA's entry into a factional struggle within the party. Once the local PLA commander decided to intervene, the action of the PLA, in the form of armed suppression, was swift and decisive. Incidents of brutal suppression of the Red Guard groups became common, and February to May 1967 was a period of bloody armed struggle in all parts of China.

PLA and the Red Guards. From the outset of its intervention in the Cultural Revolution, the PLA acted too swiftly and alienated a large segment of the Red Guard groups. The PLA commands in many localities certainly exhibited strength as well as a large amount of arrogance in carrying out their role. The tough attitude of the PLA gave the various contending factions a pretext for organized resistance. Less than a week after the general order was made for the PLA to intervene in the local power struggle, the Military Affairs Committee, on January 28, 1967, had to issue orders to restrain the assertiveness and initiative of the PLA. The Military Affairs Committee urged the troops to resolutely support the "genuine" revolutionary rebel groups—the Red Guards— without giving specific instruction as how to identify a genuine revolutionary rebel group. It warned the troops not to arrest anyone without specific orders, not to confiscate properties or mete out physical punishment indiscriminately. The Military Affairs Committee directive also revealed the existence of open attacks by the Red Guard groups upon PLA units.[30] These attacks on military organizations and public security agencies were widespread in February and March 1967.[31] In many of these incidents, the PLA, in the name of maintaining law and order, opened fire on the unruly groups and made arrests. In Jinan the PLA declared some ten Red Guards organizations, made up of workers, as counterrevolutionary and thus disbanded them. When the workers who belonged to these organizations resisted, they were arrested or were beaten up by the PLA troops. Thousands more were imprisoned in buildings commandeered by the PLA in many cities.[32]

A great deal of the PLA's problem with the Red Guard groups stemmed from the inability of the PLA commands in these local situations to distinguish which faction was the genuine revolutionary left. The moment the PLA recognized one faction in the power seizure, it was immediately attacked by the other faction or factions. In self-defense, the PLA in many of these situations used force to suppress other factions.

As complaints and criticisms arose as a result of the PLA intervention, orders were issued on April 6 by the Military Affairs Committee for the military in the provinces to curb the use of force in restoring order. Violent behavior of the contending Red Guard groups reached such an uncontrollable state, abetted by the restrictive April 6 order, that a new order had to be issued on June 6 to restore law and order in the provinces. The June 6 order, issued jointly by the Military Affairs Committee, the State Council, and the Cultural Revolution Group, revealed the extent of the chaos throughout the country. PLA troops stationed in the provinces were authorized 1. to arrest and punish, according to law, any individual or group that committed actions of looting, pillaging, or destroying of public documents or property and 2. to prevent any unauthorized arrests and assaults. Nowhere in the text of the directive was the PLA specifically given authority to use force to compel violators to comply with the directive.[33]

The June 6 order placed the PLA in an extremely vulnerable position. On one hand, there was the nationwide appeal for "struggle by reason and persuasion," reinforced by the April 6 order which restricted PLA action in cases of in-fighting between and among the factions. On the other hand, armed clashes and other disorderly conduct had to be controlled if not suppressed by force. The responsibility for restoring order and maintaining discipline among the Red Guard groups rested on the PLA's shoulders, the only effective coercive instrument available. Any action taken by the PLA for the explicit purpose of carrying out the June 6 directives would have required force, which would instantly arouse hostility and resentment among the groups being suppressed. Many PLA commands simply refused to take any action under these circumstances for fear of being criticized and reprimanded. The PLA's failure to act in maintaining law and order led to an upsurge in lawlessness carried on by the various contending factions of Red Guard groups. These anarchical activities included seizing arms and equipment from PLA troops and arsenals. In many of these incidents of seizure of PLA arms and equipment, the PLA troops simply remained passive.[34] Confronted with contradictory directives, some PLA commands acted on their own, guided by their respective regional predilections. The July 20 Wuhan incident was a good case in point.

The Wuhan Incident, July 1967. Two competing factional organizations were formed to seize power in the city of Wuhan.[35] One, the General Headquarters for Proletarian Revolution in the Wuhan area, was made up largely of university students and steel workers. The other, the One Million Heroes, was composed mainly of regular government and party cadres, elements of militia, and factory workers, and had the support of the Wuhan Military District Command under Chen Jaidao and the Wuhan party apparatus. The One Million Heroes was under the leadership of cadres from the public security agencies, who had a close working relationship with the PLA stationed in Wuhan city. The One Million Heroes dominated power-seizure activities in the Wuhan area not only because of its numerical strength but also because of the support it received from the military command and the party apparatus. It frequently employed force to suppress the opposing Red Guard groups in the area. In the first few days of July, the One Million Heroes forcefully occupied the staging centers of its rival group and thus nullified the latter's activities altogether. Beijing then appealed to the Wuhan Regional Military Command for cessation of these suppressive activities, to no avail. On July 14, two emissaries, Xi Fuzhi and Wang Li of the Central Cultural Revolution Group, were flown to Wuhan with the specific instruction from Premier Zhou to settle the factional struggle on the spot. On July 19, the Wuhan Regional Military Command called a meeting, attended by representatives of the two rival mass organizations. There Wang Li presented Zhou Enlai's directive for an investigation of the Wuhan Military District Command's mistaken activities in its support of the left, and for restoration of the good reputation of the steel workers' union.

On the evening of July 20, elements of the PLA local command, with the aid of the One Million Heroes, put the two emissaries from Beijing under house arrest. Beijing's response was to mobilize swiftly available army and naval units of the centrally controlled main force mentioned earlier for a showdown. The result was the release of the two emissaries and the disbandment of the One Million Heroes. The regional PLA commander in Wuhan, Chen Jaidao, and the political commissar were relieved of their commands and were flown to Beijing for reeducation (Chen too has been rehabilitated recently).

The Wuhan incident represented an open revolt led by a powerful regional PLA commander in defiance of the Cultural Revolution and its leaders in Beijing. It also reflected, in retrospect, two basic difficulties in the PLA's intervention: the problem of identifying "genuine" revolutionary factions among the feuding Red Guards, and the close identification of provincial and district military commanders with the established local party structure. The incident also marked the beginning of intensive use of the main force, controlled by Beijing, to restore order in many localities where the regional forces failed to perform.

China Under Military Control

By September 1967, the central authorities finally realized that chaos and violence in the country could be halted only by placing the nation under military control. In addition to the need for coercive force, military control would enable provincial party apparatus to be reorganized and transformed into the new revolutionary committees.

The Military Affairs Committee was responsible for supervising the PLA main force once it had taken control of a city or a province. Initially this included 1. maintaining revolutionary discipline and protecting proletarian revolutionary groups, 2. supporting revolutionary factions within the Public Security Bureau, and 3. purging the established public security bureau of anti-revolutionary elements. Party newspapers and all broadcasting facilities were placed under PLA supervision, and the PLA was given the responsibility of supervising economic, financial, and relief activities. Nationally, military control was imposed on the country's communication and transportation systems. There was evidence that PLA officers were assigned to a number of ministries in the State Council at the government level. Senior PLA officers with managerial expertise were identified as directors or deputy directors in the State Planning Commission and in the ministries of finance, commerce, food supply, and foreign trade.[36]

By May 1968, with the active support of the PLA, twenty-four out of twenty-eight provinces and autonomous regions had established revolutionary committees based on the principle of the Three-Way Alliance in place of the old party apparatus. Special PLA units, elements of the main force, under the exclusive direction of the Military Affairs Committee at the Central Committee level, were formed with specific instructions to help the localities to complete the formation of the new revolutionary committees.

Authority for these special units of the main force was spelled out in a directive: The central forces were to act as the "representative in full authority" of the Military Affairs Committee and, as such, they were given power to supervise the local PLA units in implementing the directives of Beijing. Any resistance on the part of local PLA units to the orders, or refusal to cooperate with the special PLA units, could mean the arrest of their commanders and the disarming of their units as fighting forces. The directive was also very explicit in the authority given to the special PLA units in dealing with the revolutionary mass organizations to curb further armed struggle: Arrest and punish those leaders of the contending factions who resist the return of seized weapons and ammunition, punish severely those who continue to incite armed bloodshed, return fire on those who continue to incite the masses to attack the PLA, bring the conflicting leaders together for negotiation in order to achieve "Great Unity," and finally, perform educational and propaganda work among these Red Guard groups.[37]

Ostensibly, the primary purpose of the special PLA units of the main force was to consolidate and accelerate the formation of the revolutionary Committees in the provinces and the autonomous regions. Its major objective was to serve notice to the local military commanders to cut their ties and regional predilection by lending their support to the revolutionary groups. Beijing had by now realized that in-fighting among the contending factions often was triggered by the alliance between the local PLA commands and the conservative party apparatus. The momentum for the speedy establishment of unity of all revolutionary groups was retarded by the incessant fighting. The dispatch of the special PLA units into the regional and provincial military districts could ensure not only the speedy formation of a united stand of the revolutionary group but could provide protection to the already hard-pressed groups loyal to Beijing. The immediate consequence resulting from the dispatch of the special PLA units was the speedy establishment of the revolutionary committees in the remaining provinces of Yunnan, Fujian, and the autonomous regions of Xizang and Guangxi.

MILITARY POLITICS SINCE
THE CULTURAL REVOLUTION

By the spring of 1969, when the Ninth Party Congress met, the military had been thrust into the dominant position in the provincial and municipal revolutionary committees by the Cultural Revolution. As we pointed out in Chapter 1, the revolutionary committees were temporary power structures established to reflect the alliance of the military, rehabilitated veteran party cadres, and the mass organizations, such as the Red Guard groups. The dominant position of the military is illustrated in Table 6.1. Of the twenty-nine chairmen for the provincial, autonomous regions and three centrally administered municipal revolutionary committees, twenty (sixty-eight perceht) were affiliated with the PLA either as commanders or political commissars for provincial or regional military dis-

TABLE 6.1: Military Dominance in Provincial Party Committees, 1968–1975

Position Held	PLA No.	PLA %	Party No.	Party %	Mass No.	Mass %	Total No.	Total %
			1968–1969					
Chairmanship of Provincial Revolutionary Committees	20	68%	9	32%	—	—	29	100%
Vice Chairmanship	63	34%	52	29%	66	36%	181	100%
			1970–1971					
Secretary of Provincial Party Committees	95	60%	53	34%	10	6%	158	100%
			1974–1975					
Secretary of Provincial Party Committees	74	47%	68	43%	16	10%	158	100%

Sources: For 1968–1969, the tabulation is based on James C. F. Wang, "The PLA in Communist China's Political Development" (unpublished doctoral dissertation, University of Hawaii, 1971).

For 1970–1971, the tabulation is based on Parris Chang, "The Decentralization of Political Power in China since the Cultural Revolution," paper presented at the Second Sino-American Conference on Mainland China, June 1972, pp. 6–7.

For 1974–1975, the tabulation is based on Robert A. Scalapino, "The CCP's Provincial Secretaries," Problems of Communism, vol. xxv, no. 4 (July–August 1976), 27.

tricts. Only nine (thirty-two) of these chairmen were party cadres, representing the old guard party bureaucratic power. Despite repeated pleas from Beijing that the Red Guard groups not be discriminated against, not a single Red Guard leader was ever appointed as chairman of a provincial-level revolutionary committee. Leaders of the Red Guard groups made a better showing in the vice-chairman distribution. Of the 181 known vice-chairmen for these twenty-nine revolutionary committees, sixty-six (thirty-six percent) were leaders of Red Guard groups. Sixty-three (thirty-four percent) were PLA commanders and political commissars, and fifty-two (29 percent) were veteran party cadres. Again the combined strength of the PLA and the veteran party cadres occupying the vice-chairmanship in the revolutionary committees for the provinces overwhelmed those who represented the Red Guard groups. One other fact points out vividly the influence of the PLA in the provincial revolutionary committee; eight out of thirteen PLA regional commanders (military regions of Guangzhou, Fuzhou, Shengyang, Nanjing, Wuhan, Xinjiang, Xizang, and Inner Mongolia) were concurrently serving as chairmen for the provincial revolutionary committees under their military jurisdictions. This alone demonstrated the ascendency of regional military's influence in Communist China's political development.

The dominant position of the military in the provinces continued in the 1970–1971 period of party rebuilding. Table 6.1 shows that, of some 158 party secretaries in various ranks for provincial party committees in 1971, about sixty percent were military officers from regional and provincial commands, thirty-four percent were veteran party cadres, and only six percent were leaders from the ranks of mass organizations.

The rapid expansion of military power in the provinces, and the continued dominance of the PLA in Chinese politics in general, following the conclusion of the Ninth Party Congress, became a major factor in the Lin Biao affair which came to a head in September 1971.[38] The key question raised in the Lin Biao affair was who should have control of the political system in China: a civilian party under Mao or the military under Lin Biao. The purge of Lin was a direct consequence of both the tensions which developed between the civilian party and the military as it expanded its power, and the tensions which had developed between the central military command and the regional military power base in the provinces. In the end, the powerful regional commanders opposed Lin and contributed significantly to his purge.[39] The Lin Biao affair was an important bench-mark in the party-army relations. It also meant that the rapid expansion of the military's role under Lin Biao had constituted a threat to the power and the authority of Mao and Zhou Enlai. Events of the post-Lin Biao period from 1971–1974 largely centered on restoring the party's control over the military, under Mao's 1929 dictum that "the party must command the gun." These events can be summarized as follows:

First, a massive purge was undertaken at the central command structure level, which had been the main base of Lin's support. In addition to the disappearance of some nine senior military leaders—including the chief of staff and the commanders of general logistics, the air force, and the navy—more than forty other ranking officers associated with the Lin group were purged.

Second, a movement was launched to reduce the involvement and role of the military in politics. A January 4, 1973, announcement issued by the State Council, headed by Zhou Enlai, and the party's Military Affairs Committee, headed by Zhou's close ally Marshal Ye Jianying, directed PLA units in all regions and provinces to strictly observe the policies of the party and pointedly noted that the PLA's role was primarily military rather than political. Public media stressed the need to observe military discipline and to concentrate on military affairs. Visitors to China began to see fewer military representatives on school and university campuses and in factories. Coincident with the campaign to play down the role of the military in Chinese society was the reappearance of many party veterans who had been vilified during the Cultural Revolution.

Third, some analysts of Chinese politics suggest that there was also a deliberate attempt by Mao and Zhou Enlai to reduce the influence of the military in the decision-making process both at the national level and at the regional and provincial levels.[40] As shown in Table 6.1, members of the military serving as party secretaries in the provinces declined from ninety-five (sixty percent) in the 1970–1971 period to seventy-four (forty-seven percent) in the 1974–1975 period. The most dramatic decline in military participation in the political process came at the powerful Politburo level. In 1969, the twenty-five-member Politburo included thirteen PLA senior officers, or sixty-three percent of the membership. In 1973, the twenty-one-member Politburo included only seven PLA senior officers, or thirty-three percent of the membership. Military representation on the Central Committee declined less drastically, from forty-three percent of the full members on the Ninth Central Committee in 1969 to approximately thirty-two percent on the Tenth and Eleventh Central Committees. Interestingly, while PLA regional or provincial commanders concurrently holding the post of provincial party secretary decreased from fourteen to eight during the post-Lin period, their representation on the Central Committee remained fairly stable, as shown in Table 6.2. This continued high participation rate in the Central Committee, by the military commanders and political commissars for the regional and provincial commands, apparently reflects their continuing importance in the Chinese political power structure.

The Tenth Party Congress of August 1973 not only officially disposed of the Lin Biao affair but approved the formation of a new power structure based on the coalition of the forces under Premier Zhou and those following the party ideologues Jiang Qing, Zhang Chunqiao, Yao Wenyuan, and the new rising star, Wang Hungwen, who was elected vice-chairman of the CCP. The new power structure of the coalition clearly revealed the ascendency of Zhou and his veteran party cadres, who in the aftermath of the dominance exercised by Lin Biao had received support from the majority of regional and provincial military commanders and political commissars. For the first time in decades, the new coalition was in a position in 1974 to make shifts in the personnel of the regional and provincial military commands: seven of the eleven commanders of the military regions were transferred or swapped posts. Ellis Joffe has pointed out several significant inferences that can be drawn from the reshuffling of the regional military commanders, many of whom concurrently held the position of first party secretary for a province. First, the removal of these military commanders from their bases of operations, some held since the early 1950s, immeasurably strengthened the center's control over the provinces. Second, the successful removal of the officers revealed their military discipline and their commitment to the center.[41]

TABLE 6.2: PLA Regional and Provincial Commanders and Political Commissars on the 9th–11th Central Committees by Military Regions

Number of Full Members on
Central Committees:

Military Regions	PLA Commanders			PLA Commissars		
	9th	10th	11th	9th	10th	11th
1. Guangzhou	3	2	1	3	2	5
2. Chengdu	1	1	1	2	3	1
3. Fuzhou	2	1	—	2	1	3
4. Kumming	1	3	2	2	1	2
5. Lanzhou	1	1	1	5	3	5
6. Shengyang	2	2	3	3	3	2
7. Nanjing	1	2	2	4	5	5
8. Beijing	2	1	1	5	3	7
9. Wuhan	2	1	1	2	3	3
10. Xinjiang	2	1	2	—	1	2
11. Xizang	—	—	—	1	1	2
12. Inner Mongolia	1	1	1	1	1	—
13. Jinan	—	1	1	2	—	2
	18	17	16	32	27	39

Source: From lists provided in Peking Review, 14 (April 4, 1969), 9: Peking Review, 35 and 36 (September 7, 1973), 9–10; and Peking Review, 35 (August 26, 1977), 14–16.

The coalition of the new power structure formed in 1973 proved to be temporary and in many ways illusory. The heart of the new power structure was the veteran party administrators, reinforced by the key military figures brought to the center by Zhou. The weakest element of the coalition was the party's radical ideologues, the Gang of Four, who had tried unsuccessfully to organize the urban militia as a countervailing force to the PLA.

This brief study on the Chinese military's role in politics clearly shows that the PLA has emerged as a major force in the party and government. Approximately thirty-one percent of the regular members on the Eleventh Central Committee of the party, elected in 1977, are representatives of the PLA. Of the sixty-two PLA representatives on the Eleventh Central Committee, fifty-five, or twenty-seven percent, are active PLA commanders and political commissars from the regional military commands. When this twenty-seven percent representation of PLA members stationed in the provinces is added to the forty percent representing provincial party secretaries of various ranks, it becomes evident that the provinces have a formidable voice in the highest decision-making council, the Central Committee.

MILITARY MODERNIZATION

The increased influence of the military at the central decision-making level inevitably revived and strengthened the PLA's demand for military professionalism and modernization. This demand most likely became more urgent after 1969, as Sino-Soviet relations deteriorated and border incidents increased. After almost twenty years of debate and neglect, the new Chinese leadership has come out squarely on the side of military modernization. In an all-army political works conference, Hua Guofeng stated that "our army must speed the improvement of its weapons and equipment and raise its tactical and technical level."[42] By this, Hua meant the acquisition of modern arms and equipment, including missiles and nuclear weapons. Marshal Ye Jianying pointed out at the same conference that "a modern war will be more ruthless and more intense than past wars" and that the Chinese military establishment must devote its efforts for "more proficient techniques and tactics, military skills, and commandership."[43]

The Chinese realize that at the foundation of military modernization is the rapid development of heavy industries, as well as research in science and technology, which takes time. To fill the large deficiencies which exist in their technology, the Chinese have embarked on an ambitious program of weapons purchase from abroad. Chinese military missions, headed by senior military officers, most of whom were vilified for advocating military professionalism during the Cultural Revolution, have shopped around in England, France, and West Germany for possible purchase of the latest weapons: tanks, anti-tank missiles, fighter planes, and helicopters. While the United States has remained opposed to sales of sophisticated modern weapons to the Chinese, it tacitly has given approval to its allies in Western Europe to sell such weapons to China.[44] The Chinese strategy may involve studying the mechanisms of the sophisticated modern weaponry purchased in limited quantities from the West, as a means of acquiring the needed weapon-making technology. This would be more beneficial for military modernization from a long-term point of view, and it would be less costly than massive purchases of the available modern weapons. It has been pointed out that if the Chinese were to purchase a sufficient number of modern battle tanks with all the service support equipment, in terms of rangefinders, ballistic computers, and combat carriers, it would cost from five to seven billion dollars, an amount most likely prohibitive.[45] While the long-range goal is a modernized military, the Chinese military leaders recognize that the old military doctrine of people's war, or guerrilla warfare, must remain a basic ingredient in their war preparedness plans for some time to come.[46] But China's month-long military action in Vietnam in the spring of 1979 may alter that military approach, for the pace of China's invasion was rather slow and casualty was high, 20,000 killed and wounded. China's invasion in Vietnam showed that its military lacked mobility which was the result of not having enough armored vehicles for combat purpose.[47] Thus the Chinese military will have to compete with other industries in China for priority in modernization.

NOTES

[1]See William Whitson, "The Field Army in Chinese Communist Military Politics," *The China Quarterly*, 37 (January–March 1969), 1–30, and Jurgen Domes, *The Internal Politics of China, 1949–1972*, (New York: Holt, Rinehart & Winston, 1973), pp. 21–26.

[2]John Gittings, *The Role of the Chinese Army* (London: Oxford University Press, 1967).

[3]Whitson, "The Field Army in Chinese Communist Military Politics," p. 7.

[4]Whitson, "The Field Army in Chinese Communist Military Politics," pp. 2–26. Also see Y. C. Chang, *Factionalism and Coalition Politics in China: The Cultural Revolution and Its Aftermath*, (New York, Praeger Publishers, 1976), p. 77.

[5]William L. Parish, Jr., "Factions in Chinese Military Politics," *The China Quarterly*, 56 (October–December 1973), 667—99 and Harvey W. Nelson, "Military Forces in the Cultural Revolution," *The China Quarterly*, 51 (July–September 1972), 444–474.

[6]See James C.F. Wang, "The Urban Militia as a Political Instrument in the Power Contest in China in 1976," *Asian Survey*, vol. xviii, no. 6 (June 1978), 541–45.

[7]Gittings, *The Role of the Chinese Army* pp. 201–24.

[8]Gittings, *The Role of the Chinese Army*, pp. 201–24.

[9]Gittings, *The Role of the Chinese Army*, pp. 201–24.

[10]Gittings, *The Role of the Chinese Army*, pp. 201–24.

[11]*Renmin Ribao*, March 17, 1969, p. 1.

[12]Philip Bridgham, "Mao's Cultural Revolution: The Struggle to Consolidate Power," *The China Quarterly*, 41, (January–March 1970), 1; Parris Chang, "Changing Patterns of Military Roles in Chinese Politics," in ed. William Whitson, *The Military and Political Power in China in the 1970s* (New York: Holt, Rinehart & Winston, 1972), pp. 47–70; Jurgen Domes, "The Cultural Revolution and the Army," *Asian Survey*, vol. viii, no. 5 (May 1968), 349–63; John Gittings, "Reversing the PLA Verdicts," *Far Eastern Economic Review*, 30 (July 25, 1968), 191–93; Ellis Joffee, "The Chinese Army in the Cultural Revolution: The Politics of Intervention," *Current Scene*, vol. viii, no. 18 (December 7, 1970), 1–25; Ellis Joffee, "The Chinese Army after the Cultural Revolution: the Effects of Intervention," *The China Quar-

terly, 55 (July–September, 1973), 450–77; Thomas Jay Matthews, "The Cultural Revolution in Szechwan," in *The Cultural Revolution in the Provinces,* Harvard East Asian Monographs, no. 42 (Cambridge, Mass.: Harvard University Press, 1971), pp. 94–146; Margie Sargent, "The Cultural Revolution in Heilungkiang," ibid., pp. 16–65; Vivienne B. Shue, "Shanghai After the January Storm," ibid., pp. 66–93; Harvey Nelsen, "Military Forces in the Cultural Revolution," *The China Quarterly,* 51, (July–September, 1972), 448–50; Ralph Powell, "The Party, the Government, and the Gun," *Asian Survey,* vol. x, no. 6 (June 1970), 441–71; William Whitson, *The Chinese Communist High Command: A History of Military Politics, 1927–69* (New York: Holt, Rinehart & Winston, 1971).

[13]*Renmin Ribao,* March 29, 1969, p. 2.

[14]Chiang Ye-shang, "Military Affairs for 1970," *The China Monthly,* 82 (January 1971), 11–12.

[15]Based on monitored provincial broadcast. See *Chung-kung yen-chiu (Studies on Chinese Communism),* vol. 6, no. 1 (January 1973), 40–41.

[16]See "Failure of 'Gang of Four's' Scheme to Set Up a 'Second Armed Forces,'" *Peking Review,* 13 (March 25, 1977), 10–12; and "'Gang of Four's' Abortive Counter-Revolutionary Coup," *Peking Review,* 25 (June 17, 1977), 22–25. Also see Wang, "The Urban Militia as a Political Instrument," pp. 545–59.

[17]"Failure of 'Gang of Four's' Scheme to Set Up a 'Second Armed Forces,'" pp. 10–12; "'Gang of Four's' Abortive Counter-Revolutionary Coup," pp. 22–25 and Wang, "The Urban Military as a Political Instrument," pp. 545–59.

[18]Nieh Jung-chen, "The Militia's Role in a Future War," *Peking Review,* 35 (September 1, 1978), 16–19.

[19]Martin Wilbur, "Military Separatism and the Process of Reunification under the Nationalist Regime, 1922–1937," In *China in Crisis,* vol. 1, b. 1, eds. Ho Pi-ting and Tang Tsou (Chicago: University of Chicago, 1968), p. 203.

[20]Wilbur, "Military Separatism and the Process of Reunification," p. 203.

[21]Wilbur, "Military Separatism and the Process of Reunification," p. 203.

[22]Treadgold, *Soviet and Chinese Communism: Similarities and Differences,* p. 25.

[23]Robert C. Tucker, "On the Contemporary Study of Communism," *World Politics,* vol. xix, no. 2 (January 1967), 242–57.

[24]Parris Chang, "Changing Patterns of Military Roles in Chinese Politics," in *The Military and Political Power in China in the 1970s,* ed. William Whitson (New York: Holt, Rinehart & Winston, 1972), p. 48.

[25]See Alice Langley Hsieh, *Communist China's Strategy in the Nuclear Era* (Englewood Cliffs, N.J.: Prentice-Hall, Inc., 1962).

[26]See Chalmers Johnson, "Lin Piao's Army and Its Role in Chinese Society," *Current Scene,* vol. iv, no. 13 (July 1, 1966), 1–10, and no. 14 (July 15, 1966), 1–11. Also see Ralph L. Powell, "The Increasing Power in Lin Piao and the Party-Soldiers 1959–1966," *The China Quarterly,* 34 (April–June, 1968), 38–65; and Ellis Joffe, "The Chinese Army Under Lin Piao: Prelude to Political Intervention," in *China: Management of a Revolutionary Society,* ed. John M.H. Lindbeck (Seattle, Wash. and London: University of Washington Press, 1971), pp. 343–74.

[27]See Mary Sheridan, "The Emulation of Heroes," *The China Quarterly,* 33 (January–March 1965), 47–72 and James C.F. Wang, "Values of the Cultural Revolution," *Journal of Communication,* vol. 27, no. 3 (Summer 1977), 41–46.

[28]Ralph L. Powell, "The Increasing Power of Lin Piao and the Party-Soldiers 1959–1966," *The China Quarterly*, no. 34 (April–June 1968), 38–65.

[29]See Lin Biao, "Long Live the Victory of People's War," *Peking Review*, no. 32 (August 4, 1967), 14–39.

[30]"Military Order Defines PLA Activities in the Cultural Revolution," *Samples of Red Guard Publications*, vol. II (U.S. Department of Commerce, Joint Publications Research), August 8, 1967.

[31]"Military Order Defines PLA Activities in the Cultural Revolution."

[32]"Comrade Hsieh Fu-chih's Speech on April 20 to the Peking Revolutionary Committee," *Hongqi (The Red Flag)*, 61 (May 6, 1967), 19–20.

[33]"Immediately Cease Physical Violence," *Renmin Ribao*, editorial (May 22, 1967), p. 1.

[34]See summary of Chiang Ching's speech on September 5 to representatives from Anhwei Province in *Renmin Ribao*, (September 17, 1967), p. 1.

[35]See Thomas W. Robinson, "The Wuhan Incident: Local Strife and Provincial Rebellion during the Cultural Revolution," *The China Quarterly*, 47 (July–September 1971), 413–38; and Deborath S. Davis, "The Cultural Revolution in Wuhan," in *The Cultural Revolution in the Provinces*, pp. 147–70.

[36]*Renmin Ribao*, September 3, 1967, p. 1.

[37]"Directive of the Central Committee, the State Council, Military Affairs Committee, and the Cultural Revolutionary Group Concerning the Dispatch of Central Support the Left Units to Regional and Provincial Military Districts," *Studies on Chinese Communism*, vol. II, no. 8 (August 31, 1968), 109–17; and *Renmin Ribao* (September 7, 1968), pp. 1–4.

[38]See Y.M. Kau, *The Lin Piao Affairs: Power Politics and Military Coup* (White Plains, N.Y.: International Arts and Sciences Press, 1975) pp. *xxxi–xxviii;* Ellis Joffe, "The Chinese Army after the Cultural Revolution," pp. 468–77; and Parris Chang, "The Changing Patterns of Military Participation in Chinese Politics," *ORBIS*, vol. xvi, no. 3 (Fall 1972), 797–800.

[39]Ellis Joffe, "The Chinese Army after the Cultural Revolution," pp. 450–77. For the account of Lin Piao's crash, see Cheng Huan, "The Killing of Comrade Lin Piao," *Far Eastern Economic Review*, July 22, 1972, pp. 11–12; *The New York Times*, July 23, 1972, pp. 1, 16. For the official version, see Chou En-lai, "Report to the Tenth National Congress of the Communist Party of China" *Peking Review*, nos. 35 and 36 (September 7, 1973), p. 18. Also see Philip Bridgham, "The Fall of Lin Piao" in *The China Quarterly*, 55 (July–September, 1973), 427–49; Ying-mao Kau and Pierre M. Perrolle, "The Politics of Lin Piao's Abortive Military Coup," *Asian Survey*, vol. xiv, no. 6 (June 1974), 558–77; and Ying-mao Kau, *The Lin Piao Affair*, pp. xix-li.

[40]See Parris Chang, "China's Military," *Current History*, 67, 397 (September 1974), 101–105; Ellis Joffe, "The PLA in Internal Politics," *Problems of Communism*, vol. xxiv, no. 6 (November–December 1975), 1–12.

[41]Ellis Joffe, "The PLA in the Internal Politics," p. 12.

[42]"Chairman Hua's Speech at All-Army Political Work Conference," *Peking Review*, 24 (June 16, 1978), 10.

[43]"Vice-Chairman Yeh Chien-ying's Speech," *Peking Review*, 25 (June 23, 1978), 12; Also *Peking Review*, 32 (August 5, 1977), 14.

[44]*The New York Times*, May 18, 1978, p. A-6.

[45]Edward N. Lutwak," Problems of Military Modernization for Mainland China," *Issues and Studies,* vol. xiv, no. 7 (July 1978), 58.

[46]Hsu Hsiang-chen, "Heighten Our Vigilance and Get Prepared to Fight a War," *Peking Review,* 32 (August 11, 1978), 8–11.

[47]For an assessment of Chinese military invasion in Vietnam, see Drew Middleton, "China's Lack of Mobility," New York Times News Service feature reprinted in *Honolulu Star Bulletin*; March 9, 1979, A-17.

Mass Participation and Political Action -- Chinese Style

7

One of the most dramatic and sometimes frightening aspects of the contemporary Chinese political scene is the participation of millions of people in mass campaigns, waged periodically by the regime for a variety of purposes—from the eradication of pests to land reform, to socialist education, and, finally, to the Cultural Revolution. There were more than seventy-four mass campaigns waged on the national level from 1950 to 1978, and perhaps a third of that number waged locally over the same period. The average length of these mass campaigns has been between seventeen and eighteen months.[1] In addition to these mass campaigns, which generally engulf the entire populace, rural peasants and urban residents have been required to regularly participate in some sort of conscious political activity—usually as participating members of "small groups,"[2] the organizational device used to assure active participation by ordinary citizens in political action. The basic purpose of the extraordinary stress upon active mass participation and periodic mass campaigns has been to inculcate new values and to induce correct attitudinal and behavioral patterns essential for making political, social, and economic changes to build a socialist society.

Before we take up such pertinent topics as the extent and manner of mass participation and the style, techniques, and significance of mass campaigns, a few words must be said about the Chinese masses.

The Chinese population was estimated at eight hundred million in the mid-1960s, with a projected two percent per annum growth rate.[3] This translates into an annual increase of approximately sixteen million people to the already enormous population. Based on this projection, there is no question that by the 1980s, China's total population will have reached one billion. The State Statistical Bureau announced in June 1979 a population of 975 million. Since only a small percentage of this total population are party members or cadres, the term *masses* refers to more than ninety percent of the people. Roughly eighty percent of the masses live in the countryside as toiling peasants, and the remaining twenty percent reside in the cities. Although China has a land area as large as that of the United States (about 3.7 million square miles), most of China's huge population is concentrated along the valleys of the two major river basins, the Huanghe and the Changjiang, and their tributaries. About eighty-five percent of the land area is hilly or mountainous and is sparsely populated.

Great strides have been made since 1949 in raising the literacy rate in China. At present, the literacy rate for adults is about fifty percent, with a higher rate for those who live in urban areas.[4] Adult education, with political education as its main content, has contributed to the gradual reduction of illiteracy among the adults in China over the past three decades. While local dialects were a serious barrier to effective political communication before 1949, adults below the age of forty-five today can converse effectively in the standard spoken language known as "Putonghua." It is a common sight for visitors to China to see the simplified Chinese written characters alongside the romanization, for standard uniform pronunciation in schools in various regions of China. The Chinese masses, both rural and urban, are constantly being exposed to the networks of the political communication system: controlled mass media in the form of newspapers, radio broadcasts, and wall posters; the organization units to which the masses in one way or another become attached; and the "small group," or "xiaozu," into which the masses have been organized and through which mass mobilization efforts are achieved. Aspects of the political communication system and the impact on mass participation and mobilization will be discussed later in this chapter.

In Chapter 2, we discussed in detail the meaning and significance of mass line in the thought of Mao. We may summarize the concept of Mao's mass line as a process by which the leaders (cadres) and the people (masses) establish a close relationship: the cadres attempt to learn the aspirations, doubts, and problems of the masses; the leaders then present ideas to solve a particular problem to the masses, and seek unanimous or majority agreement about the solution. In essence, the mass line concept, as applied in practice, is a process of "mutual education of leaders and led," by which unity among the masses is achieved on a given issue, and through which the masses can lend their overwhelming support by participating in the implementation of the decision.[5] Thus, participation in Chinese politics involves three sets of actors—the top leadership at the Politburo level, the cadres in the middle level, and the masses at the bottom—and a host of actions, which include listening, learning, reacting, summing up, interpreting or reinterpreting changing attitudes, and decision making.

It must be obvious by now that, unlike political participation in the United States, where there is a wide variation in the degree of political involvement by the American people in various socio-economic levels,[6] a vast majority of Chinese citizens must become involved in a variety of participatory modes, particularly those of a legal and formal nature, which include a great deal of ritual content. It is somewhat erroneous to assume that the vast majority of Chinese who participate in formal and legal political activities are automatically classified as activists. Chairman Mao once said that more than sixty percent of the populace must be considered fence-sitting middle-of-the-roaders, and only about twenty percent, as progressives or activists.[7] One recent study, based on responses of refugees from mainland China on frequency of political participation by mode, indicated that although a majority of Chinese do participate in various forms of political activities, their sincerity in participation varies with the mode: the more formal the mode of participation, the less the sincerity there is on the part of the participants.[8] While recognizing that there are most likely varying levels of sincerity of participation, the regime's institutionalization of mass participation in politics and in decision making has been highly successful, especially when one considers the enormous size of China's population. Let us now turn to the fundamental question: In what ways do the Chinese masses participate in politics?

FORMS OF PARTICIPATION IN CHINA

There are a variety of ways the Chinese masses participate in the "democratic management" of their political life. Mao's concept of mass line has been enshrined in the 1978 state constitution, promulgated by the Fifth National People's Congress. The constitution states, "All organs of the state must constantly maintain close contact with the masses of the people, rely on them, heed their opinions, be concerned for their weal and woe . . ."[9]

Elections and Voting

While voting in elections may be the single most important act of citizen participation in Western democracies, it is only one form of legally approved political action for the people of China. The election process in China also differs from that in Western democracies in several crucial respects.

First, the CCP manages the electoral process at all levels. Most important is the CCP control of the election committees, which prepare approved slates of candidates for all elective offices, from the national to the basic level. These slates present only one candidate for each office and thus determine the outcome of the election. The election process among the masses, therefore, is used primarily as a vehicle to arouse interest and heighten the political consciousness among the people.

Second, as we have noted, all elections above the basic level are indirect. At the basic level, the people elect the people's congress. Basic level congresses elect the county level congresses, which in turn elect the provincial congresses. The provincial congresses then elect the National People's Congress. There is no breakdown of how many national deputies each provincial people's congress was allowed to elect, even though the total number of deputies who met in March 1978 for the Fifth National People's Congress to adopt the new state constitution was 3,497. In compiling the number of deputies to the provincial people's congresses, as reported in the governmental controlled media, we arrive at the total of 28,709 deputies who met in their respective provinces or autonomous regions. Based on the reports from twenty-five provinces and autonomous regions, it averaged 1,148 deputies for each province.[10]

Third, while the frequency of elections is prescribed by law, the legal schedule seldom has been followed in practice. There have been eight local elections since the founding of the People's Republic: 1953–1954, 1956–1957, 1958, 1961, 1963, 1966, and 1978. Both the 1953–1954 and the 1956 elections had a respectable eighty-six percent voter turnout, somewhat below the usual turnout of over ninety percent for most communist countries.[11] Unfortunately, we have no information about the local elections after 1956.[12] But if the post Mao trend toward socialistic democracy continues, some form of free and direct local elections may be instituted by the NPC at the lower levels.

It should be noted that direct election of team leaders at the production team level, the lowest accounting and administrative unit in a rural commune, is more meaningful. At this level, voting takes place at regular intervals to elect cadres for the production team. Even though the slate of cadres to be elected by the team members must be approved by the brigade, the very process of election provides the team members a significant opportunity to participate in selecting their leaders and, on some occasions, in articulating the resolution of issues.[13]

Mass Organizations

In China, literally hundreds of millions of people daily participate in politics as members of a myriad of "mass organizations." These mass organizations have been described as the "organizational matrix" of the party's rule over the masses.[14] They serve not only as institutions for political education but also as what Lenin termed the "transmission belt" for party policy. They are used as vehicles to gain support for policies and to mobilize the masses for implementing policies. The enormous membership and widespread extension of the networks from these mass organizations assure participation in political action by millions of adults and youths. All of these mass organizations are formed on the basis of special interest or occupation and serve as "bridges and links" between the party and the masses.[15] The four largest and most active mass organizations—the Communist Youth League, the All-China Federation of Trade Unions, the All-China Women's Federation, and the peasants' associations—have been reactivated, following disruption during the Cultural Revolution. All held national congresses in the fall of 1978.[16]

The Communist Youth League (CYL) of China reported a membership of over forty-eight million in 1978 under a new leadership approved by the party. With the disbanding of the Red Guard organizations for secondary school students in November 1978, the CYL can be expected to increase in size and importance. In the past, the CYL has served as a vast reservoir for new party members, and has provided political and ideological education for China's youth. Many of the party's leaders have come up from the ranks of the CYL.

The All-China Federation of Trade Unions, an important mass organization in industrial centers, was most active prior to the Cultural Revolution. The upheaval disrupted the functioning of this workers' mass organization to such an extent that by January 1967 it was dissolved at both the national and the local levels. Many of the union leaders were purged by the Red Guards and were charged with being followers of the Liu Shaoqi line, being opposed to the class struggle, and placing emphasis on expertise in production.[17] From 1967 to 1973, workers were organized into revolutionary workers' congresses, dominated at the national level by radicals, such as Wang Hungwen and Ni Zhifu, who later lent his support to Hua Guofeng. For the period from 1973 to the arrest of the Gang of Four in October 1976, trade-union committees in factories functioned as adjuncts of the factory revolutionary committees. These trade union committees were primarily responsible for political education of the workers and supervision of social insurance, welfare, and factory safety measures.[18] Whatever the current organizational structure, workers in factories frequently meet and actively participate in mass action, particularly with regard to production efficiency: "to lower costs, to raise productivity, to stimulate innovation and new design, to develop aspects of decision making, to improve proletarian work style."[19] In an address to the Ninth National Trade Union Congress in October 1978, Politburo members Deng Xiaoping and Ni Zhifu urged the delegates to support the party's program for modernization and labor discipline and to observe the return to the system of decision making by the factory managers.[20]

The All-China Women's Federation once had a membership of close to one hundred million but ceased to function as a mass organization in 1967, during the Cultural Revolution. The women's federation's basic function has been to mobilize women in support of the various programs initiated by the party. Since women "shouldered half the sky," as the Chinese are fond of saying, this mass organization played an important role in the past in helping to obtain support for party programs and policies and in providing political education for its vast membership. The reactivated All-China Women's Federation selected the following items for its new program: promoting equal pay for equal work, with proper attention to conditions peculiar to women, such as pregnancies and maternity leaves; turning "petty housekeeping" into productive work and providing more time for rest and recreation; developing better educational care for the children, and supporting family planning and planned population growth; and developing friendly contacts with women of other countries.[21]

We must also mention the peasant association as another important mass organization. After inactivity during the 1950s, the peasants' associations were reestablished in 1963 to serve as watch dog agencies to oversee the work performance and to monitor the behavior of the cadres, many of whom had engaged in anti-socialist actions during the early 1960s, such as "eating too much or owning too much, extravagance and waste, nepotism, corruption, theft, and destruction of public property."[22] Under a June 1964 regulation, the peasants' associations were asked to participate in a host of governmental activities: public security surveillance over counterrevolutionary activities, propaganda and educational work among the people, administrative consultation on commune policies prior to implementing any decisions by the cadres. Since the Cultural Revolution, the party branch at the basic levels of rural communes has controlled and manipulated the mass organizations, such as the peasants' associations, the All-China Women's Federation, and the Communist Youth League. It is not uncommon on rural communes today to find the leader of the brigade concurrently serving as the party branch secretary and as the leader of the revolutionary committee. Many of the watch dog functions formerly assigned to the peasants' associations have been undertaken by the revolutionary committees at the brigade level. Further changes in mass participation on rural communes can be expected as various institutions evolve and as further experimentation takes place.

Urban residents are organized into resident groups, the lowest level of mass organization for the urban areas. As pointed out in Chapter 5, the resident group is made up of from fifteen to forty households. A small group of household representatives discusses and resolves neighborhood problems, such as housing, social welfare, sanitation, marriage, and birth control.[23] A primary function of the resident group is political education of members living in the area. Thus, the resident groups in urban areas serve as instruments both for participatory democracy and for mass mobilization. They are comparable to production teams or brigades in rural communes.

Small Study Groups

No discussion of mass participation in China is adequate without a close examination of the small group.[24] Across China, cadres in offices, workers in factories, peasants in communes, students in schools, soldiers in the armed forces, and residents in neighborhood and street committees are organized in small groups, known as the "xiaozu." Usually the groups are formed from the members of the lowest organizational unit in factories, offices, and communes.[25] Frequently, an entire class in a school, even at the primary level, becomes a small group.[26] It is a common practice to have representatives of the mass organizations, such as the peasants' association, the trade union, or the Communist Youth League, work with the party committee at the lowest unit to organize these small groups.

The most important activity of the small groups is political study. In conversation with a small study group in a May Seventh cadre school near Beijing, which I visited in 1973, it was pointed out that political study for the group began with each member studying the works of Marx, Engels, and Mao on their own.[27] Sometimes they were asked to study an important editorial or special article from the *People's Daily*. A leader was generally assigned to the study group to answer questions about the reading content. Next, the group studied collectively, both engaging in group discussion and questioning each other's understanding of the reading material. Toward the end of the group's collective study, the group leader entered into the discussion by pointing out the important theoretical points and how they related to correct thinking and behavior or simply the correct revolutionary line. After grasping the correct line, members of the group engaged in self-criticism for the purpose of making the necessary changes in their thinking and behavioral patterns. I was told that, during the self-criticism stage, unity would be reached by all members of the group on the meaning of the readings for their daily lives. In addition to political studies, small groups engage in problem solving for work units. Empirical studies, using refugees as informants, have indicated problems in the execution of small group dynamics and have raised questions about the quality and sincerity of the members' participation.[28] Boredom, disinterest, and deliberate reticence during group discussions seemed too common in many office and factory units and in production brigades in the communes.

What can be said about the effects of small groups as an organizational technique in terms of implementing Mao's concept of mass line? First, there is no question, as James Townsend has pointed out, that the small group has permitted personal participation in politics and thus made it real and meaningful.[29] Second, it is a very effective device for social control. Whyte employs a term, the "encapsulation" of the people, to describe how deviant behavior can be identified and corrected through mutual self-criticism and peer pressure.[30] The control that the regime exercises over its disciplined populace on the whole must be attributed to the workings of the small groups. Third, it is a vehicle through which the party's directives and policies can be effectively communicated to the masses and can receive the necessary support for implementation. Fourth, it is through discussion, self-criticism, and self-evaluation that Chinese masses are becoming increasingly analytical, not only about their own affairs, but about politics in general.

Mass Campaigns

A mass campaign in China can be defined as a movement, conceived at the top, which encourages and promotes active participation by the masses in collective action, for the purpose of mobilizing support for or against a particular policy or program. Rarely has an important policy or program been launched without a mass campaign to support it. It is generally easy to detect the launching of a mass campaign. Since all mass campaigns require the active participation of the masses, the signal, or message, for the start of the campaign must be conveyed either in heavily couched ideological language or in "coded names" form, as Lucian Pye has described.[31] The signal is sent through newspaper editorials, or in statements made by key party leaders and displayed in newspaper headlines. First, an important speech, made by a key leader, accompanied by an editorial highlighting the major themes, is disseminated. Soon slogans capsulating the key ideas of the campaign, as outlined in the published speech or editorial, appear in the masthead of newspapers, on walls, and on banners in communes and factories. These articles and editorials become a basic source material for small group discussion and study. During the Cultural Revolution, activists in universities and high schools displayed their wall posters (daizibao) to pinpoint a particular theme or target to be struggled against in a campaign. Photographic displays or exhibits illustrating key leaders' ideas also appear in prominent locations. It has become a standard practice, for instance, for the government-owned and controlled printing corporation, the Xinhua Bookstore, to display photo exhibits outside the walls of its branch stores all over China.

Next, massive public rallies and demonstrations are staged. The October 24, 1976, rally in Tian An Men Square, for the campaign to criticize the Gang of Four, drew a million people. In these campaign kick-offs, leading national, provincial, and local party and government cadres make repetitive speeches, outlining the purpose and targets for the campaign and exhorting the masses to participate and demonstrate their enthusiastic support.

Public rallies and demonstrations are followed by intensive study in small groups. The intensity of small group study varies from one basic unit to another. For instance, it is not unusual for some factories to require daily political study by small groups for half an hour to one hour during the evening. Such was the case at the beginning of the anti-Lin Biao campaign in 1972.[32] Generally speaking, small group meetings tend to become more numerous during a mass campaign. As the campaign intensifies, the small group study in various basic units also becomes tense, particularly when the stage of criticism and self-criticism is reached. In the early days, when the land reform program was launched and at the time of the Cultural Revolution, struggle or accusation meetings took place when campaign procedure called for attacks, mostly verbal but sometimes physical, against the "enemy." Some campaigns may call for the masses to make a sacrifice for the collective good. Sometimes the deeds of a model hero are used as examples, as in the early phases of the Cultural Revolution, when such PLA heroes as Lai Feng were used as models for emulation.[33]

From an organizational point of view, the key to the success of any mass campaign is in the cadres dispatched from the national and provincial party committees to the basic units in factories and production brigades in the communes. Work teams of these cadres were originally used during the Socialist Education Campaign in 1963–1965 to conduct on-the-spot investigations of charges made against corrupt cadres in the rural areas. Once the charges were substantiated through the team's first-hand investigation among the peasants, the members of the work teams were responsible for preparing and executing mass criticism to clean up corrupt practices within the cadre ranks. Finally, the work team was to recommend punitive measures for the wrong-doers and to institute necessary changes. During the Cultural Revolution, Mao's thought propaganda teams were recruited among the PLA units and workers, primarily to mobilize the masses through discussion and study of Mao's teachings. Members of the work team in a mass campaign are campaign supervisors, whose main task is to see that the masses participate in the movement through meetings and study sessions. Millions of cadres must have been recruited in urban areas to form these work teams during the campaign to criticize the Gang of Four.

Mass campaigns have been institutionalized and have become an indispensable part of contemporary political life. The fact that there have been more than seventy campaigns waged at the national level since the founding of the republic in 1949 testifies to the frequency of their occurrence—an average of two per year. Charles Cell has classified mass campaigns into three basic groupings:[34] 1. campaigns waged on politics and economic development programs, frequently aimed at instituting basic changes; 2. ideological campaigns waged primarily to make social reforms or to induce new social values among the populace; and 3. campaigns waged to weaken or eliminate groups or individuals who were considered enemies of the people, such as landlords, counter-revolutionaries, and rightist elements. Some major mass campaigns, however, cannot readily be classified into any of these categories because of the multiplicity of themes. The Great Proletarian Cultural Revolution of 1966–1968 is such a campaign.

Wall Posters

Wall posters, as a form of political communication closely associated with mass campaigns, have become common in major urban centers in China since the days of the Cultural Revolution. The purge of Deng Xiaoping by the Politburo, at Mao's insistence, in April 1967 was preceded by a flurry of wall posters on the streets of Beijing. Most wall posters have been written and prepared with approval from higher authorities. In the days of the Cultural Revolution, information contained in the Red Guard wall posters was purposefully leaked by the members of the Central Cultural Revolution Group, dominated by radical leaders such as Jiang Qing and Chen Boda. The hundreds of poems read by demonstrators in the Tian An Men incident during April 1976 in support of Zhou Enlai, however, were spontaneous expressions—a book of six hundred poems selected from those posted at Tian An Men has been published now that the incident has been termed a "completely revolutionary action."[35] Similarly, some of the wall posters that appeared in November 1978 protesting the treatment of Deng Xiaoping in 1976 and criticizing Mao's part in Deng's removal, were also spontaneous, motivated perhaps by a concern for civil or human rights. In the final analysis, all wall poster campaigns, like all mass campaigns of the past, can be abruptly terminated when the authorities call for a halt, even though Article 45 of the 1978 constitution stipulates that Chinese citizens "have a right to speak out freely, air their views fully, hold great debates, and write big-character posters." The flurry of free expression exhibited on the "Democracy Walls" in Beijing was abruptly halted in March 1979 by the authorities on the ground that it was too excessive in critizing the leaders and the system.

MASS CAMPAIGNS SINCE
THE CULTURAL REVOLUTION

There have been at least seven major and two minor mass campaigns waged since the conclusion of the Cultural Revolution. Table 7.1 presents a summary of the general nature and duration of these recent mass movements. The first six major campaigns—anti-Lin Biao, anti-Confucius, *Water Margin,* study of the dictatorship of the proletariat, anti-capitalist-roaders, and anti-Gang of Four—were rectification campaigns aimed at the problem of leadership tension and crisis. The modernization campaign launched in 1978 was for both economic and at-

TABLE 7.1: Mass Campaigns Since 1969

	Time Period	Type of Campaign	Targets And Goals
1. Anti-Lin Biao	1971–1973	rectification	Lin Biao and his supporters in party, government, and PLA
2. Anti-Confucius	1974–1975	ideological/ rectification	Zhou Enlai and moderates in party and government
3. *Water Margin*	1975–1976	ideological/ rectification	Zhou Enlai, Deng Xiaoping, and possibly Hua Guofeng
4. Study the Dictatorship of the Proletariat	1975	ideological/ rectification	Zhou Enlai, Deng Xiaoping, and 4th NPC programs
5. Campaign against Capitalist Roaders	Spring 1976	ideological	Deng Xiaoping
6. Anti-Gang of Four Campaign	1976–1978	rectification	the radical elements of the party
7. Emulation Campaign in Railroads	March 1977	economic/ rectification	railway efficiency, security, and discipline
8. Nationwide Sanitation campaign	1978	attitudinal	sanitation and public health
9. The Four Modernization Campaign	1978	economic/ attitudinal	economic development

titudinal purposes. The remaining two minor campaigns were directed at specific goals—railway reform and improved sanitation. Let us examine these recent campaigns in some detail.

Anti-Lin Biao Campaign, 1971–1973

The anti-Lin Biao campaign began soon after Lin's demise in September 1971, but his name was not mentioned in the mass media until after the convening of the Tenth Party Congress in August 1973. Thus, for roughly the first two years of the campaign, the general populace was quite confused about the theme and target of the campaign. For one thing, the political views of Lin Biao had been very close to those of Mao Zedong, particularly during the days of the Cultural Revolution. As a campaign with ideological content, it was difficult at the beginning to pinpoint exactly the main divergent view of Lin Biao. Part of the campaign's focus initially had to be more on Lin's "personal foibles than on errors of line."[36] As the campaign progressed, Lin Biao's alleged plot against Mao became the dominant theme of the campaign, to illustrate Lin's anti-party activities. During this campaign, an extensive purge was undertaken at the national, regional, and provincial levels to eliminate the remnants of Lin's supporters in the party, government, and the PLA. On the whole, the first stage of the anti-Lin Biao campaign from 1971–1973 was weak in ideological content and explanation but strong in rectification and the purge of Lin's supporters and sympathizers. In comparison with previous mass campaigns, including those essentially of a rectifying nature, the anti-Lin Biao campaign aroused limited mass enthusiasm. Perhaps there were more secret meetings held by the party units at all levels to explain events that had taken place two years earlier, but there was evidently less open discussion than usual by the masses and the cadres.[37]

Anti-Confucius and Anti-Lin Biao Campaign, 1973–1974

At first the anti-Confucius campaign sounded like an academic debate. It began when a noted Chinese historian and scholar, Guo Moro, published an article on ancient Chinese history in the party's theoretical journal.[38] Guo dated the transition from "slave" to "feudal" society at about 206 B.C. This began a debate among China's historians, at least on the surface, on the subject of periodization. Soon the scholars' debate veered from the question of periodization to whether Confucius was a conservative reactionary. With the public disclosure, at the Tenth Party Congress in August 1973, of Lin Biao's alleged plot against the party and

Chairman Mao, a link was established between Confucius and Lin Biao: Lin was castigated as a convert to Confucian teachings.[39] While Confucius advocated the restoration of the rule of the slave-owning society of the Western Zhou dynasty (1066–771 B.C.), Lin wanted to restore revisionist tendencies to denigrate the gains of the Cultural Revolution. The general tenor of the articles that proliferated to criticize Lin Biao and Confucius gave the appearance of a militant mass campaign comparable to a mini-Cultural Revolution. There was some upsurge in the campaign, with the participation of the masses, during most of spring 1974.[40] By mid-summer, the targets had enlarged to include problems that had surfaced with respect to a number of Cultural Revolution reforms, such as illegal entry into the universities by the "back door," the reluctance of urban youth to work in the countryside, and the failure of cadres to participate in manual labor. Between the upsurges of the mass campaign, there was a period of cautious retreat into militancy.

Even in the midst of the campaign to criticize Lin Biao and Confucius, there was confusion, particularly outside of China, about the real intended target and the authority actually directing the campaign. Some observers in the West interpreted events of the campaign as a movement directed by Premier Zhou against the radicals and the remnants of the Lin Biao clique.[41] Others viewed the campaign as an attack directed by the radicals against Premier Zhou and his attempts to return to the pre-Cultural Revolution programs, which included the return of Deng Xiaoping to power.[42] One observer, Parris Chang, divided the campaign into two different phases with two different leadership factions directing it: the radicals in control of the campaign from 1972–1973, with the joint conservative forces of the central leadership and the provincial military as its target; and Zhou Enlai's pragmatic group in control in 1974, with Lin Biao as a target, in order to downgrade the ideological impact of the radicals' attack on the conservatives.[43]

In 1977, the *Peking Review* reported that during 1974 the Gang of Four attempted to manipulate the anti-Confucius and anti-Lin Biao campaign. At a series of meetings in January 1974, they developed material, including tapes, for dissemination, which criticized those who obtained admittance to the army and the universities by the "back door," or by using private connections. At these meetings the radicals, led by Jiang Qing, evidently decided to direct the campaign against the PLA, the leaders of the party's Military Affairs Commission and Zhou Enlai. Immediately subsequent to the January meetings, the name of the eleventh century B.C. Duke of Zhou, implying Premier Zhou Enlai, was added to the targets in the mass media.[44] The anti-Lin Biao and anti-Confucius campaign faded away during the early months of 1975 and was replaced by two offshoots, the movement to study the dictatorship of the proletariat and the *Water Margin* campaign, both waged by the radicals to attack Zhou Enlai and his pragmatic programs.

Dictatorship of the Proletariat Campaign, 1975

This new campaign was personally launched by Mao on the heels of the Fourth National People's Congress in January 1975, but was managed by the radicals. The purpose of the campaign was to bring out into the open disagreement with Zhou Enlai over policies and the rehabilitation of many leaders vilified during the Cultural Revolution. In this campaign, the radicals hoped to generate the mass participation and militancy that the anti-Confucius and anti-Lin Biao campaigns had lacked. In typical fashion, the campaign began with an outpouring of theoretical articles in the mass media, mostly written by a group of radical propagandists under the name of the "mass criticism group of Beijing and Zinghua Universities."[45] At the heart of the campaign was the radicals' concern over the pragmatic policies in the economic sector: continuation of private plots and sideline enterprises of the peasants in the communes, and reliance on managers and specialists in industrial production. Zhou Enlai had advocated a modernization program in his report to the Fourth National People's Congress. The implementation of Zhou's long-range modernization plan meant major changes in the economic sphere, coupled with educational reforms to upgrade China's scientific and technological development. The arguments of the radicals focused on these areas of economic modernization, which inevitably would entail emphasis of material incentives and the creation of a new "bourgeois class" of industrial managers and specialists.

In the midst of this new campaign, labor unrest, protesting the inequal distribution of wages which placed the lower ranks of workers at a disadvantage, was reported in the industrial regions of east China.[46] Troops had to be dispatched to quell riots in Hangzhou, the capital of Zhejiang, caused by workers demonstrating for reform of the wage differential system and for wage increases.[47] When, in the summer of 1975, it became evident that the campaign for the study of the dictatorship of the proletariat lacked mass support, a new attack was mounted in August against Zhou Enlai, based on criticism of a popular novel about a peasant rebellion.

Campaign to Criticize *Water Margin,* August–November, 1975

The campaign to criticize the popular novel, *Water Margin,* was an attack against Premier Zhou by innuendo. The radicals, in their desperation to curb "bourgeois tendencies" may have felt that an emotional appeal, coupled with the vehicle of a familiar heroic folk tale, would succeed in gaining the attention of the masses where the intellectual approach had failed.

Water Margin relates how a group of 108 peasants and government officers, under the able leadership of Sung Jiang, mounted a successful rebellion against corrupt officials during the Sung Dynasty in the twelfth century. The popular novel, which was abridged in the late Ming Dynasty, ends here. The original novel went on to relate how Sung Jiang accepted a pardon from the emperor and then served the emperor in suppressing other rebellions. The Shanghai radicals criticized the ending of the popular novel, and quoted Mao as saying that Sung Jiang was a reactionary because he capitulated to the emperor and practiced revisionism.[48] By innuendo, the radicals' campaign literature called Premier Zhou Enlai and his supporters, who advocated more pragmatic programs, "present day Sung Jiangs" who practiced capitulation and revisionism.[49] The campaign lasted only about three months; its sudden disappearance from the political scene may be attributed to its ineffectiveness.

Campaign Against Capitalist-Roader, January–September 1976

This rather short-lived campaign, instigated by the radicals, was aimed at Deng Xiaoping, the vice premier of the State Council and a possible successor to the ailing Zhou Enlai. The campaign began with wall posters posted in Beijing by radical students from Beijing and Qinghua Universities.[50] As the posters began to appear, attacking him as the "capitalist-roader," Deng disappeared from the political scene. Other rehabilitated veteran cadres who had been reinstated in the government and party also were labelled as "right deviationists." When the Tian An Men incident occurred in April, Deng Xiaoping was charged with instigating this mass demonstration to disrupt the political order. As pointed out in Chapter 1, the Tian An Men incident apparently was a spontaneous demonstration in support of Zhou Enlai and Deng against the radicals. Following the Tian An Men incident, Deng was formally removed from office, and the campaign began to criticize him for attempting to reverse the "correct verdict of the Cultural Revolution,"

184

particularly in the field of education. Deng's plans to develop science and technology and to revitalize industry were attacked by the radical press.[51] Like the mass campaigns waged by the radicals in 1974 and 1975, this campaign against Deng Xiaoping not only failed to arouse popular enthusiasm but created confusion among the masses. The campaign was terminated with the arrest of the four radical leaders in early October, following Mao's death.

Campaign to Criticize the Gang of Four, December 1976 to 1978

This campaign was launched officially at the Second National Conference on Agriculture in December 1976. Hua Guofeng outlined the two-step development of the campaign: 1. to expose the radicals' plot to take over the party and state, and 2. to reveal and criticize their past "criminal" and "counterrevolutionary" activities.[52] The conduct of this campaign closely followed the pattern of past campaigns which had the sanction of the leaders in control of the party. Party committees at all levels were used as focal centers for implementation. Work teams from urban areas in each province were dispatched to the countryside to help the communes prepare and organize meetings and study sessions. It has been reported that for the first several months of 1977, some four hundred thousand cadres assigned to these work teams were sent to the countryside in Anhui, Fujian, Henan, Shanxi, and Sichuan provinces alone.[53] The campaign was conducted both in public meetings and in small study groups. The mass media presented a daily diet of criticism of the "nation's scourge" (the misdeeds of the Gang of Four), and big-character posters proliferated. In official briefings in factories and communes, foreign visitors were told that production had increased since the downfall of the Gang of Four.

Exposés of various organizational units' struggles against the Gang of Four when they were in power gave a fairly good idea of how the radical leaders "interfered" in the work of every sector of society, and shed light on the conflicts of key issues between the radicals and the Zhou Enlai group. The theoretical group of the prestigious Chinese Academy of Sciences charged that the radicals considered scientific inquiry and pure research as "bourgeois in nature."[54] The mass criticism group of the State Planning Commission revealed that the Gang of Four were opposed to centralized planning, rational industrial management, training of skilled technicians, and importation of advanced technology from abroad.[55] The theoretical study group of the Ministry of Foreign Affairs criticized Jiang Qing for "issuing statements to foreigners without authorization" and for "divulging classified information of the party and the state," as well as for creating confusion in China's foreign trade.[56]

These mass outpourings of criticism against the radical leaders were, of course, also being used to mobilize public opinion in favor of the pragmatic policies and programs of Hua Guofeng and Deng Xiaoping, which were basically those endorsed by Zhou Enlai. The exposure of the wrongdoings of the radical leaders was to help explain the sweeping reversal of the Cultural Revolution policies of the past decade. The campaign also intended to create a favorable climate for the new leaders to exercise control over their opposition. From September 1976 to the spring of 1977, there were reports of unrest and disorder in many parts of the country.[57] The intensive mass campaign allowed the new leaders to carry on the necessary purge within the party and governmental apparatus in order to consolidate their power. Hua's political report to the CCP Eleventh Party Congress in August 1977 made it very clear that the mass campaign would eradicate the Gang of Four's "pernicious influence in every field."[58] The purge was to extend to all individuals who were involved in the "conspiratory" activities of the Gang of Four.

The campaign to criticize the Gang of Four was also accompanied by two minor mass movements: the emulation campaign in railway administration and the nationwide sanitation campaign. The first, primarily aimed at the railway workers, was intended to improve the efficiency of the railways. The second was a crash program to improve China's sanitation, and was reminiscent of the mass campaigns to eradicate pests in the early 1950s.

Emulation Campaign in Railways, March 1977

The national conference on railway work in February 1977 launched the campaign by criticizing the inefficiency and lack of labor discipline among railway workers. The conference called for the railway workers to fulfill their important role in the national economy. Specifically, the conference urged that the railway services be improved to have trains run on time and to increase the volume of freight carried.[59] Workers, conductors, and drivers for all railways in China had to set up efficient service guidelines and transport quotas. Upon arriving at the train's destination, workers and representatives of passengers were required to evaluate the services rendered on the journey in terms of food, drinks, and safety measures. The coach with the best service was usually awarded a red banner to be displayed in the dinner car.[60]

Since the railway administrations in many localities had been considered strongholds of the Gang of Four, sabotage of the railways may have been the underlying cause of the emulation campaign.[61] There were reports of a large increase in the number of railway workers' accidents, as well as in security problems. In the first part of 1977, PLA units in some provinces were drafted to help manage and control the rail lines.

Nationwide Sanitation Campaign, 1978

This campaign to improve public health in urban areas was launched in 1978 by the Central Patriotic Public Health Campaign Committee, headed by Vice Premier Li Xiannian. The mass campaign, which was reported to have involved more than one million people in a single day, was to wipe out four pests—rats, bed bugs, flies, and mosquitoes—through cleaning the streets, collecting garbage, planting trees, and spraying insecticides.[62] Workers in offices and factories, students and teachers in schools, and neighborhood and street committees were mobilized in urban areas to carry out the campaign. They were augmented at times by cadres and PLA officers. This campaign may have provided the impetus for the letters-to-the-editor by residents in Beijing, published in the leading newspaper, the *People's Daily*, complaining about pollution, litter, noise, and unhealthy odors emitted by factories in the area. It may have also prompted commentaries in the *People's Daily* concerning the unsanitary processing and handling of food and the need for a conference to establish regulations for food processing. Educational campaigns on sanitation and clean food habits were conducted among the cadres in the food producing industries, as well as among youth and children. Failure to heed the aims of the campaign meant punishment; workers in restaurants in Beijing had wage reductions for noncompliance.

In addition, several other mass campaigns have been conducted recently which can be considered spin-offs from the anti-Gang of Four movement. For instance, a discrete campaign was launched by Deng Xiaoping and his supporters in January 1978 to ferret out party leaders—many, supporters of Hua Guofeng—who were reluctant to lend their wholehearted support to Deng's new policies. This type of subtle campaign resulted in reshuffling and dismissal of some provincial secretaries, as well as criticisms of Politburo members Chen Xilian, Wang Dongxing, and Wu De, mentioned earlier. Another spin-off was the campaign for "socialist democracy" and equal justice for all, which was launched soon after the convocation of the Fifth NPC and reached its height in the winter of 1978. This campaign included both the frequent appearance of wall posters, focusing on the issue of individual human rights, and numerous exposés in the mass media on the radicals' use of arbitrary arrest and detention.

The mass campaign, as we have seen in this section, is a unique form of participation for the people in China. These movements have been employed for a variety of purposes: ideological conformity, developing popular acceptance of economic programs, and resolving intra-party conflicts among leaders at the top. These mass movements also have been used to combat inertia of the masses and the cadres in implementing new economic programs, as well as a check on cadre corruption by means of mass criticism. The mass campaigns launched in the post-Cultural Revolution era of the 1970s have been mainly for rectification to resolve conflicts among the top elites. In these mass campaigns, the shifting ideological pitch and targets for attack certainly have created confusion and uncertainty for the populace as a whole. But, as Alan Liu has pointed out, the integrative effect of these mass campaigns for the Chinese nation has been valuable and lasting in terms of uniformity of language in political expression and the acquisition of organization skills demanded by mass campaigns.[63] The Chinese, through those mass campaigns, have indeed become "organization men" in a society which has traditionally been full of centrifugal tendencies.

SUMMARY

We have discussed the many ways by which the masses in China participate in political life. Like citizens in many other countries of the world, where popular elections for public or political offices are permitted, the Chinese do participate in the elections at the local, or basic, level. But unlike most countries where there are elections, the Chinese participate in politics far more extensively through many modes of participation, voluntary or pressured, in mass organizations, in small study groups, and in periodic mass campaigns. This participation has had a number of effects. Most important has been the political socialization—the formation of political beliefs and values—for the vast population. This socialization process has allowed the drastic social reform to take root in the communist Chinese experience. It has also involved the population, formerly unaware, unconcerned, and unmotivated about government, in politics in a very personal way.[64] This personal participation has spilled over into other areas of their lives and has made the people more analytical in problem solving. A familiar story among textile workers in Hongkong relates that when it comes to a problem, such as the introduction of a new machine in the factory, the mainland émigrés invariably request a meeting with their supervisors to discuss and analyze the new situation. By contrast, their coworkers from Hongkong or from Taiwan simply ask for a demonstration of how the machine works.

Perhaps as important as the political involvement by the populace is the fact that the leaders have been made responsive to the masses through study sessions, self-criticism, and open mass rectification. Whatever excesses the Cultural Revolution may have brought to the contemporary Chinese political scene, it did result in a deep awareness, among those in leadership positions, of their accountability to the masses in such campaigns.[65] The process of mass participation, one might add, has made the Chinese masses, both old and young, somewhat more "daring" in their outlook toward their leaders' policies and programs.[66] The point is best illustrated by the outpouring of feelings and criticisms in the wall posters in post Mao China.

With the major proponents of mass campaigns—Mao and the Gang of Four—removed from the political scene, what can we expect of mass campaigns in the future? It seems clear that in order to achieve the objectives of modernization, the masses will have to be mobilized to become aware of the paramount significance of modernization and to play their part in its development. This can be achieved fully only through the techniques developed for mass participation. The leadership has indicated that certain modifications will have to be introduced to make the participatory process practical as well as meaningful. Deng Xiaoping warned his colleagues at the Eleventh Party Congress that the mere incantation of slogans and the enormous amount of time spent on empty talk must be eliminated. It seems apparent that meetings for political studies at the basic levels will be reduced if they do not contribute to the solution of problems at hand. Although no one in China has said that political studies are no longer important in schools, a basic agent for socialization, it has been made clear that an excessive number of hours ought not to be devoted to political and ideological studies at the expense of hard learning. Intellectuals and scientists have been told to return to their laboratories for more research activities, but have also been reminded of the importance of raising their political consciousness through studies and self-criticism during their spare time. Thus, political study and mass campaigns, somewhat curtailed, will continue to be an essential part of political life in China.

NOTES

[1]Charles P. Cell, *Making the Revolution Work: Mass Mobilization Campaigns in the People's Republic of China,* unpublished doctoral dissertation, University of Michigan, 1973, University Microfilms, Ann Arbor, Michigan.

[2]Martin King Whyte, *Small Groups and Political Rituals in China* (Berkeley, Calif.: University of California Press, 1974).

[3]John S. Aird, "Population Growth and Distribution in Mainland China, and Recent Provincial Population Figures," *The China Quarterly,* 73 (March 1978), 35–38, 44.

[4]See Charles S. Taylor and Michael C. Hudson, *World Handbook of Political and Social Indicators* (New Haven, Conn.: Yale University Press, 1972), p. 232.

[5]See Jack Gray and Patrick Cavendish, *Chinese Communism in Crisis: Maoism and the Cultural Revolution* (New York: Holt, Rinehart & Winston, 1968) and John W. Lewis, *Leadership in Communist China* (Ithaca, N.Y.: Cornell University Press, 1963), p. 70.

[6]See Kenneth Prewitt and Sidney Verba, *Principles of American Government*, 2nd ed. (New York: Harper and Row, Pub., 1977), p. 65-67.

[7]See "Speech at the Lushan Conference, 23 July 1959" in *Chairman Mao Talks to the People*, ed. Stuart Schram (New York: Pantheon, 1974), pp. 134-39.

[8]V.C. Falkenheim, "Political Participation in the People's Republic of China" (unpublished paper presented at the 1978 annual meeting of the Association for Asian Studies, Chicago, March 31-April 2, 1978). Permission from author to make this reference in the paper.

[9]See Article 15 of the Constitution of the People's Republic of China, adopted on March 5, 1978, by the Fifth National People's Congress as reprinted in *Peking Review*, 11 (March 17, 1978), 9.

[10]*Renmin Ribao,* December 10, 1977, p. 1; December 14, 1977, p. 1; December 15, 1977, p. 1; December 20, 1977, p. 1; December 23, 1977, p. 1; December 24, 1977, p. 1; December 27, 1977, p. 1; December 29, 1977, p. 1; January 4, 1978, p. 1; January 6, 1978, p. 1; January 9, 1978, p. 1; January 10, 1978, p. 1.

[11]See James Townsend, *Political Participation in Communist China* (Berkeley, Calif.: University of California Press, 1969), p. 119. The figure of eighty-six percent turnout that Townsend used was based on Chinese reports compiled by the Union Research Service, Hongkong. For a comparative voter turnout in different counties, see Gabriel A. Almond, *Comparative Politics Today: A World View* (Boston: Little, Brown, 1974), p. 60.

[12]There are few statistics for local elections except for the 1953-1954 election. See Townsend, *Political Participation in Communist China*, pp. 115-36.

[13]John P. Burns, "The Election of Production Team Cadres in Rural China: 1958-74," *The China Quarterly*, 74 (June 1978), 273-96. For election of shop leaders in a factory, see Zhi Exiang, "The Election of Shop Heads," *China Reconstructs*, vol. xxviii, no. 5 (May 1979), 6-8.

[14]Doak Barnett, *Communist China: The Early Years, 1949-55* (New York: Holt, Rinehart & Winston, 1964), p. 30.

[15]"The PRC's New Labor Organization and Management Policy," *Current Scene*, vol. xv, nos. 11 and 12 (November-December 1977), 18-23; and Ni Chih-fu, "Basic Principle for Trade Union Work in the New Period," *Peking Review*, 44 (November 3, 1978), 7-13, 24.

[16]"Mass Organizations Reactivated," *Peking Review*, 20 (May 19, 1978), 10-13; "Women's Movement in China: Guiding Concepts and New Tasks," *Peking Review*, 39 (September 29, 1978), 5-11; See Ni Chih-fu "Basic Principle for Trade Union Work in the New Period," p. 24.

[17]See *Peking Review*, 4 (January 26, 1968), 7. Also, see "China's Trade Unions—An Interview with Chen Yu, Vice-Chairman of All China Federation of Trade Unions," *China Reconstructs*, vol. xxviii, no. 5 (May 1979), 9-12.

[18]See Charles Hoffmann, "Worker Participation in Chinese Factories," *Modern China: An International Quarterly*, vol. 3, no. 3 (July 1977), 296.

[19]Hoffmann, "Worker Participation in Chinese Factories," p. 308.

[20]"Greeting the Great Task," *Peking Review*, 42 (October 20, 1978), 5-8; and "Basic Principle for Trade Union Work," pp. 10-13.

[21]Kang Ke-ching, "Women's Movement in China: Guiding Concepts and New Tasks," *Peking Review*, 39 (September 29, 1978), 8–11. Also see "The Women's Movement in China—An Interview with Lou Qiong," *China Reconstructs*, vol. xxviii no. 3 (March 1979), 33–36.

[22]CCP Central Committee 23-Point Regulation on Cadres Policy, 1965. For details see Richard Baum, *Prelude to Revolution: Mao, the Party, and the Peasant Question, 1962–66* (New York: Columbia University Press, 1975), pp. 76–82.

[23]"The Neighborhood Revolutionary Committee" in *China Reconstructs*, vol. xxii, no. 8 (August 1973), 2–3.

[24]For in-depth study of small group, see Whyte, *Small Groups and Political Rituals in China*. Also see Townsend, *Political Participation in Communist China*, pp. 174–76.

[25]Whyte, *Small Groups and Political Rituals in China*, p. 172.

[26]Whyte, *Small Groups and Political Rituals in China*, p. 105.

[27]See James C.F. Wang, "May 7th Cadre School for Eastern Peking," *The China Quarterly*, 63 (September 1975), 524–25.

[28]Whyte, *Small Groups and Political Rituals*, pp. 212–13; and Falkenheim, "Political Participation in the People's Republic of China," a paper presented at the 1978 annual meeting of the Association of Asian Studies, Chicago, March 31–April 2, 1978. Permission to use the summary findings of the paper is given by the author.

[29]Townsend, *Political Participation in Communist China*, p. 176.

[30]Whyte, *Small Group and Political Ritual*, pp. 15–16, 233.

[31]Pye, "Communications and Chinese Political Culture," *Asian Survey*, vol. xviii, no. 3 (March 1978), 228–30.

[32]Conversation with Fred Engst, an American who worked in a factory in China from 1960–1976.

[33]See Mary Sheridan, "The Emulation of Heros," *The China Quarterly*, 33 (January–March 1968), 47–72 and James C.F. Wang, "Values of the Cultural Revolution," *Journal of Communication*, vol. 27, no. 3 (Summer 1977), 41–46.

[34]See Charles P. Cell, "Making the Revolution Work: Mass Mobilization Campaigns in the People's Republic of China" (unpublished doctoral dissertation, University of Michigan, 1973), pp. 26–28.

[35]"T'ien An Men Incident: Completely Revolutionary Action," *Peking Review*, 47 (November 24, 1978), 6. For examples of the poems posted at T'ien An Men, see David S. Zweig, "The Peita Debate on Education and the Fall of Teng Hsiao-p'ing," *The China Quarterly*, 74 (March 1978), 155–57. For a latest version of the T'ien An Men incident see "The Truth about the T'ien An Men Incident," *Peking Review*, 45 (December 1, 1978), 6–17.

[36]John Bryan Starr, "China in 1974: 'Weeding Through the Old to Bring Forth the New,' " *Asian Survey*, vol. xv, no. 1 (January 1975), 6.

[37]*The New York Times*, October 12, 1972, section 1, p. 1; and also see Thomas W. Robinson, "China in 1972: Socio-Economic Progress Amidst Political Uncertainty," *Asian Survey*, vol. xiii, no. 1 (January 1973), 8. The same experience was shared by many American visitors, like myself, who visited China in 1972 and 1973.

[38]For a detailed account of the scholarly debate on the anti-Confucius campaign and its link with the anti-Lin Biao campaign, see the following articles: Peter R. Moody, Jr., "The New Anti-Confucius Campaign in China: the First Round," *Asian Survey*, vol. xiv, no. 4

(April 1974), pp. 307–25; Starr, "China in 1974"; Parris Chang, "The Anti-Lin Biao and Confucius Campaign: Its Meaning and Purposes," *Asian Survey*, vol. xiv, no. 10 (October 1974), 871–86; and Merle Goldman, "China's Anti-Confucius Campaign, 1973–74," *The China Quarterly*, 63 (September 1975), 435–62.

[39]"Lin Biao and the Doctrine of Confucius and Mencius: by the Mass Criticism Group of Peking and Tsinghua University," *Peking Review*, 7 (February 15, 1974), 6–12.

[40]"Workers, Peasants, and Soldiers Are the Main Force in Criticizing Lin Biao and Confucius," *Peking Review*, 7 (February 15, 1974), 12–15.

[41]See Merle Goldman, "China's Anti-Confucius Campaign, 1973–74," p. 435; and Leo Goodstadt, "Back to the 'Four Cleans,'" *Far Eastern Economic Review*, vol. 83, no. 2 (January 14, 1974), 14.

[42]John Bryan Starr, "China in 1975: 'The Wind in the Bell Tower,'" *Asian Survey*, vol. xvi, no. 1 (January 1976), 43–48; and Parris Chang, "The Anti-Lin Biao and Confucius Campaign: Its Meaning and Purposes," pp. 874–77.

[43]Chang, "The Anti-Lin Biao and Confucius Campaign," pp. 880–84.

[44]"A Factual Report—'Gang of Four's' Plots in the Movement to Criticize Lin Biao and Confucius," *Peking Review*, 16 (April 15, 1977), 27–29.

[45]"Such Was This 'Writing Group,'" *Peking Review*, 50 (December 9, 1977), 16–17; and "Who is Liang Hsiao," *Peking Review*, 43 (October 21, 1977), 22–24.

[46]Saikowski, "China's Industrial Push and New Hope," *Christian Science Monitor* (Boston), July 10, 1975.

[47]Saikowski, "China's Industrial Push and New Hope."

[48]"Unfold Criticism of 'Water Margin,'" *Peking Review*, 37 (September 12, 1975), 7–8. Also, see Chu Fung-ming, "Criticism of 'Water Margin,'" *Peking Review*, 9 (February 27, 1976), 7–11.

[49]See "Unfold Criticism of 'Water Margin'": pp. 7–8 and "'Gang of Four's'" Scheme in Criticizing 'Water Margin,'"

[50]See "Tsinghua University: Mass Debate Brings Changes," *Peking Review*, 7 (February 13, 1976), 7–9; and "Tsinghua University: The Great Proletarian Cultural Revolution Continues and Deepens," *Peking Review*, 12 (March 19, 1976), 9–11.

[51]See "Grasp the Crucial Point and Deepen the Criticism of Teng Hsiao-p'ing," *Peking Review*, 35 (August 27, 1976), 5–6; and Kao Lu and Chang Ko, "Comments on Teng Hsiao-p'ing's Economic Ideas of the Comprador Bourgeoisie," *Peking Review*, 35 (August 27, 1976), 6–9.

[52]See "Speech at the Second National Conference on Learning from Tachai in Agriculture," *Peking Review*, 1 (January 1, 1977), 37.

[53]"Marching to New Victories," *Peking Review*, 10 (March 4, 1977), 13.

[54]"A Serious Struggle in Scientific and Technical Circles," *Peking Review*, 16 (April 15, 1976), 24–27.

[55]"Why Did the 'Gang of Four' Attack 'The Twenty Points'?," *Peking Review*, 42 (October 14, 1977), 5–13.

[56]"Premier Chou Creatively Carried Out Chairman Mao's Revolutionary Line in Foreign Affairs," *Peking Review*, 5 (January 28, 1977), 6–15.

[57]See Jurgen Domes, "China in 1977: Reversal of Verdicts," *Asian Survey*, vol. xviii, no. 1 (January 1978), 3–9 and "The 'Gang of Four' and Hua Kuo-feng: Analysis of Political Events in 1975–76," *The China Quarterly*, 71 (September 1977), 492.

[58]"Political Report to the 11th National Congress of the Communist Party of China, August 12, 1977," *Peking Review,* 35 (August 26, 1977), 44–45.

[59]See "Go All Out to Improve Railway Transport," *Peking Review,* 9 (February 25, 1977), 3.

[60]"Labor Emulation Drive," *Peking Review,* 17 (April 28, 1978), 14–18.

[61]"Emulation Campaigns in Railway Administrations," *Peking Review,* 11 (March 11, 1977), 5.

[62]"Nationwide Sanitation Campaign," *Peking Review,* 21 (May 26, 1978), 30.

[63]*Communications and National Integration in Communist China* (Berkeley, Calif.: University of California Press, 1971), pp. 115–16.

[64]See Whyte, *Small Groups and Political Rituals in China,* pp. 16, 234; and Townsend, *Political Participation in Communist China,* p. 176.

[65]Richard Pfeffer, "Serving the People and Continuing the Revolution," *The China Quarterly,* 52 (October–December 1972), 620–53.

[66]Whyte, *Small Groups and Political Rituals,* p. 176 and Pfeffer, "Serving the People and Continuing the Revolution," 620–53.

The Politics
of Modernization:
Economic Development,
Science and Technology

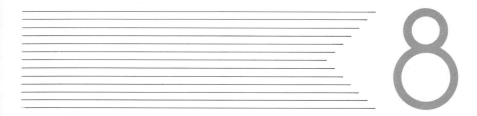

8

Our general objective is to strive to build a great socialist country. . . . How long will it really take to accomplish socialist industrialization and the socialist transformation and mechanization of agriculture and make China a great socialist country? We won't set a rigid time limit now. It will probably take a period of three five-year plans, or fifteen years, to lay the foundation. I think for us to build a great socialist country, about fifty years, or even ten five-year plans, will probably be enough . . ..[1]

Mao Zedong

The quotation above comes from a speech made by Mao in 1954, on the eve of the ratification of China's first constitution. Achievement of the regime's basic objective of industrialization and modernization depends upon policies not only for economic development but also for science and technology and education, which are necessary to support any development. Let us begin our examination of this subject with a brief review of economic development policies in China from 1953–1975.

ECONOMIC DEVELOPMENT

Overview of Economic Development Policies and Rate of Growth, 1953–1975

The development of the Chinese economy has not been what one might describe as a smooth operation. On the contrary, it has not been characterized as anything but erratic and volatile. In the initial years, 1949–1952, the regime's priority was to seek, as rapidly as possible, economic recovery and rehabilitation in the aftermath of a long period of war and the dislocation of its productive capacity. The regime then embarked on a long range planning of its economic development in 1953, by employing the Stalinist model of centralized planning with emphasis on development of heavy industries. As it was pointed out in Chapter 1, the First Five-Year Plan was followed by a shift in development strategy in 1958, which placed emphasis on mass mobilization and intensive use of human labor under the Great Leap. Economic recovery was made rapidly soon after the failure of the Great Leap, but was disrupted again by the Cultural Revolution in the mid-1960s. The post-Cultural Revolution period, 1969–1975, witnessed the development of mixed emphases, both on local economic self-reliance and self-sufficiency and on continued selective centralized management of a number of heavy industries, transport, banking, and foreign trade. A major economic policy was not formulated until 1975, when Zhou Enlai consolidated his political power in the aftermath of the Lin Biao affair.

During the period of 1953 to 1975, covered by the economic development policies discussed above, the rate of economic growth in China was approximately six percent. This is quite an impressive record when compared with other developing nations,[2] particularly in view of the size and density of China's population and the interruptions that occurred during the Great Leap and the Cultural Revolution.

Emergence of Pragmatic Development Policies

The reversal from a mass-mobilization-oriented strategy to a comprehensive and orderly planning strategy for modernization occurred at the beginning of 1975 when the Fourth National People's Congress convened to revise the 1954 constitution. Premier Zhou proposed a two-stage development for China's national economy: a comprehensive industrial system by 1980, and a comprehensive modernization program in agriculture, industry, national defense, and science and technology by the year 2000.[3] While preliminary discussions were held within the State Council's various functional ministries in regard to the guidelines for implementing comprehensive plans to step up the economy, the radicals were set to attack any action that would reverse the gains made by the Cultural Revolution and the restoration of "bourgeois rights." Yao Wenyuan, the radical's theoretical spokesman, authored an article in the party's theoretical journal, *Hongqi (Red Flag)*, in which he raised at least four major points of disagreement with Zhou on the development of the economy.[4] First, Yao argued that a gap existed between the workers and peasants, between town and country, and between mental and manual labor, and that these differences must be removed or polarization and inequality would inevitably result. A comprehensive program for national economic development eventually would place the elite technocrats in a position of power and prestige and, thus, widen these gaps in society. Second, Yao argued that once the technocrats were in power, they would "restore capitalism in the superstructure" and would redistribute capital and power according to mental power and skills, rather than on the basis of "each according to his work." Third, Yao attacked the plan for reintroducing material incentives to induce workers and peasants to produce more in the name of modernization: wage incentives to "lure the workers" represented to Yao the corrupt practice of the bourgeois right. Fourth, Yao labeled the rationale for increasing agricultural and industrial production because the peasants "lacked food and clothing" as nothing but a scheme to "undermine the socialist collective economy." Zhou's pragmatic planners wanted to step up the production on the ground that the peasants needed food and clothing. To Zhou and his supporters, to raise the living conditions of the peasants is to produce more, and the only way to encourage the peasants to produce more is to provide them with incentives such as the private plot and free markets. To the radicals, as expressed by Yao, the very idea of introducing material incentives in order to spur production is to alter the nature of the commune system which is based on "the socialist collective economy."

The pragmatic planners under Premier Zhou ignored the radicals' attacks and continued to prepare comprehensive plans for modernization. Deng Xiaoping was brought back to the party and the State Council to initiate a series of planning conferences within the central government, which also involved members of China's scientific elite from the Chinese Academy of Sciences. These planning conferences produced three documents: A guideline for the party and the nation for the modernization program, a twenty-point outline for the acceleration of industry, and a plan for the development of science and technology.[6] The radicals labeled these documents Deng Xiaoping's "three poisonous weeds." Deng, who was purged for the second time after the Tien An Men incident in April 1976, was charged with restoring centralized power in the administration of economic affairs to the State Council's functional ministries, with placing managers of enterprises in control in industrial plants, and with instituting rules and regulations in industrial plants for the purpose of restoring labor discipline.[7] Echoing the demand made by Zhang Chunqiao for the exercise of total dictatorship over the bourgeoisie, the mass criticism group of China's two leading universities—Beijing and Qinghua—argued that scientific research institutions, which were dominated by the bourgeois intellectuals before the Cultural Revolution, must be in the hands of the masses. Scientific research must be carried on in an "open door" manner so that workers are integrated with the educated elite and so that theory is integrated with practice. The radicals at these universities argued that class struggle must continue and that "nonprofessionals can lead professionals."[8]

After the arrest of the Gang of Four, Hua Guofeng reintroduced Zhou Enlai's comprehensive plan for modernization, and brought Deng

Xiaoping back to revive his guidelines for accelerated industrial and scientific development. Hua pledged his support to these economic plans at the Eleventh Party Congress in August 1977, when he declared

> We must build an independent and fairly comprehensive industrial and economic system in our country by 1980. By then farming must be basically mechanized, considerable increases in production must be made in agriculture, forestry, animal husbandry, side-line production and fishery, and the collective economy of the people's communes must be further consolidated and developed.

> Scientific research ought to anticipate economic construction, but it now lags behind, owing to grave sabotage by the "Gang of Four." This question has a vital bearing on socialist construction as a whole and must be tackled in earnest.[9]

Hua presented a detailed set of development plans to the Fifth National People's Congress in March 1978. The plan consisted of two interrelated plans, comparable to Premier Zhou's 1975 two-stage development plan: a ten-year, short-term development plan, and a twenty-three-year, long-term, comprehensive plan. The short-term plan calls for four hundred million metric tons of grain production, a sixty million ton capacity for steel production, and an overall ten percent per year increase in industrial production by 1985.[10] The ten-year plan also calls for at least "eighty-five percent mechanization in all major processes of farmwork" in the communes. The ten-year plan is to be followed by a series of five-year plans to push China "into the front ranks of the world economy."[11] Figure 8.1 presents the types and range of the capital construction projects which were planned in 1978. These huge projects include large opencast coal mines, oil field pipelines, modern iron and steel complexes, chemical fertilizer plants, farm machinery plants, and railway construction.

THE ECONOMIC PLANNING PROCESS[12]

Submission of the plan to the Fifth National People's Congress was the final step in a three-stage planning process, involving governmental agencies and party committees at all levels.[13] This process is diagramed in Figure 8.2.

At the first stage, the State Council prepares a preliminary draft of the plan, with proposed quotas and targets, as a basis for nationwide consultation. Two important central agencies under the State Council play a vital role in drafting the preliminary plan: the State Planning Commission and the State Statistical Bureau. In addition, the functional ministries of the State Council are also involved in the initial planning.

Since the Cultural Revolution, the provincial revolutionary com-

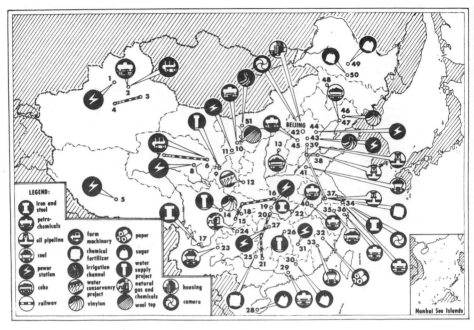

More than 1,000 major projects were started in 1978. A third has been completed or partially completed. The map shows a few of them.

1. Manas River Hydropower Station
2. Xinjiang Petrochemical Works
3. Turpan (Southern Xinjiang Railway)
4. Korla (Southern Xinjiang Railway)
5. Yangbajain Geothermal-Power Station
6. Xining (Qinghai-Xizang Railway)
7. Golmud (Qinghai-Xizang Railway)
8. Longyangxia Hydropower Station
9. Lanzhou water supply project
10. Wool top mill and oil refinery in Yinchuan
11. Qingtongxia water control project
12. Fengjiashan Reservoir
13. Coking plant of the Taiyuan Iron and Steel Company
14. Chengdu water supply project
15. Chongqing (Xiangfan-Chongqing Railway)
16. Xiangfan (Xiangfan-Chongqing Railway)
17. Panzhihua Iron and Steel Company
18. Sichuan Vinylon Mill
19. Gezhouba Hydropower Station
20. Zhicheng (Zhicheng-Liuzhou Railway)
21. Liuzhou (Zhicheng-Liuzhou Railway)
22. Wuhan Iron and Steel Company's 1.7-metre rolling mill and Wuhan Petrochemical Works
23. Housuo Coal-Dressing Plant
24. Chishui Natural Gas and Chemical Plant
25. Hechi Nitrogenous Fertilizer Plant
26. Changsha water supply project
27. Fengtan Hydropower Station

28. Yanglan Sugar Refinery
29. Guangzhou Petrochemical Works
30. Wengyuan Sugar Refinery
31. Wanan Hydropower Station
32. Nanping Paper Mill
33. Yongan Coal Mine
34. Baoshan Iron and Steel Complex, Shanghai Petrochemical Complex and Shanghai Camera Factory
35. Sintering plant of the Hangzhou Iron and Steel Works
36. Zhejiang Oil Refinery
37. Qixiashan Chemical Fertilizer Plant and Luning oil pipeline, Nanjing
38. Dongying (oil pipeline)
39. Cangzhou (oil pipeline)
40. Anqing Petrochemical Works
41. Yanzhou coal base
42. Housing construction and camera factory, Beijing.
43. Beidagang Power Plant and Tianjin Petrochemical and Chemical Fibre Complex
44. Douhe Power Plant, Tangshan
45. Renqiu Oilfield
46. Liaoyang Petrochemical and Chemical Fibre Complex
47. Coking plant of the Anshan Iron and Steel Company
48. Huolinhe Coal Mine
49. Anda Sugar Refinery
50. Zhaoyuan Sugar Refinery
51. Ancillary project of the Huanghe River irrigation area.

FIGURE 8.1: Capital Construction Projects of 1978

Source: Beijing Review, *12 (March 23, 1979).*

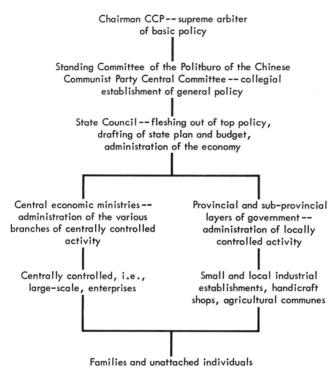

Chairman CCP -- supreme arbiter
of basic policy

Standing Committee of the Politburo of the Chinese
Communist Party Central Committee -- collegial
establishment of general policy

State Council -- fleshing out of top policy,
drafting of state plan and budget,
administration of the economy

Central economic ministries --
administration of the various
branches of centrally controlled
activity

Provincial and sub-provincial
layers of government --
administration of locally
controlled activity

Centrally controlled, i.e.,
large-scale, enterprises

Small and local industrial
establishments, handicraft
shops, agricultural communes

Families and unattached individuals

FIGURE 8.2: China's Economic Decision-making Structure

Source: Arthur G. Ashbrook, Jr., "China: Economic Overview, 1975" in China: A Reassessment of the Economy, Joint Economic Committee, Congress of the United States (Washington, D.C.: Government Printing Office, July 10, 1975), p. 48.

mittees have participated in the planning process at the second stage. With the emphasis on decentralization, many of the governmental agencies below the provincial level also have participated in the formulation of economic plans. All of these agencies engage in planning activities, which include setting quotas and determining the resources needed to meet the various targets in terms of investment, transport, revenues, labor, and social welfare.[14] This second stage, which is a departure from the Soviet planning model, allows the provincial agencies, in consultation with planning units in the enterprises and communes, to develop realistic, detailed proposals, based upon the national preliminary plan and proposed targets and quotas. At this stage, the tentative plan with detailed proposals is scrutinized by the masses, workers, peasants, staff of enterprises, and party committees of the productive units. They can offer suggestions or recommendations on the tentative plan. Thus, op-

201

portunities are provided for negotiation on the specific production proposals between the enterprises or communes and the planning officials from the center.

The final draft of the development plan is prepared by the planning officials at the various ministries in joint sessions, and is then forwarded to the State Council, which in turn submits it to the party's Central Committee for endorsement. It is this final draft plan, as approved by the Central Committee, which Hua Guofeng, in his capacity as the premier and chairman of the party, submitted to the March 1978 session of the National People's Congress for final approval. It should be noted that only after approval by the National People's Congress does the tentative plan become the official development plan. Any major readjustment of or revision to the plan must also have the final approval of the NPC. The State Council then transmits the details of the plan downward to the provinces, municipalities, counties, communes, and production units for implementation.

As an integral part of the planning process, national conferences on major concerns have been employed from time to time for the purpose of publicizing, as well as for soliciting input from experts on, major policy changes or programs to be launched. Thus, for instance, the draft Outline National Plan for the Development of Science and Technology, 1978–1985 was aired at the National Science Conference convened by the Central Committee in March 1978. It was at this major national conference that some six thousand scientific and technical personnel received detailed briefings from the top leaders at the Politburo level about the approved policies and programs under the plan for the development of science and technology.[15] Other national conferences, held since the downfall of the Gang of Four, dealtwith policy changes in the fields of education, finance and trade, and political work in the military. It has been estimated that a total of approximately twenty-two nationwide conferences were convened from the fall of 1976 to August 1977 under the leadership of Hua Guofeng and Deng Xiaoping.[16]

PROBLEMS IN AGRICULTURAL PRODUCTION

Although the overall performance of the Chinese economy has been good, with an average annual growth rate of 6 percent, there have been problems and weaknesses in some sectors of the economy. The most serious weakness has been in agricultural production, which had an average annual growth rate for grain production of only 2.4 percent from 1952 to 1976.[17] The Chinese have recognized that a continued increase in agricultural production is crucial to success in other sectors of the economy. Hua Guofeng and his predecessors have always emphasized the general guideline of "take agriculture as the foundation and industry as the leading factor." This means that expanded agricultural production is the key to China's industrialization. Without a significant increase in agricultural production, increases in the industrial sector are limited. Not only does the industrial sector depend on agriculture for raw materials and food stuffs, but new investment requires agricultural surpluses to help the economy generate savings. A report in 1978 stated[18]

> Our grain production has not increased rapidly enough, and for a long time annual grain output has remained at the level of averaging slightly over 300 kilogrammes per capita. Moreover, the output is not stable, with a vast difference between rich harvest and crop failure years. While in years of bumper harvest the country is self-sufficient and has some surplus in grain, in normal years grain production is only enough to cover needs. Production of industrial crops still cannot meet the increasing needs of economic construction and the people's livelihood.

To achieve the grain production target of four hundred million metric tons by 1985, the annual rate of growth in grain production is planned to increase from 2.4 percent to between 4 and 5 percent a year.[19] (Hua Guofeng reported to the Second Session of the Fifth NPC in June 1979 that grain output in 1978 reached over 300 million metric tons, a 7.8 percent increase over 1977.) Furthermore, population increase is to be held to about 1 percent a year. In order to meet the production targets, there must be an increase in investment for mechanization of agricultural production, water conservation programs, and fertilizer plants, and for scientific research to improve seeds and farming techniques, as well as an improvement in peasant morale.

The method of mechanizing agriculture was one of the many areas of policy dispute between Mao and Liu Shaoqi.[20] Mao contended that mutual aid teams and cooperatives should be transformed into collectivized operations prior to mechanization to enable the peasants to accumulate, on their own initiative, the necessary capital and labor to acquire agricultural machinery. Liu argued that only nationalized industries could produce quantities of machinery at low cost for the peasants, who otherwise could not possibly afford to finance their own mechanized farm implements. Even more important, Liu believed that the peasants simply lacked the organizational and technical skills to make mechanized farming a success. He therefore promoted state-owned tractor stations, which rented farm machinery to the the communes and provided operators. Mao won initially during the Great Leap Forward. By the end of 1958, about seventy percent of the tractors in China had been transferred to local cooperatives at the commune level. During the post-Leap period, the Liu forces regained control; and by the end of

1962, about eighty-eight percent of the tractors, some of which had been purchased by the communes, had been returned to tractor stations. The policy was again reversed during the Cultural Revolution, with the elimination of tractor stations and all ownership of mechanized equipment transferred to the communes.[21]

This policy of self-reliance, which has continued to the present, uses the Dazhai commune as a model. Before 1949, the old Dazhai village, located in the northwest province of Shanxi, was a barren, arid, terraced wasteland, which produced little to support the starving villages. After it was organized as a commune, the villagers, without much outside help, transformed the commune into a flowering oasis through sheer will power and hard work.[22] Dazhai relied on the members to generate funds for the purchase of farm machinery, for capital construction, and for experimentation with new farming methods. The Dazhai commune has frequently overfilled production targets and is highly mechanized, with eighty percent of plowing done by tractor.

The moderate leadership under Hua Guofeng, while following through with the Mao line of self-reliance, has recognized the difficulty for local areas to generate the necessary capital for improvements. The Fifth National People's Congress substantially increased the proportion of total state investment for agricultural investment. State credits for mechanization, capital improvements, and diversification of the economic base are to be extended to the communes. Long-term, low-interest loans will be granted for specific purposes. Poor communes may receive some direct subsidies for improvements. Interest rates on savings deposits in rural areas are to be raised to encourage savings and capital accumulation.[23] Large-scale land reclamation and water conservation projects are planned by the central government, in addition to those to be carried out by provincial and lower-level units. State investment will be increased for support industries, such as farm implement and fertilizer production. Increased agricultural research is to be conducted, particularly in seed breeding, seeking new sources of organic fertilizer, and finding optimum application of chemical fertilizer.[24]

The problem of peasant morale has also been given consideration. The Dazhai commune incentive pay system has been emulated for some time. The work points under this system are based on three factors: 1. skill and productive capacity, 2. enthusiasm for work and honesty, and 3. degree of class consciousness, a political and often hard-to-define criterion. In addition, cadres are expected to participate in productive labor. Hua Guofeng has called for adherence to the principle of "to each according to his labor," with equal pay for equal work, without prejudice to women. Typically, a production team, the basic accounting unit in a commune computes its income by deducting the gross production cost (about twenty-five percent), the public welfare funds (about thirteen percent), and state taxes (four to six percent) from the total gross income from selling its produce to the state at a fixed purchase price. The remaining net income is to be divided among the team members according to their earned work points.[25] Income derived from family-run sideline production and private plots is extra cash income for the peasants. Further incentives for increased income are given under the regime's new program to give brigade- and commune-run enterprises certain tax exemptions and some funds or materials. Private family plots and sideline enterprises are also encouraged. Rural free markets, which were outlawed during the Cultural Revolution, are permitted again.[26]

An important new income incentive is embodied in the new fixed agricultural tax and grain purchase quotas for a five-year period. These fixed taxes and quotas are to encourage overproduction. Once the quotas are set, they may not be raised for five years, despite overproduction. Excess production may be retained by the communes or sold to the state at a higher price than that for quota production. Underproduction because of natural disaster will lessen quotas for the disaster period. In addition, the gap between urban industries and rural communes will be narrowed by adjustments to the price ratio between industrial goods and farm produce, with industrial prices lowered and agricultural prices raised. Further, the quality of industrial goods is to be improved, and factories are to be responsible for repair or reimbursement for defective goods. Standardized parts for the diverse farm equipment that proliferated under Mao's decentralization program is to be promoted. The acceleration in agricultural development has generated some concern among the peasants that there might be again drastic change to the commune system. To allay such a fear the party's Eleventh Central Committee declared in the fall of 1978 that, one, the right of collective ownership and management of a commune must be respected and, two, there shall be no arbitrary interference with the small private plot of a commune member for personal use. All of these policies are intended to provide a greater degree of stability and a sense of well-being for the peasants in the countryside.

PROBLEMS IN INDUSTRIAL PRODUCTION AND MANAGEMENT

The average annual rate of growth for industrial production from 1953 to 1974 has been estimated at a very respectable rate of about eleven percent. The performance from 1975 to 1977 has been placed at a slightly lower rate, between nine and ten percent per year.[27] The official Chinese estimate put the annual growth rate from 1966 to 1977 at twelve percent.[28] Hua Guofeng told the Fifth National People's Congress that with the downfall of the radicals, it should be possible for China to surpass, in the years to come, the industrial production over the last decade.

What are the key features of the Chinese industrial system which have helped to produce such an impressive record? One obvious factor was the nationalization of basic industries. State ownership of all large enterprises since 1956 has enabled the state not only to establish a centralized budget process, but to reinvest a sizable share of earnings in new plans and equipment for further increases in production. One specialist on the Chinese economy pointed out that by the end of the First Five-Year Plan, seventy-five percent of state revenues came from the earnings of state-owned enterprises and that state revenues constituted one-third of China's national income.[29] Closely related to the capacity for reinvestment has been the policy of keeping industrial wages at low levels; income not distributed to the workers could be reinvested.

Another key factor is the initial strategy of placing emphasis on the development of heavy industries, particularly machine-tool factories and iron and steel plants. Iron and steel production remains the key to future growth of China's industries.[30] Steel plants are located strategically in eight major centers, with the largest at Anshan in the northeast, producing about twenty-five percent of the total national output. The fulfillment of Hua Guofeng's target of sixty million metric tons of steel produced by 1985 (this target has been readjusted in 1979 to forty-five million metric tons) will depend on the removal of a number of barriers to expanded production. China needs new mines for both coal and iron to feed the steel furnaces. (see Figure 8.1) In addition, efficient coal and iron mining equipment will have to be imported from abroad in order to boost production. Modern and large-scale blast furnaces are needed. Most of the furnaces in use in 1978 were built by the Soviets in the 1950s.

Finally, emphasis on the development of a large number of medium- and small-scale, labor-intensive industries has been a major factor in the rapid gains in industrial production. These decentralized, relatively small enterprises take advantage of the abundance of manpower in rural areas, using a minimum of capital goods, and thus free investment for heavy industry. The policy of "walking on two legs," therefore, simultaneously develops heavy industry, which is capital-intensive and centralized, and medium to small industry, which is labor-intensive and decentralized. The small industries, with employment ranging from fifteen to six hundred, are owned either by the state, at the county level, or by communes.[31] Many of the small- and medium-sized industries, such as cement, brick, fertilizer, and farm machinery plants, are linked to agricultural production. The importance of small-scale industries in rural communes can be illustrated by the following cycle of development: annual rainfall must be caught by dams and reservoirs, which are constructed with cement; with the availability of water for irrigation of the fields, more chemical fertilizer is needed to produce a higher yield of crops; with the prospect of a higher yield, agricultural machinery, such as tractors, harvesters, and water pumps is needed. In one year, fifty-four percent of China's synthetic ammonia was produced by about one thousand small fertilizer plants. [32] The United States' delegation on small-scale industry, which visited China in 1975, pointed out that these small-scale industries save time in construction, solve the problem of limited transport facilities for rural areas, and allow for the exploitation of available local resources.[33] These small-scale industries in rural areas also have the ideological justification of removing the urban-rural dichotomy.

Small-scale industry is also found in urban areas in the form of neighborhood enterprises managed by the street revolutionary committees. Visitors to China are frequently led to such street enterprises in the midst of a residential area for the workers. Housewives of the neighborhood may be employed in a small factory, making small items, such as bulbs for flashlights or transistors for radios. Charles Bettelheim has suggested that the housewives who worked in the neighborhood small-scale enterprises are not motivated by economic need to augment the family's income but by the ideological call to contribute to production.[34]

Like every other aspect of China's economic and political development, the management of industrial enterprises has been subject to policy alterations. The party's control over the management of enterprises waxed and waned as the development strategy vacillated from reliance on technical expertise to mass participation, from 1953 to the Cultural Revolution.[35] The Cultural Revolution placed so much emphasis on the participatory aspect of "politics-in-command" that industrial workers took over the plants and managed them through committees. For over a decade there was confusion and laxity in industrial management. Instead of "relying on experts to run the factories," groups of workers, revolutionary rabble-rousers, managed them. This mass movement in industry was exemplified by the Anshan steel and iron factory and therefore was called the Anshan Charter.[36] The essence of the Anshan Charter was to make the workers masters of socialist industry.[37] At the height of the Cultural Revolution, workers discarded factory rules and regulations, often with some justification, since these regulations were voluminous and practically incomprehensible to ordinary workers. As the Cultural Revolution intensified, a state of anarchy existed in many factories. By 1969, when the Ninth Party Congress met, efforts were made to restore order and discipline in industrial plants. Workers participated cooperatively in enacting basic rules, which required punctuality, quality control, and safety measures. The Daqing oil fields became the national model for strict observance of rules and regulations by workers and staff. After their arrest in October 1976, two radical leaders, Yao Wenyuan and Zhang Chunqiao, were attacked for rejecting rules and regulations in factories.[38] In 1977, Hua Guofeng urged his countrymen to reverse the habit of laxity in industrial production and to follow the Daqing model, a "fine example of how a good job can be done in socialist industry."[39]

A nagging problem in the industrial sector has been the remuneration system and the related question of material incentives.[40] The debate in recent years has centered on whether to have egalitarianism or disparity in income distribution. The pragmatic moderates, such as Zhou Enlai, Hua Guofeng, and Deng Xiaoping, have argued that the incentive system, based on timework, piecework, and bonuses, is the only way by which the principle of "to each according to his work" can be correctly instituted.[41] Yao Wenyuan and other radicals, on the other hand, feared that continuing wide disparity of wages could lead only to an unequal distribution of "commodities and money."[42]

Carl Riskin has pointed out that the Chinese industrial wage system is basically a bourgeois method of distribution.[43] Payment in factories is based primarily on timework, supplemented by piecework. Since 1977, the wage differential has included the level of a worker's skill and the employment of bonuses as production inducements. The 1977 wage policy allows for the elevation or promotion of workers with outstanding achievements without their climbing "the wage ladder rung by rung."[44] The present timework payment is governed by an eight-grade wage scale, from a minimum of 34 to a maximum of 110 yuan. A worker's grade within the scale is based on his skill and training, length of service, and performance record. Technicians, engineers, and plant managers come under a separate wage system.

In October 1977, a wage increase was promulgated by the State Council for about sixty percent of China's industrial workers, the first major increase since 1963. The new wage increases moved some forty-six percent of the workers, whose wages were at the lowest levels, up one grade in the scale. Workers who were receiving more than ninty yuan had no increase or adjustment. This action apparently was taken to raise workers' standards of living in line with greater prosperity and to alleviate dissatisfactions in the industrial centers. All of the effects of the new wage increases on the Chinese economy are difficult to predict. Stable prices have been maintained in large measure by keeping both wages and the supply of goods at a low level. It is most likely that the supply of consumer goods will gradually be increased to fulfill the regime's stated goal of elevating the standard of living. To reach this goal without side effects, the state will have to be vigilant in enforcing stable prices while providing more and a better variety of goods. In fact Hua Guofeng told the Second Session of the Fifth NPC in June 1979 that the government has established regulations for price control.

In addition to wage increases for the Chinese industrial workers, a varied system of bonuses also has been reintroduced into the state enterprises. Briefly, the bonus system, which is identical to the one that existed before the Cultural Revolution, calls for the distribution of an additional income allowance, usually not more than ten percent of the enterprise's total wage bill. This additional income allowance, as explained to me by the cadres in a ball bearing plant in Loyang in the summer of 1978, is given to an enterprise only if it has fulfilled the assigned quota of production. This additional allowance is then distributed to the plant's various workshops or groups, including workers' congresses of the trade union federation in large enterprises, which decide how the bonus is to be awarded. The decision may be an across-the-board distribution to all or most workers in the plant, with each worker receiving only a few yuans. At other times, the bonus consists of consumer items, such as clothing or food, for those who have been good workers and who observe work discipline. The bonus system is by no means uniform for all enterprises in China. Some enterprises adhere to the egalitarian concept of distributing bonuses to all workers regardless of the quality and quantity of individual work performed. This across-the-board distribution of bonuses to all workers in a plant has been subject to criticism as revealed in the mass media in 1979. As time goes on and as they gain more experience, the Chinese most likely will have a uniform set of principles for bonus distribution and other material incentive measures to spur production.

THE ROLE OF SCIENCE AND TECHNOLOGY IN MODERNIZATION

An historic milestone was reached in the spring of 1978 when some six thousand scientists and technicians gathered in Beijing to discuss and endorse the plans for China's development of modern science and technology. In his keynote address to the conference, Deng Xiaoping, by then vice premier of the State Council, criticized the party's past errors in not providing adequate services, supplies, and working conditions for scientists.[45] This was certainly a far cry from the days when intellectuals, scientists, and technicians were labeled, by Yao Wenyuan, as "an exploiting class" with strong bourgeois prejudices,[46] and Deng was charged with advocating the "poisonous weed" of advanced scientific development by the radicals.

Since 1949, science policy has vacillated between professional orientation and mass mobilization along with alterations in China's development policies.[47] Whitson has noted that during each alteration period, the leadership has embraced a different set of approaches toward the identifiable issues of planning, the role of self-sufficiency, and the place of technology transfers from abroad.[48] The First Five-Year Plan period saw the professionals and technical bureaucrats in a position of dominance, with the consequent emphasis on centralized planning and control over the allocation of resources, the importation of some three hundred complete industrial plants from the Soviet Union, and scientific and technical training of Chinese in the Soviet Union. Following the withdrawal of Soviet aid in 1960, the Great Leap altered the basic approach from professionalism, with heavy reliance on technological transfer from abroad, to Mao's approach of self-reliance and "disdain" for foreign technology. The alternating pattern reappeared with some variations over the periods of economic recovery from the Great Leap and the Cultural Revolution.

The Cultural Revolution disrupted the scientific community in a number of ways. Scientists and technicians were criticized for their professional sins: their aloofness from and disinterest in politics; their privileged status and high salaries; and their theoretical research, unrelated to practical problems. Established in 1958 under the supervision of the State Council, the State Scientific and Technological Commission was supposed to provide direction for scientific research, administer scientific and technological programs, and approve funds for research. The organization's leading members, however, were subject to Red Guard criticism and harassment for their elitist orientation. Many of the scientific cadres associated with the commission were sent to the countryside for rehabilitation through physical labor. And the commission disappeared as an organization.

The Academy of Sciences, which conducts research in the various physical and social sciences, both directly and through affiliate members, was subject to criticism and purges. At the height of the upheaval, it was reported that thousands of its members had been sent to the factories and communes for physical labor.[49] The president of the academy, the late Kuo Moro, a noted historian, managed to survive by making self-criticism in which he repudiated all of his previous writings. Typically, the academy's affairs were taken over by a revolutionary committee, with the PLA and the masses participating in decision making. Members were forced to spend long hours in political reeducation and ideological remolding.

Some members of the academy were sent to factories and communes to engage in applied research. Many of the research institutes of the academy decentralized their operations during the Cultural Revolution by establishing provincial and local branches, which proliferated duplicate activities. Although the Cultural Revolution strategy did not contribute to basic scientific research, some observers in the West have viewed some of the reforms in science and technology as innovative from a developmental perspective. Genevieve Dean has argued that China's urgent need was for the application of innovative native technology to solve immediate problems of development and that high-level research was too sophisticated to be of any use to the ordinary peasants and workers.[50] Oldham and Lee see the prospect of mass participation in developing native technology, based on local initiative and resources, as enriching the economic life of the Chinese.[51] Oldham noted that the mass training of ordinary workers as "amateur technicians" might be viewed as the beginning step toward the eventual formation of a "highly specialized corps of technicians."[52]

In contrast to Mao and the radicals, who questioned both the practicality and the ideological impact of modern science, both Hua Guofeng and Deng Xiaoping see the "mastery of modern science and technology" as the key to modernization. They have frankly admitted that China is lagging behind some of the advanced countries, such as the United States, by as much as fifteen to twenty years in food production.[53] To catch up with the ever-expanding body of world knowledge, China plans both to learn from the advanced nations and to develop her own scientific capabilities.

This program calls for increased imports of plants and equipment. The Chinese strategy for technology transfer in recent years has been to purchase complete industrial plants from abroad, the "turnkey" strategy. For the period from 1972 to 1975, China imported some 170 complete industrial plants, valued at 2.6 billion U.S. dollars, from eight European nations, Japan, the United States, and the Soviet Union.[54] Most of these plants were for basic industries, such as steel, electricity, petroleum, and chemical fertilizer. As noted earlier, the Chinese can expand their capital formation by copying a complete imported plant which is a "carrier of new technology."[55] China hopes to pay for some of the capital formation by acquiring agricultural surpluses through increased productivity. China can also incur large long-term debt in the form of credits, such as a one- to two- billion dollar bank loan from Japan.[56] China's total debt obligation to foreign nations was about two billion U.S. dollars at the end of 1976, and with expansion in export trade, China's debt payment will most likely reach eight percent in the 1980s, a rather manageable level by international standards.[57]

To supervise the development program in science, the Fifth National People's Congress reinstated the Scientific and Technology Commission and elevated it to ministerial status under the State Council. The program calls for the recruitment of a force of eight hundred thousand scientists and technicians.[58] A scientific exchange program is being undertaken for training abroad to raise the level of scientific knowledge in China. This exchange may not be limited only to science and technology. Hua Guofeng has stated that China must "learn the strong points of all nations and countries, to learn from them all that is truly good in politics, economics, military affairs, science, technology, literature, and art."[59] Perhaps most important for the advancement of science in China, however, is the new policy to allow scientists to pursue their work in relative peace.

Deng Xiaoping has publicly rejected the radicals' assertion that scientists are not part of the productive forces, and instead contends that "brain workers who serve socialism" are part of the working people. At the 1978 national science conference, Deng clearly repudiated the treatment of intellectuals and technicians over the past decade when he stated

> We cannot demand that scientists and technicians, or at any rate, the over-whelming majority of them, study a lot of political and theoretical books, participate in numerous social activities, and attend many meetings not related to their work.

> How can you label as "white" a man who studies hard to improve his knowledge and skills? Scientists and technicians who have flaws of one kind or another in their ideology or their style of work should not be called "white," if they are not against the party and socialism. How can our scientists and technicians be accused of being divorced from politics when they work diligently for socialist science?[60]

Deng went on to ask that the party stop interfering in the work of scientific and research institutions and restore the decision-making authority on technical matters to the directors and deputy directors of these agencies. The party committee's work in a scientific institution should be judged by the scientific results and the training of competent scientific personnel.[61]

In this chapter we have tried to present a picture of China's efforts to modernize since 1949 with focus on the post Mao era. Modernization means industrialization and economic growth, supported and strengthened by universal education, which emphasizes the acquisition of modern science and technology. The politics of modernization in China since 1949 have focused primarily, although not exclusively, on how China can be transformed as rapidly as possible into an industrialized nation, equal to nations on the forefront of technological development. Because of the lack of unity among the leaders about the answer to this question, policies and programs for modernization have vacillated from the revolutionary mass mobilization model to the professional and orderly development model. The continuous conflict and ambivalence toward these strategies for modernization has dominated the flow of Chinese politics for the past decades. But when all has been said about the struggle between the radical revolutionaries and the moderate pragmatists, there is the pervasive feeling not only among the Chinese but among the peoples of all developing nations that they want a better way of life in terms of both moral and material well-being and that it can come about only through the continuous acquisition of knowledge in science and technology.

Will China be able to achieve its goal of modernization? The answer rests on a number of factors. One is the ability of the leaders to maintain unity and some degree of cohesiveness so as to provide the needed political stability and climate for orderly development. Another factor is how fast China can develop effective intermediate and lower level leadership to implement the plans of modernization. The second factor will be to a large extent, influenced or shaped by the unity and cohesiveness at the top. Closely related to the development of effective leadership is the urgent need to acquire managerial skills in industrial and agricultural sectors for efficient production.

Managerial training for cadres at all levels in industries is also needed. In addition, China's pragmatic leaders must solve the problems in improving work efficiency such as overstaffing, administrative redtape, and liberation from endless meetings—all of these tend to delay or hamper efficient production. Another important factor in attaining her goal of modernization is funds to be made available for investment in large capital construction of needed projects, shown in Figure 8.1, and the massive technology purchase from abroad. China's economic planners had admitted that too many projects were being undertaken simultaneously resulting in wide dispersion of resources. These problems led to readjustment and temporary retrenchment in the modernization programs, until China's economic planners could work out more realistic priorities and needed corrections. Thus we may see readjustments and changes in priorities to the modernization programs in years ahead as China's economic planners begin to experience many of these developmental problems. The party leadership's decision, officially approved by the June 1979 session of the Fifth NPC, to readjust priorities in China's modernization program is a good case in point.[62] The readjustment in the national economy covered a span of three years, from 1979 to 1981, during which period a concentrated effort would be made to give top priority to rapid advancement in agriculture, in light and textile industries which require less investment but bring quick returns, in petroleum, power, and transport industries. The readjustment would also curtail the number of capital construction projects as initially proposed in 1978 (see Figure 8.1), by limiting the key projects to the rapid development of agriculture, light industry, the fuel and power industries, and the transport and communications facilities. The readjustment also called for continued importation of technology and expanded foreign trade. However, the technology import would be restricted to importation of less equipment but more technology. Or, as the Chinese leaders say: "To buy hens for them to lay eggs." The readjustment also would mean changes in economic management in that the productive enterprises would be given more autonomous power to make decisions on production, supply, and marketing. Even more significant was the decision reached in June 1979 that would place the director of a factory, the technical expert, as the chief administrator for directing the production in the entire factory.

Modernization can bring many blessings to the Chinese. But it also brings many problems. In China, the gap between rural and urban conditions may widen further, since the urban sector benefits more from modernization. If this rural-urban disparity is not reduced during the modernization process, the peasant population may become increasingly discontent. The recent demonstration by peasants in Beijing serves as a warning to Chinese economic planners of the possible consequence of widening this rural-urban disparity. Modernization also inevitably breeds elitism of specialists and the consequent evils of bureaucracy, the targets of the Cultural Revolution. If elitism and bureaucratism are not controlled or monitored effectively, another upheaval or violent swing of the pendulum to the left cannot be ruled out in the future.

NOTES

[1]"On the Draft Constitution of the People's Republic of China, June 14, 1954," *Selected Works of Mao Tse-tung,* vol. v (Peking: Foreign Language Press, 1977), pp. 141–42.

[2]See Arthur G. Ashbrook, "China: Economic Overview, 1975," in *China: A Reassessment of the Economy,* Joint Economic Committee, U.S. Congress (Washington, D.C.: Government Printing Office, July 10, 1975), p. 24; and Jan S. Prybyla, "Some Economic Strengths and Weaknesses of the People's Republic of China," *Asian Survey,* vol. x, no. 12 (December 1977), 1122.

[3]Chou En-lai, "Report on the Work of the Government," *Peking Review,* 4 (January 24, 1975), 23.

[4]Yao Wen-yuan, "On the Social Basis of the Lin Biao Anti-Party Cliquen" *Hongqi,* no. 3 (1975) as translated in *Peking Review,* 10 (March 7, 1975), 5–10

[5]Chang Ch'un-ch'iao, "On Exercising All-Round Dictatorship Over the Burgeoisie," *Hongqu,* no. 4 (1975) as translated in *Peking Review,* 14 (April 4, 1975), 5–11.

[6]For the full text of these three documents, see *Issues and Studies,* vol. xiii, no. 6 (June 1977), 107–15; no. 8 (August 1977), pp. 77–99; no. 9 (September 1977), pp. 63–70. For commen-

taries on the radical's attack on Deng's three documents, see Chi Wei, "How the 'Gang of Four' Opposed Socialist Modernization," *Peking Review* 11 (March 11, 1977), 6–9; Wang Che, "The 'Gang of Four' Pushed Anarchism," pp. 23–26; Hsiang Chun, "An Attempt to Restore Capitalism Under the Signboard of Opposing Restoration," *Peking Review,* 34 (August 19, 1977), 29–32, 37; and Mass Criticism Group of State Planning Commission, "Why Did the 'Gang of Four' Attack 'The Twenty Points'," *Peking Review,* 42 (October 14, 1977), 5–13.

[7]Kao Lu and Chang Ko, "Comments on Teng Hsiao-p'ing's Economic Ideas of the Comprador Bourgeoisie," *Peking Review,* 35 (August 27, 1976), 6–9.

[8]"Repulsing the Right Deviationist Wind in the Scientific and Technological Circles," *Peking Review,* 18 (April 30, 1976), 6–9.

[9]Hua Kuo-feng, "Political Report to the 11th National Congress of the CCP," *Peking Review,* 35 (August 26, 1977), 50.

[10]Hua Kuo-feng, "Report on the Work of the Government," *Peking Review,* 10 (March 10, 1978) 19.

[11]Hua Kuo-feng, "Report on theWork of the Government" p. 19.

[12]Thomas G. Rawski, "Chinese Economic Planning," *Current Scene,* vol. xiv, no. 4 (April 1976), 1–15; and Dwight Perkins, "China's Fourth Five-Year Plan," *Current Scene,* vol. xii, no. 9 (September 1974), 1–7. Also see E.L. Wheelwright and Bruce McFarlane, *The Chinese Road to Socialism: Economics of the Cultural Revolution* (New York and London: Monthly Review Press, 1970), pp. 129–42; Audrey Donnithorne, *China's Economic System* (London: George Allen and Unwin, 1967), pp. 457–495.

[13]Rawski, "Chinese Economic Planning," p. 2.

[14]Rawski, "Chinese Economic Planning," pp. 2–4.

[15]Fang Yi, "Outline National Plan for the Development of Science and Technology, Relevant Policies and Measures," *Peking Review,* 14 (April 17, 1978), 6–14; and "C.P.C.Central Committee Circular on Holding National Science Conference," *Peking Review,* 40 (September 30, 1977), 6–11.

[16]Chu Chun-yu, " 'Three Poisonous Weeds', Three Fragrant Flowers, and Three Great Conferences," *Ta Kung-Pao* (Hongkong), July 18, 1977, p. 1.

[17]"China's 10-Year Program for the Development of Agriculture and the National Economy (1976–1985)," *Current Scene,* vol. xvi, nos. 4 and 5 (April–May 1978), 17.

[18]Fang Tsui-nung and Chang Yi-hua, "Strive for Modernization of Agriculture," *Peking Review,* 23 (June 9, 1978), 5.

[19]"China Increases Investment in Agriculture," *Current Scene,* vol. xvi, no. 1 (January 1978), 17 and "The PRC Economy in 1976," *Current Scene,* vol. xv, nos. 4 and 5 (April–May 1977), 9; and "China's 10-Year Program For the Development of Agriculture and the National Economy (1976–1985)," p. 26.

[20]See "The Conflict Between Mao Tse-tung and Liu Shao-chi over Agricultural Mechanization in Communist China," *Current Scene,* vol. vi, no. 17 (October 1, 1968), 1–18.

[21]"The Conflict Between Mao Tse-tung and Liu Shao-chi over Agricultural Mechanization in Communist China, pp. 1–18.

[22]*The Red Sun Lights the Road Forward For Tachai* (Peking: Foreign Language Press, 1969), and "Tachai Speeds up Farm Mechanization," *Peking Review,* 28 (July 8, 1977), 6–8.

[23]Ching Hua, "How to Speed Up China's Agricultural Development," *Peking Review,* 42 (October 20, 1978), 9–10.

[24]See "Entering New Phase in Farm Mechanization," *Peking Review,* 7 (February 7, 1978), 9–10; "Farm Mechanization: Targets for 1980," *Peking Review,* 8 (February 24, 1978), 10–14; Chou Chin, "Mechanization: Fundamental Way Out for Agriculture," *Peking Review,* 9 (February 25, 1977), 11–15, 26; Fang Tsui-nung and Chang Yi-hua, "Strive for Mechanization of Agriculture," *Peking Review,* 23 (June 9, 1978), 5–7. Also, see "China's 10-Year Program for the Development of Agriculture," pp. 27–29. Also see Scott S. Hallford, "Mechanization in the PRC," *Current Scene,* vol. xiv, no. 5 (May 1976), 1–12.

[25]See Harold C. Champeau, "Five Communes in China," *Current Scene,* vol. xiv, no. 1 (January 1976), 14–15.

[26]"China's 10-Year Program for the Development of Agriculture," p. 27.

[27]See "PRC Economic Performance in 1975," *Current Scene,* vol. xiv, no. 6 (June 1976), 1–14 and "The PRC Economy in 1976," *Current Scene,* vol. xv, nos. 4 and 5 (April–May 1977), 1–10.

[28]Hua Kuo-feng, "Report on the Work of Government," *Peking Review,* p. 20.

[29]Robert F. Dernberger, "Past Performance and Present State of China's Economy," in *China's Future: Foreign Policy and Economic Development in the Post-Mao Era,* eds. Allen S. Whiting and Robert F. Dernberger (New York: McGraw-Hill, 1977), pp. 95, 140.

[30]For information on China's steel production, see Alfred H. Usack, Jr., and James D. Egan, "China's Iron and Steel Industry," in *China: A Reassessment of the Economy,* pp. 264–88.

[31]American Rural Small-Scale Industry Delegation, *Rural Small-Scale Industry in the People's Republic of China* (Berkeley, Calif.: University of California Press, 1977), p. 1. Also for an article on the evolution of China's policy toward the development of small industries, see Carl Riskin, "Small Industry and the Chinese Model of Development," *The China Quarterly,* 46 (April–June 1971), 245–73; and Carl Riskin, "China's Rural Industries: Self-Reliant System or Independent Kingdom?" *The China Quarterly,* 73 (March 1978), 77–98.

[32]Chaing Hung, "Small and Medium-sized Industries Play Big Role," *Peking Review,* 45 (November 7, 1975), 23–25.

[33]See *Rural Small-Scale Industries in the People's Republic of China;* and "Small Enterprises," *Peking Review,* 46 (November 15, 1974), 22.

[34]Charles Bettelheim, *Cultural Revolution and Industrial Organization: Changes in Management and the Division of Labor* (New York and London: Monthly Review Press, 1974), p. 47.

[35]See Stephen Andors, *China's Industrial Revolution: Politics, Planning, Management, 1949 to the Present* (New York: Pantheon, 1977); Eckstein, *China's Economic Revolution,* pp. 84–108; Barry M. Richman, *Industrial Society in Communist China* (New York: Vintage Books, 1969), pp. 671–720; and Joan Robinson, *Economic Management in China* (London: Anglo-Chinese Educational Institute, 1976).

[36]"China's Iron and Steel Industry Advances Rapidly Along Chairman Mao's Proletarian Revolutionary Line," *Peking Review,* 40 (October 3, 1968), 32–34.

[37]See three rather revealing articles on a state-owned watch factory in Shanghai entitled "The Workers Are the Master," *Peking Review,* nos. 26–28 (June 29, July 6 and 13, 1973), pp. 11–14, respectively.

[38]Wang Che, "The 'Gang of Four' Pushed Anarchism," *Peking Review,* 14 (April 1, 1977), 23–26.

[39]Hua Kuo-feng, "Report on the Work of Government," p. 20; and Li Hsien-nien, "Opening Speech at the National Conference on Learning from Taching in Industry," *Peking Review,* 18 (April 29, 1977), 15–17.

[40]See the following works for detailed information and analysis: Peter Schran, "Institutional Continuity and Motivational Change: The Chinese Industrial Wages System, 1950–1973," *Asian Survey,* vol. xiv, no. 11 (November 1974), 1014–32; Jan S. Prybyla, "A Note on Incomes and Prices in China," *Asian Survey,* vol. xv, no. 3 (March 1975), 262–78; and Carl Riskin, "Workers' Incentives in Chinese Industry," in *China: Reassessment of the Economy,* pp. 199–224.

[41]"Implementing the Socialist Principle 'To Each According to His Work,' " *Peking Review,* 33 (August 18, 1978), 11–19.

[42]"Implementing the Socialist Principle 'To Each According to His Work," p. 13; and "After Wages Went Up," *Peking Review,* 18 (May 5, 1978), 21.

[43]Carl Riskin, "Workers' Incentives in Chinese Industry," p. 199.

[44]"Implementing the Socialist Principle," p. 16.

[45]Teng Hsiao-p'ing, "Speech at Opening Ceremony of National Science Conference, March 18, 1978," *Peking Review,* 12 (March 24, 1978), 17.

[46]Theoretical Group of the Chinese Academy of Sciences, "A Serious Struggle in Scientific and Technical Circles," *Peking Review,* 16 (April 15, 1977), 24–27.

[47]Richard Suttmeier, "Science Policy Shifts, Organizational Change and China's Development," *The China Quarterly,* 62 (June 1975), 207–41. Also see William W. Whitson, "China's Quest for Technology," *Problems of Communism,* xii (July–August 1973), 16–30.

[48]Whitson, "China's Quest for Technology," p. 17–18.

[49]Bruce J. Esposito, "The Cultural Revolution and China's Scientific Establishment," *Current Scene,* vol. xii, no. 4 (April 1974), 2–3.

[50]Genevieve Dean, "China's Technological Development," *New Scientist* (May 18, 1972), pp. 371–73.

[51]C.H.G. Oldham, "Technology in China: Science for the Masses?" *Far Eastern Economic Review* (May 16, 1968), pp. 353–55; and Rensselaer W. Lee, III, "'The Politics of Technology in Communist China," in *Ideology and Politics in Contemporary China,* ed. Chalmers Johnson (Seattle, Wash. and London: University of Washington Press, 1973), pp. 301–25; Jonathan Unger, "Mao's Million Amateur Technicians," *Far Eastern Economic Review* (April 3, 1971), pp. 115–118; and *China: Science Walks on Two Legs* (New York: Avon Books, 1974).

[52]Oldham, "Science and Technological Policies," *China's Developmental Experience,* Michel Oksenberg, ed. (Praeger Publishers, New York, Washington, and London, 1973), pp. 80–94.

[53]Teng Hsiao-p'ing, "Speech at Opening Ceremony of National Science Conference," p. 10; and Hua Kuo-feng, "Raise the Scientific and Cultural Level of the Entire Chinese Nations," March 24, 1978, *Peking Review,* 13 (March 31, 1978), 6–14.

[54]See Dave L. Denny, "International Finance in the People's Republic of China" in *China: A Reassessment of the Economy,* 701–702. Also see Kent Morrison, "Domestic Politics and Industrialization in China: The Foreign Trade Factor," *Asian Survey,* vol. xviii, no. 7 (July 1978), 690–98.

[55]Shannon Brown, "Foreign Technology and Economic Growth," *Problems of Communism,* xxvi (July–August, 1977), 30–32.

[56]Brown, "Foreign Technology and Economic Growth," p. 35; and Susumu A. Wanohara, "China Looks for More Credit," *Far Eastern Economic Review* (May 27, 1977), p. 78; and Henry Scott-Stokes, "Japan Will Lend China $1–2 Billion," New York Times Service as reprinted in *Honolulu Star-Bulletin* (September 12, 1978), sec E, p. 10.

[57]Brown, "Foreign Technology and Economic Growth," p. 36.

[58]Fang Yi, "Outline National Plan for the Development of Science and Technology, Relevant Policies and Measures," p. 7.

[59]"Raise the Scientific and Cultural Level of the Entire China Nation," p. 12.

[60]"Speech at Opening Ceremony of National Science Conference," p. 15.

[61]"Speech at Opening Ceremony of National Science Conference," p.17.

[62]Hua Guogeng, "Report on the Work of the Government: Delivered at the Second Session of the Fifth NPC on June 18, 1979," *Beijing Review*, no. 27 (July 6, 1979), pp. 11–21 and Shi Zhengwen, "Readjusting the National Economy: Why and How?" *Beijing Review*, no. 26 (June 29, 1979), pp. 13–23.

The Politics of Education

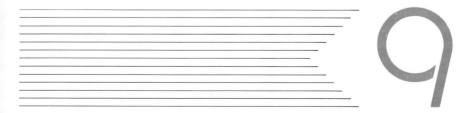

9

Two important factors have influenced, if not dominated, Chinese educational policies since 1949. First, education has been used as an instrument for the inculcation of new values and beliefs to build a new socialist revolutionary society. Second, changes in the content and form of education invariably have been intertwined with the shifting policies and strategies of economic development. Although the basic goal of the regime has been to construct a socialist state, the implementation of this basic goal has involved periodic shifts in emphasis between "red" (politics) and "expert" (technology). Let us begin our discussion by examining educational policies which governed the administration of schools and universities prior to the advent of the Cultural Revolution in 1966.

EDUCATIONAL POLICIES BEFORE THE CULTURAL REVOLUTION

The very first governmental decree on education, "Decision of the Reformation of the Education System," promulgated in October 1951, was intended to provide formal education, stressing both technical training and ideological education of the new socialist values.[1] The Chinese educational reform in the early 1950s was modeled on the Soviet approach to education, which stressed technical training to develop specialized skills. This emphasis on technical training was in harmony with the need to develop manpower for the First Five-Year Plan, covering the period from 1953 to 1957. There was a manifold increase in special technical schools at the secondary and university levels to help produce skilled workers to fill the estimated one million positions that would be required by the industrial plants transferred from the Soviet Union.[2] In many instances, the length of schooling at the secondary and university levels was increased to ensure the quality of technical training. In addition, spare-time educational opportunities were made available for workers and peasants who were to be trained as semi-skilled workers.[3] Student enrollment in spare-time primary and middle schools increased from a combined total of less than two million in 1953 to about nine million in 1957.[4] The Great Leap placed increased emphasis on the need to combine education with productive labor. With the introduction of communes in the countryside and the stress on self-sufficiency, local communities assumed the full responsibility for maintaining schools. A summary of the Chinese educational system on the eve of the Cultural Revolution follows.

Primary Schools

On the advice of Soviet advisers, the length of primary schooling was initially reduced by one year, to a term of five years, to extend the system and to produce more graduates. By 1953 the length of primary schooling had reverted back to six years. In rural areas the length of primary schooling was usually limited to perhaps three or four years, with many of the schools on a half-study and half-work basis. Initially, primary school was neither compulsory nor universal. During the first ten years of the regime's rule, enrollment in primary schools increased from a little over twenty-four million in 1949 to fifty-one million in 1953 and to over eighty-six million in 1958.[5] During the period from 1953 to 1958, approximately twenty-seven and a half million adult peasants and workers enrolled in spare-time primary schools.[6] The curriculum for primary schools contained a heavy emphasis on political and ideological value formation as well as the usual subjects of Chinese language, arithmetic, and introduction to general science.

Secondary Schools

There were several types of secondary, or middle, schools prior to the Cultural Revolution. First were the general, academically oriented secondary schools, which included three years at the junior level and three more years at the senior level. These academically oriented schools were found exclusively in urban areas before 1958. Second were vocational schools, which emphasized practical training and teacher education. The length of these vocational secondary schools was usually three to four years. Third were specialized polytechnic schools that prepared students for work in industry, agriculture, public health, and commerce and trade. These specialized secondary schools emphasized little solid academic instruction and were almost exclusively found in urban areas before 1958. Most of the vocationally oriented and specialized schools were on half-study and half-work basis. The Great Leap and the communization programs expanded the half-study and half-work vocational secondary schools into the communes, where agricultural production became the main content of instruction. There were enormous increases in enrollment at all types of secondary schools.[7] In 1953, enrollment in middle schools, including spare-time, was at 3.3 million; secondary technical schools, including spare-time, was about 1.7 million. By 1958, enrollment for middle schools, including spare-time, was over 9 million; and secondary technical schools, including spare-time, was 1.4 million. A large percentage of the middle-school enrollment was in the countryside. By 1958, the educational thrust was to teach whatever was required by the communes to help agricultural production. In addition to a heavy emphasis on agricultural subjects, rural middle schools' curriculum included political and ideological studies and arithmetic. Spare-time rural secondary specialized schools now began to teach machinery repair and tractor driving.

The mushrooming of secondary schools, and their tremendous increase in enrollment, soon presented problems for the job situation in the urban areas. The First Five-Year Plan's economic acceleration had encouraged migration to the urban areas, but the number of jobs generated by the economy simply could not keep pace with the potential workers who flocked to the urban areas. Two basic changes in China's educational policy were made to meet this problem: first, the number of spare-time specialized secondary schools was reduced; and second, all graduates from primary and secondary schools who could neither find jobs in factories nor go on to technical colleges or universities were sent to the countryside to engage in agricultural production. This was the beginning of the youth rustication program, which will be discussed separately.

The problems of rapid growth in urban population and the resultant unemployment in urban areas were solved in 1958 by the Great Leap, which called for mass mobilization and labor-intensive production in the countryside. Students were told to participate as farmers or workers after school. Expansion of half-study and half-work schools resumed in both urban and rural areas. In addition, political education became an even more essential part of the curriculum to inculcate the values of being both "red" and "expert."[8]

Higher Education

Leo Orleans identified five different types of higher educational institutions in China prior to the Cultural Revolution.[9] There were comprehensive universities, comparable to any American universities, with the traditional academic departments. These were four-year institutions of higher learning with full-time students. Then there were the polytechnic institutions, such as the famous Qinghua University, located in Beijing—a sort of Chinese M.I.T. Below these two types of universities were the new institutions of higher learning that proliferated during and after the Great Leap: 1. vocationally organized, specialized colleges; 2. enterprise-controlled spare-time industrial colleges, for workers already employed by the industries; and 3. the low-quality and highly questionable institutions, known as workers and peasants colleges, that mushroomed during the Great Leap. While comprehensive and polytechnic universities numbered between twenty and forty before 1966, the new institutions grew by the hundreds. Enrollment in institutions of higher education in 1949 was about 117,000. In 1959, the total figure had reached 810,000.[10]

Entrance to comprehensive and polytechnic universities was based on passing the entrance examination. A large percentage of students who were admitted to university work, in the period under discussion, were those who wanted to be engineers and scientists. The areas of specialization were determined according to the state plan and manpower needs in the scientific and technological fields. During my visits in 1973 to Beijing University, Qiao dung University in Xian, and Fudan University in Shanghai, it was pointed out by the faculties that before 1960 science instruction at the university level was under the influence of the Soviet Union, in terms of textbooks, laboratories, and equipment. Before the withdrawal of Soviet aid in June 1960, some seventy-five hundred Chinese students had gone to the Soviet Union for either post-graduate work or specialized training. According to Leo Orleans, the total number of graduates from these institutions of higher learning from 1949 to 1966 was 1.7 million, with thirty-four percent in engineering, twenty-seven percent in education, eleven percent in medicine, eight percent in agriculture and forestry, six percent in natural sciences, and five percent in finance and economics.[11]

Chinese university education before the Cultural Revolution was modeled on the European system, with a great deal of formalism and rigidity. The role of the professor was to give formal lectures in class, with no opportunity for questions and answers or interaction between the instructor and the students. As doors of higher education opened to students of worker and peasant background (in 1957 about thirty-six percent of the university student body in China came from that social background) a serious problem of academic deficiency occurred among the students. Instructors were unwilling to provide remedial work for those who needed it, and were often contemptuous of those who were academically ill-prepared for university work.[12] Tension, therefore, existed in the relationship between the students and their professors, coupled with feelings of resentment on the part of students who could not reach their instructors.[13] We will see later how this "feudal relationship" was corrected after the Cultural Revolution.

THE CULTURAL REVOLUTION
AND EDUCATIONAL REFORM

The Cultural Revolution's greatest impact was in the area of education. Some far-reaching consequences resulted from the revolutionary reforms introduced during the upheaval to overhaul the educational system at all levels. In the following pages we will discuss some of the changes and innovations in Chinese education introduced during the Cultural Revolution and its aftermath.

It must be kept in mind that for at least two years, from 1966 to 1968, all schools and universities were closed because of the disruption caused by the students' participation in the Cultural Revolution. When the central government ordered the schools to be reopened and students to return to their classes in late 1967 and early 1968, the normal combined length of attendance for both primary and middle schools was shortened from twelve years to nine years.[14] Most rural areas shortened the combined length of attendance in both primary and middle schools to a bare seven years. It was reasoned that by the time the youngsters completed their middle-school education they would be fifteen or sixteen, "a suitable age to begin taking part in farm work." Those who finished the shortened secondary education in urban areas were expected to work in factories to gain practical experience. Upon reaching the age of fifteen or sixteen, all youths who had completed secondary education were required to render at least three years of practical work or service before considering entrance to higher education. This requirement for three years of practical work experience relieved some of the pressure for entrance to colleges and universities. University education, particularly at technical colleges, was similarly shortened to three years or less.

Then drastic changes were made in the curriculum in both schools and universities. Primary school instruction revolved around subjects on politics and ideology and rudimentary agriculture or industry. Language arts and arithmetic were barely squeezed in between these political and practical subjects. At the secondary schools, academic subjects, such as language arts, arithmetic, and history, were taught in conjunction with productive labor, political, and military training. Mao's principle that "education must serve proletarian politics and be combined with productive labor" became the key factor in developing instructional content in all schools. Primary and secondary education was mainly devoted to the acquisition of knowledge which had immediate application to economic production. Many primary and secondary schools were structured on the half-study and half-work basis. Rural education was to cultivate pride for being peasants, appreciation of agricultural work, and a desire for "striking roots" in the countryside. The attitude developed by many rural students, that "the first year they are still country folks, the next year they become different, and the third year they look down on their parents," was to be condemned as revisionist.[15] University book learning, which was impractical and irrelevant to problem solving, was expanded to integrate theory and practice. To implement this integration, universities established factories on campus to manufacture marketable products. In addition, long-time factory workers who had practical experience were allowed to enroll in university classes on physics, chemistry, or mechanical engineering. Visitors to Chinese universities in the 1970s, as a rule, were shown the facilities on campus where experienced factory workers worked alongside of young students on some aspect of science, such as solid state physics and transistor making. One of China's leading scientists and educators, Professor Zhou Peiyuan, vice president of the Chinese Academy of Science and president of Beijing University said in 1973

> Beijing University has shortened the period of schooling, enrolled students from among workers, peasants, and soldiers with practical experience, and changed the road and approach in conducting education. The faculty of sciences has established direct contact with factories, and the university has set up its own workshops. Teachers and students spend a certain amount of time in productive labour at factories where teaching and scientific research are done in combination with practice. . . . The university has seven factories and twenty-seven workshops, plus a farm, and has established regular contact with sixty-five industrial enterprises. This has effectively promoted changes in the system, contents, and method of teaching.[16]

The Cultural Revolution severely condemned the system of evaluating student performance by examination. Entrance examinations and the practice of holding students back a year for failure to pass the examinations were labeled as the "revisionist line of education." Entrance examinations for universities were abolished when these institutions were reopened in 1970. In their place, a system of nominations and recommendations was adopted for all institutions of higher learning. The new system called for the following methods of nomination: 1. self-nomination by individual students, 2. nomination by the masses, and 3. recommendation by the party leadership. High school graduates thus nominated then had to be approved by the institutions. The purpose of the new system was to enable youngsters from a "revolutionary social background"—workers, poor and lower-middle peasants, members of the army, and youth who had gone down to live with the peasants—to have the opportunity to enter universities. Clearly, the new system was designed to meet complaints at the time that the universities, the road to one's future station in life, had become the preserve of the elites and tended to exclude those who had become political activists endowed with revolutionary fervor. The new admissions policy was aimed not only at greatly increasing recruitment of youths from the proper "revolutionary social background," but it limited admissions to those who had acquired practical experience, either as workers in factories or in communes. In 1970, most universities required two to three years of practical experiences prior to entrance. Thus, under the new system with its lack of entrance examinations, 150,000 workers, peasants, and PLA servicemen were admitted to universities from 1970 to 1973. With the admission of large numbers of students who did not have adequate preparation, academic standards had to be lowered and remedial classes organized.

The administration and management of education during the Cultural Revolution was taken out of the hands of the professional educators. Local revolutionary committees began taking control of the schools in October 1968 through the dispatch of "worker and peasant," Mao's Thought Propaganda Teams, with the active participation of PLA soldiers.[17] These teams ended strife among the students[18] and worked with the students and teachers to reorganize the educational content, placing more stress on the study of Mao's thought and relating education to productive labor. In addition to revolutionary committees which administered the schools and universities, there was the "Revolution in Education Committee" on campus to provide daily guidance for the reform measures being carried out in these institutions, particularly in higher education.[19] Members of these educational committees were cadres and teachers. At Fudan University in Shanghai, which I visited in 1973, cadres who were workers in the revolutionary committee dominated the university's administration; the leading cadre who directed Fudan University was a skilled worker in a textile factory in Shanghai.

In rural areas, primary schools were run by the production brigades, and secondary schools by the communes. This meant that these revolutionary committees on the communes were in full charge of education. Two reasons were generally given for the reform. One was on a purely ideological level: "Since the fundamental question of revolution is political power" and the "fundamental question of revolution in education is also the question of power," proletarian education must be in the hands of the people in order to prevent the growth of the revisionist educational line. The second was on a practical level: "We (lower-middle peasants) can decide the teaching contents and, in a way we see fit, plan when classes take place."[20] Another important fact was that in brigade-run schools teachers were members of the same commune, "eating the same kind of food and living in the same kind of housing as the poor and lower-middle peasants."[21] In urban areas, primary schools were generally run by neighborhood revolutionary committees or street committees; secondary schools were run by neighborhood revolutionary committees and factories located in the area. The new revolutionary management of schools by local units reflected the overall thrust of the Cultural Revolution for decentralization. It also relieved the state from spending enormous amounts of money for primary and secondary education.

A number of innovative educational experiments were undertaken during the Cultural Revolution and its aftermath, most notably in extension work at agricultural colleges and in short-term courses for workers in "July 21" workers' colleges. Many agricultural colleges extended their teaching to practical learning situations in the countryside. Traditionally, an agricultural college insisted on learning from textbooks, in individual classes, arranged by stages in the curriculum: for instance, a basic course on botany, followed by a specialized course in plant physiology and crop cultivation. Under the reform, students were taught the rice seedlings process simultaneously with basic course on plant physiology and a specialized course on crop cultivation.[22] Also, short extension courses were provided for older peasants to help them understand the scientific methods.[23] The first experiment for a workers' college was made by the Shanghai Machine Tools Plant, in response to Mao's directive of July 21, 1968 for shortening the length of schooling and revolutionizing education.[24] These "July 21" workers' colleges selected experienced workers from the plant, and capable students from the middle school administered by the plant, to form a technical college with short-term instruction on instruments and their components. This training of semi-skilled workers to become skilled technicians in a short period was comparable to the on-the-job or manpower retraining programs funded by the United States government in recent years. Typically, the curriculum at these workers' colleges consisted of political education, militia activities, mathematics, mechanical engineering, and related technical subjects. Encouragement was often given to the workers' college to design machinery for the plant. There was a phenomenal growth of workers' colleges in many provinces. In one year, Liaoning Province claimed an increase from 52 to 270 such colleges, with a total student enrollment of 25,300. Heilongjiang had 333 such institutions, with enrollment of 17,800, or twenty percent of all students in higher education in that province.[25] Both agricultural extension work and short-term on-the-job training were designed to raise the scientific capability of the peasants and workers, in the nation's quest for rapid scientific and technological development. As one participant in the workers' college explained: "We should . . . build a magnificent contingent of working-class intellectuals, with socialist culture and technical knowledge, and adept in production."[26]

REVERSAL OF THE CULTURAL REVOLUTION EDUCATIONAL POLICY

The reforms and innovations introduced during the Cultural Revolution and its aftermath created a host of problems. As the Chinese leaders reviewed the educational field in the 1970s, they discovered that the quality of education had fallen and that the gap between China and the industrial nations in science and technology had widened rather than narrowed over the past decade.[27] The disappearance of a large number of scientific research institutes reflected the almost complete abandonment of basic research in science and technology.[28] The deterioration in educational quality was attributable to the inordinate amount of classroom time spent on ideological and political studies, the absence of examinations to measure students' performance, and the lack of discipline in schools.[29] The morale of the country's nine million teachers and educational workers was at a low ebb.

Premier Zhou was the first leading party and government official to take action to arrest the declining state of education. In 1973, the State Council under Zhou's direction reinstated entrance examination requirements for universities and colleges. Zhou called for more research by both scientific institutions and universities. The premier asked that certain academically superior students be enrolled in universities directly after graduation from secondary school. All these measures were designed to improve the quality of education and to recruit potential young scientists. The radical ideologues, of course, waged a campaign of criticism against these educational policies, which reversed the reforms introduced by the Cultural Revolution. At first the attack focused on the question of entrance examination to universities. In June 1973, a number of universities in several provinces began the cultural examination system, which required nominees to pass both an oral and a written test prior to admission. The oral portion of the test dealt with political studies and experience gained through labor; the written portion dealt with academic knowledge, with emphasis on mathematics, physics, and chemistry. The cultural examination became a public issue after the protest by a student who was sent to a commune in 1968. Following nomination to to the university by his commune brigade in 1973, he took the entrance test but refused to answer questions in physics and chemistry. Instead, at the instigation by the radicals, he wrote a protest letter on his examination paper, stating that he had followed Chairman Mao's directive to go down to the countryside to engage in collective productive labor for almost five years. Since he had to work long hours as a captain of a production team in the commune, he had found no time to review the subjects learned five years earlier in secondary school. Following this protest, articles in the *People's Daily* and the *Red Flag*, the party's theoretical journal controlled by the radicals, criticized abuse in the application of the cultural examinations.[30] They argued that this examination system failed to take into account the importance of a student's revolutionary fervor and practical experience and that there had been cases of favoritism where cadres had wrangled admission for their children "through the back door." A week before the convening of the Tenth Party Congress, an editorial, reputedly written by Mao, appeared in the *People's Daily*, supporting the campaign against the unfair entrance examination system and urging everyone to "go against the tide"—a slogan reminiscent of the 1966 Cultural Revolution's "dare to rebel."[31]

Now the battle line had been drawn on educational policies. The initial skirmishes were won by the radicals who attacked the Minister of Education during 1975 and 1976 and succeeded in removing him from that office. The radicals charged 1. that the revisionsists had dominated China's education for seventeen years, from 1949 to 1966, and 2. that most teachers and students were so bourgeois as to be ranked as "the stinking ninth category of class enemy of socialism."[32]

THE NEW EDUCATIONAL POLICY AFTER MAO

With the downfall of the Gang of Four, the regime moved to expand and improve education throughout the system. Hua Guo-feng announced plans to guarantee eight years of schooling in all rural areas and ten years in all urban areas by 1985. In 1977, the total primary school enrollment of 146 million students in 9.8 million schools probably did not provide all youngsters with a five-year primary education.[33] The new policy will mean that all students will receive at least three years of secondary education beyond the five years in primary school. The quality of education also will be improved, with more classroom time devoted to learning academic subjects and less to political ideology. Special classes for the gifted and a dual track of "quick" and "slow" learner system have been instituted. Primary school curriculum will emphasize arithmetic, general science, and foreign language (English, Russian, Japanese, or German in the third year). Other subjects will include the Chinese language, political education, and physical culture. Discipline is to be tightened, and an improved examination system introduced.

Competitive university entrance examinations have already been reintroduced. In the summer of 1977, approximately 5.7 million young people took these entrance exams, which were administered on a nationwide basis. The leading universities admitted over eleven hundred successful candidates, with a large percentage from peasant and cadre family backgrounds.[34] The present university entrance system combines the nomination system of the Cultural Revolution period and the academic entrance examinations. Candidates for university entrance first apply for nomination to the communes or factories where they work or to the schools they attend. Then the county or municipal enrollment committee screens the applicants to determine who will be eligible to take the entrance examination. The candidates who successfully pass the entrance examination are further screened by both the university and the provincial or minicipal enrollment committees to assure their political (devotion to the party and socialism as well as love of labor) and physical qualifications. The universities decide which candidates from the final list are to be admitted, on the basis of the candidate's major field of interest.[35] This new enrollment system is obviously intended to insure that students who receive a university education will be both "red" and "expert."

Other features of the new educational policy include 1. the transfer of governance of universities from the revolutionary committees to the institution's administrators, to eliminate political interference by non-professionals; 2. the continuation of spare-time education for adults, on-the-job in workers' colleges and at agricultural middle schools, as a way of broadening scientific knowledge among the masses; 3. improvement of working conditions and salaries for the nation's intellectuals and nine million teachers, and the adoption of incentive awards for excellence; 4. increased funds for improvement of education, including such needed projects as new modern libraries for schools and universities and instructional television and radio.[36]

The new education program will continue the practice of sending urban youth into the countryside. It has been estimated that over twenty million middle-school graduates were sent down to the countryside to work in communes from the beginning of the Cultural Revolution in 1966 to 1977. Hua Guofeng has called this vast army of educated young people now working in the countryside a "new force in our contingent of intellectuals."[37] This massive transfer of urban secondary-school graduates to rural areas and sparsely populated autonomous regions was designed to accomplish a number of objectives.[38] Ideologically, the transfer to the countryside was supposed to reduce the gap created by the differences in urban and rural living standards and to remove elitist tendencies prevalent among educated urban intellectuals who generally looked down upon the peasants. Pragmatically, it was seen as a means of solving the urban unemployment problem and, at the same time, bolstering rural economies where intensive labor was the strategy for development.

This annual migration of educated youths has proved of some benefit to rural development. First, their physical labor has contributed to sorely needed food production. In addition, these youths who possess a certain amount of technical knowledge frequently serve as "agents of technological change." Many have become agricultural technicians or rural paramedics, "barefoot doctors" in public health and paramedical work.[39] Others gradually have become leaders in production teams or brigades.

These tangible benefits of the program to transfer urban youths to the countryside have often been marred by problems. The peasants frequently have looked upon these urban youths as an additional burden.[40] Too often the peasants have felt that the urban youths were not really suited to the hard labor in the fields and have resented spending time to teach them how to do simple manual work. Young male and female students from the cities often found the work too hard and the rural backwardness too difficult to take for a long period of time. These youths were reluctant to remain on the communes for any longer than was necessary, and viewed their stay as only transitory. Some escaped the misery of their hard life on the communes by smuggling themselves back to the cities; without a job or food coupons they soon became wanderers on the city streets or sheltered by friends and relatives. Hua Guofeng admits that these problems need to be corrected.[41] With the leadership's determination to move speedily toward agricultural mechanization, these millions of urban youths certainly could make a valuable contribution. Hua has hinted rather strongly that one of the measures that might boost the morale of these urban youths working in the countryside would be improvement in living conditions. There have been reports of poor housing and inadequate diet for the inexperienced urban youths who are not able to earn the minimum number of work-points to allow for an adequate standard of living. Innovative experiments to link the urban youths in the countryside with the factories in their home cities, to provide for resettlement when they return, have become popular in recent years.[42] Other improvements designed to reduce bitterness and resentment of the urban youths in the countryside are in the offing, including the sending down of rural youth to state farms or collectively owned farms set up especially for them, instead of sending them to work as members of production teams in a commune.

In this chapter we have tried to justify the thesis that the educational content, form, and policies over the past decades have been influenced by shifting policies and development strategies. As China moves into the post-Mao era, the new leadership is determined to repair some of the damage to the educational system brought about by the Cultural Revolution and its aftermath, particularly in the area of educational quality. What we need to emphasize here is that, despite the disruptive effects of the Cultural Revolution, there have been enormous strides made, in terms of student enrollment in educational institutions at all levels. In 1965, the enrollment for China's primary schools was about 116 million; by 1977, enrollment exceeded 146 million students in 9.8 million schools. This enrollment can be expected to rise further as China moves toward her goal of eight years of primary education for rural children and ten years for urban children. At the same time, China is committed to expanding and upgrading secondary and university education in order to provide trained manpower for scientific and technological work. Chinese official figure now shows that nearly two hundred institutions of higher learning were added in 1978, bringing the total of institutions of higher learning to five hundred and ninety-eight, with a total university and college student enrollment of 850,000. Enrollment in secondary technical schools now reach   880,000.[43] Expanded and improved education will require not only long term investment and political commitment, but also the willingness and ability to make educational innovations in the years to come.

NOTES

[1]Hung-ti Chu, "Education in Mainland China," *Current History*, vol. 59, 349 (September 1970), 168–70; and Leo A. Orleans, "Communist China's Education: Policies, Problems, and Prospects," in *India and China: Studies in Comparative Development*, ed. Kuan-I Chen and Jogindar Uppal (New York: Free Press, 1971), pp. 276–77.

[2]Joel Glassman, "Educational Reform and Manpower Policy in China: 1955–1958," *Modern China*, vol. iii, no. 3 (July 1977), 265–66.

[3]Glassman, "Educational Reform and Manpower Policy in China," pp. 268–69.

[4]Glassman, "Educational Reform and Manpower Policy in China," p. 272.

[5]The figure for 1949 was taken from "Primary Schools in China," *Peking Review*, 36 (September 8, 1978), 15. Figures for 1953 and 1958 were taken from State Statistical Bureau of 1960 as reprinted in Joel Glassman, "Educational Reform and Manpower Policy in China," pp. 212, 281.

[6]Glassman, "Educational Reform and Manpower Policy in China," pp. 212, 281.

[7]Glassman, "Educational Reform and Manpower Policy in China," p. 268.

[8]Glassman, "Educational Reform and Manpower Policy in China," p. 280; Hung-Ti Chu, "Education in Mainland China," p. 181; and Orleans, "Communist China's Education," p. 282.

[9]Orleans, "Communist China's Education," pp. 282–83.

[10]Hung-Ti Chiu, "Education in Mainland China," p. 169; and Orleans, "Communist China's Education," p. 282.

[11]Orleans, "Communist China's Education," p. 288.

[12]Philip E. Ginsburg, "Development and Educational Process in China," *Current Scene,* vol. xiv, no. 3 (March 1976), 3–4. Also see *Survey of China Mainland Press* (SCMP), no. 784, pp. 22–23.

[13]Ginsburg, "Development and Educational Process in China," p. 4.

[14]"It is Essential to Rely on the Poor and Lower-Middle Peasants in the Educational Revolution in the Countryside," *Peking Review,* 39 (September 27, 1968), 21.

[15]"It is Essential to Rely on the Poor and Lower-Middle Peasants," p. 20; and "A New-Type School Where Theory Accords with Practice," *Peking Review,* 44 (November 1, 1968), 4–8.

[16]*Hsinhua News Agency* (NCNA), a special for October 1, 1975, p. 22. My own notes in a briefing session given by Professor Zhou on the campus of Peking University in January 1973 contained similar expression.

[17]See Ellen K. Ong, "Education in China since the Cultural Revolution," *Studies in Comparative Communism,* vol. iii, nos. 3 and 4 (July–August 1970), 158–75.

[18]See William Hinton, *Hundred Day War: The Cultural Revolution at Tsinghua University* (New York and London: Monthly Review Press, 1972).

[19]Robert McCormich, "Revolution in Education Committees," *The China Quarterly,* 57 (January–March 1974), 134–39.

[20]"Power is the Fundamental Question of Revolution in Education," *Peking Review,* 51 (December 20, 1968), 8.

[21]"Power Is the Fundamental Question of Revolution," p. 8.

[22]"An Agricultural College in the Countryside," *Peking Review,* 48 (September 29, 1974), 25–26; and "Peasants-College Graduates-Peasants," *Peking Review,* 7 (February 14, 1975), 13–15.

[23]"Peasants-College Graduates-Peasants," p. 13.

[24]" 'July 21' Workers' Colleges," pp. 16–20; and "A Worker after Graduating College," *Peking Review,* 37 (September 12, 1975), 16–19, 21–22.

[25]"A Worker after Graduating College," p. 12.

[26]"Shifts in Higher Education Policy," *Current Scene,* vol. xiii, no. 9 (September 1975), 26.

[27]See Hua Guofeng, "Report on the Work of Government," p. 27; and Fang Yi, "On the Situation in China's Science and Education," *Peking Review,* 2 (January 13, 1978), 15.

[28]Deng Xiaoping, "Speech at the National Educational Work Conference," *Peking Review,* 18 (May 5, 1978), 7–8.

[29]Fang Yi., "On the Situation in China's Science and Education," p. 15.

[30]*Renmin Ribao,* February 2, 1974, p. 1.

[31]*Renmin Ribao,* August 13, 1973, p. 1.

[32]"A Great Debate on the Educational Front: Repudiating the Gang of Four's 'Two Estimates,' "*Peking Review,* 51 (December 16, 1977), 4–9.

[33]"Primary Schools in China," p. 15.

[34]"New College Students," *Peking Review,* 16 (April 21, 1978), 11.

[35]"New College Students," p. 12. Also see "TV University," *Beijing Review,* no. 7 (February 16, 1979), 7

[36]"New College Students," p. 12.

[37]See Hua Guofeng, "Report on the Work of Government," p. 28; Deng Xiao ping, "Speech at the National Educational Work Conference," pp. 7-12; Fang Yi, "On the Situation in China's Science and Education," pp. 16-18; "New College Students," pp. 11-13; and "Educational Policy: Questions and Answers," *Peking Review,* 15 (April 14, 1978), 13-15.

[38]The following works on the youth to the countryside movement may be of interest to readers: Thomas P. Bernstein, *Up to the Mountains and Down to the Countryside: The Transfer of Youth from Urban to Rural China* (New Haven, Conn.: Yale University Press, 1977); and "Urban Youth in the Countryside: Problems of Adaptation and Remedies," *The China Quarterly,* 69 (March 1977), 75-108; D. Gordon White, "The Politics of Hsia-Hsiang Youth," *The China Quarterly,* 59 (July–September 1974), 491-517; Laurence J.C. Ma, "Counterurbanization and Rural Development: The Strategy of Hsia-hsiang," *Current Scene,* vol. xv, nos. 8 and 9 (August–September), 1-12, "1975 Down-to-the-Countryside Program," *Current Scene,* vol. xiv, no. 2 (February 1976), 16-18.

[39]Laurence J.C. Ma, "Counterurbanization and Rural Development," p. 8.

[40]"Urban Youth in the Countryside," pp. 85-86.

[41]"Report on the Work of Government," p. 30.

[42]"1975 Down-to-the-Countryside Program," p. 16.

[43]State Statistical Bureau, "Communique on Fulfillment of China's 1978 National Economic Plan," *Beijing Review,* no. 27 (July 6, 1979), p.41.

China's Role
in
World Politics

STAGES OF EVOLUTION IN CHINESE FOREIGN POLICY

This chapter will focus on current themes and issues in China's foreign policy. It will be necessary at the very outset, however, to briefly sketch the evolution of present day Chinese foreign policy to provide an overview for an understanding of China's role in world politics. We need to point out that China's foreign policy is invariably shaped by a number of factors; among the most important are her geography, history, political ideology, the flow and ebb in her internal politics, and the exertion of international pressures at any given moment which may force China to make realistic adjustment in her policy. An examination of the development of China's foreign relations since 1950 reveals four distinct stages of evolution: 1. the concern for border settlement and security, 1950–1953; 2. the pattern of oscillation between militancy and peaceful coexistence, 1954–1965; 3. China's self-imposed isolation during the Cultural Revolution, 1966–1968; 4. China's return to conventional diplomacy under international pressure, and her increased tempo of international contacts, from 1969 on.

Concern for Border Settlement and Security, 1950–1953

Much of China's external activity during the years of consolidation was devoted to securing her frontiers with her neighbors and attempting to regain her lost territories, such as Xizang (Tibet) and Taiwan. China also wanted to eliminate foreign influence in neighboring countries with shared borders. In pursuing these objectives, the Chinese employed force during the early 1950s. After the successful landing of General MacArthur's United Nations forces in Inchon in September 1950, which cut the North Korean forces in half and paved the way for a rapid advance of UN forces deep into the territory of North Korea and up to the Yalu River that separated China and North Korea, the Chinese watched the deteriorating situation in Korea with fear and apprehension. The fear that the United States forces, under the United Nations command, would cross the Yalu in Manchuria finally prompted the Chinese to intervene in the Korean conflict in October 1950.[1] Before the Chinese intervention in the Korean War, China sought to regain the Island of Taiwan by force—her attempt was met by the United States determination to protect the Nationalist-held island in the Formosa Strait. Similarly, Chinese forces marched into Xizang in October 1950, despite protests from India. During much of this period, China was viewed by the rest of the world as a revolutionary nation, belligerent, and determined to employ armed struggle for the purpose of securing her frontier from unfriendly foreign influences and to regain her lost territories. Because of China's belligerent behavior and seemingly expansionist mood, as evidenced by her action in Xijiang, a containment policy was imposed on China by the United States, which in essence extended the United States defense perimeter to the Pacific coast of China from Japan, to Okinawa, to Formosa, to the Philippines. Later, the containment policy was bolstered by the formation of the Southeast Asian Treaty arrangement to provide a defensive curtain on the land mass bordering China's southwest provinces.

Influence of Domestic Politics on the Oscillation Pattern of China's Foreign Policy, 1954–1965

The record of Chinese foreign policy from 1954 to 1965 reveals a striking pattern of oscillation between militancy and peaceful coexistence. These alternating periods of tension and relaxation in China's relations with other nations were closely related to changes in her internal politics. They reflected both the style of leadership and the developmental strategy for achieving socialism and the goals of industrialization. Thus, when China entered the arena of world politics at the Geneva Conference of 1954 and the Bandung Conference of 1955—the golden age of Chinese diplomacy—her policy and behavior reflected the confidence of the regime and the cohesion of its leaders in launching the orderly and pragmatic developmental program of the First Five-Year Plan at home.

The Geneva Conference of 1954 was convened by the foreign ministers of France, the Soviet Union, the United Kingdom, and the United States for the purpose of settling the problems of Indochina (Cambodia, Laos, and the Vietnams), as well as the unification problem of Korea, following cessation of hostility and the signing of the Korean armistice agreement in the summer of 1953. A French victory in the Indochina war waged against the Viet Minh forces was already very doubtful. A political settlement aimed at preventing an armed takeover by the forces of Ho Chih-min in Indochina was the basic motivation for the Geneva Conference of 1954. The conference did produce a declaration prohibiting foreign military bases or forces in the three states of Vietnam, Laos, and Cambodia. In addition, separate agreements were signed for the eventual independence of the three Indochina states through elections to be supervised by an International Control Commission. The conference failed to provide any political settlement for the unification of Korea. The Geneva Conference marked China's debut in conventional international diplomacy. It gave the outside world an opportunity to see the affable Zhou Enlai confront John Foster Dulles of the United States and Anthony Eden of Great Britain in the intricate games of international diplomacy.

In the spring of 1955, Zhou Enlai and Nehru played a dominant role in the first Bandung Conference, which brought together for the first time the nonaligned nations of Asia and Africa as a third world force in a bipolarized world of Soviet and United States orbits. The Bandung Conference produced the famous five principles—mutual respect for sovereignty and territorial integrity, mutual nonaggression, noninterference in each others' internal affairs, equality and mutual benefit, and peaceful coexistence—as the guide for relations among the nations participating in the conference.

When dissension over developmental strategy surfaced among China's leaders, as was the case during the Great Leap from 1958 to 1961, the posture of China's foreign relations became militant, calling for worldwide revolutionary struggle. Tension mounted in the Formosa Strait during the summer of 1958, as the Chinese bombarded the Nationalist held offshore islands of Mazu and Jinmen, only twelve miles away from the Chinese mainland. When the Chinese realized the United States' firm intention was to back up the Nationalists by using the Seventh Fleet to escort ships to the offshore islands and Krushchev's policy was to not provoke the United States into a war in the Far East, they reverted to a conciliatory attitude, resumed ambassadorial talks with the United States, and temporarily stopped bombardment of the offshore islands. The Chinese later resumed bombardment on odd-numbered days only.

When moderation in economic development was resumed during 1962, after the fiasco of the Great Leap and the related crash programs, interaction with other countries increased at a fantastic rate. Premier Zhou visited fourteen countries in Asia, Africa, and Europe from late

1963 to early 1965. Liu Shaoqi, as the chief of state for the People's Republic of China, paid state visits to countries of South and Southeast Asia in 1963. These expanded diplomatic activities were designed to win friends among the third world countries of Asia and Africa, most of whom were not aligned with either of the two superpowers. By June 1960, the rift between China and the Soviet Union began to be noticed by the outside world from the arguments they hurled at each other and from the zeal exhibited by the Chinese in trying to win friends in the underdeveloped third world, at the expense and discomfort of the Soviet Union.

Chinese Foreign Policy During the Cultural Revolution, 1966–1968

In many ways, the Cultural Revolution represented the lowest point of the regime's foreign relations. During this period there were almost no major pronouncements in foreign policy, and contact with other nations consisted mainly of visits from friendly nations and occasional state receptions for visiting dignitaries. In the midst of the upheaval, more than forty of China's envoys were recalled from abroad, with no replacement sent to many countries with which China had established diplomatic relations. Behavior of extreme militancy was evident in the treatment of foreigners in Beijing during the early stages of the Cultural Revolution.

For a brief period, the Cultural Revolution evidently paralyzed China's very instrument for conducting foreign relations, the Ministry of Foreign Affairs. China's foreign minister, Chen Yi, was under attack by the radicalized Red Guards, who actually seized the ministry in the summer of 1967. Liu Shaoqi, for a time a leading foreign policy maker in the early 1960s, was purged. Red Guard attacks on Liu Shaoqi and the Ministry of Foreign Affairs practically immobilized the senior foreign policy personnel.[2] Recent disclosures also reveal that during the Cultural Revolution the radicals not only attempted "to meddle in foreign affairs work," but tried "to seize the diplomatic power of the central leading organs."[3] With this in-fighting and turmoil, it is little wonder that Chinese foreign policy during the Cultural Revolution period was directionless. Some observers have thought that the issues debated among the dissenting top leaders in China during the upheaval had been triggered by the United States' escalation of war in Vietnam. For example, Robert Scalapino argued in 1968 that the Cultural Revolution represented a victory for Mao and his supporters because of the need to readopt guerrilla strategy to fight an imminent invasion of China by the United States forces in Southeast Asia.[4] Similarly, Donald Zagoria argued that the

United States involvement in Vietnam in 1965 was a "catalyst" that brought about open disagreement among top Chinese leaders on the policy most suitable to meet the threat poised on China's southwest border, a debate that eventually engulfed the whole nation in an unprecedented upheaval.[5]

The spillover of Cultural Revolution demonstrations and riots to neighboring countries, such as those in Hongkong and Burma in 1967, had led some observers to conclude that the export of Mao's revolutionary thought and the Chinese revolutionary experience had become the main objective of China's foreign policy.[6] Recent disclosures by Chinese officials on these incidents abroad, as well as the anti-foreign campaign conducted inside China during the early stages of the Cultural Revolution, have raised doubt about this. For a short period Zhou Enlai apparently lost control over the direction of foreign policy.[7] In a speech, the deputy chief for the Hongkong branch of the New China News Agency revealed that the 1967 campaign waged in Hongkong and Macao, under the banner "opposing British, resisting brutality," was carried out by Lin Biao in opposition to Mao's and Zhou's policies.[8] The implication of the statement is that Zhou Enlai, who was responsible for China's foreign affairs, was unable to prevent these occurrences. Thus, the Chinese are now saying that the export of China's revolutionary model during the Cultural Revolution was not a part of the legitimate Chinese foreign policy design.

China's Return to Conventional Diplomacy, 1969–1976

From the post-Cultural Revolution period to Mao's death in 1976, Chinese foreign policy contained fewer ideological polemics and was more conventional and pragmatic. Admittedly, there were differences among the leaders, with respect to a number of domestic problems emanating from the Cultural Revolution, but these differences on domestic policies had little impact on China's foreign policy. The armed clashes along the Sino-Soviet frontier in the spring of 1969 had awakened the Chinese to the stark reality that China could be completely isolated and vulnerable to the Soviet military power amassed along the border. It seemed possible to the Chinese that the Soviet Union might very well try to repeat its 1968 military invasion of Czechoslovakia by attacking China. Doak Barnett called this China's "military-security concerns."[9] The breakdown in China's relations with the rest of the world during the Cultural Revolution had to be repaired to check the Soviets. This could be done by a well executed pragmatic foreign policy designed to strengthen China's international position in general and to restore the power balance in Asia. Gestures, as well as intention, of peaceful coexistence became pronounced in China's post-Cultural Revolution foreign policy, including moves toward a rapprochement with the United States. The signing of the Shanghai communiqué in February 1972 by President Nixon and Premier Zhou Enlai represented an unprecedented diplomatic victory for Zhou; it provided China with the needed leverage to check the threat posed by the Soviet Union. Coupled with this major thrust in China's new foreign policy was China's desire to reestablish or cement her friendship with fraternal communist nations of East Europe, North Korea, and North Vietnam. Chinese diplomatic efforts even penetrated into Western Europe where China supported Britain's entry into the Common Market. At the same time, Chinese propaganda depicted the Soviet Union as one of the two superpowers bent on "imperialist" domination of the world.

All mention of export of the Chinese revolutionary model, a primary theme of the Cultural Revolution days, disappeared from the media and official pronouncement during the 1970s. When the Paris Peace Agreement was signed in 1973 to terminate the United States involvement in the Vietnam War, China supported it. At the same time, China indicated that she would now welcome United States presence in Asia by deliberately refraining from her usual criticism of the United States security arrangement between Japan and United States bases in the Pacific. Meanwhile, diplomatic overtures were made by the Chinese to woo former members of the Southeast Asian Treaty group, such as the Philippines and Thailand. The shape of the new Chinese foreign policy was clearly outlined by Premier Zhou in his reports on the government to the Tenth CCP Congress in August 1973 and to the Fourth National People's Congress in January 1975. These two important speeches revealed the dominance of Zhou Enlai in the formulation of a new conciliatory pragmatic foreign policy. It is in this regard that we need to briefly review Zhou's perception of the international situation and China's relation to it.

The main concern expressed by Premier Zhou in these speeches was the possibility of a "surprise attack on our country by Soviet revisionist social-imperialism."[10] Zhou complained that in 1975 the Soviets had refused to sign an agreement with China to prevent armed conflict on the border and to disengage the two nations' armed forces in the disputed area along the Ussuri River.[11] Zhou was rather conciliatory when he directed his remarks to the Soviet leadership, despite the longstanding differences between the two countries. Zhou noted that these differences should not have obstructed "the maintenance of normal state relations" between the two countries. With deterioration of relations, Zhou became even more concerned about talk of détente or "collusion" between the two superpowers, the United States and Soviet Union. Zhou saw the collusion of the two nuclear powers as only temporary because, in the long run, the two must contend for global hegemony, the cause of tension in the world. Zhou pointed out that the Soviet Union had stepped up her contention with the United States not only in the Third World, but in Western Europe as well. Based on Zhou's new concept of world politics was China's appeal to the rest of the world to form a united front to resist Soviet Union-United States détente, disguised form of superpower hegemonism that eventually would lead to war:

> Their fierce contention is bound to lead to world war some day. The people of all countries must get prepared. Détente and peace are being talked about everywhere in the world; it is precisely this that shows there is no détente, let alone lasting peace, in this world.[12]

China's foreign policy, as Zhou pointed out in 1973 and 1975, was to support not only the countries of the Third World War against this new form of imperialism or hegemonism, but those in the West and Japan. In this process of forming a united front with other nations against superpower hegemonism, China woukd, however, continue to improve her relations with the United States and, at the same time, do all she could to isolate the Soviet Union in the Asian power balance. It is this strategy, as outlined by Zhou Enlai in 1973 and 1975, that constitutes the foundation of China's present day foreign policy.

MAJOR THEMES IN CHINESE FOREIGN POLICY UNDER HUA GUOFENG

Since his ascendency to the leadership of the party, Hua Guofeng not only has visited Korea, Romania, Yugoslavia, and Iran, but has articulated themes and issues on the international situation and China's foreign policy. In reviewing four recent key official documents on China's foreign policy, we can identify three major themes in China's foreign policy for the 1970s and beyond:[13] Mao's theory of three worlds; anti-superpower hegemonism; and anti-détente, Strategic Arms Limitation Treaty (SALT), and China's nuclear capability.

Mao's Theory of Three Worlds

The Chinese generally attributed the origin of the "three worlds" concept to a quotation from Mao, from his talk in February 1974 with either Kaunda of Zambia or Boumediene of Algeria:

> In my view, the United States and the Soviet Union form the first world. Japan, Europe, and Canada, the middle section, belong to the second world. We are the third world. . . . The third world has a huge population. With the exception of Japan, Asia belongs to the third world. The whole of Africa belongs to the third world, and Latin America, too."[14]

Actually, the concept was formed back in 1955 by Zhou Enlai, Nehru, and Tito at the Bandung Conference when they called for unity against imperialism and nonalignment. Deng Xiaoping officially announced China's concept of three different worlds to the international community at the Sixth Special Session of the United Nation's General Assembly in April 1974.[15] In his political report to the Eleventh Party Congress in August 1977, Hua Guofeng adhered to the three-worlds concept and proposed a broad united front to oppose capitalist and socialist imperialism of the United States and the Soviet Union.[16] Hua expanded this thesis in his 1978 speech to the Fifth National People's Congress by declaring that China would be willing to develop relations with all countries on the five principles of peaceful coexistence endorsed by the 1955 Bandung Conference.[17]

What is the significance of China's concept of the three worlds? First, the Chinese have realistically seen the world in terms of the widening disparity between a vast majority of the world's people who live in developing countries and the affluent people who live in the developed countries. Deng Xiaoping, speaking in 1974 at the Sixth Special Session of the United Nations Assembly on the question of world distribution of wealth and raw materials, stated that the superpowers continue to exploit the peoples of the third world by paying low prices for the raw materials from the developing countries and raising the export prices of the manufactured products sold to them. This was the main concern of practically all Asian, African, and Latin American countries at that special United Nations conference. Second, a three-fold, differentiated world, with contradictions between the parts, fits well into the Chinese communist traditional ideological framework. The struggle between the first world and the third world (the poor nations), with the support of the second world (Japan, Canada, and Western Europe), is looked upon by the Chinese as present day class struggle on a world scale.[18] Third, the Chinese policy to support the third world allows her to develop a broad coalition to alienate the Soviet Union from the developing nations. The Soviet Union's interference in Angola and elsewhere in Africa was seen as an example of social-imperialism that the developing nations must guard against. In a general debate in the United Nations Assembly, Huang Hua, the Chinese Foreign Minister, recently stated:

> To further its aggression and expansion, social-imperialism is trying to fool people by flaunting the signboard of "a natural ally of the developing countries" who "supports the national-liberation movements." Besides, it is doing its utmost to sow discord among the third world countries. It confers on you the title "progressive" on one day, but labels you "reactionary" the next. Now supporting one against another, now the other way round, it stops at nothing in creating dissension and undermining the unity of the third world countries.[19]

Fourth, the theory of the Third world represents a clear departure from the Cultural Revolution stance of China as a revolutionary model to be emulated by others. Hua Guofeng made it very clear at the Eleventh Party Congress in August 1977 that "revolution cannot be exported."[20] Instead, China's new orientation in world politics is to, first of all, identify "the main revolutionary forces, the chief enemies, and the middle forces that can be won over and united" to form an international coalition. This new orientation in China's foreign policy of a united front implies a realignment in the existing international relations, which included China's moves to establish relations with the European Common Market countries and Tito's Yugoslavia.

Anti-superpower Hegemony

The concept that no nation should exercise its preponderant influence over another was one of the principles that the United States and China agreed on in the Shanghai communiqué of February 28, 1972, signed by President Nixon and Premier Zhou Enlai: "Neither should seek hegemony in the Asia-Pacific region and each is opposed to efforts by any other country or group of countries to establish such hegemony."[21] Anti-hegemonism has become a major objective in Chinese foreign policy; one communiqué after another, signed by China and various friendly nations, has contained this expression in varying degrees of intensity.[22] While the United States is one of the two superpowers, the Chinese seem to focus their attack on the Soviet Union and her social imperialism. Hua Guofeng singled out the Soviet Union's role in world politics as "the most dangerous source of a new world war" on the ground that "The Soviet Union relies mainly on its military power to carry out expansion; yet it goes about flaunting banners of 'socialism' and 'support for revolution' to dupe people and sell its wares."[23] The United States is viewed by the Chinese as the superpower which is "striving to preserve its vested interests" and is thus less dangerous than the Soviet Union, which is "trying hard to extend its sphere of influence."[24] The Chinese have made a point to catalog the Soviet Union's penetration into Europe, Africa, the Middle East, the Persian Gulf region, and the Asian-Pacific basin in recent years, to prove that "social imperialism is the more aggressive and adventurous of the two superpowers and is the major threat to world peace and security."[25] While the Chinese deny that they consider the Soviet Union the more dangerous superpower because it occupied the disputed areas along the Sino-Soviet frontier, the military might of the Soviet Union, and her war-making capability, is a major consideration in their perception. The Chinese perceive that the entire Soviet economy has been placed on a "military footing," and they are keenly aware that there are Soviet troops stationed in foreign countries, particularly in Czechoslovakia, which "is completely under prolonged (actually indefinite) military occupation."[26]

Some time ago, Deng Xiaoping stated that a superpower "is an imperialist country which everywhere subjects other countries to its aggression, interference, control, subversion, or plunder, and strives for world hegemony."[27] The Chinese believe that a number of local wars have begun through the interferences of the two superpowers in the affairs of third world countries, and that more local wars may result from the Soviet Union's strategic deployment around the world in contention with the United States. The Chinese seem to believe that the contention between the two superpowers will inevitably lead to world war. The Chinese formula for averting the outbreak of wars was outlined by her foreign minister in a recent speech at the United Nations: 1. make third world countries aware of the "growing danger of war" and be prepared for such an eventuality; 2. frustrate the superpowers' expansion and aggression; and 3. make no compromises or actions of appeasement in dealing with the superpowers.[28] In addition, the Chinese feel that the struggle against hegemonism can be waged on the economic front by the third world. Since the superpowers, as the Chinese perceive them, are becoming more dependent upon the supplies of raw materials from the third world, a united effort must be formed to establish "a new international economic order" by defending not only the economic rights and interests of the third world countries, but the price for the raw materials from them.[29] This new international economic order calls for the stabilization of primary commodity prices such as coffee, cocoa, and sugar through negotiations at the United Nations, reduction or cancellation of debts incurred by the poor third world countries, more funds for development, and an easing of credit conditions and restraints on the transfer of technology and scientific knowledge.[30] All these measures proposed by the Chinese are aimed at winning the support of the third world countries, which in the past have demanded the enactment of these programs to relieve their economic plight in the councils of the United Nations.

Detente, SALT Talks, Disarmament, and China's Nuclear Capability

The time was late November 1974; the places were Ulan Bator in the People's Republic of Mongolia and a conference room in the Great Hall of the People on Tian An Men Square in Beijing. While attending an anniversary celebration in Ulan Bator, Mongolia, Soviet Party Chief Leonid Brezhnev announced that he had rejected the Chinese proposal for the withdrawal of troops along the disputed Sino-Soviet frontier as a precondition for establishing normal relations between the two countries. In Beijing, meanwhile, Secretary of State Henry Kissinger was trading jokes with Deng Xiaoping, the Chinese deputy premier, before briefing the Chinese on the Ford-Brezhnev nuclear arms agreement reached at the Vladivostok summit conference. Kissinger flew directly to Beijing after the summit in order to assure the Chinese that there were no secret protocols reached between the United States and the Soviet Union which might be construed by the Chinese as unfriendly toward them. This extraordinary mission by Secretary of State Kissinger was undertaken with the full realization that the Chinese were opposed to any accord on the strategic limitation of nuclear and other sophisticated weapons between the two superpowers. In 1972 at the United Nations, the Chinese made known to the world their opposition to the policy of détente and efforts to relax the nuclear arms race. As the Chinese chief delegate to the United Nations said recently, "How can we afford to relax and to sleep when a superpower has deployed a million troops along our border?"[31]

The Chinese wasted no time in castigating the theme of détente at the conclusion of the Helsinki summit in the fall of 1975, when some progress was made in the Strategic Arms Limitation (SALT) talks between the United States and the Soviet Union. This time the Chinese called the talk of détente by Moscow a fraud to mask Soviet expansion in other parts of the world, as demonstrated by its intervention in Angola.[32] To the Chinese, détente is synonymous with nuclear arms expansion: "Therefore, in the interest of 'détente' it is necessary to feverishly step up manufacturing even more 'weapons of mass destruction.' "[33] The Chinese view the SALT talks as a veil for intensifying the nuclear arms race between the two superpowers, and the negotiations on SALT as "a form of struggle by which each side tries to restrict the other's expansion and build up its own strength."[34] The Chinese also see détente between the two superpowers and the SALT talks as a design by the Soviet Union to create a false sense of security for many nations in Western Europe and, thus, as an opportunity to greatly strengthen their relative military position and nuclear capability vis à vis Western Europe. The Chinese think that the countries of Western Europe must bolster their national defenses: to accept détente and disarmament is to appease Soviet expansionism.[35] One might add that it is probable that détente has made it increasingly difficult for China to isolate the Soviet Union, and therefore she is vehemently opposed to the détente even at the risk of jeopardizing her rapprochement with the United States.

In the special session of the United Nations General Assembly on disarmament, the Chinese seemed to take three positions with respect to universal disarmament.[36] First, the Chinese believe that general disarmament must begin with the Soviet Union and the United States, the two superpowers. China resented Soviet Foreign Minister Gromyko's appeal to all other members of the United Nations to take steps to halt the armament race. The Chinese argue that medium and small countries must strengthen their defenses in order to protect themselves against the threat posed by the military might of the superpowers. Second, the Chinese objected to the Soviet view that the real threat to world peace lies in nuclear armaments, since the superpowers have accumulated an enormous arsenal of conventional weapons in preparation for a possible conventional war. The Chinese position, therefore, is that genuine disarmament must involve both nuclear and conventional weapons. Third, the Chinese also objected to the Soviet proposal for an international convention for guaranteeing the security of nonnuclear states. To the Chinese, the purpose of this proposal is "to bind, hand and foot, the numerous small and medium-sized countries and deprive them of their capabilities for self-defense" by restricting the possession of nuclear armaments to the superpowers alone.[37] The Chinese counterproposal is that a superpower like the Soviet Union should be the first to declare the nonuse of nuclear weapons "under whatever conditions against the nonnuclear countries, instead of playing tricks of one kind or another."[38]

China decided to undertake a costly program for nuclear development, in terms of both atomic devices and missiles, in 1957, after prolonged debate within the party and the military hierarchy.[39] It was a hard decision because of the cost involved, as well as the realization that a nuclear weapons program had to be developed without Soviet aid or advice. Since then, the Chinese have considered the nuclear program the supreme example of self-reliance and determination. China had her first nuclear test in October 1964, her first thermonuclear test of about two hundred kilotons in May 1966, and her first atmospheric test of several megatons in November 1971. During the fourteen years from 1964 to 1978, at least thirty-six nuclear tests were conducted in the Xinjiang and Inner Mongolian desert areas. China has also developed a system of about twenty intermediate ballistic missiles with a range of up to one thousand miles, as well as one hundred medium-range ballistic missiles with a range of five hundred to seven hundred fifty miles. Both systems are capable of carrying nuclear warheads. Since April 1970, when China sent her first satellite orbiting around the world, she has successfully launched six more satellites. Although China is lagging behind in other aspects of scientific and technological development, her nuclear and space programs have been progressing steadily, and she must be regarded as a nuclear power.

Even though she has become a member of the exclusive "nuclear club," China has consistently opposed the test ban and the nonproliferation treaties, based on the contention that 1. the test ban treaty was designed by the superpowers to prevent the less developed nations from acquiring nuclear weapons, and 2. China's nuclear program was purely for defensive purposes. Zhou Enlai once declared for the Chinese government that unless there was total disarmament, including the destruction of all nuclear weapons by all powers and the dismantling of foreign military bases, China would continue to develop her own nuclear weapons for defensive purposes.[40] Certainly China's nuclear capability was one of the several factors which compelled the United States to seek rapprochement with China in 1971. The growth of China's nuclear capability not only altered the power balance in Asia but also made the world realize that any arms control program, such as the SALT talks, would be meaningless in the long run unless the Chinese were brought into the discussion and became a part of the international cooperative effort toward global arms limitations.

SINO-SOVIET CONFLICT
AND THE BORDER DISPUTE

At the founding of the People's Republic of China in 1949, the Soviet Union was China's only ally. The alliance was cemented in a thirty-year Sino-Soviet treaty of peace and friendship, ratified in April 1950, after months of hard negotiation by the Chinese. Although the treaty provided an automatic extension for five additional years, the Chinese decided in April 1979 to terminate the treaty at its expiration in April 1980. This decision by the Chinese to not renew the treaty represented a benchmark in the two nations' turbulent relations over the past three decades.

The first signs of the rupture in the Sino-Soviet alliance appeared in 1953–1954. At the conclusion of the Korean War, China was eager to obtain a commitment from the Soviet Union for support in confronting the containment policy imposed by the United States in Asia. The Soviet Union's stance at that time was to move toward a global policy of peaceful coexistence. As the United States extended its protection to Taiwan by concluding a mutual defense treaty with the Chinese Nationalists in 1954, Chinese uneasiness was demonstrated in her militancy toward the Taiwan issue, which reached a crisis proportion in 1958. In the face of nuclear threat from the United States, the Chinese sought a commitment from the Soviet Union for nuclear protection. When Khrushchev refused the Chinese request, the rupture in the Sino-Soviet relations became enlarged and at times quite explosive. Thus, 1958 was a turning point in Sino-Soviet relations. Not only did a serious difference develop in the two nations' approach toward the Asian power balance situation vis à vis the United States containment policy, but at that critical juncture the Chinese decided to switch their economic development strategy from centralized planning with emphasis on heavy industry, requiring heavy dependence on Soviet aid, to mass mobilization of the Great Leap and the commune programs. It was, then, a combination of differences, over both the changing Asian situation and the appropriate economic development model, that provided the fuel for the on-going ideological dispute as to which system was more purely Marxist-Leninist. The Soviet Union's decision to withdraw aid from China's economic development in 1960 added more bitterness to the already rapidly deteriorating relationship. From 1960 until the Cultural Revolution, the Sino-Soviet conflict was manifested in several forms. First, both countries engaged in a continuous verbal duel in the form of polemics (arguments) heavily couched in ideological terms. For instance, Mao's ninth polemic in 1964 charged that the brand of communism practiced by the Soviet Union under Khrushchev was a "phoney" one and deviationist. Second, China had, by the mid-1950s, decided to compete with the Soviet Union for influence in the third world. The major role played by China at the 1955 Bandung Conference of neutral and nonaligned nations of Asia and Africa was indicative of China's changing policy approach. After Bandung, Chinese economic and technical aid became an important instrument for wooing countries of the third world to the Chinese side, in competition with the Soviet Union and the Chinese Nationalists. Third, China seized every opportunity to engage in propaganda warfare against the Soviet Union on issues of revolutionary war, superpower hegemony, détente, and disarmament. Fourth, the Sino-Soviet conflict and competition became more intense and acute when it involved influence over fraternal communist countries bordering China, such as North Korea and North Vietnam . The 1979 Sino-Vietnam conflict must be viewed in this light. The chain of actions which prompted China to take "punitive" military action against Vietnam in the spring of 1979 was triggered by the Vietnamese moving away from Chinese influence to Soviet influence, culminating in the Soviet-Vietnamese treaty of alliance, signed in November 1978. The Chinese could not take lightly this Soviet alliance with an Asian nation bordering her territory. As incidents along the unmarked border increased, and as successive expulsions of overseas Chinese from Vietnam occurred, the Chinese became more impatient. When, in January 1979, the Chinese-backed Cambodian regime of Pol Pot collapsed under the pressure from the invading Vietnamese army, the Chinese leaders, possibly with some dissenting voices in the inner council, reached their decision to take military action. The action, according to Deng Xiaoping, was taken to "teach the Vietnamese a lesson." One might add that this action was directed at Moscow as well as at Hanoi.

At the heart of Sino-Soviet relations is the question of the disputed borders along their common frontiers. Specifically, the disputed areas are north of the Amur River, east of Ussuri River on China's northeast, and the part of the Ili Valley on China's northwest Xinjiang region, as shown in Figure 10.1. The Chinese claimed that 12,700 square miles of territory north of the Amur River was Chinese but was ceded to Czarist Russia under pressure in 1860. The Ili Valley was taken by Russian troops in 1867 when the Muslims in Xingjiang rebelled against Chinese rule.

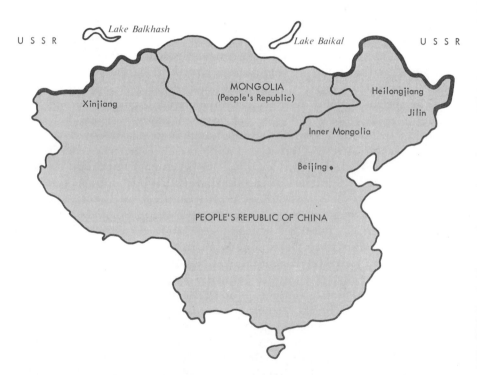

FIGURE 10.1: Disputed Border Along the Sino-Soviet Frontier (Indicated by heavy lines)

The border dispute between China and the Soviet Union did not surface in public until the 1963–1964 period. From March to September of 1963, Chinese mass-media editorials and open letters raised the question of the unsettled frontier north of the Ili Valley in the Xinjiang autonomous region.[41] In the fall of 1963, the Soviet Union responded by presenting an account of Chinese violations of the border from 1960 to 1963. According to the Soviet account, there were over five thousand border violations committed by the Chinese in 1962 alone.[42] Incidents along the 4,000 mile frontier may reach dozens per day, including smuggling and other illegal entry into China. In 1964 amidst charges and countercharges, negotiations were begun to demarcate the border and to fix navigation lines on the boundary rivers of Amur and Ussuri. While these negotiations made little progress toward the mutual agreement on the disputed border, there were no serious flare-ups along the frontier until March 1969. For a two-week period, March 2–15, 1969, Chinese and Soviet troops clashed over the ownership of an island named "Chenpaotao" by the Chinese and "Damansky" by the Soviets (see Figure 10.2). These clashes, or deliberate ambushes of each other's border patrols, resulted in some casualties on both sides. The immediate consequence of these March 1969 border clashes, irrespective of motives or linkage to domestic politics,[43] was the intensified fortification of military installations on both sides of the frontier, which led to further tension in Sino-Soviet relations.

Curiously, the border clashes of 1969 also brought both sides much closer to an agreement on means for reducing tension and for settling disputed areas. We now know that in September 1969 top-level negotiations were conducted in Beijing, which produced the so-called September 11 Agreement of Understanding between Soviet Premier Aleksei Kosygin and Premier Zhou Enlai. The Chinese claim that the Soviet Union agreed to the following framework for further negotiation toward reducing tension between the two countries: 1. "The armed forces of the Chinese and Soviet sides disengage by withdrawing from, or refraining from entering, all the disputed areas along the Sinov-Soviet border," and 2. "both sides reach an agreement on the provisional measures for maintaining the status quo of the border."[44] In 1973, Premier Zhou indicated to Sulzberger of *The New York Times* that Kosygin had agreed to these two provisions but that the Soviet Union had done nothing since to move toward the implementation of any of the points agreed upon.[45] What Zhou did not point out to Sulzberger was that the Soviet Union had, in January 1971, proposed to the Chinese a treaty on the nonuse of force by both sides in settling their border disputes.[46] By the summer of 1971, not only had Chinese attitudes toward the conciliatory moves by the Soviet Union stiffened, but a basic policy change with the United States was also in the offing. The signing of the Shanghai communiqué in February 28, 1972 marked both a major turning point in the Sino-United States relations and the beginning of a period of deterioration in Sino-Soviet relations. The obtaining by the Chinese of the United States agreement to not seek superpower hegemony in Asia and the

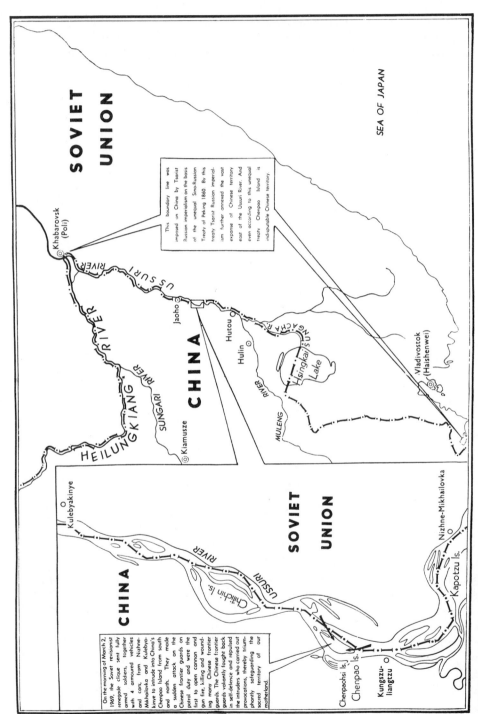

FIGURE 10.2: Sino-Soviet Boundary Line and Disputed Area in the 1969 Clash

Source: Peking Review 11 (March 14, 1969), 15–16

Pacific and to oppose other nations that establish such hegemony was aimed at the Soviet Union. As a countermeasure to the gradual rapprochement between the United States and China, the Soviet Union, in 1973, offered to the Chinese a draft treaty of mutual nonagression, which contained a provision that read, "Each party to the treaty pledges itself not to invade the other party on land, sea, or air with any types of arms or threaten it with such invasion."[47] The Chinese rebuffed the Soviet offer and argued, instead, for the implementation of the September 11, 1969 Agreement of Understanding between Kosygin and Zhou, which called for the withdrawal of armed forces from the disputed areas. From 1973 to 1976, Sino-Soviet negotiation toward the settlement of the border disputes was at a standstill, accompanied, nevertheless, by verbal barrages hurled at each other. When Mao Zedong died in September 1976, the Soviet Union thought at first that this was an opportunity to improve Sino-Soviet relations. Not only did Brezhnev send the fraternal party's condolences on Mao's death, but all media criticisms of China were halted for several months. In addition, Ambassador Illichev returned to Beijing after more than a year's absence. But if the Soviet Union expected improved Sino-Soviet relations with the new leadership in China, which their gestures after Mao's death certainly indicated, the illusion was soon shattered by Hua Guofeng's harsh words at the Eleventh Party Congress in August 1977. Hua charged that "the Soviet leading clique has betrayed Marxism-Leninism" and that it wanted to exert its hegemony everywhere in the world.[48] Hua blamed the Soviet Union for the impasse in Sino-Soviet border negotiations over the previous eight years. He challenged the Soviet leaders by saying that "If it really has any desire to improve the state relations between the two countries, this clique should prove it by concrete deeds."[49] Undauted by the Chinese intransigence, the Presidium of the U.S.S.R. Supreme Soviet sent a conciliatory letter, in February 1978, to the Standing Committee of the Chinese National People's Congress, on the eve of the convocation of its Fifth Congress. The letter proposed a joint statement by both countries that their relations be based on the five principles of peaceful coexistence advocated by Zhou Enlai: equality, mutual respect for sovereignty, territorial integrity, noninterference in internal affairs, and nonuse of force in the settlement of disputes (see Appendix D). The Chinese responded by charging that such a joint statement on the five principles of peaceful coexistence would be only a "hollow statement" at best. The Chinese wanted the Soviet Union to admit that it had agreed to the September 11, 1969 Agreement of Understanding. The Chinese then made a counterproposal which provided for not only the disengagement of the armed forces on both sides in the disputed border areas but the withdrawal of Soviet forces now stationed along the Sino-Soviet border and in the People's Republic of Mongolia as well. Thus, the Chinese have insisted that the Soviet Union must accept a precondition before negotiations on the normalization of relations can proceed: "When you have a million troops deployed on the Sino-Soviet border, how can you expect the Chinese people to believe that you have a genuine and sincere desire to improve the relations between our two countries?"[50]

The subsequent border incursion, which occurred two months after the exchange of notes between the parliaments of the two countries, seems to have strengthened the argument presented by the Chinese side for the withdrawal of the Soviet armed forces from the disputed border areas. On May 9, a Soviet army helicopter intruded into China's air space by crossing the border river and penetrating four kilometers (about two and a half miles) into the production center of a commune in Heilongjiang province on the northeast. The Chinese protested and charged that thirty Soviet troops landed in Chinese territory and fired at and seized the inhabitants.[51] On May 12, the Soviet Ministry of Foreign Affairs apologized to the Chinese and stated that the intrusion had occurred in order to arrest an armed criminal. In spite of the Soviet admission of the intrusion and the apology for the incident, the Chinese oral statement to the Soviet Ambassador to China, V.S. Tolstikov, was hostile. To the Chinese, the border intrusion was not "a case of inadvertent trespass into the Chinese territory" but was simply a deliberate "military provocation organized by the Soviet side, a bloody incident created by Soviet troops."[52]

The future settlement of the border disputes, the heart of the Sino-Soviet relations, hinges on the triangular relationship between the Soviet Union, United States, and China. The 1969 border clashes made the Chinese realize their vulnerability and isolation in a contest with the Soviet Union. China's abrupt shift in foreign policy toward rapprochement with the United States in 1969–1970 was indicative of that concern. As China moved closer to the United States, she became more intransigent toward overtures by the Soviet Union for negotiations to settle the border problem. The Sino-United States rapprochement also made the Soviet Union more cautious in its handling of China's intransigence in the border settlement. On the other hand, as United States-Soviet relations improved, through détente and progress in SALT talks, the Soviets felt somewhat more belligerent toward China in terms of both the massive display of armed forces along the Sino-Soviet frontier and diplomatic hints that it would not be unthinkable for the Soviet Union to launch a preemptive attack on China and her nuclear installations in nearby Inner Mongolia. It may be that Washington is holding its trump "Chinese card" in a poker game with the Soviet Union in the SALT talks.

There has also been some slight movements on both sides of the

Sino-Soviet dispute toward a rapprochement. The conciliatory note sent in February 1978 by the Presidium of the U.S.S.R. Supreme Soviet to the Chinese for renewed negotiations of their differences; the Soviet Union's cautious refraining from taking military action along the Sino-Soviet border during the Chinese military incursion into Vietnam in March 1979; and the Chinese proposal for negotiations "for the solution of outstanding issues and the improvement of relations between the two countries" in April 1979, when they announced their intention not to renew the peace and friendship treaty when it expires in 1980, were all positive signs for possible improved relations in the future.

SINO-UNITED STATES NORMALIZATION OF RELATIONS AND THE TAIWAN PROBLEM

The move for a rapprochement between the United States and China came at the time when there was a change in the perception of each other's intentions. In the United States, both public and political opinion toward China had turned from hostility, which reached its height during the Korean War, to an increasing desire for understanding and contact. China's cautious attitude in refraining from involvement in the Vietnam War in Southeast Asia certainly had moderated the hardline attitude previously taken by the policy makers in Washington. The Chinese had learned at the early stages of the United States involvement in Vietnam that it was not the design of the United States to invade China. In addition to this was China's worry over the menace of the Soviet Union, exemplified by the Soviet interference in the internal affairs of fraternal socialist countries, such as Czechoslovakia in 1968, and by her amassing of military strength along the Sino-Soviet frontier, following the 1969 border clashes. Thus, when Henry Kissinger slipped quietly into Beijing for top-level talks in the summer of 1971, both sides were ready to explore rapprochement. Furthermore, the two-decade-long United States policy to contain and isolate China no longer had any practical meaning after China was seated in the United Nations in the fall of 1971. A new era had to begin, and rapprochement with China was already high on the political agenda of Richard Nixon, who planned to seek his second term as president of the United States in 1972.

The new era in Sino-United States relations began with the signing of the Joint Communiqué, or the Shanghai communiqué, by President Nixon and Premier Zhou Enlai on February 28, 1972 (see Appendix C). The Shanghai communiqué contains three parts: a candid review of the international situation, as viewed separately by the United States and

China; an acceptance of a set of principles to govern the conduct of the two countries' foreign relations; and the agreed steps for the eventual normalization of relations between the two nations, including the settlement of the Taiwan question.[53]

On the question of Taiwan, the United States finally declared in the communiqué that "there is but one China and that Taiwan is a part of China." This ended a long debate on both sides of the Pacific over the status of Taiwan. Having made a major pledge to the Chinese that Taiwan is a part of China, the United States then expressed its desire that the question be settled peacefully by the Chinese themselves. The United States pledged that it would withdraw all of its forces when the Taiwan question was finally settled peacefully. In the meantime, the United States will "progressively reduce its forces and military installations on Taiwan as tension in the area diminishes." It was obvious that neither the Chinese nor the Americans wanted to solve the Taiwan question with one stroke of the pen; it was in reality simply not possible. But the mere recognition of Taiwan as a part of China in principle was a giant step for the United States, and the Chinese knew it. In addition, China had obtained pledges from the United States not to seek or support hegemony in Asia and the Pacific region and not to collude with another against other countries; both of these pledges were aimed at gaining United States support to check the Soviet Union, whom the Chinese now perceived as a more dangerous enemy than the United States ever was.

Other tangible measures were agreed on by China and the United States to improve their relations, with a view toward their eventual normalization. First, increased people-to-people contact and exchanges in the fields of science, technology, culture, sports, and journalism were to be undertaken by both sides in order to broaden understanding between the two countries. Second, trade relations were to be developed between the two countries. Third, liaison offices were to be established in each other's capitals for official contact and consultation. In many ways the establishment of liaison offices in Beijing and Washington was unique in international diplomacy. For one thing, the liaison offices are in fact embassies, even though there is no official recognition of formal diplomatic relations between two countries. The Chinese in the past have refused to send envoys to any capital where there was diplomatic representation from the government of Taiwan. Evidently, in her desire to improve relations, China made a departure in this case from past practice. In the late spring of 1973, China sent a high-ranking experienced diplomat, Huang Zhen, a participant in the Long March and a former Chinese ambassador to France, as her chief of mission. The United States dispatched one of the foreign service's most respected senior career officers, David Bruce, to Beijing. It was then assumed by many that the establishment of these liaison offices was merely a preliminary to the formal exchange of ambassadors as soon as the United States officially recognized the People's Republic of China.

Sino-United States relations remained at a standstill during 1972–1973 and most of 1974–1975. Whatever Nixon might have planned for normalizing relations became inoperative as he sank deeply into the morass of the Watergate scandal. The Chinese were also preoccupied with their own internal struggle as the radicals mounted an assault against Zhou Enlai and his pragmatic policies under the anti-Confucius campaign. Zhou Enlai's reference to the Sino-United States relations in his report to the Fifth National People's Congress in January 1975 was vague. He noted that improvements had been made in the past three years and that he believed the relations would continue to improve "as long as the principles of the Sino-American Shanghai communiqué are carried out in earnest."[54] In contrast, Zhou devoted more time to outlining the impasse in Sino-Soviet relations and appealed to the Soviet leaders to "sit down and negotiate honestly."

When President Ford arrived in Beijing on December 2, 1975, he was the second American president to sit down with the aging but still alert Mao Zedong. Zhou Enlai was already dying of cancer. The Chinese leader with whom Ford and Kissinger negotiated was Deng Xiaoping, a man about to be purged for the second time by the radicals and their supporters. Because of the conclusion of the Helsinki agreement on the SALT talks in the fall of 1975, the Chinese saw détente between the two superpowers as a major concern. Deng opened his speech at the welcoming banquet by singling out the agreement between China and the United States in the 1972 Shanghai communiqué, to not seek hegemony, as an "outstanding common point." While Deng did not mention the stumbling block of the Taiwan question, he stated that "so long as the principles of the Shanghai communiqué are earnestly observed," normalization of relations "will eventually be realized through the joint efforts of our two sides." He went on to say, "At present, a more important question confronts the Chinese and American people—that of the international situation." He discussed the intensified contention for world hegemony, which would lead to war: "Rhetoric about 'détente' cannot cover up the stark reality of the growing danger of war."[55] After two days of lengthy sessions with the Chinese, each lasting more than two and a half hours, there was no new ground broken in the bilateral relationship. At the farewell banquet hosted by the Americans, President Ford seemed to reassure the Chinese: "I reaffirmed that the United States is committed to complete the normalization of relations with the People's Republic of China on the basis of the Shanghai communiqué."[56]

At the end of the five-day visit, there was no joint communiqué as there had been at the end of the Nixon visit in 1972. What specific agreement, if any, was reached by President Ford and the Chinese became a subject for speculation. Had either Kissinger or Ford secretly promised the Chinese that the United States would sever the diplomatic relations with Taiwan after the presidential election in 1976, in order to facilitate the normalization of relations with Beijing? Deng Xiaoping has been quoted as remarking in the fall of 1977 that President Ford had indeed promised that he would break relations with Taiwan upon reelection in 1976. Former President Ford has denied that such a promise was made to the Chinese during his visit in 1975. The fact remains, leaving aside the question of the alleged verbal promise by Ford, that Deng Xiaoping's remark indicates the strain in the Sino-United States relations during the mid-1970s.

With the change in the administration in Washington, following the 1976 presidential election, the Chinese waited patiently for the Carter administration to make the move. The succession struggle after the deaths of Zhou Enlai and Mao in 1976 had prevented the Chinese from being overly concerned about the normalization of relations. With the arrest of the Gang of Four and the emergence of a new leadership in China, the focus in Sino-United States relations was brought once again to the question of Taiwan, the obstacle to the normalization of relations.

In his keynote address to the Eleventh Party Congress on August 18, 1977, Hua Guofeng proposed a formula for ending the impasse in Sino-United States relations. The formula contained three specific actions to be taken by the United States: 1. break diplomatic relations with Taiwan; 2. withdraw all United States forces and military installations from the island and from the Taiwan Strait; and 3. repeal the 1954 Mutual Defense Treaty signed by the United States and the Taiwan government.[57] Perhaps Hua was responding to a signal sent by President Carter in June when Carter said that he was looking for "a formula which can bridge some of the difficulties that still separate us."[58] Secretary of State Cyrus Vance was sent to Beijing on August 22 to try to break the deadlock and to initiate exploratory talks on Hua's three-point formula. While Vance spent four days in Beijing discussing the formula proposed by Hua Guofeng, there was little official indication from either side as to what had been discussed or what agreement, if any, had been reached. Then, within ten days after Vance's departure from China, Vice Premier Deng Xiaoping revealed some substance of the consultation with Vance in an interview with a delegation of executives from the Associated Press.[59] Deng confided that the Vance visit represented a setback in Sino-United States relations, since the Secretary of State had failed to sever diplomatic relations with Taiwan after the 1976 election, as Deng claimed President Ford had promised during his December 1975 trip to China. Deng also revealed that China had rejected Vance's offer of full diplomatic relations with Beijing coupled with changing the United States embassy in Taiwan to a liaison office. It was obvious that the Chinese were not satisfeid with the United States response to Hua Guofeng's formula for the settlement of the Taiwan question. The Carter administration was then deeply involved in the negotiation of the Panama treaty and was actively seeking a solution to the Mid-East problem. Normalization of relations with China was a basic objective of the administration's foreign policy but was certainly not a top priority at that time. The Chinese seemed to have stood firmly on the three-point formula and the Shanghai communique, which recognized Taiwan as an integral part of China. Hua Guofeng said, in 1977, that to tell China what she should do about Taiwan, and in what manner, was in itself an infringement into China's domestic affairs.

China experts in the American academic community have offered a number of proposals intended to enable the United States to break the deadlock on the Taiwan question. These experts, both in and out of the government, agree that United States relations with China must be normalized on a basis similar to her relations with the Soviet Union and that normalized relations with China is crucial to stabilization in Asia, a basic objective in the overall United States foreign policy. Curiously, it was primarily because of United States concern over the stability of Asia, immediately after the Korean War, that the Mutual Defense Treaty was consummated with the Chinese Nationalists in Taiwan; now this very defense treaty impedes normalization of relations with the People's Republic of China. Focusing on the problem of the Mutual Defense Treaty of 1954, Jerome Cohen of Harvard University suggested that some sort of guarantee be given to ensure peaceful settlement of Taiwan at the time when the United States and China establish full relations with each other. Such a guarantee could be made either unilaterally or bilaterally.[60] For instance, the Chinese could unilaterally declare that China has the right to claim Taiwan by force but elects not to do so or has no intention of doing so. The United States could unilaterally declare her determination to maintain peace and security in the Pacific. Similarly, both countries could jointly declare that the Taiwan Strait is a demilitarized zone. Doak Barnett of the Brookings Institution, on the other hand, suggested that the United States must impress upon the Chinese that they should set aside the Taiwan question for the present and deal with the United States on other problems. For example, China and the United States might cooperate in the area of military security. It would be in the interest of both countries to cooperate in improving China's defense capabilities in the face of the Soviet military threat on her border.[61] In many respects, the strategy outlined by Doak Barnett seems to have been followed for a while by President Carter's national security advisor, Zbigniew Brzezinski, in his visit to Beijing during May 1978. Brzezinski assured the Chinese that the United States also is concerned and apprehensive about the Soviet Union's interference around the world and about the Soviet threat to the Chinese. He told the Chinese, "The United States does not view its relationship with China as a tactical expedient. We recognize—and share—China's resolve to resist the effort of any nation which seeks to establish global or regional hegemony."[62] Then he expanded by saying that the Sino-United States friendship was based on three beliefs: Sino-United States relationship would be beneficial to world peace; a secure and strong China was in America's interest; and a strong and powerful United States was in China's interest.[63] Brzezinski's remarks certainly pleased the Chinese, in view of the May 1978 Soviet incursion into Chinese territory on the Ussuri River. These remarks, however, were certainly anti-Soviet Union and bearbaiting. Brzezinski also continued the practice established by Kissinger of briefing the Chinese on the United States position on the SALT talks with the Soviet Union. He perhaps went a step further than Kissinger by disclosing secret thinking of the United States on security and strategic goals.[64] Brzezinski's trip to China did not provide any immediate break in the negotiation for normalizing relations between the two countries. There was also a rising vocal opposition in the United States to immediate normalization of relations with China at the expense of Taiwan.[65]

The breakthrough in the negotiations for normalizing diplomatic relations between China and the United States finally did occur in the fall of 1978. At a meeting with the head of the Chinese liaison office in Washington in September 1978, the Carter administration proposed that the United States would recognize the government of the People's Republic of China immediately if the Chinese would waive their insistence on the simultaneous repeal of the United States 1954 Mutual Defense Treaty with Taiwan. From then on, the Chinese began to hint to visitors from abroad that the "Japan formula," would break the deadlock with the United States over the question of normalization of relations. These hints were also given to Japanese reporters by Vice Premier Deng Xiaoping on his trip to Japan to sign the Sino-Japanese Peace Treaty in October 1978. The "Japan formula" meant that China would not object to continued United States economic, trade, and cultural relations with Taiwan once the United States formally recognized the People's Republic. These diplomatic gestures led to a series of intensive secret negotiations between Beijing and Washington, which produced the joint communiqué of December 15, 1978, calling for the establishment of normal diplomatic relations on January 1, 1979 (see Appendix F).

The joint communiqué states that while the United States would recognize the government of the People's Republic as the sole and legal government of China on January 1, 1979, it nevertheless would continue to maintain "cultural, commercial, and other unofficial relations with the people of Taiwan." In addition, both sides reaffirmed the principles contained in the Shanghai communiqué of 1972: the anti-hegemony provision, recognition of Taiwan as an integral part of China, and the pledge for reduction in international military conflict in Asia. An exchange of ambassadors and the establishment of embassies between Beijing and Washington was to commence on March 1, 1979.

The joint communiqué, as a formal diplomatic instrument, does not reveal all of the concessions, made by each side, that led to the final agreement for normalization of relations. The areas or points of concession are to be found mainly in other statements. The joint communiqué does indicate clearly that one point of the three-point formula laid down by Hua Guofeng in 1977—the severance of United States diplomatic relations with Taiwan—was met. The United States agreement on the other two points was revealed in a separate United States statement (see Appendix F-4) that announced that 1. The United States would notify Taiwan of her intention to repeal the 1954 Mutual Defense Treaty on January 1, 1980, giving a year's notification for cancellation of the treaty obligations, as prescribed by the treaty itself, and 2. the United States would withdraw the remainder of its military personnel, about 750 people, from Taiwan by April 1979.

What concessions did the United States obtain from China? First, the United States made a unilateral declaration (see Appendix F-4) that she desired a peaceful settlement of the Taiwan issue. The official United States statement said

> The United States is confident that the people of Taiwan face a peaceful and prosperous future. The United States continues to have an interest in the peaceful resolution of the Taiwan issue and expects that the Taiwan issue will be settled peacefully by the Chinese themselves.

In his nationwide broadcast on the normalization of relations, on December 15, 1978, President Carter declared:

> As the United States asserted in the Shanghai communiqué in 1972, we will continue to have an interest in the peaceful resolution of the Taiwan issue.
>
> I have paid special attention to insuring that normalization of relations between the United States and the People's Republic will not jeopardize the well-being of the people of Taiwan.

Neither of the above statements, nor the United States' clear intention to continue "cultural, commercial, and other unofficial relations with the people of Taiwan," has been contradicted or challenged by the Chinese.

Furthermore, the United States evidently told the Chinese during the negotiations for normalization of relations that it intended to sell to Taiwan selective defensive weapons after the termination of the Mutual Defense Treaty with Taiwan in 1980. In an interview with MacNeil and Lehrer on December 18, Dr. Brzezinski, the president's national security advisor, said that such sale of arms to Taiwan would be authorized, "if in fact such requests are needed," as governed by the presence or absence of any future "tension, hostility, and conflicts" in the area. Discussing possible future United States arms sales to Taiwan, CCP Party Chairman Huo Guofeng, in a Chinese television interview, said that the Chinese, at the time of the negotiations, "absolutely would not agree to this" after the abrogation of the Mutual Defense Treaty. Then Hua also revealed that "Nevertheless, we reached an agreement on the joint communiqué." That the issue of arms sales to Taiwan by the United States did not become a stumbling block to normalization of relations certainly was a major concession on the part of the Chinese. Possible arms sales to Taiwan and the continued patrolling of the Formosan Strait by the United States Seventh Fleet could be considered a reasonable substitute for the abrogated Mutual Defense Treaty of 1954. It seems to be the judgment of the United States, based on "the implicit understanding with the Chinese," as indicated by Dr. Brzezinski in the interview with MacNeil and Lehrer, that there will be no violent resolution of the Taiwan issue and that there will be expanded close cooperation and friendship between China and the United States in the changing international strategic situation on a global scale. Both President Carter and Dr. Brzezinski emphasized that, from a purely military point of view, it would be not only costly but very risky for the Chinese to launch an invasion of Taiwan. An invasion of that scope would require air and naval superiority across one hundred miles of water, an unobtainable position for China for some time to come.

The recognition by the United States of the People's Republic of China in January 1979 ended thirty years of ill-feeling and conflict between the two countries. In addition, the normalization of relations will, in the long run, provide stability in the power situation in East Asia. For the Chinese, friendship with the United States provides support in their confrontation with the Soviet Union and thus serves as a check on Soviet expansion of power in East Asia. Sino-United States normalization will also bring some immediate benefit to both countries in terms of trade, and for the Chinese in terms of technological transfer. China's ten-year development plan, as described in the preceding chapter, calls for purchases from abroad, amounting to eight to ten billion dollars per year (these figures have been readjusted) for several years after 1978. China's total foreign trade for 1978 has been estimated at twenty billion dollars and is expected to increase at an annual rate of at least ten percent per year for the next decade or so. With the establishment of diplomatic relations, trade between China and the United States is expected to reach over two billion dollars in 1979, double the volume of trade for 1977, and about five billion dollars by 1985. For the 1978–1979 period, the Chinese government has concluded agreements with major United States industrial and manufacturing concerns for more than three billion dollars worth of purchases, including one billion dollars of iron ore mining and processing facilities from the United States Steel Co., over one billion dollars for construction of hotels in major cities in China, and eight hundred million dollars of copper mining technology and facilities. With the signing of the United States-China claims agreement over the frozen assets in March 1979, regular banking, credit, and shipping arrangements can now be made to facilitate the expected expansion in trade for the future. The signing of United States-China trade agreement in May 1979 will undoubtedly enable American businessman to sell large quantities of technology and machinery to China in the future. Thus, normalization of relations between China and the United States will not only contribute to the peace and stability of Asia, where we fought three wars in less than forty years, but to the prosperity of both America and China.

SINO-JAPANESE PEACE TREATY AND TRADE RELATIONS

Although most nations view Japan as a modernized and westernized nation because of her technological and industrial capacity, the Chinese see Japan as a member of the second world in their three-world perception. Hua Guofeng said at the Eleventh Party Congress in 1977 that China would support second world countries, European nations and Japan, "in their struggle against control, intimidation and bullying by the superpowers."[66] The countries of the second world, according to the Chinese, are no longer the main force that dominate and oppress the third world countries. Instead, the countries of the second world are subject to "interference" and "bullying" by the superpowers. China would like to form a united front with the second world countries against this superpower hegemony. Japan, naturally, has figured prominently in China's strategy for a united front with the second world.

The normalization of relations between China and Japan, from the Chinese point of view, was a "protracted struggle." In the 1950s and 1960s, Japan's official contact with China was restricted by the United States containment policy and concerns for the security of the Pacific. Furthermore, Japan politically and economically supported the Chinese

Nationalists in Taiwan. The Chinese, on the other hand, used trade to lure Japanese businessmen for increased contacts. Special trade agreements were awarded to selected Japanese firms on a non-governmental basis. By the late 1950s, trade between China and Japan exceeded one hundred million dollars per year. By 1960, some two hundred Japanese firms, such as Toyota Motors, Tokyo Electric, and Anzai Fertilizer Co., had a large volume of trade with China under the "friendly firms" arrangement. Under this arrangement, the Chinese permitted trade only with those Japanese firms that were sympathetic to China and that accepted the principles of no hostility toward China, no support for the "two-China" policy, and no hinderance to normal relations. The Chinese limited contracts for "friendly firms" to only one year, making long-term planning impossible for the Japanese. The desire of these private "friendly firms" for long-term contracts led to the signing of the Liao-Takasaki Agreement in November 1962. Under the agreement, the "friendly firms" were to receive a five-year contract, provided they adhered to the political principles mentioned above. Trade between China and Japan then soared, reaching over three hundred million dollars a year for the next several years. Then, to accelerate the trade relations, the Chinese supplemented the Liao-Takasaki Agreement with other short-term arrangements, usually one-year contracts, known as "memorandum trade." By 1971, trade had reached 820 million dollars a year and pressure was beginning to build up within Japan's ruling Liberal Democratic Party for a change in Japan's policy toward China, particularly in Japan's adherence to United States policy. Visits to China by Japanese trade missions and political delegations became more frequent. Within the Liberal Democratic Party, there was increasing criticism of Japan's support for a "two-China" policy and Japan's loyalty to Taiwan. The Chinese intensified their drive for normalized relations with Japan. Persuasive pressure was applied for changes in Japan's China policy to every Japanese delegation visiting China. When President Nixon announced, in July 1971, that he would visit China soon (the "Nixon shock") and the United States resolution for a two-China policy failed in the United Nations, Japan's two-China policy, as advocated by Prime Minister Eisaku Sato of the ruling Liberal Democratic Party, began to collapse. At this time the Chinese mounted a propaganda campaign against the build-up of Japan's military capability. Zhou Enlai, in his lengthy interview with James Reston of *The New York Times,* expressed his concern about development of militarism in Japan.[67] On the eve of Nixon's departure for China, the Chinese Ministry of Foreign Affairs issued a strongly worded statement criticizing the reversion of Okinawa to Japan as a fraud, because the reversion agreement included several islands claimed by China. A Chinese statement on the inclusion of the islands belonging to China in the reversion agreement revealed their feelings: "Japanese militarism and U.S. imperialism are colluding in speeding up implementation of the scheme to annex China's territory."[68] The Shanghai communiqué, which declared that Taiwan was an integral part of China and that the United States would ultimately withdraw its military complex from the island, forced the Sato government to abandon its China policy, as Gene Hsiao has pointed out.[69]

Sato's successor, Prime Minister Tanaka, lost no time in recovering from the "Nixon shock" by accepting an invitation from China to move speedily toward normalization of relations. Tanaka arrived in Beijing on September 25, 1972, and five days later a joint statement was issued which contained a nine-point agreement for terminating "the abnormal state of affairs" between the two countries. Specifically, Japan recognized the People's Republic of China as the "sole legal government of China" and Taiwan as "an inalienable part of China." Both countries agreed to the immediate establishment of full diplomatic relations and pledged not to seek hegemony in the Asia-Pacific region. The agreement also provided for conclusion of a peace treaty and negotiations for agreements on trade, navigation, aviation, and fisheries.[70] It will be recalled that the People's Republic of China was not a party to the San Francisco peace treaty, which ended the allied occupation of Japan in 1954.

One interesting development occurred soon after the signing of the Tanaka-Zhou agreement for the normalization of relations in 1972. It was the emergence of the "Japan formula" for continuing Japan's economic ties with Taiwan. When diplomatic relations with Taiwan were terminated, Japan's investment in the island was over five hundred million dollars and the volume of trade was at eight-hundred-million-dollars-a-year level.[71] This economic relationship was maintained between Japan and Taiwan by a nongovernmental arrangement: The Japanese embassy and consular services in Taiwan were replaced by the Japan Interchange Association, a semi-private, incorporated entity for coordinating economic and trade relations. The Chinese Nationalists formed the East-Asia Relations Association in Japan to conduct trade relations between the two countries. Beijing raised no objection to these arrangements. By the mid-1970s, trade between Japan and Taiwan had exceeded 2.9 billion dollars a year.[72] Trade between China and Japan also flourished after the 1972 normalization agreement, reaching 3.2 billion dollars by 1974.[73] Hong Kim has indicated that the two major factors for the increased trade with China were Japan's willingness to extend the necessary credit to China and China's need for steel, machinery, and technology.[74]

While a direct consequence of the Tanaka-Zhou agreement on normalization of relations was a flourishing trade, China and Japan remained deadlocked, for almost six years, over the conclusion of a treaty of friendship and peace. The slow progress in negotiations for a peace treaty was attributable to the emergence of the Soviet Union as an issue. Japan had resisted the Chinese insistence that an anti-hegemony clause, which was essentially aimed against the Soviet Union, be included in the treaty. During this time, Japan was having difficulty in her negotiation with the Soviet Union over the important issue of fishery rights, one of the many delicate problems facing the two countries. Japan was not very comfortable when China's propaganda criticized the Soviet Union for behaving like an overlord and intimidating the Japanese in the fishery negotiations over the boundaries of the two-hundred-mile economic zone, formulated at the United Nations Law of the Seas Conference.[75] Nor was the stand taken by the Chinese, that the Soviet Union return the four northern islands off Hokkaido in the Kuril Islands to the Japanese, diplomatically welcome. The Soviet Union had warned Japan that they oppose the anti-hegemony clause, and offered to have Japan join in their new "Asian security system." The deadlock over a Sino-Japanese peace treaty was broken after Japan concluded an agreement on fishery rights with the Soviet Union. To overcome the Chinese insistence on and the Soviet Union's opposition to the anti-hegemony clause, the Japanese finally persuaded the Chinese to accept an additional clause in the treaty which would read "The present treaty shall not affect the position of either contracting party regarding its relations with third countries." With the inclusion of this additional clause, the Japanese could tell the Soviet Union that the anti-hegemony clause should not be considered as anti-Soviet Union. The peace treaty between China and Japan was finally signed in Beijing on August 12, 1978 (see Appendix E). The treaty was to be in force for ten years, during which time both countries pledged to adhere to the five principles of peaceful co-existence (respect sovereignty and territorial integrity, mutual nonaggression, noninterference in international affairs, equal and mutual benefit, and mutual respect), to see no hegemony in the Asia-Pacific region, to promote cultural and economic relations, and to promote the exchange of peoples.

What are the implications of the Sino-Japanese peace treaty? First, it officially ended the long-standing animosity between the two countries and opened a new chapter of equal relations between China and Japan. Second, the anti-hegemony clause aimed at the Soviet Union was a victory for the Chinese. With this peace treaty and the Shanghai communiqué, which also contained an anti-hegemony clause, China felt perhaps less isolated in a new Asian balance of power. Third, the

Chinese could look forward to expanded long-term trade agreements with Japan. This was particularly important for China's long-term program of modernization, since Japan could supply a large portion of China's requirements for machinery and technology.[76] Similarly, Japan could count on China to supply needed raw materials and even light industrial goods, which were more expensive for her to produce. Fourth, conclusion of the Sino-Japanese peace treaty showed that neither the Taiwan problem nor the United States Security Treaty, originally aimed at containing possible Chinese communist expansion in Asia, was a barrier to permanent relationships based on friendship and mutual respect. Finally, the Chinese flexibility and accommodation on the anti-hegemony issue in the peace treaty with Japan may have provided clues for strategies to normalize relations between China and the United States.[77]

In conclusion, China's perception of three worlds, China's fear of the threat posed by the Soviet Union, the normalization in Sino-United States relations, and the ratification of the peace treaty with Japan all seem to point to the development of a new international pattern in Asia and the Pacific. The region is no longer dominated by one or two powers. Now there is a new but delicate power balance, based on four power centers: Beijing, Moscow, Tokyo, and Washington. China, because of her geographic location and population size, will hold one of the keys to the balance and future stability of the region.

NOTES

[1]See Allan Whiting, *China Crosses the Yalu* (Stanford: Calif: University Press, 1960); and Trumbull Higgins, *Korea and the Fall of MacArthur* (Cambridge: Oxford University Press, 1960).

[2]Daniel Tretiak, "The Chinese Cultural Revolution and Foreign Policy," *Current Scene,* vol. viii, no. 7 (April 1, 1970), 1–26; and Melvin Gurtov, "The Foreign Ministry and Foreign Affairs in the Cultural Revolution," *The China Quarterly,* 40 (October–December 1969), 65–102.

[3]The Theoretical Study Group of the Ministry of Foreign Affairs, "Premier Chou Creatively Carried Out Chairman Mao's Revolutionary Line in Foreign Affairs," *Peking Review,* 5 (January 28, 1977), 15.

[4]"The Cultural Revolution and the Chinese Foreign Policy," *Current Scene,* vol. vi, no. 13 (August 1, 1968), 1–15.

[5]*Vietnam Triangle: Moscow, Peking, Hanoi* (New York: Pegasus, 1967).

[6]Peter Van Ness, *Revolution and Chinese Foreign Policy* (Berkeley, Calif.: University of California, 1970), pp. 232–36.

[7]"Premier Chou Creatively Carried Out Chairman Mao's Revolutionary Line in Foreign Affairs," p. 15.

[8]*Ming Pao* (Hongkong), September 7, 1978, p. 8.

[9]"Peking and the Asian Power Balance," *Problems of Communism,* xxi (July–August 1976), 36–40.

[10]Chou En-lai, "Report to the Tenth National Congress of the Communist Party of China," *Peking Review,* nos. 35 and 36 (September 7, 1973), 24.

[11]Chou En-lai, "Report on the Work of the Government," *Peking Review,* 4 (January 24, 1975), 24.

[12]Chou En-lai, "Report on the Work of the Government," p. 24.

[13]Foreign policy themes and issues are culled from the following official documents: Hua Kuo-feng, "Political Report to the 11th National Congress of Communist Party of China," *Peking Review,* 35 (August 26, 1977), 39–43; Hua Kuo-feng, "Unite and Strive to Build a Modern, Powerful Socialist country!" *Peking Review,* 10 (March 10, 1978), 35–39; Theoretical Group of the Ministry of Foreign Affairs, "Premier Chou Creatively Carried out Chairman Mao's Revolutionary Line in Foreign Affairs," *Peking Review,* 5 (January 28, 1977), 6–15; and Huang Hua, "The International Situation and China's Foreign Policies," *Peking Review,* 40 (October 10, 1978), 12–17, 35.

[14]Editorial Department of *Remin Ribao,* "Chairman Mao's Theory of the Differentiation of the Three Worlds Is a Major Contribution to Marxism-Leninism," *Peking Review,* 45 (November 4, 1977), 11.

[15]"Speech By Teng Hsiao-p'ing, Chairman of Delegation of People's Republic of China," Supplement to *Peking Review*, no. 15 (April 12, 1974), pp. I–II.

[16]"Political Report to the 11th National Congress," p. 43.

[17]"Unite and Strive to Build a Modern, Powerful Socialist Country," pp. 36–37.

[18]"Chairman Mao's Theory of the Differentiation of the Three Worlds," p. 11; and Hua Kuo-feng's "Political Report to the 11th Party Congress," p. 41.

[19]Huang Hua, "The International Situation and China's Foreign Policies," *Peking Review,* 40 (October 6, 1978), 14.

[20]"Political Report to the 11th National Congress," p. 42.

[21]"Joint Communiqué," *Peking Review,* 9 (March 3, 1972), 5.

[22]See Joachim Glaubitz, "Anti-Hegemony Formulas in Chinese Foreign Policy," *Asian Survey,* vol. xvi, no. 3 (March 1976), 205–15.

[23]"Unite and Serve to Build a Modern, Powerful Socialist Country," p. 36.

[24]Huang Hua, "The International Situation and China's Foreign Policy," p. 12.

[25]Huang Hua, "The International Situation and China's Foreign Policy," pp. 12–13; and "Unite and Strive to Build a Modern, Powerful Socialist Country," pp. 40–41.

[26]"Chairman Mao's Theory of the Differentiation of the Three Worlds," pp. 21, 23. Also see "History Has a Lesson to Teach,"*Peking Review,* 34 (August 25, 1978), 21–22.

[27]"Speech by Teng Hsiao-p'ing," p. v.

[28]"The International Situation and China's Foreign Policy," p. 13.

[29]"Third World Countries Unite Against Hegemony in Economic Sphere," *Peking Review,* 47 (November 18, 1977), 23–25.

[30]"The International Situation and China's Foreign Policy," p. 17.

[31]Huang Hua, "Superpower Disarmament Fraud Exposed," *Peking Review,* 22 (June 2, 1978), 9.

[32]"Soviet Détente Fraud Exposed," *Peking Review,* 3 (January 14, 1977), 31–32.

[33]"Soviet Détente Fraud Exposed," p. 32.

[34]"Soviet-U.S. Nuclear Talks: An Analysis," *Peking Review,* 51 (December 16, 1977), 22. Also see "What Do Moscow-Vaunted 'Détente' and 'Disarmament' Add Up to?", *Peking Review,* 50 (December 9, 1977), 22–24.

[35]"France and Germany: Voices Against Appeasement," *Peking Review,* 6 (February 10, 1978), 23–25; and "Soviet Détente Exposed," p. 32.

[36]See "Who Should Disarm First?" *Peking Review,* 24 (June 16, 1978), 25–26; "Nuclear and Conventional Armaments Must Be Reduced Simultaneously," *Peking Review,* 25 (June 23, 1978), 27–29; "The International Situation and China's Foreign Policies," pp. 15–16.

[37]"The International Situation and China's Foreign Policies," p. 16.

[38]"The International Situation and China's Foreign Policies," p. 16.

[39]See Alice Langley Hsieh, *Communist China's Strategy in the Nuclear Era* (Englewood Cliffs, N.J.: Prentice-Hall, Inc., 1962).

[40]*Peking Review,* 42 (October 16, 1964), 2–4.

[41]"Letter of the Central Committee of the CCP of February 29, 1964 to the Central Committee of CPSU," *Peking Review,* 19 (May 8, 1964), 12–18.

[42]"Letter of the Central Committee of the CCP of February 29, 1964 to the Central Committee of CPSU."

[43]See Thomas Robinson, "The Sino-Soviet Dispute," *The American Political Science Review,* vol. xvi, no. 4 (December 1972), 1175–1202, and Neville Maxwell, "Why the Russians Lifted the Blockade at Bear Island," *Foreign Affairs,* vol. 57, no. 1 (Fall 1978), 138–45.

[44]The text of the agreement of understanding is to be found in "Real Deeds, Yes; Hollow Statements, No!", *Peking Review,* 13 (March 31, 1978), 15. Also see an interview by C.L. Sulzberger of *The New York Times* with Chou En-lai, "Chou Attacks the Soviet for Delaying Border Pact," *The New York Times* (October 29, 1973), pp. 1, 8.

[45]*The New York Times,* October 29, 1973, p. 8.

[46]"Real Deeds, Yes; Hollow Statements, No!", p. 14.

[47]"Real Deeds, Yes; Hollow Statements, No!" p. 15.

[48]"Political Report to the 11th National Congress of CCP," pp. 42–43.

[49]"Political Report to the 11th National Congress of CCP," p. 43.

[50]"Chinese Foreign Ministry's Note to the Soviet Embassy in China," *Peking Review,* 13 (March 31, 1978), 18.

[51]"Protest against Soviet Military Provocation," *Peking Review,* 20 (May 19, 1978), 3–4; and "Chinese Foreign Ministry's Oral Statement to the Soviet Ambassador," *Peking Review,* 21 (May 26, 1978), 20–21.

[52]"Chinese Foreign Ministry's Oral Statement," p. 21.

[53]For the text of the Joint Communiqué, see Appendix C which is published in *Peking Review,* 9 (March 3, 1972), 4–5.

[54]"Report on the Work of the Government," p. 24.

[55]"Vice Premier Teng Hsiao-p'ing's Toast at Banquet Honoring President Ford," *Peking Review,* 49 (December 5, 1975), 8.

[56]"President Ford's Toast at Farewell Banquet by President Ford," *Peking Review*, 50 (December 12, 1975), 6.

[57]"Political Report to the 11th National Congress of the Communist Party of China," p. 42.

[58]*Department of State Bulletin* (June 13, 1977), p. 625.

[59]See Louis D. Boccardi, "China Says Vance's Visit Was a Setback," Associated Press release as reprinted in *Honolulu Star-Bulletin*, September 6, 1977, p. A-1. Also see *Ming Pao Daily News*, (Hongkong), September 9, 1977, p. 1; and *The New York Times*, September 9, 1977, sec. 1, p. 1.

[60]"A China Policy for the Next Administration." *Foreign Affairs*, vol. 55, no. 1 (October 1976), 34–35.

[61]"Military-Security Relations between China and the United States," *Foreign Affairs*, vol. 55, no. 2 (April 1977), 584–97 and *A New U.S. Policy Toward China* (Washington, D.C.: Brookings Institution, 1971), pp. 68–69.

[62]"Dr. Brzezinski in Peking," *Peking Review*, 21 (May 26, 1978), 5.

[63]"Dr. Brzezinski in Peking," p. 5.

[64]*The New York Times*, May 28, 1978, sec. 1, pp. 1, 6.

[65]"Military-Security Relations between China and the United States," pp. 584–97. Richard H. Solomon, "Thinking Through the China Problem," *Foreign Affairs*, vol. 56, no. 2 (January 1978), 341. Solomon, a former member and China expert on Kissinger's national security staff, analyzed all the major arguments in the United States that were opposed to the normalization.

[66]"Political Report to the 11th National Congress," p. 42.

[67]"Official Transcript of Reston's Conversation with the Chinese Premier in Peking," *The New York Times*, August 10, 1971, p. C-14.

[68]"Statement of the Ministry of Foreign Affairs of the PRC," and "Tiaoyu and Other Islands Have Been China's Territory since Ancient Times," *Peking Review*, 1 (January 7, 1972), 12–14.

[69]"The Sino-Japanese Rapprochement: A Relationship of Ambivalence," in *Sino-American Détente and Its Policy Implications*, ed. Gene Hsiao (New York: Holt, Rinehart & Winston, 1974), p. 165.

[70]"Joint Statement of the Government of PRC and the Government of Japan," *Peking Review*, 40 (October 6, 1972), 1–13.

[71]See Gene Hsiao, "The Sino-Japanese Rapprochement," p. 175.

[72]Hong N. Kim, "Sino-Japanese Relations since the Rapprochement," *Asian Survey*, vol. xv, no. 7 (July 1975), 561.

[73]Kim, "Sino-Japanese Relations since the Rapprochement," p. 561.

[74]Kim, "Sino-Japanese Relations since the Rapprochement," p. 561. Also see S.H. Chou, "China's Foreign Trade," *Current History*, vol. 71, no. 419. (September 1976), 85–87.

[75]"Japan-U.S.S.R. Fishery Talks: Hegemonism Goes against the Will of the People" *Peking Review*, 17 (April 22, 1977), 46, 48; "Support Japanese People's Just Struggle," *Peking*

Review, 20 (May 13, 1977), 17–18; "Why Are the Fishery Overlords Satisfied?" *Peking Review,* 34 (August 19, 1977), 43–44.

[76]See "Vice Premier Teng at Tokyo Press Conference: New Upsurge in Friendly Relations between China and Japan," *Peking Review,* 44 (November 3, 1978), 15.

[77]During President Ford's visit to China in December 1975, the Chinese had suggested the "Japan Model" to the U.S. as an acceptable means to normalize the Sino-U.S. relations. See Ron Nesson, *It Sure Looks Different from the Inside* (New York: Playboy, 1978), p. 139.

Appendix A

THE CONSTITUTION OF
THE PEOPLE'S REPUBLIC OF CHINA*

Contents

Preamble

*Peking Review, 11 (March 17, 1978), 5–14. (Adopted on March 5, 1978 by the Fifth National People's Congress of the People's Republic of China at its first session)

Preamble

After more than a century of heroic struggle the Chinese people, led by
the Communist Party of China headed by our great leader and teacher Chairman Mao Zedong, finally overthrew the reactionary rule of imperialism,
feudalism, and bureaucrat-capitalism by means of people's revolutionary war,
winning complete victory in the new-democratic revolution, and in 1949
founded the People's Republic of China.

The founding of the People's Republic of China marked the beginning of
the historical period of socialism in our country. Since then, under the leadership of Chairman Mao and the Chinese Communist Party, the people of all our
nationalities have carried out Chairman Mao's proletarian revolutionary line in
the political, economic, cultural, and military fields and in foreign affairs, and
have won great victories in socialist revolution and socialist construction through
repeated struggles against enemies, both at home and abroad, and through the
Great Proletarian Cultural Revolution. The dictatorship of the proletariat in our
country has been consolidated and strengthened, and China has become a
socialist country with the beginnings of prosperity.

Chairman Mao Zedong was the founder of the People's Republic of China.
All our victories in revolution and construction have been won under the guidance of Marxism-Leninism-Mao Zedong thought. The fundamental guarantee
that the people of all our nationalities will struggle in unity and carry the
proletarian revolution through to the end is always to hold high and staunchly to
defend the great banner of Chairman Mao.

The triumphant conclusion of the first Great Proletarian Cultural Revolution has ushered in a new period of development in China's socialist revolution
and socialist construction. In accordance with the basic line of the Chinese
Communist Party for the entire historical period of socialism, the general task
for the people of the whole country in this new period is to persevere in continuing the revolution under the dictatorship of the proletariat; to carry forward the
three great revolutionary movements of class struggle; the struggle for production, and scientific experiment; and to make China a great and powerful socialist
country with modern agriculture, industry, national defense, and science and
technology by the end of the century.

We must persevere in the struggle of the proletariat against the
bourgeoisie and in the struggle for the socialist road against the capitalist road.
We must oppose revisionism and prevent the restoration of capitalism. We must
be prepared to deal with subversion and aggression against our country by
social-imperialism and imperialism.

We should consolidate and expand the revolutionary united front, which is
led by the working class and based on the worker-peasant alliance, and which
unites the large numbers of intellectuals and other working people, patriotic
democratic parties, patriotic personages, our compatriots in Taiwan, Hongkong,
and Macao, and our countrymen residing abroad. We should enhance the great
unity of all the nationalities in our country. We should correctly distinguish and
handle the contradictions among the people and those between ourselves and
the enemy. We should endeavour to create among the people of the whole

country a political situation in which there are both centralism and democracy, both discipline and freedom, both unity of will and personal ease of mind and liveliness, so as to help bring all positive factors into play, overcome all difficulties, better consolidate the proletarian dictatorship, and build up our country more rapidly.

Taiwan is China's sacred territory. We are determined to liberate Taiwan and accomplish the great cause of unifying our motherland.

In international affairs, we should establish and develop relations with other countries on the basis of the five principles of mutual respect for sovereignty and territorial integrity, mutual nonaggression, noninterference in each other's internal affairs, equality and mutual benefit, and peaceful coexistence. Our country will never seek hegemony, or strive to be a superpower. We should uphold proletarian internationalism. In accordance with the theory of the three worlds, we should strengthen our unity with the proletariat and the oppressed people and nations throughout the world, the socialist countries, and the third world countries; and we should unite with all countries subjected to aggression, subversion, interference, control, and bullying by the social-imperialist and imperialist superpowers to form the broadest possible international united front against the hegemonism of the superpowers and against a new world war, and strive for the progress and emancipation of humanity.

CHAPTER ONE

General Principles

Article 1. The People's Republic of China is a socialist state of the dictatorship of the proletariat led by the working class and based on the alliance of workers and peasants.

Article 2. The Communist Party of China is the core of leadership of the whole Chinese people. The working class exercises leadership over the state through its vanguard, the Communist Party of China.

The guiding ideology of the People's Republic of China is Marxism-Leninism-Mao Zedong Thought.

Article 3. All power in the People's Republic of China belongs to the people. The organs through which the people exercise state power are the National People's Congress and the local people's congresses at various levels.

The National People's Congress, the local people's congresses at various levels and all other organs of state practice democratic centralism.

Article 4. The People's Republic of China is a unitary multinational state.

All the nationalities are equal. There should be unity and fraternal love among the nationalities and they should help and learn from each other. Discrimination against, or oppression of, any nationality, and acts which undermine the unity of the nationalities are prohibited. Big-nationality chauvinism and local-nationality chauvinism must be opposed.

All the nationalities have the freedom to use and develop their own spoken and written languages, and to preserve or reform their own customs and ways.

Regional autonomy applies in an area where a minority nationality lives in a compact community. All the national autonomous areas are inalienable parts of the People's Republic of China.

Article 5. There are mainly two kinds of ownership of the means of production in the People's Republic of China at the present stage: socialist ownership by the whole people and socialist collective ownership by the working people.

The state allows nonagricultural individual laborers to engage in individual labor involving no exploitation of others, within the limits permitted by law, and under unified arrangement and management by organizations at the basic level in cities and towns or in rural areas. At the same time, it guides these individual laborers step by step onto the road of socialist collectivization.

Article 6. The state sector of the economy, that is, the socialist sector owned by the whole people, is the leading force in the national economy.

Mineral resources, waters, and those forests, undeveloped lands, and other marine and land resources owned by the state are the property of the whole people.

The state may requisition by purchase, take over for use, or nationalize land under conditions prescribed by law.

Article 7. The rural people's commune sector of the economy is a socialist sector collectively owned by the masses of working people. At present, it generally takes the form of three-level ownership, that is, ownership by the commune, the production brigade, and the production team, with the production team as the basic accounting unit. A production brigade may become the basic accounting unit when its conditions are ripe.

Provided that the absolute predominance of the collective economy of the people's commune is ensured, commune members may farm small plots of land for personal needs, engage in limited household sideline production, and in pastoral areas they may also keep a limited number of livestock for personal needs.

Article 8. Socialist public property shall be inviolable. The state ensures the consolidation and development of the socialist sector of the economy owned by the whole people and of the socialist sector collectively owned by the masses of working people.

The state prohibits any person from using any means whatsoever to disrupt the economic order of the society, undermine the economic plans of the state, encroach upon or squander state and collective property, or injure the public interest.

Article 9. The state protects the right of citizens to own lawfully earned income, savings, houses, and other means of livelihood.

Article 10. The state applies the socialist principles: "He who does not work, neither shall he eat" and "from each according to his ability, to each according to his work."

Work is an honorable duty for every citizen able to work. The state promotes socialist labor emulation, and, putting proletarian politics in command, it applies the policy of combining moral encouragement with material reward, with the stress on the former, in order to heighten the citizen's socialist enthusiasm and creativeness in work.

Article 11. The state adheres to the general line of going all out, aiming high and achieving greater, faster, better, and more economical results in building socialism; it undertakes the planned proportionate and high-speed development of the national economy; and it continuously develops the productive forces, so as to consolidate the country's independence and security and improve the people's material and cultural life step by step.

In developing the national economy, the state adheres to the principle of building our country independently, with the initiative in our own hands; and through self-reliance, hard struggle, diligence and thrift, it adheres to the principle of taking agriculture as the foundation and industry as the leading factor; and it adheres to the principle of bringing the initiative of both the central and local authorities into full play under the unified leadership of the central authorities.

The state protects the environment and natural resources and prevents and eliminates pollution and other hazards to the public.

Article 12. The state devotes major efforts to developing science, expands scientific research, promotes technical innovation and technical revolution, and adopts advanced techniques wherever possible in all departments of the national economy. In scientific and technological work we must follow the practice of combining professional contingents with the masses, and of combining learning from others with our own creative efforts.

Article 13. The state devotes major efforts to developing education in order to raise the cultural and scientific level of the whole nation. Education must serve proletarian politics and be combined with productive labor, and must enable everyone who receives an education to develop morally, intellectually, and physically and to become a worker with both socialist consciousness and culture.

Article 14. The state upholds the leading position of Marxism-Leninism-Mao Zedong thought in all spheres of ideology and culture. All cultural undertakings must serve the workers, peasants, and soldiers and must serve socialism.

The state applies the policy of "letting a hundred flowers blossom and a hundred schools of thought contend" so as to promote the development of the arts and sciences and bring about a flourishing socialist culture.

Article 15. All organs of state must constantly maintain close contact with the masses of the people, rely on them, heed their opinions, be concerned for their weal and woe, streamline administration, practice economy, raise efficiency, and combat bureaucracy.

The leading personnel of state organs at all levels must conform to the requirements for successors in the proletarian revolutionary cause, and their composition must conform to the principle of the three-in-one combination of the old, the middle-aged, and the young.

Article 16. The personnel of organs of state must earnestly study Marxism-Leninism-Mao Zedong thought, wholeheartedly serve the people, endeavour to perfect their professional competence, take an active part in collective productive labor, accept supervision by the masses, be models in observing the constitution and the law, correctly implement the policies of the state, seek the truth from facts, and must not have recourse to deception or exploit their position and power to seek personal gain.

Article 17. The state adheres to the principle of socialist democracy, and ensures to the people the right to participate in the management of state affairs and of all economic and cultural undertakings, and the right to supervise the organs of state and their personnel.

Article 18. The state safeguards the socialist system, suppresses all treasonable and counter-revolutionary activities, punishes all traitors and counter-revolutionaries, and punishes newborn bourgeois elements and other bad elements.

The state deprives of political rights, as prescribed by law, those landlords, rich peasants, and reactionary capitalists who have not yet been reformed, and at the same time it provides them with the opportunity to earn a living so that they may be reformed through labor and become law-abiding citizens supporting themselves by their own labor.

Article 19. The chairman of the Central Committee of the Communist Party of China commands the armed forces of the People's Republic of China.

The Chinese People's Liberation Army is the workers' and peasants' owned armed force led by the Communist Party of China; it is the pillar of the dictatorship of the proletariat. The state devotes major efforts to the revolutionization and modernization of the Chinese People's Liberation Army, strengthens the building of the militia, and adopts a system under which our armed forces are a combination of the field armies, the regional forces, and the militia.

The fundamental task of the armed forces of the People's Republic of China is to safeguard the socialist revolution and socialist construction; to defend the sovereignty, territorial integrity, and security of the state; and to guard against subversion and aggression by social-imperialism, imperialism, and their lackeys.

CHAPTER TWO

The Structure of the State

Section 1. The National People's Congress

Article 20. The National People's Congress is the highest organ of state power.

Article 21. The National People's Congress is composed of deputies elected by the people's congresses of the provinces, autonomous regions, and municipalities directly under the Central Government, and by the People's Liberation Army. The deputies should be elected by secret ballot after democratic consultation.

The National People's Congress is elected for a term of five years. Under special circumstances, its term of office may be extended or the succeeding National People's Congress may be convened before its due date.

The National People's Congress holds one session each year. When necessary, the session may be advanced or postponed.

Article 22. The National People's Congress exercises the following functions and powers:

1. to amend the constitution;
2. to make laws;
3. to supervise the enforcement of the constitution and the law;
4. to decide on the choice of the premier of the State Council upon the recommendation of the Central Committee of the Communist Party of China;
5. to decide on the choice of other members of the State Council upon the recommendation of the premier of the State Council;
6. to elect the president of the Supreme People's Court and the chief procurator of the Supreme People's Procuratorate;
7. to examine and approve the national economic plan, the state budget, and the final state accounts;

8. to confirm the following administrative devisions: provinces, autonomous regions, and municipalities directly under the central government;
9. to decide on questions of war and peace; and
10. to exercise such other functions and powers as the National People's Congress deems necessary.

Article 23. The National People's Congress has the power to remove from office the members of the State Council, the president of the Supreme People's Court and the chief procurator of the Supreme People's Procuratorate.

Article 24. The Standing Committee of the National People's Congress is the permanent organ of the National People's Congress. It is responsible and accountable to the National People's Congress.

The Standing Committee of the National People's Congress is composed of the following members:

the chairman;
the vice chairman;
the secretary-general; and
other members.

The National People's Congress elects the Standing Committee of the National People's Congress and has the power to recall its members.

Article 25. The Standing Committee of the National People's Congress exercises the following functions and powers:

1. to conduct the election of deputies to the National People's Congress;
2. to convene the sessions of the National People's Congress;
3. to interpret the constitution and laws and to enact decrees;
4. to supervise the work of the State Council, the Supreme People's Court, and the Supreme People's Procuratorate;
5. to change and annul inappropriate decisions adopted by the organs of state power of provinces, autonomous regions, and municipalities directly under the central government;
6. to decide on the appointment and removal of individual members of the State Council upon the recommendation of the premier of the State Council when the National People's Congress is not in session;
7. to appoint and remove vice presidents of the Supreme People's Court and deputy chief procurators of the Supreme People's Procuratorate;
8. To decide on the appointment and removal of plenipotentiary representatives abroad;
9. to decide on the ratification and abrogation of treaties concluded with foreign states;
10. to institute state titles of honor and decide on their conferment;
11. to decide on the granting of pardons;
12. to decide on the proclamation of a state of war in the event of armed attack on the country when the National People's Congress is not in session; and
13. to exercise such other functions and powers as are vested in it by the National People's Congress.

Article 26. The chairman of the Standing Committee of the National People's Congress presides over the work of the Standing Committee; receives foreign diplomatic envoys; and in accordance with the decisions of the National People's Congress or its Standing Committee, promulgates laws and decrees, dispatches and recalls plenipotentiary representatives abroad, ratifies treaties concluded with foreign states, and confers state titles of honor.

The vice chairmen of the Standing Committee of the National People's Congress assist the chairman in his work and may exercise part of the chairman's functions and powers on his behalf.

Article 27. The National People's Congress and its Standing Committee may establish special committees as deemed necessary.

Article 28. Deputies to the National People's Congress have the right to address inquiries to the State Council, the Supreme People's Court, the Supreme People's Procuratorate, and the ministries and commissions of the State Council, which are all under obligation to answer.

Article 29. Deputies to the National People's Congress are subject to supervision by the units which elect them. These electoral units have the power to replace at any time the deputies they elect, as prescribed by law.

Section 2. The State Council

Article 30. The State Council is the Central People's Government and the executive organ of the highest organ of state power; it is the highest organ of state administration.

The State Council is responsible and accountable to the National People's Congress, or, when the National People's Congress is not in session, to its Standing Committee.

Article 31. The State Council is composed of the following members:

the premier;
the vice premiers;
the ministers; and
the ministers heading the commissions.

The premier presides over the work of the State Council and the vice premiers assist the premier in his work.

Article 32. The State Council exercises the following functions and powers:

1. to formulate administrative measures, issue decisions and orders, and verify their execution, in accordance with the constitution, laws, and decrees;
2. to submit proposals on laws and other matters to the National People's Congress or its Standing Committee.
3. to exercise unified leadership over the work of the ministries and commissions and other organizations under it;
4. to exercise unified leadership over the work of local organs of state administration at various levels throughout the country;
5. to draw up and put into effect the national economic plan and the state budget;
6. to protect the interests of the state, maintain public order, and safeguard the rights of citizens;
7. to confirm the following administrative divisions: autonomous prefectures, counties, autonomous counties, and cities;
8. to appoint and remove administrative personnel according to the provisions of the law; and
9. to exercise such other functions and powers as are vested in it by the National People's Congress or its Standing Committee.

Section 3. The Local People's Congresses and the Local Revolutionary Committees at Various Levels

Article 33. The administrative division of the People's Republic of China is as follows:

1. The country is divided into provinces, autonomous regions, and municipalities directly under the central government;
2. Provinces and autonomous regions are divided into autonomous prefectures, counties, autonomous counties, and cities; and
3. Counties and autonomous counties are divided into people's communes and towns.

Municipalities directly under the central government, and other large cities, are divided into districts and counties. Autonomous prefectures are divided into counties, autonomous counties, and cities.

Autonomous regions, autonomous prefectures, and autonomous counties are all national autonomous areas.

Article 34. People's congresses and revolutionary committees are established in provinces, municipalities directly under the central government, counties, cities, municipal districts, people's communes, and towns.

People's congresses and revolutionary committees of the people's communes are organizations of political power at the grass-roots level, and are also leading organs of collective economy.

Revolutionary committees at the provincial level may establish administrative offices as their agencies in prefectures.

Organs of self-government are established in autonomous regions, autonomous prefectures, and autonomous counties.

Article 35. Local people's congresses at various levels are local organs of state power.

Deputies to the people's congresses of provinces, municipalities directly under the central government, counties, and cities divided into districts are elected by people's congresses at the next lower level by secret ballot after democratic consultation; deputies to the people's congresses of cities not divided into districts, and of municipal districts, people's communes, and towns are directly elected by the voters by secret ballot after democratic consultation.

The people's congresses of provinces and municipalities directly under the central government are elected for a term of five years. The people's congresses of counties, cities, and municipal districts are elected for a term of three years. The people's congresses of people's communes and towns are elected for a term of two years.

Local people's congresses at various levels hold at least one session each year, which is to be convened by revolutionary committees at the corresponding levels.

The units and electorates which elect the deputies to the local people's congresses at various levels have the power to supervise, remove, and replace their deputies at any time according to the provisions of the law.

Article 36. Local people's congresses at various levels, in their respective administrative areas, ensure the observance and enforcement of the constitution, laws, and decrees; ensure the implementation of the state plan; make plans for local economic and cultural development and for public utilities; examine and approve local economic plans, budgets, and final accounts; protect public property; maintain public order; safeguard the rights of citizens and the equal rights of minority nationalities; and promote the development of socialist revolution and socialist construction.

Local people's congresses may adopt and issue decisions within the limits of their authority as prescribed by law.

Local people's congresses elect, and have the power to recall, members of revolutionary committees at the corresponding levels. People's congresses at county level and above elect, and have the power to recall, the presidents of the people's courts and the chief procurators of the people's procuratorates at the corresponding levels.

Deputies to local people's congresses at various levels have the right to address inquiries to the revolutionary committees, people's courts, people's procuratorates, and organs under the revolutionary committees at the corresponding levels, which are all under obligation to answer.

Article 37. Local revolutionary committees at various levels, that is, local people's governments, are the executive organs of local people's congresses at the corresponding levels and they are also local organs of state administration.

A local revolutionary committee is composed of a chairman, vice chairmen, and other members.

Local revolutionary committees carry out the decisions of people's congresses at the corresponding levels as well as the decisions and orders of the organs of state administration at higher levels, direct the administrative work of their respective areas, and issue decisions and orders within the limits of their authority as prescribed by law. Revolutionary committees at county level and above appoint or remove the personnel of organs of state according to the provisions of the law.

Local revolutionary committees are responsible and accountable to people's congresses at the corresponding levels and to the organs of state administration at the next higher level, and work under the unified leadership of the State Council.

Section 4. The Organs of Self-Government of National Autonomous Areas

Article 38. The organs of self-government of autonomous regions, autonomous prefectures, and autonomous counties are people's congresses and revolutionary committees.

The election of the people's congresses and revolutionary committees of national autonomous areas, their terms of office, their functions and powers, and also the establishment of their agencies should conform to the basic principles governing the organization of local organs of state as specified in Section 3, Chapter 2, of the constitution.

In autonomous areas where a number of nationalities live together, each nationality is entitled to appropriate representation in the organs of self-government.

Article 39. The organs of self-government of national autonomous areas exercise autonomy within the limits of their authority as prescribed by law, in addition to exercising the functions and powers of local organs of state as specified by the constitution.

The organs of self-government of national autonomous areas may, in the light of the political, economic, and cultural characteristics of the nationality or nationalities in a given area, make regulations on the exercise of autonomy and also specific regulations and submit them to the Standing Committee of the National People's Congress for approval.

In performing their functions, the organs of self-government of national autonomous areas employ the spoken and written language or languages commonly used by the nationality or nationalities in the locality.

Article 40. The higher organs of state shall fully safeguard the exercise of autonomy by the organs of self-government of national autonomous areas, take into full consideration the characteristics and needs of the various minority nationalities, make a major effort to train cadres of the minority nationalities, and actively support and assist all the minority nationalities in their socialist revolution and construction and thus advance their socialist economic and cultural development.

Section 5. The People's Courts and the People Procuratorates

Article 41. The Supreme People's Court, local people's courts at various levels and special people's courts exercise judicial authority. The people's courts are formed as prescribed by law.

In accordance with law, the people's courts apply the system whereby representatives of the masses participate as assessors in administering justice. With regard to major counter-revolutionary or criminal cases, the masses should be drawn in for discussion and suggestions.

All cases in the people's courts are heard in public except those involving special circumstances, as prescribed by law. The accused has the right to defense.

Article 42. The Supreme People's Court is the highest judicial organ.

The Supreme People's Court supervises the administration of justice by local people's courts at various levels and by special people's courts; people's courts at the higher levels supervise the administration of justice by people's courts at the lower levels.

The Supreme People's Court is responsible and accountable to the National People's Congress and its Standing Committee. Local people's courts at various levels are responsible and accountable to local people's congresses at the corresponding levels.

Article 43. The Supreme People's Procuratorate exercises procuratorial authority to ensure observance of the constitution and the law by all departments under the State Council, the local organs of state at various levels, the personnel of organs of state, and the citizens. Local people's procuratorates and special people's procuratorates exercise procuratorial authority within the limits prescribed by law. The people's procuratorates are formed as prescribed by law.

The Supreme People's Procuratorate supervises the work of local people's procuratorates at various levels and of special people's procuratorates; people's procuratorates at the higher levels supervise the work of those at the lower levels.

The Supreme People's Procuratorate is responsible and accountable to the National People's Congress and its Standing Committee. Local people's procuratorates at various levels are responsible and accountable to people's congresses at the corresponding levels.

CHAPTER THREE

The Fundamental Rights and Duties of Citizens

Article 44. All citizens who have reached the age of eighteen have the right to vote and to stand for election, with the exception of persons deprived of these rights by law.

Article 45. Citizens enjoy freedom of speech, correspondence, the press, assembly, association, procession, demonstration, and the freedom to strike, and have the right to "speak out freely, air their views fully, hold great debates, and write big-character posters."

Article 46. Citizens enjoy freedom to believe in religion and freedom not to believe in religion and to propagate atheism.

Article 47. The citizens' freedom of person and their homes are inviolable.

No citizen may be arrested except by decision of a people's court or with the sanction of a people's procuratorate, and the arrest must be made by a public security organ.

Article 48. Citizens have the right to work. To ensure that citizens enjoy this right, the state provides employment in accordance with the principle of overall consideration, and, on the basis of increased production, the state gradually increases payment for labor, improves working conditions, strengthens labor protection, and expands collective welfare.

Article 49. Working people have the right to rest. To ensure that working people enjoy this right, the state prescribes working hours and systems of vacations and gradually expands material facilities for the working people to rest and recuperate.

Article 50. Working people have the right to material assistance in old age, and in case of illness or disability. To ensure that working people enjoy this right, the state gradually expands social insurance, social assistance, public health services, cooperative medical services, and other services.

The state cares for and ensures the livelihood of disabled revolutionary armymen and the families of revolutionary martyrs.

Article 51. Citizens have the right to education. To ensure that citizens enjoy this right the state gradually increases the number of schools of various types and of other cultural and educational institutions and popularizes education.

The state pays special attention to the healthy development of young people and children.

Article 52. Citizens have the freedom to engage in scientific research, literary and artistic creation, and other cultural activities. The state encourages and assists the creative endeavours of citizens engaged in science, education, literature, art, journalism, publishing, public health, sports, and other cultural work.

Article 53. Women enjoy equal rights with men in all spheres of political, economic cultural, social, and family life. Men and women enjoy equal pay for equal work.

Men and women shall marry of their own free will. The state protects marriage, the family, and the mother and child.

The state advocates and encourages family planning.

Article 54. The state protects the just rights and interests of overseas Chinese and their relatives.

Article 55. Citizens have the right to lodge complaints with organs of state at any level against any person working in an organ of state, enterprise, or institution for transgression of law or neglect of duty. Citizens have the right to appeal to organs of state at any level against any infringement of their rights. No one shall suppress such complaints and appeals or retaliate against persons making them.

Article 56. Citizens must support the leadership of the Communist Party of China, support the socialist system, safeguard the unification of the motherland and the unity of all nationalities in our country and abide by the constitution and the law.

Article 57. Citizens must take care of and protect public property, observe labor discipline, observe public order, respect social ethics, and safeguard state secrets.

Article 58. It is the lofty duty of every citizen to defend the motherland and resist aggression.

It is the honorable obligation of citizens to perform military service and to join the militia according to the law.

Article 59. The People's Republic of China grants the right of residence to any foreign national persecuted for supporting a just cause, for taking part in revolutionary movements, or for engaging in scientific work.

CHAPTER FOUR

The National Flag, the National Emblem, and the Capital

Article 60. The national flag of the People's Republic of China has five stars on a field of red.

The national emblem of the People's Republic of China is Tien An Men in the center, illuminated by five stars, and encircled by ears of grain and a cogwheel.

The capital of the People's Republic of China is Peking.

Amendments to the Constitution*

The Second Session of the Fifth National People's Congress, having examined the motion on amendments to some provisions of the Constitution (for the full text, see issue No. 11, 1978) submitted by the Standing Committee of the Fifth National People's Congress, agreed that standing committees be established for local people's congresses at and above the county level, that local revolutionary committees at various levels be changed into local people's governments, that deputies to the people's congresses of counties be elected directly by the voters, and that the relationship between higher and lower people's procuratorates be changed from that of supervision to one of leadership.

The N.P.C. Standing Committee gave the following explanation on the necessity for these changes:

1. As the focus of our work is being shifted to socialist modernization and the local organs of power at various levels, particularly those at and above the county level, are shouldering heavy tasks, it is necessary to separate the organ of power (people's congress) from the administrative organ (people's government) and establish standing committees in people's congresses at and above the county

*Source: *Beijing Review*, no. 28 (July 13, 1979), p. 10.

level. When people's congresses at and above the county level are not in session, standing committees will perform their functions and powers as the permanent organs of the people's congresses at their respective levels. This will help broaden the scope of people's democracy, strengthen the socialist legal system, and improve the people's congress as an institution.

2. The revolutionary committee, a provisional institution which appeared during the Cultural Revolution, is no longer able to meet the needs of the new period of socialist modernization. The change from local revolutionary committees to local people's governments will not only help strengthen democracy and the legal system but will give distinctive expression to the close relationship between the government and the people.

With the change from local revolutionary committees to local people's governments, the titles of the leading members of the local governments will be changed to governor and deputy governors (of a province), chairman and vice-chairmen (of an autonomous region inhabited in compact communities by minority nationalities), mayor and deputy mayors (of a city), head and deputy heads (of a county) and director and deputy directors (of a commune administrative committee).

3. The electoral law for the National People's Congress and local people's congresses promulgated in 1953 stipulated that deputies to the people's congresses at the county level and above would be elected indirectly by the congresses at their next lower levels respectively. In view of the fact that tremendous changes have taken place in China and a considerable rise has occurred in people's political and educational standards over the last two decades or so, it is now necessary and possible to broaden the scope of direct election of an organ of power to the county level. The aim is to give fuller scope to people's democracy and improve China's electoral system step by step.

4. In order to maintain the independence of the procuratorates, it is necessary to change the relationship between people's procuratorates at different levels from that of supervision to one of leadership, that is, the Supreme People's Procuratorate should offer leadership to local people's procuratorates and special procuratorates, and a higher procuratorate should offer leadership to a lower one.

Appendix B

CONSTITUTION OF THE COMMUNIST
PARTY OF CHINA*

General Program

The Communist Party of China is the political party of the proletariat, the highest form of its class organization. It is a vigorous vanguard organization composed of the advanced elements of the proletariat, which leads the proletariat and the revolutionary masses in their fight against the class enemy.

The basic program of the Communist Party of China for the entire historical period of socialism is to persist in continuing the revolution under the dictatorship of the proletariat, eliminate the bourgeoisie and all other exploiting classes step by step, and bring about the triumph of socialism over capitalism. The ultimate aim of the party is the realization of communism.

Marxism-Leninism-Mao Zedong thought is the guiding ideology and theoretical basis of the Communist Party of China. The party persists in combating revisionism, dogmatism, and empiricism. The party upholds dialectical materialism and historical materialism as its world outlook and opposes the idealist and metaphysical world outlook.

Our great leader and teacher Chairman Mao Zedong was the founder of

*Peking Review, 36 (September 2, 1978), 16–22. (Adopted by the Eleventh National Congress of the Communist Party of China on August 18, 1977)

the Communist Party of China and the greatest Marxist-Leninist of our time. Integrating the universal truth of Marxism-Leninism with the concrete practice of the revolution, Chairman Mao inherited, defended, and developed Marxism-Leninism in the struggles against imperialism and the domestic reactionary classes, against right and left opportunist lines in the party, and against international modern revisionism. He led our party, our army, and our people in winning complete victory in the new-domocratic revolution and in founding the People's Republic of China, a state of the dictatorship of the proletariat, through protracted revolutionary struggles and revolutionary wars, and then in achieving tremdous victories in the socialist revolution and socialist construction through fierce and complex struggles between the proletariat and the bourgeoisie, and through the unparalleled Great Proletarian Cultural Revolution. The banner of Chairman Mao is the great banner guiding our party to victory through united struggle.

Socialist society covers a historical period of considerable length. In this period classes, class contradictions, and class struggle—the struggle between the socialist road and the capitalist road—and the danger of capitalist restoration invariably continue to exist; and there is the threat of subversion and aggression by imperialism and social-imperialism. The resolution of these contradictions depends solely on the theory and practice of continued revolution under the dictatorship of the proletariat.

China's Great Proletarian Cultural Revolution was a political revolution carried out under socialism by the proletariat against the bourgeoisie and all other exploiting classes to consolidate the dictatorship of the proletariate and prevent the restoration of capitalism. Political revolutions of this nature will be carried out many times in the future.

The Communist Party of China adheres to its basic line for the entire historical period of socialism. It must correctly distinguish and handle the contradictions among the people and those between ourselves and the enemy, and consolidate and strengthen the dictatorship of the proletariat. The party must rely on the working class wholeheartedly, and rely on the poor and lower-middle peasants, unite with the vast numbers of intellectuals and other working people, mobilize all positive factors, and expand the revolutionary united front led by the working class and based on the worker-peasant alliance. It must uphold the proletarian nationality policy and strengthen the great unity of the people of all nationalities in China. It must carry on the three great revolutionary movements of class struggle and the struggles for production and scientific experiment; it must adhere to the principle of building our country independently, with the initiative in our own hands, and through self-reliance, diligence, and thrift, and to the principle of being prepared against war and natural disasters, doing everything for the people, so as to build socialism by going all out, aiming high, and achieving greater, faster, better, and more economical results. The party must lead the people of all nationalities in making China a powerful socialist country with modern agriculture, industry, national defense, and science and technology by the end of the century.

The Communist Party of China upholds proletarian internationalism and opposes great-nation chauvinism; it unites firmly with the genuine Marxist-Leninist parties and organizations the world over, unites with the proletariat, the oppressed people, and nations of the whole world, and fights shoulder to shoulder with them to oppose the hegemonism of the two superpowers, the Soviet Union and the United States, to overthrow imperialism, modern revisionism and all reaction, and to wipe the system of exploitation of man by man off the face of the earth, so that all mankind will be emancipated.

The correctness or incorrectness of the ideological and political line decides everything. All party comrades must implement Chairman Mao's proletarian revolutionary line comprehensively and correctly and adhere to the three basic principles: Practice Marxism, and not revisionism; unite, and don't split; be open and aboveboard, and don't intrigue and conspire. They must have the revolutionary boldness in daring to go against any tide that runs counter to these three basic principles.

The whole party must adhere to the organizational principle of democratic centralism, and practice centralism on the basis of democracy and democracy under centralized guidance. It must give full scope to inner-party democracy and encourage the initiative and creativeness of all party members and party organizations at all levels, and combat bureaucracy, commandism, and warlordism. The whole party must strictly observe party discipline, safeguard the party's centralization, strengthen its unity, oppose all splittist and factional activities, oppose the assertion of independence from the party and oppose anarchism. In relations among comrades in the party, all members should apply the principle of "Say all you know and say it without reserve" and "Blame not the speaker but be warned by his words," adopt the dialectical method, start from the desire for unity, distinguish between right and wrong through criticism or struggle, and arrive at a new unity. The party must strive to create a political situation in which there are both centralism and democracy, both discipline and freedom, both unity of will and personal ease of mind and liveliness.

The party must conscientiously follow the proletarian line on cadres, the line of "appointing people on the merit" and oppose the bourgeois line on cadres, the line of "appointing people by favoritism." It must train and bring up in mass struggles millions of successors in the revolutionary cause of the proletariat in accordance with the five requirements put forward by Chairman Mao. Special vigilance must be exercised against careerists, conspirators, and double-dealers so as to prevent such bad types from usurping the leadership of the party and the state at any level and to ensure purity of the leadership at all levels.

The whole party must keep to and carry forward its fine tradition of following the mass line and seeking truth from facts; it must keep to and carry forward the style of work characterized by integration of theory with practice, close ties with the masses and criticism and self-criticism, the style of modesty, prudence, and freedom from arrogance and impetuosity, and the style of plain living and hard struggle; and the whole party must prevent party members, especially leading party cadres, from exploiting their position to seek privileges, and wage a resolute struggle against bourgeois ideology and the bourgeois style of work.

A member of the Communist Party of China should at all times and in all circumstances subordinate his personal interests to the interests of the party and the people; he should fear no difficulties and sacrifices, work actively for the fulfillment of the program of the party, and devote his whole life to the struggle for communism.

The Communist Party of China is a great, glorious, and correct party, and it is the core of leadership of the whole Chinese people. The whole party must always hold high and resolutely defend the great banner of Marxism-Leninism-Mao Zedong Thought and ensure that our party's cause will continue to advance triumphantly along the Marxist line.

CHAPTER ONE

Membership

Article 1. Any Chinese worker, poor peasant, lower-middle peasant, revolutionary soldier, or any other revolutionary who had reached the age of eighteen and who accepts the constitution of the party and is willing to join a party organization and work actively in it, carry out the party's decisions, observe party discipline, and pay membership dues may become a member of the Communist Party of China.

Article 2. The Communist Party of China demands that its members should

1. conscientiously study Marxism-Leninism-Mao Zedong thought, criticize capitalism and revisionism, and strive to remold their world outlook;
2. serve the people wholeheartedly and pursue no private interests either for themselves or for a small number of people;
3. unite with all the people who can be united inside and outside the party, including those who have wrongly opposed them;
4. maintain close ties with the masses and consult with them when matters arise;
5. earnestly practice criticism and self-criticism, be bold in correcting their shortcomings and mistakes, and dare to struggle against words and deeds that run counter to party principles;
6. uphold the party's unity, refuse to take part in, and moreover oppose, any factional organization or activity which splits the party;
7. be truthful and honest to the party, observe party discipline and the laws of the state, and strictly guard party and state secrets; and
8. actively fulfill the tasks assigned them by the party and play an exemplary vanguard role in the three great revolutionary movements of class struggle and the struggles for production and for scientific experiment.

Article 3. Applicants for party membership must go through the procedure for admission individually. An applicant must be recommended by two full party members, fill in an application form for party membership, and be examined by a party branch, which must seek opinions extensively inside and outside the party; he or she may become a probationary member after being accepted by the general membership meeting of the party branch and being approved by the next higher party committee.

Before approving the admission of an applicant for party membership, the higher party committee must appoint someone specially to talk with the applicant and carefully examine his or her case.

Article 4. The probationary period of a probationary member is one year. The party organization concerned should make further efforts to educate and observe him or her.

When the probationary period has expired, the party branch to which the probationary member belongs must promptly discuss whether he or she is qualified for full membership. If qualified, he or she should be given full membership as scheduled; if it is necessary to continue to observe him or her, the probationary period may be extended but by no more than one year; if he or she is found to be really unfit for party membership, his or her status as a probationary members should be annulled. Any decision either to transfer a probationary member to full membership, to prolong the probationary period, or to annul his or her status as a probationary member must be adopted by the general membership meeting of the party branch and approved by the next higher party committee.

The probationary period of a probationary member begins from the day when the higher party committee approves the applicant's admission. The party standing of a party member begins from the day when he or she is transferred to full membership.

A probationary member does not have the right to vote and to elect or be elected, enjoyed by a full member.

Article 5. When a party member violates party discipline, the party organization concerned should give the member education and, on the merits of the case, may take any of the following disciplinary measures—a warning, a serious warning, removal from his or her post in the party, being placed on probation within the party, and expulsion from the party.

The period for which the party member concerned is placed on probation should not exceed two years. During this period, he or she does not have the right to vote and to elect or be elected. If the party member concerned has been through the period of probation and has corrected his or her mistake, these rights should be restored; if the member clings to the mistake instead of correcting it, he or she should be expelled from the party.

Proven renegades, enemy agents, absolutely unrepentant persons in power taking the capitalist road, alien class elements, degenerates, and new bourgeois elements must be expelled from the party and not be readmitted.

Article 6. Any disciplinary measure taken against a party member must be decided on by a general membership meeting of the party branch to which the member belongs and should be submitted to the next higher party committee for approval. Under special circumstances, a primary party committee or a higher party committee has the power to take disciplinary action against a party member.

Any decision to remove a member from a local party committee at any level, to place on probation, or to expel the member from the party must be made by the said party committee and be submitted to the next higher party committee for approval.

Corresponding provisions on disciplinary measures against members of the party committees, at all levels in the army units, should be laid down by the Military Commission of the Central Committee in accordance with the party constitution.

Any decision to take a disciplinary measure against a member or alternate member of the Central Committee must be made by the Central Committee or its Political Bureau.

When a party organization takes a decision on a disciplinary measure against a member, it must, barring special circumstances, notify the members that he or she should attend the meeting. If the member disagrees with the decision, he or she may ask for a review of the case and has the right to appeal to higher party committees, up to and including the Central Committee.

Article 7. A party member whose revolutionary will has degenerated, who fails to function as a communist, and who remains unchanged despite repeated education may be persuaded to withdraw from the Party. The case must be decided by the general membership meeting of the party branch concerned and submitted to the next higher party committee for approval.

A party member who fails to take part in party life, to do the work assigned by the party, and to pay membership dues over six months and without proper reason is regarded as having given up membership.

When a party member asks to withdraw from the party or has given up membership, the party branch concerned should, with the approval of its general membership meeting, remove his or her name from the party rolls and report the case to the next higher party committee for the record.

CHAPTER TWO

Organizational System of the Party

Article 8. The party is organized on the principle of democratic centralism.

The whole party must observe democratic centralist discipline: The individual is subordinate to the organization, the minority is subordinate to the majority, the lower level is subordinate to the higher level, and the entire party is subordinate to the Central Committee.

Article 9. Delegates to party congresses and members of party committees at all levels should be elected by secret ballot after democratic consultation and in accordance with the five requirements for successors in the revolutionary cause of the proletariat and with the principle of combining the old, the middle-aged, and the young.

Article 10. The highest leading body of the party is the National Congress and, when it is not in session, the Central Committee elected by it. The leading bodies of party organizations at all levels in the localities and in the army units are the party congresses or general membership meetings at their respective levels and the party committees elected by them. Party congresses at all levels are convened by party committees at their respective levels. The convocation of party congresses at all levels in the localities and in the army units, and the composition of the party committees they elect, are subject to approval by the next higher party committee.

Article 11. Party committees at all levels operate on the principle of combining collective leadership with individual responsibility under a division of labor. They should rely on the political experience and wisdom of the collective; all important issues are to be decided collectively, and at the same time each individual is to be enabled to play his or her due part.

Party committees at all levels should set up their working bodies in accordance with the principles of close ties with the masses and of structural simplicity and efficiency. Party committees at the county level and upwards may send out their representative organs when necessary.

Article 12. Party committees at all levels should report regularly on their work to party congresses or general membership meetings, constantly listen to the opinions of the masses both inside and outside the party, and put themselves under their supervision.

Party members have the right to criticize party organizations and working personnel in leading posts at all levels and make proposals to them and also the right to bypass the immediate leadership and present their appeals and complaints to higher levels, up to and including the Central Committee and the chairman of the Central Committee. It is absolutely impermissible for anyone to suppress criticism or to retaliate. Those guilty of doing so should be investigated and punished.

If a party member holds different views with regard to the decisions or directives of the party organizations, he or she is allowed to reserve these views and has the right to bring up the matter for discussion at Party meetings and the right to bypass the immediate leadership and report to higher levels, up to and including the Central Committee and the chairman of the Central Committee, but the member must resolutely carry out these decisions and directives.

Article 13. The Central Committee of the party, local party committees at the county level and upwards, and party commitees in the army units at the regimental level and upwards should set up commissions for inspecting discipline.

The commissions for inspecting discipline at all levels are to be elected by the party committees at the respective levels and, under their leadership, should strengthen party members' education on discipline, be responsible for checking on the observance of discipline by party members and party cadres, and struggle against all breaches of party discipline.

Article 14. State organs, the People's Liberation Army, and the militia and revolutionary mass organizations, such as trade unions, the Communist Youth League, poor and lower-middle peasant associations, and women's federations, must all accept the absolute leadership of the party.

Leading party groups should be set up in state organs and people's organizations. Members of leading party groups in state organs and people's organizations at the national level are to be appointed by the Central Committee of the party. Members of leading party groups in state organs and people's organizations at all levels in the localities are to be appointed by the corresponding party committees.

CHAPTER THREE

Central Organizations of the Party

Article 15. The National Congress of the party should be convened every five years. Under special circumstances, it may be convened before its due date or postponed.

Article 16. The plenary session of the Central Committee of the party elects the Political Bureau of the Central Committee, the Standing Committee of the Political Bureau of the Central Committee, and the chairman and vice chairmen of the Central Committee.

The plenary session of the Central Committee of the party is convened by the Political Bureau of the Central Committee.

When the Central Committee is not in plenary session, the Political Bureau of the Central Committee and its Standing Committee exercise the functions and powers of the Central Committee.

CHAPTER FOUR

Party Organizations in the Localities and the Army Units

Article 17. Local party congresses at the county level and upwards, and party congresses in the army units at the regimental level and upwards, should be convened every three years. Under special circumstances, they may be convened before their due date or postponed, subject to approval by the next higher party committees.

Local party committees at the county level and upwards, and Party committees in the army units at the regimental level and upwards, elect their standing committees, secretaries, and deputy secretaries.

CHAPTER FIVE

Primary Organizations of the Party

Article 18. Party branches, general party branches, or primary party committees should be set up in factories, mines, and other enterprises, people's communes, offices, schools, shops, neighborhoods, companies of the People's Liberation Army, and other primary units in accordance with the need of the revolutionary struggle and the size of their party membership, subject to approval by the next higher party committees.

Committees of party branches should be elected annually, committees of general party branches and primary party committees should be elected every two years. Under special circumstances, the election may take place before its due date or be postponed, subject to approval by the next higher party committees.

Article 19. The primary organizations of the party should play the role of a fighting bastion. Their main tasks are

1. to lead party members and people outside the party in studying Marxism-Leninism-Mao Zedong thought conscientiously, educate them in the ideological and political line and in the Party's fine tradition, and give them basic knowledge about the Party;

2. to lead and unite the broad masses of the people in adhering to the socialist road, in criticizing capitalism and revisionism, in correctly distinguishing and handling the contradictions among the people and those between ourselves and the enemy, and in waging a resolute struggle against the class enemy;

3. to propagate and carry out the line, policies, and decisions of the party, and fulfill every task assigned by the party and the state;

4. to maintain close ties with the masses, constantly listen to their opinions and demands, and faithfully report these to higher party organizations, and be concerned about their political, economic, and cultural life;

5. to promote inner-party democracy, practice criticism and self-criticism, expose and get rid of shortcomings and mistakes in work, and wage struggles against violations of the law and breaches of discipline, against corruption and waste, and against bureaucracy and all other undesirable tendencies; and

6. to admit new party members, enforce party discipline, and consolidate the party organizations, getting rid of the stale and taking in the fresh, so as to purify the party's ranks and constantly enhance the party's fighting power.

Appendix C

JOINT COMMUNIQUE
BY CHINA AND THE UNITED STATES*

(The Chinese and U.S. sides reached agreement on a joint communiqué on February 27 in Shanghai. Full text of the communiqué is as follows.)

President Richard Nixon of the United States of America visited the People's Republic of China at the invitation of Premier Chou En-lai of the People's Republic of China from February 21 to February 28, 1972. Accompanying the President were Mrs. Nixon, U.S. Secretary of State William Rogers, Assistant to the President Dr. Henry Kissinger, and other American officials.

President Nixon met with Chairman Mao Tsetung of the Communist Party of China on February 21. The two leaders had a serious and frank exchange of views on Sino-U.S. relations and world affairs.

During the visit, extensive, earnest and frank discussions were held between President Nixon and Premier Chou En-lai on the normalization of relations between the United States of America and the People's Republic of China, as well as on other matters of interest to both sides. In addition, Secretary of State William Rogers and Foreign Minister Chi Peng-fei held talks in the same spirit.

President Nixon and his party visited Peking and viewed cultural, industrial, and agricultural sites, and they also toured Hangchow and Shanghai where, continuing discussions with Chinese leaders, they viewed similar places of interest.

The leaders of the People's Republic of China and the United States of America found it beneficial to have this opportunity, after so many years without

*Peking Review, 9 (March 3, 1972), 4–5.

contact, to present candidly to one another their views on a variety of issues. They reviewed the international situation in which important changes and great upheavals are taking place and expounded their respective positions and attitudes.

The Chinese side stated: Wherever there is oppression, there is resistance. Countries want independence, nations want liberation and the people want revolution—this has become the irresistible trend of history. All nations, big or small, should be equal; big nations should not bully the small and strong nations should not bully the weak. China will never be a superpower and it opposes hegemony and power politics of any kind. The Chinese side stated that it firmly supports the struggles of all the oppressed people and nations for freedom and liberation and that the people of all countries have the right to choose their social systems according to their own wishes and the right to safeguard the independence, sovereignty, and territorial integrity of their own countries and oppose foreign aggression, interference, control, and subversion. All foreign troops should be withdrawn to their own countries. The Chinese side expressed its firm support to the peoples of Vietnam, Laos, and Cambodia in their efforts for the attainment of their goal and its firm support to the seven-point proposal of the Provisional Revolutionary Government of the Republic of South Vietnam and the elaboration of February this year on the two key problems in the proposal, and to the Joint Declaration of the Summit Conference of the Indochinese Peoples. It firmly supports the eight-point program for the peaceful unification of Korea put forward by the government of the Democratic people's Republic of Korea on April 12, 1971, and the stand for the abolition of the UN Commission for the Unification and Rehabilitation of Korea." It firmly opposes the revival and outward expansion of Japanese militarism, and firmly supports the Japanese people's desire to build an independent, democratic, peaceful, and neutral Japan. It firmly maintains that India and Pakistan should, in accordance with the United Nations resolutions on the India-Pakistan question, immediately withdraw all their forces to their respective territories and to their own sides of the ceasefire line in Jammu and Kashmir, and firmly supports the Pakistan Government and people in their struggle to preserve their independence and sovereignty and the people of Jammu and Kashmir in their struggle for the right of self-determination.

The U.S. side stated: Peace in Asia and peace in the world requires efforts both to reduce immediate tensions and to eliminate the basic causes of conflict. The United States will work for a just and secure peace: just, because it fulfills the aspirations of peoples and nations for freedom and progress; secure, because it removes the danger of foreign aggression. The United States supports individual freedom and social progress for all the peoples of the world, free of outside pressure or intervention. The United States believes that the effort to reduce tensions is served by improving communication between countries that have different ideologies so as to lessen the risks of confrontation through accident, miscalculation, or misunderstanding. Countries should treat each other with mutual respect and be willing to compete peacefully, letting performances be the ultimate judge. No country should claim infallibility and each country should be prepared to reexamine its own attitudes for the common good. The United States stressed that the peoples of Indochina should be allowed to determine their destiny without outside intervention; its constant primary objective has been a negotiated solution; the eight-point proposal put forward by the Republic of Vietnam and the United States on January 27, 1972 represents a basis for the attainment of that objective; in the absence of a negotiated settlement, the United States envisages the ultimate withdrawal of all U.S. forces from the region, consistent with the aim of self-determination for each country of Indochina. The United States will maintain its close ties with and support for the Republic of Korea; the United States will support efforts of the Republic of Korea to seek a relaxation of tension and increased communication in the Korean peninsula. The United States places the highest value on its friendly relations with Japan; it will continue to develop the existing close bonds. Consistent with the United Nations Security Council Resolution of December 21, 1971, the United States favors the continuation of the ceasefire between India and Pakistan and the withdrawal of all military forces to within their own territories and to their sides of the ceasefire line in Jammu and Kashmir; the United States supports the right of the people of South Asia to shape their own future in peace, free of military threat, and without having the area become the subject of great power rivalry.

There are essential differences between China and the United States in their social systems and foreign policies. However, the two sides agreed that countries, regardless of their social systems, should conduct their relations on the principles of respect for the sovereignty and territorial integrity of all states, nonaggression against other states, noninterference in the internal affairs of other states, equality and mutual benefit, and peaceful coexistence. International disputes should be settled on this basis, without resorting to the use or threat of force. The United States and the People's Republic of China are prepared to apply these principles to their mutual relations.

With these principles of international relations in mind, the two sides stated that:

— progress toward the normalization of relations between China and the United States is in the interests of all countries;
— both wish to reduce the danger of international military conflict;
— neither should seek hegemony in the Asia-Pacific region and each is opposed to efforts by any other country or group of countries to establish such hegemony; and
— neither is prepared to negotiate on behalf of any third party or to enter into agreements or understandings with the other directed at other states.

Both sides are of the view that it would be against the interests of the peoples of the world for any major country to collude with another against other countries, or for major countries to divide up the world into spheres of interest.

The two sides reviewed the long-standing serious disputes between China and the United States. The Chinese side reaffirmed its position: The Taiwan question is the crucial question obstructing the normalization of relations between China and the United States; the government of the People's Republic of China is the sole legal government of China; Taiwan is a province of China which has long been returned to the motherland; the liberation of Taiwan is China's internal affair in which no other country has the right to interfere; and all U.S. forces and military installations must be withdrawn from Taiwan. The Chinese government firmly opposes any activities which aim at the creation of "one China, one Taiwan," "one China, two governments," "two Chinas," and "independent Taiwan," or advocate that the "status of Taiwan remains to be determined."

The U.S. side declared: The United States acknowledges that all Chinese on either side of the Taiwan Strait maintain that there is but one China and that

Taiwan is a part of China. The United States Government does not challenge that position. It reaffirms its interest in a peaceful settlement of the Taiwan question by the Chinese themselves. With this prospect in mind, it affirms the ultimate objective of the withdrawal of all U.S. forces and military installations from Taiwan. In the meantime, it will progressively reduce its forces and military installations on Taiwan as the tension in the area diminishes.

The two sides agreed that it is desirable to broaden the understanding between the two peoples. To this end, they discussed specific areas in such fields as science, technology, culture, sports, and journalism, in which people-to-people contacts and exchanges would be mutually beneficial. Each side undertakes to facilitate the further development of such contacts and exchanges.

Both sides view bilateral trade as another area from which mutual benefit can be derived, and agreed that economic relations based on equality and mutual benefit are in the interest of the peoples of the two countries. They agree to facilitate the progressive development of trade between their two countries.

The two sides agreed that they will stay in contact through various channels, including the sending of a senior U.S. representative to Peking from time to time for concrete consultations to further the normalization of relations between the two countries and continue to exchange views on issues of common interest.

The two sides expressed the hope that the gains achieved during this visit would open up new prospects for the relations between the two countries. They believe that the normalization of relations between the two countries is not only in the interest of the Chinese and American peoples but also contributes to the relaxation of tension in Asia and the world.

President Nixon, Mrs. Nixon, and the American party expressed their appreciation for the gracious hospitality shown them by the government and people of the People's Republic of China.

February 28, 1972

Appendix D

THE CHINESE FOREIGN MINISTRY'S NOTE TO THE SOVIET EMBASSY IN CHINA*

(Yu Chan, vice minister of the Chinese Foreign Ministry, entrusted by the Standing Committee of the Chinese National People's Congress, on March 9 delivered to the Soviet Ambassador to China, Vasily S. Tolstikov, a note of the Chinese Foreign Ministry to the Soviet Embassy in Beijing. The note was a reply to the suggestion of the Soviet side that the two countries issue a joint statement on the principles of mutual relations and that a meeting of representatives of both sides be held for this purpose.

The Soviet suggestion was stated in a letter from the Presidium of the Supreme Soviet of the U.S.S.R. to the Standing Committee of the Chinese N.P.C. The letter was delivered by Viktor F. Maltsev, Soviet first vice foreign minister, to Tien Tseng-pei, charge d'affaires ad interim of the Chinese Embassy in Moscow, on February 24 this year. A copy of it was delivered by Ambassador Tolstikov to the Chinese Foreign Ministry on February 27.

On March 20, TASS released to the public the text of the letter of the Presidium of the Supreme Soviet. Following is the full text of the Chinese Foreign Ministry's note to the Soviet Embassy in Peking with that of the Soviet letter as an appendix which has been published in the Chinese newspapers.)

The Soviet Embassy in the People's Republic of China

The Ministry of Foreign Affairs of the People's Republic of China is entrusted by the Standing Committee of the National People's Congress to reply to

*Peking Review, 13 (March 31, 1978), 17–18.

the letter of February 24, 1978 from the Presidium of the Supreme Soviet of the U.S.S.R. as follows:

China and the Soviet Union used to be friendly neighboring countries, and our two peoples have forged a profound friendship in their long revolutionary struggles. Responsibility for the deterioration of the relations between our two countries to what they are today does not lie with the Chinese side; China is the victim.

It is known to all that there exist differences of principle between China and the Soviet Union. The debate over these differences will go on for a long time. However, proceeding from the fundamental interests of the Chinese and Soviet peoples, the Chinese side has always held that the differences of principle should not impede the maintenance of normal state relations between the two countries on the basis of the Five Principles of Peaceful Coexistence. And to this end it has made unremitting efforts.

In September 1969, the Chinese premier and the Soviet chairman of the Council of Ministers held talks in Peking and reached an understanding on the normalization of relations between the two countries. The Chinese side has ever since abided by this understanding, and for its full implementation has earnestly and patiently held boundary negotiations with the Soviet side for as long as eight years. However, the Soviet side not only is unwilling to implement the understanding reached by the heads of government of the two countries, it even denies the existence of the understanding itself. As a result, the boundary negotiations remain fruitless to this day. In the meantime, the Soviet Union has unceasingly increased its armed forces on the Sino-Soviet border and in the People's Republic of Mongolia, and there is not the slightest change in the Soviet policy of hostility to China. In these circumstances, the Presidium of the Supreme Soviet of the U.S.S.R. has proposed in its letter that the two countries issue a hollow statement on principles guiding mutual relations, a statement which does not solve any practical problem. Its purpose in so doing is obviously not to improve Sino-Soviet relations, but lies elsewhere.

If the Soviet side really desires to improve Sino-Soviet relations, it should take concrete actions that solve practical problems. First of all, it should sign, in accordance with the 1969 understanding between the premiers of the two countries, an agreement on the maintenance of the status quo on the border, averting armed clashes and disengaging the armed forces of the two sides in the disputed border areas, and then proceed to settle through negotiations the boundary questions; and it should withdraw its armed forces from the People's Republic of Mongolia and from the Sino-Soviet border so that the situation there will revert to what it was in the early 60s. When you refuse to take such minimum actions as maintenance of the status quo on the border, averting armed clashes, and disengaging the armed forces of the two sides in the disputed border areas, what practical purpose would it serve to issue a worthless "statement of principles guiding mutual relations" except to deceive the Chinese and Soviet peoples and the world public! When you have a million troops deployed on the Sino-Soviet border, how can you expect the Chinese people to believe that you have a genuine and sincere desire to improve the relations between our two countries? Isn't it fully reasonable to ask you to withdraw your armed forces from the Sino-Soviet border and restore the situation that prevailed in the early 60s?

The normalization of relations between China and the Soviet Union is the common desire of our two peoples and it accords with their fundamental interests and those of the people of the world. For its part, the Chinese side will, as always, make efforts toward this end. What the Chinese side likes to see is real deeds and not hollow statements.

The Ministry of Foreign Affairs avails itself of this opportunity to renew to the Embassy the assurances of its high considerations.

Ministry of Foreign Affairs
of the People's Republic of China

Peking, March 9, 1978

Letter from the Presidium of the U.S.S.R.
Supreme Soviet to the Standing Committee
of the Chinese N.P.C.

The Standing Committee of the Chinese National People's Congress: Soviet-Chinese relations assumed over the recent years a nature that cannot but cause serious concern. The existing state of affairs leads to the creation of the atomosphere of mutual distrust, to the heightening of tensions in interstate relations. The vital interests of the Soviet and Chinese peoples require adoption of definite practical measures aimed at normalizing Soviet-Chinese relations in accordance with the aspirations and hopes of the peoples of the Soviet Union and the People's Republic of China.

The Soviet government repeatedly advanced concrete proposals aimed at bringing the relations between the U.S.S.R. and the PRC back to the road of good neighborliness, and expressed the U.S.S.R.'s readiness to normalize relations with China on the principles of peaceful coexistence. The government of the People's Republic of China for its part had officially stated that the PRC could build relations with the U.S.S.R. on the principles of peaceful coexistence. The Soviet people sincerely wish to see China a friendly prosperous power.

The Presidium of the U.S.S.R. Supreme Soviet, expressing the will and aspirations of the Soviet people, is once again stating its readiness to put an end to the present abnormal situation in the relations between the U.S.S.R. and the PRC and to stop the dangerous process of further aggravation of relations which may lead to serious negative consequences for our countries and peoples, for the destinies of peace in the Far East, in Asia, and throughout the world.

In order to materialize the desire expressed by the two sides to base their relations on the principles of peaceful co-existence and embody it in a tangible international act, the Presidium of the U.S.S.R. Supreme Soviet is suggesting that our countries come forward with a joint statement on the principles of mutual relations between the Union of Soviet Socialist Republics and the People's Republic of China. It is believed in the Soviet Union that a joint statement that the sides will build their relations on the basis of peaceful coexistence, firmly adhering to the principles of equality, mutual respect for sovereignty and territorial integrity, noninterference in the internal affairs of each other, and nonuse of force could advance the cause of normalization of our relations.

We suggest that, if the very idea of making such a statement is acceptable for the Chinese side, a meeting of representatives of both sides should be held at a sufficiently high level to agree on a mutually acceptable text of the statement in the shortest possible time.

The Soviet Union is prepared to receive representatives of the People's Republic of China. If the Chinese side deems it expedient that Soviet representatives should arrive for the aforementioned purpose in Peking, we agree to this. On our part, we are prepared to consider proposals of the PRC aimed at normalization of Soviet-Chinese relations.

The Presidium of the U.S.S.R.
Supreme Soviet

February 24, 1978

Appendix E

TREATY OF PEACE AND FRIENDSHIP BETWEEN
THE PEOPLE'S REPUBLIC OF CHINA AND JAPAN*

The People's Republic of China and Japan,

Recalling with satisfaction that since the government of the People's Republic of China and the government of Japan issued a joint statement in Peking on September 29, 1972, the friendly relations between the two governments and the peoples of the two countries have developed greatly on a new basis,

Confirming that the abovementioned joint statement constitutes the basis of the relations of peace and friendship between the two countries and that the principles enunciated in the joint statement should be strictly observed,

Confirming that the principles of the charter of the United Nations should be fully respected,

Hoping to contribute to peace and stability in Asia and in the world,

For the purpose of solidifying and developing the relations of peace and friendship between the two countries,

Have resolved to conclude a treaty of peace and friendship and for that purpose have appointed as their plenipotentiaries:

The People's Republic of China: Huang Hua, Minister of Foreign Affairs

Japan: Sunao Sonoda, Minister for Foreign Affairs

Who, having communicated to each other their full powers, found to be in good and due form, have agreed as follows:

*Peking Review, 33 (August 18, 1978), 7–8.

Article I

1. The contracting parties shall develop durable relations of peace and friendship between the two countries on the basis of the principles of mutual respect for sovereignty and territorial integrity, mutual nonaggression, noninterference in each other's internal affairs, equality and mutual benefit, and peaceful co-existence.

2. In keeping with the foregoing principles and the principles of the United Nations Charter, the contracting parties affirm that in their mutual relations, all disputes shall be settled by peaceful means without resorting to the use or threat of force.

Article II

The contracting parties declare that neither of them should seek hegemony in the Asia-Pacific region or in any other region and that each is opposed to efforts by any other country or group of countries to establish such hegemony.

Article III

The contracting parties shall, in a good-neighborly and friendly spirit and in conformity with the principles of equality and mutual benefit and noninterference in each other's internal affairs, endeavor to further develop economic and cultural relations between the two countries and to promote exchanges between the peoples of the two countries.

Article IV

The present treaty shall not affect the position of either contracting party regarding its relations with third countries.

Article V

1. The present treaty shall be ratified and shall enter into force on the date of the exchange of instruments of ratification which shall take place at Tokyo. The present treaty shall remain in force for ten years and thereafter shall continue to be in force until terminated in accordance with the provisions of Paragraph 2 of this Article.

2. Either contracting party may, by giving one year's written notice to the other contracting party, terminate the present treaty at the end of the initial ten-year period or at any time thereafter.

In witness whereof the respective plenipotentiaries have signed the present treaty and have affixed thereto their seals.

Done in duplicate in the Chinese and Japanese languages, both texts being equally authentic, at Peking, this twelfth day of August 1978.

For the People's Republic of China:	For Japan:
Huang Hua	Sunao Sonoda
(Signed)	(Signed)

Appendix F

ESTABLISHMENT OF DIPLOMATIC RELATIONS
BETWEEN THE PEOPLE'S
REPUBLIC OF CHINA AND THE U.S.A.

1. Joint Communiqué on the Establishment of Diplomatic Relations between the People's Republic of China and the United States of America[1]

The People's Republic of China and the United States of America have agreed to recognize each other and to establish diplomatic relations as of January 1, 1979.

The United States of America recognizes the government of the People's Republic of China as the sole legal government of China. Within this context, the people of the United States will maintain cultural, commercial, and other unofficial relations with the people of Taiwan.

The People's Republic of China and the United States of America reaffirm the principles agreed on by the two sides in the Shanghai communiqué and emphasize once again that:

—Both wish to reduce the danger of international military conflict.

—Neither should seek hegemony in the Asia-Pacific region or in any other region of the world and each is opposed to efforts by any other country or group of countries to establish such hegemony.

—Neither is prepared to negotiate on behalf of any third party or to enter into agreements or understandings with the other directed at other states.

[1]*Peking Review,* 51 (December 22, 1978), 8.

—The government of the United States of America acknowledges the Chinese position that there is but one China and Taiwan is part of China.

—Both believe that normalization of Sino-American relations is not only in the interest of the Chinese and American peoples, but also contributes to the cause of peace in Asia and the world.

The People's Republic of China and the United States of America will exchange ambassadors and establish embassies on March 1, 1979.

2. Statement of the Government of the People's Republic of China[2]

The government of the People's Republic of China on December 16 issued a statement on the establishment of diplomatic relations between China and the United States. The full text of the statement reads as follows:

As of January 1, 1979, the People's Republic of China and the United States of America recognize each other and establish diplomatic relations, thereby ending the prolonged abnormal relationship between them. This is a historic event in Sino-U.S. relations.

As is known to all, the government of the People's Republic of China is the sole legal government of China and Taiwan is a part of China. The question of Taiwan was the crucial issue obstructing the normalization of relations between China and the United States. It has now been resolved between the two countries in the spirit of the Shanghai communiqué and through their joint efforts, thus enabling the normalization of relations so ardently desired by the people of the two countries. As for the way of bringing Taiwan back to the embrace of the motherland and reunifying the country, it is entirely China's internal affair.

At the invitation of the U.S. government, Deng Xiaoping, vice premier of the State Council of the People's Republic of China, will pay an official visit to the United States in January 1979, with a view to further promoting the friendship between the two peoples and good relations between the two countries.

3. President Carter's Address to the Nation, Announcing Establishment of Diplomatic Relations between the United States and the People's Republic of China, December 15, 1978[3]

I would like to read a joint communiqué which is being issued simultaneously in Peking at this moment by the leaders of the People's Republic of China:

"Joint communiqué on the establishment of diplomatic relations between the United States of America and the People's Republic of China, January 1, 1979.

"The United States of America and the People's Republic of China have agreed to recognize each other and to establish diplomatic relations as of January 1, 1979.

"The United States of America recognizes the government of the People's Republic of China as the sole legal government of China. Within this context, the

---

[2]*Peking Review,* 51 (December 22, 1978), 8.

[3]*U.S. Policy Toward China: July 15, 1971–January 15, 1979,* Selected Documents, No. 9. Bureau of Public Affairs, The Department of State (Washington, D.C.), January 1979, pp. 45–46.

people of the United States will maintain cultural, commercial, and other unofficial relations with the people of Taiwan.

"The United States of America and the People's Republic of China reaffirm the principles agreed on by the two sides in the Shanghai communiqué and emphasize once again that:

"Both wish to reduce the danger of international military conflict.

"Neither should seek hegemony in the Asia-Pacific region or in any other region of the world and each is opposed to efforts by any other country or group of countries to establish such hegemony.

"Neither is prepared to negotiate on behalf of any third party or to enter into agreements or understanding with the other directed at other states.

"The United States of America acknowledges the Chinese position that there is but one China and Taiwan is part of China.

"Both believe that normalization of Sino-American relations is not only in the interest of the Chinese and American peoples but also contributes to the cause of peace in Asia and in the world.

"The United States of America and the People's Republic of China will exchange ambassadors and establish embassies on March 1, 1979."

Yesterday, the United States of America and the People's Republic of China reached this final historic agreement.

On January 1, 1979, our two governments will implement full normalization of diplomatic relations.

As a nation of gifted people who comprise one-fourth of the population of the earth, China plays an important role in world affairs—a role that can only grow more important in the years ahead.

We do not undertake this important step for transient tactical or expedient reasons. In recognizing that the government of the People's Republic is the single government of China, we are recognizing simple reality. But far more is involved in this decision than a recognition of reality.

Before the estrangement of recent decades, the American and Chinese people had a long history of friendship. We have already begun to rebuild some of those previous ties. Now, our rapidly expanding relationship requires the kind of structures that diplomatic relations will make possible.

The change I am announcing tonight will be of long-term benefit to the peoples of both the United States and China—and I believe, to all the peoples of the world.

Normalization—and the expanded commercial and cultural relations it will bring with it—will contribute to the well-being of our own nation and will enhance stability in Asia.

These more positive relations with China can beneficially affect the world in which we and our children will live.

We have already begun to inform our allies and the Congress of the details of our intended action. But I wish also to convey a special message to the people of Taiwan, with whom the American people have had and will have extensive close and friendly relations.

As the United States asserted in the Shanghai communiqué in 1972, we will continue to have an interest in the peaceful resolution of the Taiwan issue.

I have paid special attention to insuring that normalization of relations between the United States and the People's Republic will not jeopardize the well-being of the people of Taiwan.

The people of the United States will maintain our current commercial, cultural, and other relations with Taiwan through nongovernmental means. Many other countries are already successfully doing this.

These decisions and actions open a new and important chapter in world affairs.

To strengthen and to expedite the benefits of this new relationship between the People's Republic of China and the United States, I am pleased to announce that Vice Premier Deng has accepted my invitation to visit Washington at the end of January. His visit will give our governments the opportunity to consult with each other on global issues and to begin working together to enhance the cause of world peace.

These events are the result of long and serious negotiations begun by President Nixon in 1972, and continued by President Ford. The results bear witness to the steady, determined bipartisan effort of our own country to build a world in which peace will be the goal and responsibility of all countries.

The normalization of relations between the United States and China has no other purpose than this: the advance of peace.

It is in this spirit, at this season of peace, that I take special pride in sharing this news with you tonight.

4. Text of U.S. Statement, December 15, 1978[4]

As of January 1, 1979, the United States of America recognizes the People's Republic of China as the sole legal government of China. On the same date, the People's Republic of China accords similar recognition to the United States of America. The United States thereby establishes diplomatic relations with the People's Republic of China.

On the same date, January 1, 1979, the United States of America will notify Taiwan that it is terminating diplomatic relations and that the Mutual Defense Treaty between the United States and the Republic of China is being terminated in accordance with the provisions of the treaty. The United States also states that it will be withdrawing its remaining military personnel from Taiwan within four months.

In the future, the American people and the people of Taiwan will maintain commercial, cultural, and other relations without official government representation and without diplomatic relations.

The administration will seek adjustment to our laws and regulations to permit the maintenance of commercial, cultural, and other nongovernmental relations in the new circumstances that will exist after normalization.

The United States is confident that the people of Taiwan face a peaceful and prosperous future. The United States continues to have an interest in the peaceful resolution of the Taiwan issue and expects that the Taiwan issue will be settled peacefully by the Chinese themselves.

The United States believes that the establishment of diplomatic relations with the People's Republic will contribute to the welfare of the American people, to the stability of Asia where the United States has major security and economic interest, and to the peace of the entire world.

[4]U.S. Policy Toward China: July 15, 1971–January 15, 1979, Selected Documents No. 9, Bureau of Public Affairs, the Department of State (Washington, D.C.) January 1979, p. 48.

Index